M000206507

GANGSTER STATE

GANGSTER STATE

Unravelling Ace Magashule's Web of Capture

PIETER-LOUIS MYBURGH

PENGUIN BOOKS

Published by Penguin Books
an imprint of Penguin Random House South Africa (Pty) Ltd
Reg. No. 1953/000441/07
The Estuaries No. 4, Oxbow Crescent, Century Avenue, Century City, 7441
PO Box 1144, Cape Town, 8000, South Africa
www.penguinrandomhouse.co.za

First published 2019

1 3 5 7 9 10 8 6 4 2

Publication © Penguin Random House 2019
Text © Pieter-Louis Myburgh 2019

All rights reserved. No part of this publication may be reproduced,
stored in a retrieval system or transmitted, in any form or by any means,
electronic, mechanical, photocopying, recording or otherwise,
without the prior written permission of the copyright owners.

PUBLISHER: Marlene Fryer
MANAGING EDITOR: Robert Plummer
EDITOR: Bronwen Maynier
PROOFREADER: Lisa Compton
COVER DESIGNER: Ryan Africa
INDEXER: Sanet le Roux

Set in 11 pt on 14.5 pt Minion

Printed by **novus print**, a Novus Holdings company

ISBN 978 1 77609 374 8 (print)
ISBN 978 1 77609 375 5 (ePub)

For the journalists, whistleblowers, sources and activists
who have fought and continue to fight to turn the tide.

Contents

Introduction

One Friday evening in mid-2013 my cellphone rang just as I was about to put a few takeaway pizzas in my car. I had been working at a Sunday newspaper in Johannesburg and it was not unusual to get work-related calls over the weekend. Not recognising the number flashing on my phone's screen, I hesitated. It had been a long week and I was looking forward to enjoying hot pizza and a few beers with friends. But curious journalists rarely ignore phone calls, so I answered. The person on the other end of the line introduced himself as Ace Magashule, the premier of the Free State.

My first thought was that someone was playing a prank on me, but I soon realised it was indeed him. At the time, I was researching a tender awarded to a Bloemfontein-based company for organising the annual South African Sport Awards. The company's owner was said to be closely connected to top government leaders and had apparently clinched the contract in an irregular manner. While Magashule and his provincial government did not feature in the story,[1] I may have sent out queries to officials regarding the company's work in the Free State. Magashule had somehow got word of my interest in the contractor and had decided to give me a call. I don't recall verbatim what was said, but he tried to convince me that his administration and the company in question had nothing to hide.

The call was strange, to say the least. Top-level government leaders do not normally contact young, relatively unknown journalists, at least not directly. I got the sense that Magashule was worried about what I might uncover. I also think he wanted me to know that he was aware that I was looking into the matter. I later learnt that, over the years, Magashule contacted other journalists in a similar fashion. To me, this conduct betrayed a degree of nervousness about the media's interest in his province's affairs. His apparent habit of contacting reporters also carried a hint of subtle intimidation. At least one Free State journalist I spoke to claimed to have abandoned an investigation into a provincial tender after receiving such a call.

Magashule had every reason to be worried about nosy journalists. I believe the government deals unpacked in this book, along with previous revelations, sufficiently implicate him as the head of a well-organised state-capture network in his home province.

Compared to the most prominent tender bandits in national government, however, Magashule's anxiety must have been considerably more manageable during his stint as premier. For a start, Jacob Zuma's time in charge of the country saw government's law-enforcement arm become as ineffective as a gangrened limb. There was no need for the likes of Magashule to be concerned about being investigated or brought to book. Media outlets, civil society organisations and the general public, meanwhile, were largely focused on scandals involving Zuma, his state-capture enablers and rent-seeking at national departments and large state-owned companies such as Transnet and Eskom. Public-sector looters and their private-sector accomplices in provinces like the Free State were left to execute their schemes without drawing too much attention. While there have been great examples of investigative work on Magashule and his administration over the years, such reports have been too sporadic to produce the sustained outrage and pressure necessary to bring about meaningful change.

More than a few sources in the Free State's political set-up referred to Magashule as 'Mr Ten Percent' for allegedly demanding a 10 per cent cut from each government contract in the province. During his nine-year run as premier, the Free State's cumulative annual expenditure totalled over R200 billion. While it is unlikely that 'Mr Ten Percent' skimmed off R20 billion, considering what I uncovered while writing this book I do believe substantial amounts of money ended up in his broader capture network. This includes his family, friends, former business associates and political allies.

Magashule had been extremely careful in his alleged dealings with contractors and other businesspeople, some of his former associates told me. Kickbacks due to him from government contracts would be paid in cash, they all alleged, ensuring that any financial links to dodgy contractors were kept to a minimum. Furthermore, Magashule apparently often used trusted security guards, drivers and other aides to do his dirty work. He also avoided electronic communication and preferred to discuss 'funny money' and related matters in person. Some of my sources feared that if the Hawks and other law-enforcement bodies were to one day wake from their Zuma-induced slumber, they would have a difficult time finding any conclusive evidence of Magashule's involvement in corrupt government deals.

But no one can erase their entire past. In April 2018, while I was still working at *News24*, I looked into a R255-million 'asbestos audit' contract awarded by the Free State's Department of Human Settlements. I linked the contract to Igo Mpambani, a high-flying tender mogul who had been gunned down in Sandton in 2017.[2] I stayed on Mpambani's trail and eventually got hold of a bulky stack of emails, bank records and related material that detailed some of the murdered businessman's dealings. For ease of reference, I refer to these documents as the IgoFiles. In order to protect my sources, I cannot divulge any information about how these documents came into my possession. It was my 'mini-#GuptaLeaks' moment. Although not nearly as large as the dataset that laid bare the Gupta family's murky conduct, the IgoFiles were undoubtedly a valuable find when it came to linking Magashule to possible corruption. 'Premier requested that you pay full amount of R470 000,' reads a snippet of one email in the IgoFiles. Part VII fully unpacks the dubious asbestos audit contract and explains how Magashule may have received as much as R10 million from the deal.

In this book I examine the undemocratic means with which Magashule and his political allies clung to power in the Free State. I also unpack a fresh revelation about a trip to the former Gupta estate in Johannesburg, allegations of shady meetings with other connected businessmen, and indications that Jacob Zuma may have scored a 'thank-you fee' from one of the Free State's failed housing projects. All of these stories should strengthen calls for a proper investigation into Magashule's dealings as premier.

In researching and writing this book, I relied partly on the experiences of an extensive list of individuals who, at varying times during Magashule's political career, moved very close to him. I interviewed about ten political figures who all once formed part of his inner circle. They were able to provide me with invaluable insights into Magashule's conduct and habits, especially those pertaining to his alleged state-capture ploys. Another ten or so businesspeople and other connected types added to the story. A few politicians from opposition parties were also of great help. Apart from the IgoFiles, I relied on heaps of tender documents, company records and related material to construct this partial account of what I consider to be

Magashule's history as a state captor. I call it a partial account because there is certainly much more to uncover. Magashule's ties to a certain business family from Vereeniging, for example, do not feature in this book and warrant further exploration. In fact, we might need a separate commission of inquiry to help get to the bottom of the rot that infected the Free State government during Magashule's time in charge.

Magashule was given a fair opportunity to comment on the issues explored in *Gangster State*, but he chose not to make use of it. More than sixty questions sent to ANC spokesperson Dakota Legoete for the attention of his boss remained unanswered

In April 2017, I ended my first book, *The Republic of Gupta*, with a word of caution to the ruling African National Congress (ANC) that many other observers have also issued: elect better leaders to your top structures, or risk losing further support in the face of continuing state-capture and corruption scandals.

Then Nasrec happened. In December 2017, political spectators watched – some with horror, others with bemusement – as, at its fifty-fourth national conference, the ANC enacted the political equivalent of shooting itself in the foot with an anti-aircraft gun. The election of Ace Magashule and fellow 'premier leaguer' David Mabuza as the party's new secretary-general (SG) and deputy president respectively ensured that allies of the disgraced Zuma would continue to besmirch the party's name and reputation. Their presence in the ANC's Top Six would also jeopardise President Cyril Ramaphosa's so-called 'new dawn', meant to revive the party's founding values. Mabuza has since craftily repositioned himself within the ANC's broader power dynamics, and has been remarkably quiet.

It is Magashule who, in my view, now most prominently embodies the ruling party's glaring departure from the vision for the ANC and South Africa upheld by earlier leaders such as Albert Luthuli, Oliver Tambo and Nelson Mandela.

There has been much talk in the past about 'criminal elements' within the ANC. Ironically, Magashule made one such remark in 2012 when service-delivery protests in a few Free State towns turned violent.[3] This sentiment became particularly popular when the Guptas' state-capture project was exposed. The narrative was that a handful of alleged criminals, Zuma being one of them, had infiltrated an organisation that was otherwise still dominated by good, honest people. It was a hopeful notion. Less sympathetic observers called it naive. Whatever the case, it is now obvious that the ANC suffers from a chronic inability to correct past mistakes by dealing with these alleged 'criminal elements'.

Zuma's dramatic recall as state president may well have been a result of Ramaphosa's ascent to power. But the latter was bound to encounter resistance from shady characters around every corner if he attempted to navigate the ANC and the country out of the maze of corruption. In a cruel twist, the power of some of these questionable characters was actually bolstered by the internal ANC voting machine that delivered Ramaphosa and the 'renewalists' their marginal victory.

The elevation of Magashule to one of the party's most powerful positions reaffirms the organisation's reckless nonchalance with regards to its image and reputation. There are still questions around whether he won the contest to become secretary-general in a fair manner, but the ANC has effectively buried the matter for the sake of 'unity'. It is, however, Magashule's nine years as Free State premier that will have even graver implications for the ruling party. At the time, there were enough allegations of misconduct for the ANC to at least consider axing him, yet the party chose to look the other way. The fact that Magashule and other high-profile people have managed to escape censure for their alleged crimes for so long leads me to a disturbing conclusion: what we have witnessed since at least 2009 is not the work of mere 'criminal elements' within the ANC, but rather the effect of the outright criminalisation of the party as a whole.

In this regard, *Gangster State* is at once a book about Ace Magashule *and* the political organisation to which he belongs. The simple fact of the matter is that Zuma, Magashule and others were able to do so much damage to the ANC and the country because the party failed to stop them.

Can all of this still be turned around? I believe so, but by this I mean the country, not the ANC. The ruling party's appointment of its very own 'secretary-gangster' to a position as visible and important as the one Magashule now occupies can be seen as a broad endorsement of criminality. If Magashule did indeed 'steal' the position, the ANC's failure to deal with this only further supports my argument. The party's chronic inability to stem the criminalisation of its internal leadership structures will one day be viewed as a key reason for the ANC's final implosion.

'The measure of a man is what he does with power' – Plato

Prologue
Death of a Bentley bagman

On the day of the murder, Tshepo Thabane[*] had been at his usual spot on the corner of South Road and Bowling Avenue since dawn.

Like the other regular beggars and casual labourers who had made this intersection their base, the young man from the nearby Alexandra township usually arrived in time for the great procession of luxury sedans and SUVs that trickled past towards Sandton's business district each weekday. His earnings from that morning's peak-hour traffic had been pretty good. With noon fast approaching, Tshepo's mind started to drift towards thoughts of food. As he counted the coins in one of his trouser pockets, he could almost hear his stomach berating him for having skipped breakfast.

Tshepo was just about to leave his spot to go and buy lunch somewhere nearby when his eye caught the grey Bentley Continental GT driving in a southerly direction on Bowling Avenue, towards the intersection. The car glided into the turn-off lane that feeds into South Road. The impressive machine stood out even among the other expensive cars Tshepo had become accustomed to seeing at this crossing. The robot was red, and there was just one car in front of the Bentley. At the next flash of the traffic light's green arrow, it was destined to turn right into South Road and cruise towards the CBD.

Meanwhile, Tshepo noticed that a silver Audi A4 had snuck into the slipway that carries Bowling Avenue's traffic into South Road going in the opposite direction, away from the CBD and towards Alexandra. It had come to a halt on the side of the slipway, less than fifteen metres from where the Bentley waited at the traffic light.

Then two men got out of the Audi. Both brandished handguns and

---

[*] Not his real name.

wore hoodies drawn over their heads. The car had tinted windows, but Tshepo could make out the silhouette of a third man who remained waiting behind the steering wheel.

The two men were young, Tshepo noticed. He thought that they couldn't have been older than twenty-five. Tshepo thought he could hear the men exchange a few words in Zulu.

Later, as he replayed the scene in his head for the umpteenth time, Tshepo would note that time didn't freeze or slow down at all that day. If the movies were anything to go by, action scenes were supposed to unfold in slow motion. What he saw next, however, happened at a frighteningly normal pace.

The two men walked towards the stationary Bentley. Wearing a grey hoodie, the shorter of the two gunmen positioned himself in front of the sleek sedan. His accomplice, a tall, slender man wearing a blue top, stood right next to the driver's window.

'Open the door!' Tshepo heard the taller man shout in English.

The Bentley driver understandably disobeyed the order.

The tall gunman then tried to break the Bentley's window by smashing it with his weapon, but he was unsuccessful.

The driver and sole occupant of the Bentley now clearly realised that he would have to take drastic action if he wanted to live. He let the car shoot forward, forcing the gunman in grey to hop out of the way. The Bentley smashed into the car in front of it. The latter's driver panicked and sped off over the crossing, undeterred by the red robot.

The Bentley, however, failed to follow the other car over the crossing to get away from the gunmen. The engine had either stalled or the driver was paralysed with fear.

At this point, the two assassins had had enough. The taller man pointed his gun at the driver and, without hesitation, fired off a few shots in quick succession. Tshepo couldn't see if the bullets hit the driver, but he somehow knew the man was done for.

The two gunmen headed back to the silver Audi. Tshepo again noted that their actions contrasted with those of the characters he had seen making getaways on television. Instead of sprinting back to the car, the young men simply strolled towards it, their relaxed pace in step with the nonchalance with which they had just carried out their grim task.

The Audi left the scene in an equally orderly manner. Without the theatrics of screeching tyres or frantic swerving, it simply slipped up South Road, vanishing from view.

Tshepo moved towards the Bentley. Peeking inside, he saw blood gushing from the driver's head and neck. He didn't have much time to assess the gory scene, because the car's powerful six-litre twin-turbocharged engine suddenly roared to life. Tshepo jumped back as the Bentley lunged forward. He would never be sure whether this was the result of the dying man's final conscious actions or whether his death spasms had somehow kicked the car into motion.

The grey sedan accelerated over South Road, careened to the left and narrowly avoided colliding with the traffic island and robot on the far side of the intersection. It continued down Bowling Avenue in a southerly direction, passing a BP fuel station on its left, before finally smashing into a lamp post on another traffic island. The car's spooky last dash had carried it some 135 metres from where the driver was shot.

A group of people from the fuel station and elsewhere started to gather at the scene. The first emergency responders and police cars arrived not long thereafter, probably at about 12 p.m.

Tshepo watched as that part of Bowling Avenue became busier and busier. By 12:05, some of the police officers and paramedics on site had removed the driver's body from the car.

The body of Phikolomzi Ignatius 'Igo' Mpambani, who was thirty-seven at the time of his violent death on Tuesday 20 June 2017, was placed on the traffic island next to the Bentley and covered with a silver first-aid blanket.

Tshepo would not have been aware of this, but the first responders found a soft cooler bag bearing the logo of a major supermarket chain in the footwell of the front passenger seat. Dark blue, it had the word 'goodness' printed on one side. It was stuffed, not with fresh groceries, but with several stacks of banknotes held together with elastic bands. A quick glance at the cash would have been enough to realise that it was a lot of money. In fact, the cooler bag contained just R100 shy of half a million rand.

There was another R500 000 in the boot. This second stash was also made up of several bundles of banknotes, but instead of being stuffed in a cooler bag, this money simply lay loose among some documents and a briefcase.

When Tshepo later heard about the R1 million that had been found in the car, he was by no means surprised that the gunmen had left behind all of that money. The young men who shot Mpambani weren't there to steal something, Tshepo would tell people in the days and weeks after the murder. They were the type of men who got paid to kill someone.

As the months went by, Mpambani's death featured less and less in conversations among the community of beggars and job-seekers at Tshepo's intersection. It seemed certain that the story about the young businessman's gruesome end would soon fade into oblivion.

A certain Elias Sekgobelo Magashule, for one, would have been relieved about the fact that Mpambani's demise did not draw too much attention. The man popularly known as 'Ace' intended to be elected to one of the most powerful political positions in South Africa at the ruling party's elective conference in December of that year. Any investigation into his murky dealings with the slain tender mogul would have posed a serious threat to his political ambitions.

PART I

CREDENTIAL STRUGGLES

1

The Tumahole 'treasonist'

Parys is one of the Free State's northernmost settlements. It clings to the southern banks of the Vaal River, the inland equivalent of a coastal holiday town, an identity that it has come to embrace over the years. On weekends, its streets overflow with visitors flocking to restaurants, cafés, art galleries and antique shops. From the riverfront, the town radiates to the south-east until it meets a winding railway line that mimics the river's bends and curves.

Beyond the train track a small industrial zone doubles as a buffer between Parys proper and the township of Tumahole, an enduring reminder of the old apartheid government's racially motivated spatial-planning policies. It was here in this township, in November 1959, little more than a decade into the National Party's rule, that Elias Sekgobelo 'Ace' Magashule was born.

The environment Magashule entered was fundamentally unjust. It would shape a generation of agitators, activists and operatives deter-mined to destroy the oppressive regime that governed through racist laws. Magashule today counts himself among this generation, having referred to his contribution to the fight against apartheid on numerous occasions, both in his former capacity as premier of the Free State and in his current role as secretary-general of the African National Congress. Indeed, his account of his struggle past has served him well, given the ANC's practice of awarding its members valuable political capital based on their contri-bution to the liberation movement.

Yet the story of Magashule the freedom fighter is as controversial and problematic as the accounts of his later years as a senior government official. I did not have to look hard to discover that his version of his struggle history is replete with half-truths, ample embellishment and a few outright lies.

Although a rare early interview with Magashule for the ANC Oral History Project provides a first-hand account of his childhood and his years in the liberation movement, this record, like his public utterances, demands scrutiny and fact-checking. It begins in Tumahole.

'Well, my mother had only Standard Three [Grade Five], my father passed away when I was very young – when I was three years old. So I wouldn't know much about him,' Magashule told his interviewer.[1]

A source from his childhood confirmed that Magashule was raised in a single-parent household. The same source said that his mother may have worked as a domestic worker at some point, but that she was best known for running a Mo-China operation from her home. Mo-China, a gambling game that involves betting on numbers, was popular in some South African townships during the 1960s and 1970s. According to my source, Magashule's mother, described as 'a wonderful woman', used some of the proceeds of her gambling operation to support young political activists who sometimes spent time at her house.

In his ANC Oral History Project interview, Magashule recalled that his mother encouraged him from an early age to follow his own path. 'Do you know what my mother always used to say to me? She only used to say "do what will satisfy you; anything which will make you happy you must do". That was the message always.'

He described Tumahole as a 'nice community', where people knew one another, 'from number one to the last house in the township'. 'You remember in the old days when somebody had passed away, he's your neighbour or a person you knew in the township, you'd take some mealie-meal to that house, take some coal or take some wood. That's how we grew up.'

But even this tight-knit community could not shelter the young Magashule from the harsh realities of apartheid South Africa. 'When I was in Standard Five, I can't remember the year, but I grew up in that environment where we were treated by young white boys as ... we were calling them *baas* at that time – *klein baas*. We grew up knowing that they are better off; they know better than us ... We grew up knowing that white people in South Africa don't like us – that's how we grew up because of the type of education we were doing.'

Magashule gradually became aware of the ANC, its affiliated organisations and the broader struggle movement. As a boy he heard the story about the 'One Pound a Day' minimum-wage campaign that had been initiated by the ANC-aligned South African Congress of Trade Unions (SACTU) in the late 1950s.

'As time went on this is the type of information which we managed to get from old people who had been staying in that township,' Magashule explained. 'Well, we just knew the ANC as this organisation which was banned; people left the country to take up arms and fight white people because they were ill-treating us. I faintly remember the ANC – an organisation which will free black people. That's how I remember it.'

According to Magashule, his political consciousness was ignited when the Soweto uprising of 1976 spread to Tumahole. '[I]n 1976 some of the schools in the area were burned. So the Soweto influence actually spread to some of the areas in [the] country, and Parys was one of those areas. We were the last people who did Standard Six. And that's the time when we were doing our studies in Afrikaans.'[2]

Magashule was attending Phehellang Secondary School in Tumahole when the unrest broke out. 'I know the school in Parys where I was [–] it was called higher primary [–] was burned down, and some of the students were arrested. We were fortunate not to be arrested at that time, because we were not involved in those activities. But that's when I became more active.'

During this time, the young Magashule was a keen boxer and soccer player. It was his skills with a football that earned him the nickname 'Ace'.[3]

Although he grew up without a father, he had older male figures to look up to, at least in a political sense. The most prominent was Fezile Dabi, a political activist who was three years Magashule's senior and for whom the district municipality that includes Parys is now named.

According to historian Tshepo Cyril Moloi, Dabi 'played a central role in conscientising some of the young people in Tumahole', helping in the late 1970s and early 1980s to establish the Tumahole Students Organisation (TSO), which tapped into Steve Biko's Black Consciousness Movement for its ideological inspiration. The TSO staged plays with strong political messages and hosted 'symposiums which highlighted the social evils of [their] community'.[4]

Magashule appeared in some of these plays, landing him in the cross-hairs of the apartheid authorities: 'Police were always after us even when … we started with simple dramatic societies. We were actors. We'll act and after acting police would come and say "but your drama is a political drama, you don't want whites".'[5]

According to a hagiographic profile of Magashule that appeared on the Free State provincial government's website while he was premier (and which now appears on his own website), he 'became a founder member of the Congress of South African Students (COSAS) in 1979'.[6] His alleged involvement in COSAS also surfaced in his interview for the ANC Oral History Project: 'I was part of COSAS during its early stages when it was formed,' he is recorded as saying.

But Papi Kganare, a struggle stalwart, former trade unionist and one of COSAS's co-founders, says Magashule played no role in the formation of the organisation. 'I am one of the founding members of COSAS with the likes of Oupa Masuku and so on. Ace was not a founding member,' he told me.

An article that appeared in 2015 in the Free State community newspaper *Express* supports this. Penned by COSAS's first chairperson in the province, it lists the organisation's top Free State leadership during the struggle years. Magashule is not among them.[7]

Magashule's online biography goes on to claim that he also 'participated in the founding of the United Democratic Front [UDF] in the 1980's'. His interview for the ANC Oral History Project includes further details in this regard: '[W]e established the UDF in the Free State in 1984. The UDF was established in '83. In Free State we were responsible ... Comrades like comrade Popo [Molefe], Aubrey Mokoena, Terror [Lekota] was there also, Trevor Manuel. In the Free State we had Dennis Bloem and the others. So we were the pioneers of the UDF in the Free State.' Yet almost all of those UDF pioneers cited by Magashule openly denied that he was involved in setting up the organisation.

Dennis Bloem, a former ANC member who later joined Kganare in the opposition Congress of the People (COPE), said there was no way that Magashule helped to establish the UDF. 'I was a founding member of the UDF in the Free State and nationally, and I can guarantee that Ace was not one of the founding members,' he told me.

Popo Molefe, chairperson of the state-owned logistics company Transnet, concurred. 'That guy is lying, he has never been in the UDF,' he said. 'By the time I was in the Delmas [Treason] Trial [in 1985], we knew everyone from the UDF in the Free State, and Ace was not there. The main UDF guys from Tumahole and its surrounding areas were people like Vuyo Dabi and Bernard Molekane. Ace was not in the thick of things.'

Kganare agreed. 'I organised buses from Bloemfontein to Cape Town [where the UDF was formally launched in August 1983],' he said. 'I know exactly who represented the Free State, and Ace was not one of them.'

Minutes from one of the UDF's first meetings, held in Durban in September 1983, confirm that Magashule was not present during the organisation's early days, at least not as one of its leaders. The document lists about twenty UDF figures who either attended or sent apologies, including Molefe and Lekota. Magashule's name does not appear.[8]

Bloem also explained that prior to the UDF's launch there had been much preparation in the Free State. He was adamant that Magashule played no role in these processes. As a political activist and UDF member from Kroonstad, another northern Free State town not far from Parys, Bloem said he would have known if Magashule had been involved in any major political activities during that time.

In the early 1980s, Bloem and some of his fellow activists campaigned against the so-called Koornhof Bills, a series of proposed laws that sought to establish a segregated tricameral parliament in South Africa. 'We were working on the ground all over the Free State, including in the north. We were putting up posters and painted walls to encourage people to oppose the Koornhof Bills. Magashule was nowhere to be seen during this,' Bloem insisted.

The University of Fort Hare in the Eastern Cape forms the backdrop to perhaps the most egregious and best circulated of Magashule's struggle fibs.

In 1980, after matriculating from Residensia Secondary School in Sebokeng in Gauteng, Magashule began his tertiary education at Fort Hare. It is unclear what degree he pursued, but sources familiar with his background said he obtained a Bachelor of Arts.

It was while enrolled at Fort Hare that Magashule apparently became embroiled in one of that era's most famous campus revolts. 'In 1983 [sic] when I was a student at Fort Hare we were arrested, there were twenty-two of us, Bheki Mlangeni, Fezile Dabi and others,' Magashule related in his ANC Oral History Project interview. 'I was arrested during that time and the charge was treason, high treason, in an attempt to assassinate the State President of Ciskei, [Lennox] Sebe, at Fort Hare during the graduation ceremony, where we did not want Sebe to come into the campus.' This claim has made it onto the ANC's official website ('Whilst a student, he was arrested and charged with high treason in 1982'[9]) and a variety of other public platforms.

Along with genocide, crimes against humanity and war crimes, treason is viewed as one of the most serious criminal offences.[10] In South Africa in the 1980s, a guilty verdict on a charge of high treason could have resulted in the death penalty. Furthermore, being charged with treason for his political convictions would have secured Magashule a place in the struggle's proverbial hall of fame, along with the likes of Treason trialists Nelson Mandela, Oliver Tambo, Walter Sisulu and Albert Luthuli, or Mosiuoa 'Terror' Lekota, his contemporary from the Free State and one of the Delmas trialists.

That Magashule does not hold such status calls into question his alleged treason charge. In fact, old newspaper reports excavated from the archives beneath the Johannesburg City Library, a book on Fort Hare's history, court records and a few sources tell a far less dramatic story.

On 1 May 1982, 'one of the most significant protests of the early eighties' occurred at Fort Hare, researcher and academic Rico Devara Chapman writes in his book *Student Resistance to Apartheid at the University of Fort Hare*.[11] The trouble started when a motorcade carrying then Ciskei prime minister Lennox Sebe and members of his government neared the university's Alice campus, where students were getting ready for a graduation ceremony. In those days, the town of Alice formed part of Ciskei, one of the apartheid government's so-called Bantustans. As participants in the homeland system, black leaders like Sebe were reviled by the liberation movement in near equal measure to apartheid's white enforcers.

When the cavalcade entered the campus, students hurled rocks at Sebe's car, flashed black-power salutes and shouted for the Ciskei leader to leave, according to an eyewitness account included in Chapman's book. The Ciskei police were quick to respond with live ammunition, batons and whips. The authorities shot two students and arrested twenty-two people. This is the origin of Magashule's 'high treason' story.

Newspaper reports from 1982 further help determine what really happened. On 5 May 1982, the *Daily Dispatch* reported on the 'tense atmosphere' at Fort Hare following Sebe's run-in with the students. Major-General Charles Sebe, the prime minister's brother and Ciskei's director of state security, told the newspaper that twenty-two people had been arrested on the campus and that they were to be charged in accordance with the Riotous Assemblies Act.[12]

On 19 May, the *Daily Dispatch* followed up on the story, reporting that 'twenty people appeared in the Magistrate's Court [in Alice] ... yesterday on charges of public violence arising out of disturbances at the university earlier this month'. According to the article, 'those in court yesterday were part of a group of 22 arrested'. The authorities had apparently decided to let two of the detainees go.[13] It would seem that the protesters were charged with public violence, not high treason as Magashule claimed.

The report from 19 May proved particularly useful. It included the initials and surnames of all those who had been arrested, bar the two who had been let off the hook. Accordingly, one 'E. Marashula [sic]' was detained and charged. (A later report, in a partial correction, listed 'Elias Magashule' as one of the accused.)[14] The report also named 'B. Mlangeni'. This would be Bheki Mlangeni, one of the men Magashule referred to in his ANC Oral History Project interview. Mlangeni was later killed in a bomb attack planned by apartheid assassin Eugene de Kock.[15]

One former Fort Hare student who helped plan the protest action confirmed to me that Magashule was among those arrested and shed more light on the events of 1982. 'Fort Hare did not have a student representative council [SRC], so we banded together as the Azanian Students Organisation [AZASO],' this source told me. 'We planned to disrupt Sebe's visit to the campus because we did not recognise his government's authority and we wanted to get rid of him.'

As with COSAS, Magashule also claimed to have been a member of AZASO: 'And when I went to Fort Hare I became a part of AZASO.'[16] But my Fort Hare source tells a different story. 'I was in my second year in 1982 and I knew all the activists on campus,' he said. 'Ace was not among those I knew to be activists, and he certainly was not a member of AZASO. He definitely did not help plan the disruption of Sebe's visit.'

There was also never any intention to assassinate Sebe or any other member of the Ciskei government. 'We [AZASO] planned to disrupt the visit,' my source indicated, '[but] there was no plan to kill Sebe.'

In the chaos that broke out after the Ciskei police arrived on campus, the authorities rounded up anyone they could catch. As a result, Magashule may have become an accidental activist that day. 'Some of the people who were detained were part of the planned action against Sebe, but others were just bystanders,' my source said. 'I think Ace was unlucky to have been apprehended.'

According to this source, AZASO members helped raise funds for their detained fellow students. The organisation also sought the services of attorney Hintsa Siwisa to represent the group. 'That is when I first heard about Ace Magashule, when we had to get legal assistance for those who were detained,' my source explained.

Before the uprising, Magashule was apparently not a regular fixture at political gatherings on campus. 'There were AZASO meetings on campus where people like Bheki Mlangeni made speeches that lasted until 3 a.m. Ace did not attend any of these gatherings before the unrest during Sebe's visit,' the source said.

Magashule and his co-accused were eventually convicted on charges relating to 'public violence committed at a university'. They were each given 'a fine of R400 plus a suspended sentence of 300 days' imprisonment'. But the case went on appeal and dragged on until 1985, when Ciskei's Supreme Court dismissed the appeals and increased the sentences. Magashule was among sixteen of the accused whose sentences were increased to jail time ranging from one to three years.[17] It was still a far cry from being found guilty on charges of high treason, and by all indications Magashule did not end up serving any of his prison time.

Court records and old newspapers provide clues as to where Magashule may have found the creative inspiration for his story about the supposed assassination attempt and subsequent 'treason' trial.

In a summary of the protest action in their appeal ruling, the Ciskei Supreme Court judges noted the following: 'During the confusion of the riot appellants Nos 1 and 2 brought a thick pipe filled with cement and stone and some 90 cm long and together they threw it through the left side of the rear window of the motor vehicle in which Mr Namba Sebe [another brother of Prime Minister Sebe], the then Minister of Transport, was travelling. He was seated at the left rear of the vehicle and on reading the record one can only conclude that it was merely fortuitous that he was not killed or at least very seriously injured.' Magashule, who was listed as appellant No. 12, was not responsible for the attack on the minister's car.[18]

In addition, at the time of the students' court case, a terror trial was being heard in the Ciskei Supreme Court. Four men from Mdantsane outside East London were accused of being members of the then banned ANC, participating in terrorist activities and recruiting people to undergo military training.[19] These sound like the kind of struggle activities Magashule would later claim to have been involved in.

In 1984, after completing his studies at Fort Hare, Magashule enrolled for a Higher Education Diploma at the University of the Witwatersrand, but he was only there for a few months. 'I couldn't survive because I did not have the money, so I left Wits, it was around March or April,' he said in his ANC Oral History Project interview.

He then began working as a teacher. After a stint at Moqhaka Secondary School in Sebokeng, he returned to his old school, Phehellang Secondary in Parys, in 1985. A source from this phase of Magashule's life said he taught English and Bible studies.

It was in November 1985 that he ran into trouble with the apartheid government's notorious police force. While he was teaching at Phehellang, he was nabbed by the police under Section 29 of the Internal Security Act. The Act allowed for political detainees to be held in solitary confinement so that they could be interrogated.

'I spent nine months in solitary confinement,' Magashule later recalled. 'That's the most terrible and horrible type of detention. That's the worst time in my life because I was alone in the cell. I wanted to commit suicide.'[20]

He repeated this story in a 2008 interview with journalist Fiona Forde: 'I can assure you that Section 29 is serious torture. You know, I wanted to commit suicide after that. I was completely and emotionally destroyed.'[21]

My source, who was around at the time, remembered the arrest but seemed to recall that Magashule was detained for six months, not nine. 'The police alleged that he was encouraging unrest in Tumahole and in the general area,' the source told me. 'He was held at several police stations in the area during those months, including the one at Koppies [a small town near Parys].'

This wouldn't be Magashule's last encounter with the apartheid security forces.

2

Hillbrow days

At some point after his 'treason' trial at Fort Hare, Magashule slipped into the secretive world of the ANC's underground armed struggle, at least according to his own recollection.

An article penned in 2014 by two of Magashule's spokespeople for the government-owned magazine *Public Sector Manager* included a description of the then Free State premier's alleged clandestine activities for Umkhonto we Sizwe (MK), the ANC's armed wing.[1] The tax-funded puff piece's introduction is a clumsy attempt at espionage prose in the vein of a John le Carré spy novel:

> The Jan Smuts International Airport in Johannesburg is packed to capacity, with people coming in and out of the country, and some travelling locally. A lanky fellow with somewhat of an unkempt beard, clinching onto his teddy bear, snakes his way through the imposing crowd, and makes his way to customs.
>
> This was during the 1980s when Ace Magashule used to go in and out of the country as a courier. He would travel to the ANC offices in Lusaka to get money and smuggled it back into South Africa. At times, he would also take many people out of the country for military training.
>
> 'I had to carry cash with me so I stuffed the money into a teddy bear. I would deliberately carry more than two bags and at the airport would ask someone, preferably a white lady, to help me. "Please lady, I have a lot of luggage. Please hold this teddy bear for me," I would beg. After we had passed through customs, I took the teddy bear back saying, "Thank you very much, have a good day," before disappearing into the airport crowd. It was an exciting and dangerous life.'[2]

I showed the piece to one Free State politician who had spent a considerable amount of time with Magashule in the 1980s. His unequivocal assessment of the teddy-bear story was that it was 'bullshit'. 'I was with Ace the whole time during those years, and I can guarantee that it did not happen,' he told me.

A second source, who also spent time with Magashule during the 1980s, agreed. 'It is true that Ace worked with money for struggle operations, but that thing is not true,' this source said. 'It simply did not work like that.'

Several other ANC stalwarts and former MK operatives agreed that Magashule's teddy-bear tale sounded outlandish. ANC veteran Khulu Mbatha, who wrote *Unmasked: Why the ANC Failed to Govern*, said it was highly unlikely that an underground operative would have used such tactics to bring money into the country. 'There was nothing like that in those days,' Mbatha told me. 'Even if this were an actual MK method of transporting money, a real MK operative would not dare to disclose this.'

Another former MK operative, who served in one of the government's intelligence agencies after 1994, called Magashule's story 'unrealistic' and 'bizarre', telling me, 'This is not how an MK operative would have gone about it.'

Magashule's interview for the ANC Oral History Project included further details about his alleged cloak-and-dagger activities: 'Well, we were all over the country. We'll pretend to be lawyer[s] sometimes, put on a tie, take a bag, stay in hotels, change names, facilitate certain things, when people were coming into the country we had to look after [them by] giving them some money.'

From his own telling, it would appear that Magashule was a point man for operatives sneaking back into the country from one or other of the ANC's foreign bases: 'We would welcome them and accommodate them, brief them about particular areas where they were supposed to go and operate from. That's the type of work we were doing.'

Elsewhere in the interview, Magashule elaborated on this responsibility. 'And what happened, as I said, a lot of comrades were infiltrated into our townships, they would engage us and we wouldn't know that this man comes from exile, is in the underground. As people were engaging in that struggle people would identify that this one can go for a crash course, come back, and be trained quickly and sent back into the country to fight. Others were trained inside the country.'

When asked how and by whom he had been recruited into MK,

Magashule replied: 'There's an old man from Bophelong [near Vanderbijl-park], we always referred to him as "old man", I [have] just forgotten his surname ... ntate Soku or something like that in Bophelong. He was the main person who was actually recruiting people in the underground.'

A former MK member from the area around Parys disputed Magashule's version. This source was able to provide detailed information on the 'old man' and his underground cell. 'That man [Magashule] referred to was Ernest Sotso. It is true that he recruited people into MK, but Ace was not one of them.'

My source said that he worked with Sotso during that time, and that he would have known if Magashule was part of this network. 'If Ace was really recruited by Sotso, he would have had no problem remembering his name and surname.'

He added that Tate Makgoe, the current member of the executive council (MEC) for education in the Free State, was a member of that MK cell. 'Ask Tate if Ace was in that cell, or if he was even in MK,' he urged me. Unfortunately, Makgoe chose not to respond to my queries.

When asked to provide a more concrete description of his role in the MK underground for the ANC Oral History Project, Magashule seemed vague on the details: 'Well, I have done a lot of groundwork internally in the country. As I said there was this internal high team, in the early 80s, '83, '84 upwards. That's when we became more active in the underground work.' He added that he had been 'given some instructions to remain in the country, [to] remain operating underground'.

My source from MK in the Parys area asked who gave Magashule these instructions. Papi Kganare was also curious. 'Who else was in his cell? Who was his commander? Ace has not been able to provide such details because he was not in MK,' he insisted.

According to Magashule, he interacted with and received instruction from the very top echelon of the ANC's leadership structure in the late 1980s. When asked about his commanders for the ANC Oral History Project, he replied with the following: 'As I said I've been working with, eh ... some of those comrades have passed away who were my commanders. One of my commanders was a simple guy called Benji Tsholota. You know, because of my high-profile activities I was not made any commander I was just commanded by young guys of which I appreciated. But there were guys from exile in the underground who commanded me the likes of

Winnie Mandela had direct contacts with Chris Hani and, as I said, Steve Tshwete and many others ... Steve Tshwete, Chris Hani, Thabo Mbeki, Jacob Zuma – those four ... I was in the main accounting direct in the underground to comrade Chris [Hani]. But I would always ... At times when I left the country to go to Zambia I would meet the four.'

Kganare struggled to believe any of this. 'Chris Hani is dead, so he can't verify this, but there are people who worked with Chris who can verify,' he said. 'When did Chris mentor him and where?' And the former MK member from the Parys area said the only Benji he knew from that time was a student leader who had no affiliation to MK.

Requests sent to then ANC spokesperson Pule Mabe to help fill in some of these blanks went unanswered, as did queries sent to the Thabo Mbeki Foundation about Mbeki's interaction with Magashule during that time.

For someone who claims to have been so prominent in the struggle movement that he rubbed shoulders with the likes of Hani and Mbeki, Magashule left a surprisingly faint mark in the memories of his struggle contemporaries. This holds true for both the movement's underground and formal structures.

Mbatha said he first heard about Magashule at the ANC's forty-eighth national elective conference, held in Durban in 1991, after the unbanning of the ANC the year before.

One of my sources, the former MK member turned government spook, said he never encountered Magashule during the struggle. 'I did not meet him in my world,' he maintained. 'I only got to know about him after the unbanning.'

Written accounts of the period reflect a similar dearth of information concerning Magashule's role in the struggle. Hugh Macmillan's *The Lusaka Years: The ANC in Exile in Zambia, 1963–1994* does not mention Magashule once. If Magashule did indeed meet with the ANC's top brass at the organisation's Zambian base, it had to have been a highly secretive affair, for Macmillan's thorough study of that epoch does not reference any such meeting.

Thula Simpson's *Umkhonto we Sizwe: The ANC's Armed Struggle* is equally silent on Magashule's alleged involvement in underground activities. Simpson's book has been praised for being 'brilliant at laying out events and actions carried out by both prominent and less known members of MK'.[3] Magashule, who claims to have held such an important position within MK that he reported directly to someone of Hani's stature, must feel aggrieved at being overlooked by Simpson.

To be fair to Magashule, there does appear to be some truth in his narrative. Between 1985 and the end of the decade, the UDF's ability to operate as a unified resistance movement was severely hampered by successive states of emergency, the detainment of its leaders and, eventually, the apartheid government's decision to ban the organisation.[4] It was during this troubled phase of the UDF's existence that Magashule did in fact attain a degree of prominence within the movement. It was also during this time that he played a role in something at least resembling an MK cell. Sources who were at his side or who had contact with him in this period were able to verify this.

In 1986, in the depth of winter, President P.W. Botha's government declared yet another state of emergency. In the evening after the announcement, Magashule and a group of about twenty comrades from Parys arrived at Matthew Chaskalson's home in Johannesburg. Matthew's father, Arthur, had been part of the legal team that had defended Mandela and his fellow accused in the Rivonia Trial in 1963–64, and he would later become South Africa's chief justice. In the 1980s, Matthew was making his own mark as a lawyer, and his home would sometimes be used as a temporary place of shelter for activists.

'Ace was the leader of this group of people from Parys who were now on the run because of the state of emergency,' Chaskalson remembered. 'They were sleeping on the floor at my house for a couple of days, and I was trying to find them more permanent accommodation.'

Eventually, Chaskalson found an apartment for Magashule and some of his associates in Hillbrow. 'I paid the first month's rent, and after that I didn't really see much of Ace again,' he recalled. 'He was an enterprising guy, so he soon tapped into other sources of funding to sustain himself.'

This marked the start of Magashule's time in 'internal exile' in Johannesburg, which would last from mid-1986 to 1989. One source who was at Magashule's side during this period said the group did start functioning as an MK unit, and did report to the top brass.

'This was a difficult time for the entire movement, also for the underground structures,' this source told me. 'The government crackdown that came with the states of emergency disrupted everything, so we had to make other plans ... We were instructed by Chris Hani, Mbeki and Tshwete to operate from Johannesburg because things were too hot on the ground in rural areas like the Free State.'

But their contact with these leaders was infrequent. My source admitted that they only met with the top leadership on about two occasions at the ANC's Zambian headquarters in Lusaka. He said their unit's main task was 'coordination', which included facilitating communication between active underground units and helping to establish new structures. 'We communicated with actual operatives who were sent into South Africa from Lusaka, we were their contact point,' he elaborated. But he scoffed at Magashule's attempts to paint himself as the struggle's James Bond. 'I don't know why he is doing that,' he shrugged.

The group did make use of fake passports to travel overseas, but nobody smuggled cash into the country using children's toys. 'We were idle for the most part,' my source said, 'like a sleeper cell, but we needed to keep on moving around because we were being watched or chased around by the security police.'

On one occasion, around 1986, Magashule and some other members of the Hillbrow group flew to Stockholm, Sweden, to meet with several anti-apartheid organisations. A Swedish group funded the trip, and Magashule and his comrades used the opportunity to raise money for the Tumahole Civic Association. When they returned to South Africa, they once again melted into Hillbrow's busy streets. One of the places the group used as a base was the Fontana Inn, an apartment block and hotel in the heart of Hillbrow.

Magashule's time in Hillbrow coincided with a second stint at Wits, where he enrolled for a law degree in 1987. Once again, he did not finish his studies, opting instead to do a marketing course through the University of South Africa (UNISA).[5]

It was during this time that Magashule became known as someone with access to money and who liked flaunting cash. 'At university, Ace got all the girls and he had lots of money with him,' recalled one of his former comrades from the Free State. 'Questions were raised about where the money had come from.'

One of the people Magashule looked out for during this time was Hantsi Mayeza, a younger girl from Parys who was getting her high-school education at a small college in Braamfontein in Johannesburg. According to several sources, Mayeza and Magashule are extremely close.

A source who knows both individuals said that her family sheltered Magashule from time to time when he was on the run in the 1980s, and that he helped pay for Mayeza's living expenses. Mayeza, who has since taken the surname Matseke, would later become a business partner to one of Magashule's children. She also became the chairperson of the Free State Development Corporation (FDC), a state-owned entity that has been at the centre of some of the dodgiest financial dealings involving Magashule and his family.

Dennis Bloem remembered the UDF leadership asking how Magashule and the Hillbrow group could afford to stay at the Fontana Inn. 'They were there for a long time,' Bloem said. 'They bought food and paid their rent. The question is how they had funded all of that.'

His suspicions are rooted in a long-standing rift between the group from Tumahole and the Free State power bloc centred on Mosiuoa Lekota and his allies. Although Lekota and Bloem were both born in the northern Free State town of Kroonstad, they would later align with the southern Free State faction in Bloemfontein and its surrounds, while Magashule and his allies from Parys and other towns near the Vaal River would form the nucleus of what became known as the northern Free State faction.

The Lekota bloc has always been deeply critical of the fact that Magashule and his associates remained in Hillbrow, from where they supposedly contributed to the liberation movement's activities in the Free State. There is consensus among these critics that the Hillbrow group wasted valuable resources meant for their home province while doing very little to further the cause. 'We told those guys that the security police wanted them to be in Hillbrow so that they couldn't do any damage on the ground in the Free State,' said a former UDF member from Bloemfontein.

'Myself and many other comrades who are still alive were very active in the then Orange Free State at that time,' Bloem said in a public statement after Winnie Madikizela-Mandela passed away in April 2018. 'We were harassed and tortured by the brutal apartheid police. All that I know of Ace, is that he was staying in [the] Fontana Inn in Hillbrow, Johannesburg, with a group of youngsters from Parys.'[6]

As the struggle against apartheid intensified during the late 1980s, the faction that broadly aligned itself with Lekota wondered whether Magashule and his Hillbrow group were not in fact hampering the liberation movement's operations.

A source sympathetic to the Hillbrow group's struggle legacy said Magashule and his comrades had little choice but to go into hiding in Hillbrow. He used the Free State Youth Congress as a case in point.

The UDF-aligned Free State Youth Congress was established primarily to mobilise non-student youths in the Free State, but circumstances forced its leadership to begin operating from Johannesburg in the period after the first states of emergency. 'One of the [Free State Youth Congress] leaders was arrested near Sasolburg, which showed that it was necessary to move the whole operation to Johannesburg,' this source told me. 'It was just easier to blend in and disappear in Hillbrow.'

Two sources from his Hillbrow days explained where at least some of Magashule's cash came from: fundraising. 'Ace was very good at tapping into sources of funding,' said one of the sources. 'He got money from the South African Council of Churches [SACC] and even from Beyers Naudé, whom he was very close to. He also continued to get money from Swedish donors.'

There was considerable unhappiness among some Free State UDF members about this money, which was meant to assist activists and help fund struggle activities in the Free State. As Magashule and the Hillbrow group amassed more money, rumours and suspicions started to circulate within the broader UDF environment that some of these funds were being misappropriated.

According to one former UDF leader, the late Eric Molobi once accused Magashule of abusing liberation funds. Molobi had been the chairperson of the National Education Crisis Committee (NECC) and apparently somehow got wind of Magashule's alleged transgressions. 'We knew Ace was a fellow that we had to treat with a degree of caution, because there were issues over money that were never resolved,' this source explained. 'This made us wary of him.'

A former struggle activist who later became a senior political leader in the Free State, and one of Magashule's many enemies after 1994, described one particular instance where Magashule was allegedly 'caught' with a bag stuffed with cash. 'During their Hillbrow days Ace stole money that was meant for the liberation movement, so it never surprised me when he started looting the Free State's coffers,' claimed this person.

It is almost impossible to verify whether Magashule stole money meant for the liberation movement. After the banning of the UDF and its affiliate organisations in 1987, these structures could no longer receive donations in their official bank accounts. Therefore, contributions during this period were received in cash. Moreover, when donors gave money for the cause, they generally remained anonymous and hardly demanded accountability or transparency with regards to how the funds were being spent. Sources who were active in the underground movement described how they literally received suitcases and bags stuffed with cash. There were directives as to how the money needed to be spent, but there were no auditors, accountants or other watchdogs to keep track of what the struggle operatives were doing with the cash.

Azhar Cachalia, the UDF's treasurer during the last few years of the organisation's existence, recalled how difficult it was to manage the movement's finances around the time of the states of emergency. 'Money was literally being passed around in shoeboxes, so things were difficult in terms of accountability,' he said.

While we will probably never know whether Magashule stole money meant for the liberation of his people, his reaction to one such accusation in the 1980s is indicative of his disdain for anyone who questions him when it comes to matters involving money. The episode also highlights the more thuggish tactics Magashule is willing to employ to silence those who dare to look into his financial conduct.

In January 1987, struggle activist Zingile Dingane was released from Grootvlei Prison outside Bloemfontein. Dingane, a UDF member from the southern Free State region, had been arrested on the eve of the second state of emergency announced in June the previous year.

After spending more than 200 days in prison, Dingane re-entered society at the height of the government's harsh crackdown on the UDF and the broader struggle movement. But he was eager to start rebuilding some of the activist structures that had been dismantled during the states of emergency, especially in the sphere of education.

Dingane had been a member of the Free State branch of the UDF-aligned National Union of South African Students (NUSAS), which provided bursaries to poor students, among other activities. When Dingane approached the UDF's interim leadership for funding, he was told that Magashule had already taken money on behalf of the Free State. Like Molobi, Dingane started to ask questions on UDF platforms about what Magashule and his Hillbrow crew were doing with the cash that they had been collecting for the struggle.

One day, not long thereafter, a convoy of five cars filled with people stopped outside Dingane's house in the Bloemfontein township of Rocklands. It was Magashule and his group from Hillbrow. They had come to confront Dingane about the questions he was asking.

According to sources from both sides of the Free State divide, Magashule, who apparently led the Hillbrow group, was particularly aggressive towards Dingane. 'Things got very heated,' recounted one source. 'Ace was putting his finger right in Dingane's face. I think there would have been violence that day if it weren't for the fact that Dingane also had quite a lot of people with him.'

Those familiar with the saga recalled that Magashule's message to Dingane was clear: if you question how we use our struggle resources, we will come and deal with you. Dingane, who later became secretary to Parliament before a stint as an MEC in Magashule's provincial government, did not deny the incident, but said that he did not want to discuss the matter.

3

Exile

Of the late 1980s, Magashule had this to say: 'I was a high profile person during those times in the UDF. In '86, '87 I was part when other leaders were arrested and became part of the National Executive Committee [NEC] of the UDF.'[1]

The term 'high profile' may be a bit of a stretch. While it is true that Magashule did begin to take a more active leadership role in the UDF in the second half of the decade, his ascendancy needs to be assessed against the backdrop of the crises facing the organisation after 1985.

After Mosiuoa Lekota, Popo Molefe and other members of the core leadership were detained, the UDF was forced to form interim leadership structures. 'Ace only rose in the UDF ranks after the second state of emergency [in June 1986] and after the UDF was listed as an affected organisation,' said one of Magashule's struggle-era contemporaries from the Free State. 'There were coordinators from the various provinces who formed something like an NEC, but unlike the earlier NEC, the leaders weren't elected to this structure.'

There may have been some resentment in the Lekota camp about the fact that Magashule's group had wriggled into more prominent positions within the movement while the likes of Lekota had been rendered politically inactive because of the Delmas Treason Trial.

In his comprehensive book on the UDF, Jeremy Seekings details the historic rift between the Free State UDF's southern and northern factions. Seekings notes that 'a regional committee was eventually elected in April 1986 but apparently excluded activists from the southern Free State'.[2]

Azhar Cachalia, the organisation's former treasurer, said that whatever leadership structure Magashule had formed a part of would have been an interim arrangement. Before the states of emergency in 1985 and 1986, the UDF held elective conferences where its members elected formal

NECs. But this practice was halted when the UDF was banned. Magashule was therefore most likely not officially elected to any leadership position in the UDF.

'I cannot recall how many meetings he attended but it would not have been often,' said Cachalia. 'I also do not know whether he was formally elected to attend. He was not, however, a central figure in the UDF's national decision-making structures.' This is glaringly at odds with Magashule's own portrayal of himself as a top leader.

Apart from his role as a point of contact for incoming underground operatives, Magashule has also claimed that he helped to take MK recruits out of the country. 'We made sure that a lot of people leave after '84 ... up to '90,' he said in his ANC Oral History Project interview. 'We were actually in charge of ensuring that people leave the country ... others who were already really targeted by police would be the type of people we would want to take out of the country, because they were hunted day in and day out. A lot of people in the [Free State] province were taken out ... As I say, eh, they were networks throughout the country, there were people in charge of those networks. The likes of Winnie Mandela and the others played a very important role, particularly in the Free State in terms of this type of coordination.'

The former MK member from around Parys claimed this was an 'absolute lie'. 'There is no one who would be able to corroborate that claim,' he insisted.

After Winnie Madikizela-Mandela's death, Magashule visited the mother of slain struggle activist Stompie Seipei, who also hailed from Tumahole. The event received a fair amount of media coverage, and Magashule spoke about his involvement with Madikizela-Mandela during the late 1980s.

Dennis Bloem took umbrage at Magashule's claims. 'Yesterday I listened ... while he [Magashule] sat with Stompie Seipei's mother, telling the nation how he took more than 100 young comrades out of the country for military training with Mama Winnie,' an angry Bloem said in a statement. 'He knows that he did not do this, only Mama Winnie did.'[3]

According to one of Magashule's former associates from the time of their 'internal exile' in Hillbrow, the truth lies somewhere in the middle. 'Our unit in Johannesburg did assist people to get out of the country, and Winnie did help us to get people out, but it wasn't anywhere near a hundred people,' said this source. 'I can only think of about twenty people that we helped to get out.'

In an apparent attempt to latch on to the renewed popularity of Madikizela-Mandela in the days after her death, Magashule used his visit with Seipei's mother to reiterate a widely circulated view that Madikizela-Mandela had not been responsible for Seipei's death in the late 1980s, and that the apartheid government's security and intelligence apparatus had instead fabricated her involvement as part of a smear campaign. In doing so, he made claims about his activities during the struggle that appear to be untrue.

'We knew [she did not kill Seipei], because we had been working with Mama Winnie, we have been there all the time,' Magashule told journalists. 'We all ran away from the Free State and we were there, we trained Stompie and the others how to use an AK-47, how to use a hand grenade, at Mama Winnie's place.'[4]

Two of Magashule's struggle compatriots from the Hillbrow days, one former MK operative from the Free State and a former UDF leader all said Magashule was talking nonsense. 'Is he saying he trained a child to be a soldier? If that is the case, whatever they were doing there was not an MK operation,' said the former UDF leader, whose proximity to Madikizela-Mandela was such that she visited the hospital when one of his children was born.

Previously, Magashule claimed to have received his own military training 'inside the country'. 'When I left [South Africa] I had already received a lot of thorough training,' he said.[5] But the former MK member from the Parys area insisted that Magashule was not trained by anyone from MK. 'If he learnt how to use an assault rifle or hand grenades, he needs to tell us who taught him that.'

One of the sources from the Hillbrow crew said Magashule never underwent any military training and that he was in no way capable of handling an AK-47 or a hand grenade, never mind instructing anyone else on how to use them. 'We once received a bag full of firearms and ammunition that we needed to get to actual MK operatives, and Ace wanted to check them out and handle them,' recalled this source. 'We were in a hotel, and I told him to leave the things, he was going to get himself killed or he was going to expose us.'

In his public statement, Bloem accused Magashule of abusing Madikizela-Mandela's legacy for his own political gain. 'It is very painful for me to see and listen [to] how some people are using Mama Winnie's passing to promote their own names and egos,' he fumed. 'It is very sad that people such as Mr Ace Magashule can stoop so low.'

The statement tied into a broader public spat over Magashule's relationship with Madikizela-Mandela and his provincial government's apparent disregard for her legacy. At one of the struggle icon's memorial services, former finance minister Trevor Manuel lambasted Magashule because the Free State government had failed to restore a house in the town of Brandfort where Madikizela-Mandela had lived under banning orders during the 1980s. There were also indications that millions of rands earmarked for the restoration had gone missing, an issue that had deeply upset Manuel.[6]

Magashule was not going to take this beating on the chin. He was quick to accuse Manuel of sowing disunity in the ruling party, and careful to sidestep the issue of the Brandfort house and the missing money. 'When you talk about unity of the movement, don't use memorial services of revolutionaries to attack other leaders,' Magashule fired back. 'When you don't attack other leaders, you are not a coward. You are a disciplined member of the movement ... Inside internal meetings of the ANC, we talk. We can criticize you but, when I attack and criticize another leader, I am weakening the movement and this is the culture we must understand – we must nurture it.'[7] Curiously, Magashule chose to ignore Bloem's comments about his struggle history.

Bloem later told me that he had been in regular contact with Caleb Motshabi, an MK operative who established and oversaw the primary network through which the Free State's underground recruits were transported from Thaba 'Nchu, near Bloemfontein, to Lesotho. According to Bloem, Motshabi never mentioned that Magashule was in any way involved in the process. 'After I exposed Ace, many ANC comrades contacted me and told me someone needed to say this, this thing needed to come out,' Bloem told me.

As expected, Bloem's public accusations drew criticism from people sympathetic to Magashule. In a letter to the Sunday Independent, former MK member and public service and administration minister Ayanda Dlodlo came to his aid. 'There is more than enough evidence to prove that Magashule was indeed in the liberation struggle not as a planted enemy, but as a freedom fighter,' she wrote. 'All too often, we tend to want to erase those that we do not like for whatever reason, in a quest to satisfy our hate.'[8]

In her defence of Magashule, Dlodlo cited an indictment document that formed part of the Delmas Treason Trial. The document sets out some of the accuseds' activities in Tumahole in the mid-1980s.[9] One was a campaign that saw UDF-aligned organisations like the Tumahole Students Organisation allegedly intimidate and attack ward councillors from Tumahole who were viewed as 'sell-outs' and 'puppets' of the apartheid government. 'On 24 March 1985 the house of a woman councilor [sic] ... was petrol bombed,' reads the document. 'On the next day it was attacked with stones. Present were Ace Magashule, Vuyo Dabi and [Lister] Skosana.'

The attacks on this councillor's home continued even after she had resigned. According to the document: 'Her husband thereupon fetched Ace Magashule, Mosepidi and Thabane who said that they did not know the reason for the attacks as they had told the children to accept this councilor back into the community.' Mosepidi and Thabane, whose first names are not disclosed in the document, were members of the Tumahole Civic Association (TCA).

Other records from the Delmas trial further detail Magashule's role in protest activities. One witness, Matthews Thekiso, testified that Magashule spoke at a TCA meeting in February 1985. The purpose of the gathering had been to address rent increases imposed on Tumahole residents, and Magashule apparently urged residents to stand together in their opposition to the increases.[10]

Magashule was not one of the twenty-two accused in the Delmas trial, but these court records do confirm that he at least participated in struggle activities. However, the documented proof of his presence in the broader struggle environment seems to be at odds with the tales Magashule has told in an apparent attempt to embellish his struggle record.

Dlodlo maintained that there was 'anecdotal evidence from comrades' that enabled her to 'positively place Magashule in the trenches'. 'A senior commissar of uMkhonto weSizwe remembers meeting Magashule in Botswana, he had come with three others from Tumahole to seek training,' she claimed.[11] But this contradicted Magashule's own version of events. As mentioned earlier, he told the ANC Oral History Project that he was trained 'inside the country'.

Dlodlo's assertion also refuted those of my sources who were with Magashule during that time, and who all maintained that he never received any military training. Requests to Dlodlo's spokesperson for information on the 'senior commissar' she mentioned in her article went unanswered.

It is also worth noting that Stompie Seipei's mother, Mananki, does not share Magashule's view that Madikizela-Mandela was not involved in her son's death.

I went to her home in Tumahole several months after Magashule's visit. Mananki's daughter translated her heartbreaking recollection of Stompo, which is the original nickname his family gave him because of his diminutive figure. His mother does not know when 'Stompo' became 'Stompie'.

Mananki was upset that some media reports had suggested that she too believed Madikizela-Mandela was innocent. 'The stories that said Stompie's mom believes Winnie did not kill Stompie are not true, she never said that,' explained Mananki's daughter. 'What she said was that she forgave whoever was responsible for his death. All she knows about his death is that he was last seen going to Winnie's house.'

There is a backstory to the Seipei saga that might explain why Magashule wants to create the impression that Stompie's mother shares his belief in Madikizela-Mandela's innocence.

In November 1988, about a month before Seipei's brutal murder at the hands of members of Madikizela-Mandela's infamous Mandela United Football Club, Magashule showed up at Reverend Paul Verryn's office at the South African Council of Churches' headquarters.[12] In those days, the SACC's offices were at the Central Methodist Church in downtown Johannesburg. Verryn had had intermittent contact with Magashule's group of internal exiles, and had even conducted the ceremony when Magashule married his wife, Seipati, at the Central Methodist Church in 1987.

When Magashule came to Verryn at the end of 1988, he had with him a young boy whom Verryn would later come to know as Stompie, a fourteen-year-old political activist from Magashule's hometown in the Free State. According to Verryn, Magashule was also accompanied by Matthew Chaskalson. Chaskalson, however, recalled that Magashule or one of the other comrades from Parys had come to fetch Seipei from his house in Johannesburg, after which he never saw the boy again.

Whatever the case, Magashule wanted Verryn to take Seipei into his care at his parsonage in Soweto, which was near Madikizela-Mandela's house. Magashule was concerned for Seipei's safety, as he had been recently apprehended by the security police and risked re-arrest. Verryn agreed to take Seipei in.

But shortly after he arrived in Soweto, members of the Mandela United Football Club kidnapped Seipei and three other youths from the parsonage. They were taken to Madikizela-Mandela's house, where 'Mama Winnie' and other club members viciously assaulted them and accused Seipei of being a spy for the security police, according to the testimony of one of the surviving youths at the Truth and Reconciliation Commission (TRC).[13] A week later, Seipei's body was found near Madikizela-Mandela's house. His throat had been cut.

Jerry Richardson, one of Madikizela-Mandela's bodyguards, later told the TRC that he had 'slaughtered' Seipei 'like a sheep' after Madikizela-Mandela had ordered him to do so.[14] While Madikizela-Mandela was later only convicted on charges of kidnapping and accessory to assault, she will forever remain a key figure in the story of Seipei's murder.

Is it possible that Magashule, who had all but delivered his young comrade from Tumahole to death's door, felt guilty about his role in this dark part of our history? It might explain why he was all too willing to absolve Madikizela-Mandela of any apartheid-era atrocities, especially concerning Seipei.

Magashule did not speak directly about the incident during his ANC Oral History Project interview, but he addressed, in broad terms, the killing of innocents who had been accused of collaborating with the apartheid state. 'They say in any struggle obviously there would be victims,' he said. 'A lot of people, I think, were innocent. I know even in the country here when we were still fighting inside there were some of the comrades [who] were labeled by most of us in the country as enemies, infiltrators and spies. And it turned out not to be true.'

In February 1989, the Mass Democratic Movement (MDM), which had been formed in the wake of the government's clampdown on the UDF, formally distanced itself from Madikizela-Mandela. The Seipei saga had been the final straw in a series of reports about how her so-called football club had been terrorising the people of Soweto.[15]

Several sources familiar with events say Magashule was one of the few people who defended Madikizela-Mandela. He tried to persuade the MDM to reconsider its decision, but to no avail. 'Ace was a very vocal supporter of Winnie,' said one such source. 'He campaigned very hard for the movement not to abandon her.'

When asked why Magashule continued to support her, one of his former associates from the Hillbrow unit had this to say: 'His motivation was money. Winnie raised a lot of money for the movement, and some of that money came Ace's way.'

Madikizela-Mandela and Magashule maintained close ties during this period, but things were not always smooth between them. The same source told me that Magashule once crashed a car that belonged to Madikizela-Mandela. 'Ace was driving Winnie's Volkswagen Golf in Soweto when he crashed and rolled the car near the Moroka police station. It was a bad crash, and we were all nearly killed. We had to quickly get out of there because the incident happened so close to a police station.'

The accident apparently sparked conflict between Magashule and lawyer Dali Mpofu, a close companion of Madikizela-Mandela who later became her legal representative following Seipei's death. 'Dali made a lot of trouble for us,' my source said, 'because he told Winnie that we were drunk. But that wasn't the case. Ace just lost control of the car because he was a bad driver.'

Magashule's Hillbrow days came to an end not long after Seipei's murder.

At some point in 1989, the group of internal exiles was staying in a flat in the Vistaero apartment building in Berea. 'We were living next to another MK guy,' said one source. 'He had been sent to establish a route out of the country via Swaziland, but he was arrested in Nelspruit.'

The arrest sparked panic among Magashule's group. 'There were no cellphones, so we didn't really know what was going on,' the source continued, 'but we suspected that our neighbour had spilled the beans on us when he was interrogated. We saw a white guy in the street who was checking out our apartment, so we decided to move to another flat in the same building.'

One night shortly thereafter, police raided the old apartment. 'The cops stormed the apartment and practically tore it to pieces. They arrested one guy who did not move out with us, and they also took Ace's son, who was also still in the apartment.' The son was Tshepiso, Magashule's firstborn child with Seipati and a young boy at the time.

Magashule referred to the incident in his interview for the ANC Oral

History Project, although he placed it somewhat earlier in the timeline of events. 'My first-born child was arrested at John Vorster [the police head-quarters in downtown Johannesburg], I can't remember, in 1987, when they were looking for me, and he was only four years [old]. They thought I would hand over myself and I did not do so.'

According to one of my Hillbrow sources, Tshepiso was released and Seipati took care of him from that point onwards.

The raid set in motion the Hillbrow group's period of actual exile. 'We never intended to leave the country, but that incident forced us to do so,' said one source. 'We stayed at the Carlton Hotel for about three weeks after the raid, but it was getting too expensive, so we decided to go to Zambia.'

The group left the country through Swaziland, arriving in Zambia in October 1989. Magashule left behind Seipati, Tshepiso and his youngest son, Thato, who had been born in January 1988.[16]

'My family did not follow me,' Magashule told the ANC Oral History Project, 'I had to leave them behind. It was difficult.' He may have left his family, but he did take a young woman named Adelaide with him.

When they arrived in Zambia, the group was allowed to stay in Chris Hani's house in Lusaka. Magashule took pride in the fact that he rubbed shoulders with Hani. 'I did even stay with comrade Chris for some time when I was in Zambia,' he later said. 'He was one of those people who had a very serious impact on my life.'[17]

But one of his fellow exiles from the Hillbrow unit recalls that Hani did not approve of Magashule's behaviour. 'Look, Ace is a ladies' man. He likes to always have women with him. So during that time, apart from having Adelaide with him, he was also bringing other women to Hani's house.' This landed Magashule's crew in hot water with Hani and the rest of the ANC's top brass. 'They said we were putting the house at risk by bringing strange women there, so we were kicked out,' my source revealed.

The group then moved on to Tanzania, where the ANC maintained some bases, arriving in December 1989. A source from this time said they were better off in Tanzania than in Zambia, seeing as they had more free-dom away from the ANC's top leadership.

But Magashule's memory of this period seems to be mostly negative. 'I remember when I arrived in Tanzania ... I was with some comrades [and] we were eating sweet potato with tea. It was horrible. There wasn't nice food there, life was not nice, completely not nice. For young women, it was not nice, it was difficult.'[18]

He also had to deal with the death of a cousin. 'I left with one of my cousins, unfortunately he passed away whilst in Tanzania.' One of Magashule's former struggle associates said the cousin, who drank heavily, had suffered from stomach ulcers.

There was also the constant threat of disease. 'If you go to Tanzania there was an area called M'hlaba,' recalled Magashule for the ANC Oral History Project, 'a lot of our comrades were affected by malaria. So they were insane. If you walk around there you'd see them walking naked. I mean, it was a painful moment to see some of these comrades now naked. A lot of comrades died in exile.'

Then Adelaide fell pregnant with Magashule's child. One of his struggle compatriots recalled that Magashule became particularly frustrated during this time. 'He wanted to come home really badly,' said this source.

His impatience would land him in trouble. 'Ace went to the United Nations' [UN] offices in Tanzania to ask if there was any way they could help him go back to South Africa,' my source told me. Magashule had apparently gone over the heads of the ANC's leadership. But he would get caught. 'There was an intelligence line between the UN offices and the ANC,' my source explained, 'so the leadership heard about his attempt to leave Tanzania without their permission. This got him in trouble again.'

Then, on 2 February 1990, President F.W. de Klerk made the landmark announcement that would pave the way for South Africa's transition to a democratic state. Nelson Mandela would be released from prison, and the ANC and its affiliates were officially unbanned.

Magashule jumped at the opportunity to go home. He boarded a bus bound for South Africa around the time of De Klerk's announcement, one of my sources told me. He had been in exile for a total of just five months, although he later claimed it was 'almost 18 months'.[19] Circumstances apparently did not allow for Adelaide to travel home with him, and so he left her, pregnant and alone in a strange country.

Magashule relished being reunited with his family in South Africa. 'The fact that the ANC was unbanned and we had to come back home and be welcomed ... our friends were there, our mothers were still alive, my mother was still alive and my brother. Everybody was happy for us to come back, I was also happy,' he said in his ANC Oral History Project interview.

Back in Tanzania, Adelaide gave birth to Magashule's daughter, Thoko, in July 1990. Father and daughter were reunited about two decades later, by which time Magashule was premier of the Free State. Any lingering anger Thoko may have felt at being abandoned with her mother in a foreign country was likely assuaged by the contracts she later clinched from her father's provincial government.

PART II

PREMIER IN WAITING

4

An early scandal

The unbanning of the ANC sparked optimism in the broader liberation movement, but it did nothing to quell tensions between the two rival political factions in the Free State. In fact, the animosity between the two groups would only intensify in the years after South Africa took its dramatic turn towards democracy and freedom.

In early 1990, just before he was about to be released from Victor Verster Prison near Paarl, Nelson Mandela met with ANC leaders from the country's various regions and provinces. It was an opportunity for regional leaders to brief Mandela on what had been happening with their respective structures.

Dennis Bloem recalled that the Free State was the last province to brief Mandela before his release. 'There were fifteen of us, including myself, Sekhopi Malebo, Zingile Dingane and Papiki Ngesi,' he said.

The northern Free State faction was not invited, highlighting Magashule's position as a political minnow, at least as far as the ANC's top brass were concerned. It also clearly signalled which of the two Free State factions the national leadership would prefer to work with once the ANC came to power.

At the ANC's first national elective conference after the unbanning, held in Durban in 1991, the Free State's northern and southern regions were represented by two separate delegations. But seeing as the party envisioned only one structure for each province, it was clear that the two bodies would eventually have to merge to form one Provincial Executive Committee (PEC) in the Free State. Come 1993, Magashule and his faction were hard at work laying the foundation for their eventual ousting of the Lekota bloc.

Magashule had grasped early on that ascendancy within the ANC had little to do with winning the support of the general population. Instead, the road to the top was built on the very foundation of the organisation's power structure, namely its branches. 'If you control enough branches, you control a region,' explained a source who worked with Magashule in the early 1990s. 'If you control enough regions, you control a province. And if you control a province, you get a seat at the big table.'

The northern Free State faction's proficiency in establishing branches has been documented by historians and political commentators. 'During this period the ANC in the province was dominated by northerners because of the party's development in the north in as far as branches were concerned,' historian Chitja Twala noted. 'The situation was expected to change after 1994, when the ANC was seen expanding its support in Thaba Nchu [outside Bloemfontein] where it had little support.'[1]

As the April 1994 election drew near, the northern faction's branch-building started yielding results. Magashule, and not Lekota, now enjoyed the number-one spot on the ANC's provincial list. This should have secured him the position of premier, but after the election, the national leadership appointed Lekota instead.

Although premiers are technically voted into power by each province's own legislature, the ANC's NEC decides who the candidates for the job will be. At the party's 2007 national conference, the rules were altered to allow provinces to have a bigger say in the appointment of premiers. Since 2007, each PEC may submit the names of three 'cadres' for the role of premier to the NEC. But the final decision still lies with the NEC.[2] The job of premier is therefore a prerogative of whoever rules the roost at Luthuli House, the ANC's headquarters. So it was that in 1994 Magashule was once again snubbed by the party's senior leaders.

In an interview more than a decade later, Magashule reflected on the development. 'I volunteered to step down in favour of an older person. [Lekota] was not even on the provincial list. I enjoy working with the masses,' he told the *Mail & Guardian* in 2005.[3]

Some commentators have framed the move as a case of the national leadership imposing a political 'outsider' on the province in defiance of the people's preference for the supposedly popular Magashule. In his book *South African Politics Since 1994*, Tom Lodge noted that although Lekota grew up in Kroonstad, he spent significant amounts of time outside the province before the first democratic election.[4]

While there may be some merit to this argument, it has its holes. After all, Magashule spent three years at the University of Fort Hare in the early

1980s before his years in 'internal exile' in Johannesburg and his eventual stint outside the country in the latter half of the decade. It is likely that the northern faction's superior branch-building skills, which allowed it to dictate the Free State's leadership preferences, played a bigger role in the portrayal of Magashule as the 'popular choice' than province-wide consensus or ground-level support.

According to some accounts, the national leadership asked Magashule to step aside because of Lekota's seniority. But given Magashule's track record in the struggle, which included rumours about financial misconduct, insubordination and bad discipline, one wonders whether the issue of seniority was foremost on everyone's minds. It seems plausible that the ANC top brass decided to keep Magashule away from the provincial throne simply because they thought he would be disastrous for the province. His conduct after the election certainly supports this theory.

Lekota's short term as Free State premier was marred by the ongoing political feud between the opposing power blocs. Papi Kganare recalled how Magashule's camp used 'dirty tricks' to undermine the premier at every opportunity. 'Magashule and his faction were behind this idea that Lekota was against QwaQwa [the former homeland in the Free State's eastern corner] because he wanted the province's capital to be in Bloemfontein and not in QwaQwa,' Kganare explained. 'They were fuelling negative sentiments against Lekota in that part of the province.'

In November 1994, the Free State ANC finally held its first provincial elective conference as a unified province. It was held in QwaQwa, which did not bode well for the southern faction. Lekota, who may have been lulled into a false sense of security because of the support he enjoyed from the ANC's national leadership, did not do much lobbying ahead of the conference.[5]

The results were disastrous for the Lekota camp. Pat Matosa, one of Magashule's allies from the north, defeated Lekota by seventy-three votes for the position of provincial chairperson, while Magashule became deputy chairperson.[6]

There is an oft-repeated misconception that Magashule became chair in 1994, to the extent that this inaccuracy now stands as a commonly accepted fact when political journalists write about him. 'As the longest-serving provincial party boss – he has held his position since 1994 – Magashule has served under all of SA's four presidents, from Nelson Mandela to

Jacob Zuma,' wrote Marianne Merten in a 2012 edition of the *Sunday Independent*.[7] And in 2017, in the build-up to the ANC's national elective conference at Nasrec, *Sunday Times* political scribe Qaanitah Hunter also wrote that Magashule had been the 'ANC provincial chairman since 1994'.[8]

There are no indications that Magashule has ever tried to state the true facts. And why would he? The inaccuracy is a useful footnote in the narrative that portrays Magashule as the province's top dog since the advent of democracy.

Nevertheless, the ANC's vision of having one person serve as both premier and party chairperson, which may have stemmed the tide of rival power blocs, was now in tatters. While Lekota held on to the province's executive decision-making powers, Magashule and his faction now ran the party's affairs.

Lekota made some efforts to accommodate the northerners in the provincial government. In 1994, Magashule was appointed as the Free State MEC for economic affairs and tourism in Lekota's first cabinet. But the fault lines in the province's power dynamics ran deep, and any peace that this may have brought about was bound to be tentative and fragile.

Twala documented how 'the aggrieved northerners led by Matosa and Magashule made life difficult for Lekota and accused him of ruling the Free State illegitimately'.[9] According to Twala, a year after the first provincial cabinet was constituted, the political cold war escalated to open warfare when Lekota first suspended housing MEC and Magashule ally Vax Mayekiso over a dodgy property deal. Mayekiso had allegedly used his position as MEC to put pressure on and threaten the owner of a fuel station in Welkom to sell his business. It had then emerged that Mayekiso's wife had a stake in the deal.

Magashule was next in the firing line. In June 1996, Lekota axed him when he reshuffled his cabinet, accusing Magashule of 'insubordination'. When Matosa and other northerners threatened to institute a vote of no confidence in Lekota in the provincial legislature, the ANC's national leadership was forced to intervene. Steve Tshwete helped the two factions find some common ground, and Lekota subsequently reinstated Magashule.[10] However, he was appointed as MEC for transport, a move that was seen as a demotion.[11]

It became increasingly clear that Lekota had initially fired Magashule over something more dubious than mere insubordination. In July, the same month in which Magashule was reinstated, Lekota drew attention to some questionable dealings at the Department of Economic Affairs and Tourism. Under Magashule's watch, the department had secretly set up two Section 21 or non-profit companies without approval from the executive council or the provincial treasury. The two entities, called the Free State Investment and Promotion Agency and the Free State Tourism Company, had received nearly R6 million from Magashule's department. A report by the Free State's director-general found that the agencies had made questionable loans to staff members and had also splurged some of the money on trips abroad and even on pub lunches and CDs.[12] Lekota suspended five senior officials in Magashule's former department, three of whom belonged to Magashule's ANC branch.[13] This further fuelled tensions between the two camps.

Magashule's own fingerprints were on some of the dodgy dealings involving the department and its agencies. It was alleged that he had played a role in questionable loans granted by the Free State Development Corporation to companies associated with or linked to him. The FDC is the state-owned entity that would later absorb the functions of the Free State Investment and Promotion Agency after the latter was closed. The loans were made to funeral parlours, a pharmacy and a car dealership, among other businesses, and Magashule apparently approved the transactions himself.[14]

Lekota appointed Peter Goldhawk, a chartered accountant who had helped establish accounting giant PricewaterhouseCoopers' forensic unit, to probe the allegations. The Goldhawk report was released towards the end of 1996, and it made some scathing findings. The FDC had made 'irregular' loans totalling about R3 million without following proper procedure, the report found.[15] Goldhawk could not find any evidence that Magashule or anyone close to him had benefited from the loans, but he did conclude that the former MEC had unlawfully interfered in the decision-making processes of the FDC board.[16]

In August 1996, the *Mail & Guardian* reported that police were investigating some of the allegations around the Department of Economic Affairs and Tourism. Magashule's alleged 'fraud' formed part of their probe.[17]

Kganare and a former member of Magashule's camp said there was much more going on at Magashule's department than what came out in the media at the time. 'When Ace was MEC, he awarded a tender for cleaning services to a company that would have massively overcharged government,' Kganare claimed. 'We're talking about paying R200 for a one-kilogram box of Omo washing powder, R100 for a bar of soap that costs R6.' He said that the businessman would have made a 500 per cent profit through the deal, and that it was someone connected to Magashule. 'This was the start of Ace's looting,' Kganare observed.

'Terror [Lekota] picked up that Ace was issuing instructions for companies to get paid by the Department of Economic Affairs, and it was unclear what some of these payments were for,' the former member of the Magashule camp told me. 'In some of the cases there were huge amounts involved.'

The auditor-general's (AG's) subsequent report on the department's affairs, released at the end of 1996, pegged the unauthorised expenditure at almost R8 million and further validated suspicions about Magashule's handling of public funds. 'The contents of this report clearly document substantial disregard for due process and proper procedure by individuals in positions of public trust. It is clear that the interests of the taxpayer and that of good governance have not been served in this instance,' acting AG J.A.J. Loots said in his report.[18]

In June the following year, the province's public accounts committee concluded an investigation that shed further light on the financial improprieties involving Magashule. The FDC loans granted on Magashule's insistence were paid without obtaining securities from the various recipients, and no repayments had been made, the committee found. It also identified 'irregularities' in the awarding of a contract for cleaning products and recommended that legal action be taken against the supplier in question.[19] This appears to be the same contract referred to by Kganare.

Lekota, meanwhile, kept upping the ante in his ongoing assault on the northerners. He was accused of leading a witch-hunt driven by political motivations. There is probably some merit to this view, but it is not like the northerners made it difficult for their enemies to find dirt on them.

Lodge has documented how Lekota appeared on radio shows to inform the public about Magashule's alleged corruption. He also aired the dirty laundry of some of Magashule's allies, including an incident in which Matosa allegedly pointed a firearm at a traffic official after being stopped for reckless driving.[20]

But Lekota's tactic backfired on him. His attacks over the airwaves were viewed as a step too far by the ANC's national leadership, which has always preferred resolving its conflicts internally and as quietly as possible. In November 1996, Lekota and his cabinet were asked to resign. The national leadership tasked a 'caretaker committee' headed by then labour minister Tito Mboweni to take over the reins in the conflict-ridden province.[21] The ANC also disbanded the PEC chaired by Matosa.

To some, the move was seen as a serious censure levelled at Lekota and his camp. This may be true to some extent. Mandela and his fellow party leaders would not have been happy with how the Free State had degenerated into a political war zone under Lekota's watch. However, some of those who were present when the matter came to a head within the ANC's top leadership structures say Mandela saved the bulk of his wrath for the Magashule faction.

Before a meeting at Shell House, the ANC's head office at the time, Mandela summoned the foremost individuals from both sides of the divide to his residence in Cape Town. Among those in attendance were Magashule, Matosa, Mayekiso, Lekota and Gregory Nthatisi. Apparently Mandela was especially furious about how the northern camp had undermined Lekota's authority as premier. 'Mandela told Pat [Matosa] that he was showing bad leadership as chairperson by not taking responsibility for the infighting, and for allowing himself to be influenced by others,' said one source who attended the meeting. This person believes the latter remark was a reference to Magashule, who was viewed by some as the true power behind Matosa.

In public, Mandela tried to be as diplomatic about the crisis as he could. 'Of course, healthy competition between individuals for election posts is a natural part of any democratic organisation,' he said at an ANC gathering in November 1996, in reference to the fighting in the Free State. 'But when personal competition starts to absorb all one's energies, when political programmes are forgotten and when solid grassroots work is neglected, then matters become very serious.'[22]

To help quash hostilities, the national leadership decided to redeploy Lekota to Cape Town, where, in February 1997, he became chairperson of the National Council of Provinces (NCOP).[23] Ivy Matsepe-Casaburri, then board chair of the South African Broadcasting Corporation (SABC), was appointed as the Free State's new premier.[24]

Because the ANC had also dissolved the Free State PEC, a special elective conference was convened in February 1997. It was held in Welkom, a stronghold for the northern camp, but by now the national leadership's interventions had weakened Magashule's faction. Lodge described the event as a 'sullen' affair,[25] and one can understand why Free State party members would have been less than enthusiastic, given the lashing that both factions had recently received from their political seniors.

The national leadership, which hoped to finally achieve its ideal of having the positions of chair and premier reside in one person, nominated Matsepe-Casaburri to lead the party in the province. But Zingile Dingane, a Lekota ally, comfortably beat Matsepe-Casaburri to become the new chair. The conference was a resounding victory for the southerners, who won practically all the positions up for grabs and thereby retook control of the ANC in the Free State.[26] However, their dominance would be short-lived, as would Matsepe-Casaburri's stint as premier.

Magashule, meanwhile, was supposed to become an ordinary member of Parliament (MP), but he was set adrift in political limbo pending the outcome of the probes into his former department's affairs. He was effectively cast into the political wilderness, and it was up to the ANC's top leadership to decide his fate.

In June 1997, the ANC's National Working Committee (NWC) held a meeting to discuss the findings of the reports compiled by the AG and the public accounts committee. Among those present were Mandela, ANC chairperson Jacob Zuma and acting secretary-general Cheryl Carolus. Despite the AG's grave assessment of Magashule's conduct and evidence of his reckless approach to the management of public monies, as highlighted by the public accounts committee, the NWC gave him a free pass. They maintained that Magashule had not been found guilty of any impropriety and announced that he would take up his seat in Parliament when it reconvened in August that year.[27]

The ANC's national conference at the end of 1997 brought about changes to the organisation's constitution, some of which affected the mechanics of the provincial structures. As a result, the Free State and some other provinces had to convene fresh provincial conferences in 1998.

In August 1998, the party's provincial membership gathered at the Central University of Technology in Bloemfontein. This time, Magashule was elected as the ANC's new chair in the province.[28] Matsepe-Casaburri did not even secure a nomination from the branches.

Lodge attributed the Magashule camp's victory to renewed branch-level organisation in northern towns like Sasolburg, in the goldfields around Welkom and in far-flung QwaQwa.[29] But the northern faction's consolidation of its branch-level support base was accompanied by rumours of voting irregularities.[30]

According to sources involved in the party's provincial structures back then, there were indications that some branches in the northern region had made use of 'ghost members' to increase the number of delegates the north could send to the conference. 'We found that there were members in a branch in Welkom who were fully paid up, but when we checked, they were people who had been dead for a long time,' said one source.

According to this former ANC leader, they managed to track down a woman whose dead son had signed the attendance register for a branch meeting during which delegates were elected to attend the provincial conference. 'This old lady told us that if her dead son was still haunting branch meetings, he could at least pop in at home to greet his parents,' he told me.

Although banished to Cape Town, Magashule could now start reclaiming the levers of power his faction had lost under Lekota and Matsepe-Casaburri. The new PEC ensured that Lekota's foes, including Mayekiso, were once again appointed to the Free State's executive council.[31]

Come 1999, Magashule must have felt sure that the time had finally come for him to be appointed premier. After all, he was the ruling party's chairperson in the Free State, and the ANC had been very clear that it desired one person to lead both the provincial party and government. His supporters had been calling him the 'premier in waiting',[32] and they were convinced that their man would finally get the nod from the ANC's top brass.

But Thabo Mbeki, who took over from Mandela as ANC president in 1997, and as the man in charge of the country after the 1999 elections, dashed these hopes. Mbeki, who clearly shared Mandela's reservations about Magashule, shocked the latter's support base by appointing Botshabelo local and NCOP member Winkie Direko as premier.

Like Lekota and Matsepe-Casaburri before her, Direko was labelled by the Magashule camp as an outsider who had been imposed on the Free State by a national leadership that chose to ignore the wishes of its ground-level members. They went as far as calling her an 'Mbeki appointee',[33] signalling that the ANC infighting in the province would continue unabated.

But Direko was tough, and it quickly became clear that she would not be intimidated by those who refused to accept her authority. 'Magashule made life difficult for Winkie, just as he had done with Terror and Ivy, but she did not take any nonsense from him,' said a Free State politician who was in the trenches during those heady days of factional fighting.

By mid-2000, the ongoing conflict, which was driven in part by allegations that the 1998 provincial conference had been rigged, necessitated yet another drastic intervention from the ANC's national leadership. The NWC disbanded the Magashule-led PEC and appointed an interim committee to lead the party in the province.[34] This body was led by Godfrey Mosala, a former official in the provincial education department, and Noby Ngombane, who was later shot dead in what is deemed to have been the most high-profile assassination as a result of the province's political discord (see Chapter 8).

During the years of the interim committee's reign, Magashule found his feet as an MP in Cape Town, where he was a member of Parliament's portfolio committees on communications and provincial and local government. Judging by Hansard records, Magashule contributed to committee meetings from time to time, but his mind was no doubt consumed with thoughts of his inevitable comeback in his home province.

One source who was an MP in the National Assembly in those days said Magashule was often absent from Parliament because he was spending a lot of time in the Free State. 'During some weeks, Ace would maybe attend committee meetings or sittings in Parliament on the Monday and the Tuesday, but on Wednesday he would hop on a plane and fly to Bloemfontein, where he would spend the rest of the week,' said the source. 'He knew he risked becoming weak in the Free State if he spent too much time outside the province, so he maintained his presence there.'

The opportunity for Magashule to once again grab hold of the ANC's top position in the Free State presented itself in 2002, when the party was due to hold another provincial elective conference. Mbeki, of course, wanted Direko to become chair. Her name appeared on the ballot, but Magashule comfortably defeated her by about 100 votes. Matosa, Magashule's longtime ally, found himself elected to the position of provincial secretary.[35] The victory marked the start of a fifteen-year run of nearly uninterrupted rule by Magashule as chairperson of the ANC in the Free State.

The ANC's national leadership would again disband the Magashule-led Free State PEC in 2012, but this was yet another temporary setback.

5

Free State capture
and the 'cattle thief'

The 2002 victory was crucial for Magashule's subsequent dominance of party politics in the Free State, as well as his iron grip on the provincial government's finances. 'The Free State's current troubles started in 2002,' observed one of his former associates. 'This is when Ace started to consolidate his power and when he started to mastermind his capture of every level of government in the province.'

Magashule and his followers first focused on gaining control of the municipalities. As ANC chairperson and chair of the party's deployment committee, Magashule used his power and influence to ensure that 'his people' were appointed to key municipal positions all over the province, explained my source.

The most important positions were those of mayor and municipal manager. The Magashule-led PEC determined who the mayor of each municipality would be. And while the appointment of municipal managers was a prerogative of each municipality's council, ANC members who took instruction from the PEC dominated those councils. The management tier that fell under the post of municipal manager was also stacked with Magashule allies. This included directors and chief financial officers (CFOs).

A former mayor from one of the Free State's northern regions said he was axed in those years because he expressed his discomfort with how Magashule's allies were being appointed as directors in his municipality. He was also opposed to how his municipality was dishing out contracts to people associated with Magashule.

A second source, who later served as an MEC in Magashule's cabinet, agreed that the capture process began in 2002. 'There is a pattern of municipal managers appointed from 2002 who were from Fezile Dabi [the district around Magashule's hometown of Parys] or who were otherwise close to him,' he said.

Two years after Magashule became provincial chairperson, his banishment to Cape Town came to an end. He returned to the Free State in 2004, where he briefly joined the provincial legislature as an MPL.

After the national election in April 2004, Mbeki appointed Beatrice Marshoff as the Free State's new premier. Marshoff, who had been the MEC for social development in Direko's cabinet, was apparently 'shocked' when Mbeki appointed her ahead of Magashule.[1]

It is unlikely that Magashule would have been similarly shocked by yet another snub from the party's national leadership.

Marshoff said that Magashule and his cronies approached her right after she became premier. 'We had a meeting at Kopano Nokeng [a lodge and conference centre outside Bloemfontein] where they cornered me with a list of demands for people they wanted me to appoint as MECs,' she told me. 'I said, "No, I'll decide who is going to get appointed."' At that stage, she had no intention to include Magashule or any members of his clique in her government. 'I had been warned by Terror [Lekota] how much time and energy it took to keep his [Magashule's] trouble under control,' Marshoff told me.

Nevertheless, in yet another attempt to try to heal the province's festering political wounds, the national leadership asked Marshoff to make room for Magashule.

It took quite an effort to convince the new premier. 'I had sent my list of MECs to Mbeki, the SG [Kgalema Motlanthe] and the NEC, and it didn't include the names of Magashule or Casca Mokitlane, one of Magashule's allies whom that camp also wanted in the executive council,' explained Marshoff.

Essop Pahad, who led the NEC's provincial committee for the Free State, asked Marshoff if she would consider making room for Magashule and some of his people to 'protect the peace' in the Free State. The national leadership put further pressure on her during a meeting at Luthuli House. According to Marshoff, a senior party leader told her that, for the sake of stability in the province, she should appoint Magashule in a department where there were not many resources for him to plunder.

Magashule apparently wanted to be MEC for public works or economic affairs, but those departments were seen as too well-funded and important. Marshoff finally budged and agreed to appoint Magashule as the MEC for agriculture, a move she now regrets. 'There is not a lot of money in that department, but it has access to or control over lots of resources, so it is still a very important portfolio,' she said. 'It was a big mistake to appoint him there.'

With this appointment, the new premier managed to enforce a ceasefire, but the peace was as fragile as ever. Right from the get-go, Magashule and his allies showed their contempt for Marshoff's leadership. An example of this was the lack of respect they displayed for the provincial government's processes and traditions. Magashule and nine other new MECs were supposed to be sworn in at the provincial legislature on 30 April 2004, but on the day they were nowhere to be found and the event had to be postponed.

When they were eventually sworn in on a later date, Marshoff warned them that 'they would not have the luxury of settling into their posts', but would instead have to get to work immediately.[2]

As agriculture MEC, Magashule showed a willingness to directly involve himself in matters affecting the industry. As an example, when an emerging black farmer near Heilbron decided to sell his farm and equipment because of a lack of support and mentorship, the MEC intervened by personally phoning the auctioneer to put a stop to the auction and telling the farmer that he was not allowed to sell the land because the transaction would have worked against government's land-reform objectives. Magashule's department then promised the farmer funding of more than R300 000 to convert the farm into a dairy and cattle venture.[3]

Other emerging farmers were not as lucky. Shortly after Magashule's appointment, his department froze a development programme that had been funded by the European Union. Magashule maintained that the programme showed signs of irregular expenditure, but the Democratic Alliance (DA) accused him of leading its beneficiaries to financial ruin.[4] The DA in the province later stated that Magashule had 'totally failed' in his role as MEC for agriculture.[5]

Less than a year into his tenure, in April 2005, Marshoff dropped Magashule when she reshuffled her executive council. Another victim of the reshuffle was economic affairs MEC Benny Malakoane. Both men were shifted to the provincial legislature.[6]

Marshoff was rather cryptic about her reasons for axing the duo, saying at the time that the reshuffle was meant to improve service delivery in the province. She told the *Mail & Guardian* that the axed MECs had admitted that their performances were not up to scratch, but Magashule and Malakoane both denied this.[7]

The reshuffle caused a stir, especially given the fact that Magashule was ANC chair. His axing risked amplifying political tensions in the province. The story soon died down, however, and the public never learnt exactly why Magashule was fired.

In an interview with Marshoff in 2018, she revealed to me the real reasons behind her decision. One Friday after work, she was at home in Bloemfontein when her phone rang. It was one of her staffers, calling to inform her about a pending political fiasco involving Magashule, his ANC region in the north and the Glen College of Agriculture, a state-funded agricultural college situated about twenty-five kilometres outside Bloemfontein. The college fell under the leadership of Magashule's Department of Agriculture.

'This person told me that Ace had instructed staff members at the college to slaughter the college's calves and to put the meat into separate parcels,' recalled Marshoff. At the time, the ANC's Fezile Dabi region was about to hold a regional conference in Sasolburg. 'The meat parcels were meant to be distributed among ANC members who were going to attend the conference so that they would vote for Magashule's slate,' she explained.

The heist was still under way by the time the premier got word of it, so she phoned the police to try to stop it. 'The police managed to intercept three Department of Agriculture bakkies that were full of meat parcels and that were on their way to Sasolburg.'

Marshoff later learnt that there were more vehicles carrying meat than just the three apprehended, and that some of the conference attendees did get their meat parcels courtesy of Magashule. 'The department staff who were driving the bakkies confirmed that Ace had ordered them to take the meat up north,' Marshoff said. 'That is when I decided to fire Ace. This is what Ace does, he buys people's support and he uses government resources to do that.'

Dumbfounded by these revelations, I endeavoured to find out more about Magashule's alleged theft of state-owned cattle. A long-serving staff member at Glen College confirmed the incident. 'If I remember correctly, there were about thirty-two cattle that were slaughtered, and the meat was taken to a political event somewhere up north,' he told me.

Magashule's habit of abusing the college's resources apparently continued after he became premier. 'It became quite normal for them to fetch or slaughter cattle here when there were political funerals or other political events,' this source told me in August 2018. 'It is a scandal because it is the state's property, not theirs to just take. It has since become less common [after Magashule's departure from the province]. They have only come to fetch two [cattle] so far this year.'

Marshoff, meanwhile, took the cattle incident and some of Magashule's other shortcomings as MEC for agriculture to the national leadership and asked them if she could fire him. 'Apart from the cattle thing, his department was generally in a mess,' she explained. 'There was no coordination, he sometimes failed to attend ExCo meetings and he didn't submit the necessary reports for his department.'

She told Mbeki that she could not work with Magashule, and the president agreed that she needed to remove him. 'It caused a lot of problems for me in the ANC, seeing as I had dared to remove the all-powerful Ace,' recalled Marshoff.

After being booted out of the Department of Agriculture, Magashule became the ANC's chief whip in the provincial legislature. He now no longer had direct access to government coffers or contracts, but it seems he still managed to involve himself in dodgy deals.

A *Mail & Guardian* report implicated Magashule and other politicians in an alleged scheme in 2007 to extract kickbacks from a property developer in exchange for their help in resolving a dispute over the sale of a piece of land owned by the Mangaung metropolitan municipality. Magashule denied the allegations, but did concede that he had met with the developer.[8]

'I attended the meeting [with the property developer] in my capacity as the provincial chairperson of the ANC and I was approached by both parties to facilitate an amicable solution,' he told the newspaper when it broke the story in 2009. 'It is not uncommon for me to intervene in matters of governance, since the ANC is the ruling party in government and has to obviously provide leadership and strategic guidance on all matters of policy, especially those aimed at empowering our people.'

In 2007, the national leadership asked Marshoff once again to make room for Magashule in her executive council. 'They wanted me to place him in another department that did not have access to a lot of money,' she said. Publicly, the national leadership's motivation was to try to secure peace and harmony in the battle-ridden province. Behind the scenes, the Mbeki camp was on political manoeuvres.

In August, Magashule was appointed the Free State's new MEC for sport, arts, culture and recreation.[9] His presence in this new government environment caused friction and problems. Rachel Sempe, the department's then head, apparently had her hands full trying to stop Magashule from doing things that ran against the Public Finance Management Act and other rules and regulations. Magashule allegedly tried to force the department to employ people whom he had promised jobs.

'People went to the department and said Ace told them to go and work there, but there were no jobs advertised and the jobs weren't budgeted for,' said Marshoff. 'When Ace promised to give someone a job, he would make sure that person got the job.' She reiterated a claim made by almost every source I spoke to: Magashule deftly used the promise of employment in provincial and municipal structures to his advantage. As he did with the meat parcels from Glen College, he handed out jobs to buy patronage.

After less than a year in the Department of Sport, Arts, Culture and Recreation, Magashule was once again fired by Marshoff. But his political power kept growing. By that stage, the influence he wielded as ANC Free State chair and chairperson of the party's deployment committee had turned him into the province's most formidable political force.

'He determined who became mayor, municipal manager or CFO at all the municipalities,' explained Marshoff. 'He abused this scenario and influenced people at those municipalities to give tenders to people close to him or to people he needed to support him.'

Municipal officials who failed to comply were apparently swiftly dealt with. 'Ace had the ability to instil a deathly fear in people,' said Marshoff. 'Those who did not obey his orders were threatened with redeployment, suspension or demotion. He was in control of people's careers, their futures, so they did as he asked them to do.'

A former municipal official in the Fezile Dabi district confirmed that Magashule had his hands on the municipality's finances long before he became premier. 'The municipal manager decides where a municipal tender should go,' this source explained. 'They appoint a tender committee, which usually consists of the municipal manager, the CFO and some junior staffers from procurement. The municipal manager and the CFO would report to Ace, so it was easy to control the committee.'

He gave an example of how Magashule meddled in the municipality's finances. In around 2002 or 2003, after Magashule became ANC provincial chair, the Fezile Dabi district municipality was asked to provide money for a music festival at the Abrahamsrust holiday resort near Sasolburg. The event was supposedly initiated to create awareness around HIV/AIDS.

'Our municipality decided not to contribute funding, because we thought there were better ways to combat HIV/AIDS,' the source told me. But they did not have much choice. 'We got instructions from Ace's people to make the money available, and that was the end of the matter,' explained the former official.

Sixteen years later, the district municipality is still pouring money into what has become an annual concert, despite a directive from Treasury that municipalities should stop sponsoring such events.[10]

6

Crushing the Scorpions

South Africa's political calendar in 2007 was dominated by the build-up to the ANC's watershed elective conference in Polokwane in December.

As the year came to an end, commentators and analysts tried to take a reading of the political winds swirling around the main power blocs led by Thabo Mbeki and Jacob Zuma. On the surface, neither leader seemed to be getting much love from Magashule's Free State ANC.

One news report described how Magashule had 'mastered the art of fence-sitting' by not openly throwing his weight behind either Zuma or Mbeki.[1] Considering the snubs that he had endured under previous presidents, his cautious approach is perhaps understandable.

Mbeki had an obvious disadvantage. As president, he had already denied Magashule the Free State premiership. But Zuma had also played a role in blocking Magashule's appointment. When he served as deputy president under Mbeki, Zuma was one of the national leaders in favour of 'banishing' Magashule to Cape Town in the late 1990s to try to quash the faction-fighting in the Free State. 'Zuma himself said that Ace needed to go to Parliament to help the Free State ANC survive,' said Marshoff.

A former ally confirmed that Magashule was not a fan of either Zuma or Mbeki. 'Mbeki had already disappointed him, but he was not sure if he could trust Zuma,' said this source.

While Magashule made up his mind about whom he would support, the ANC in the Free State remained fractured, and threatened to weaken the province's contribution to the Polokwane conference.

The trouble started in early 2007, when a group of disgruntled party members obtained an interim interdict against all decisions taken at the party's Fezile Dabi regional conference.[2] Allegations of vote-rigging and other irregularities at branch and regional level added to the chaos, and there was even talk at one point that the Free State ANC would split.[3] One court ruling determined that some of the province's branches were unfit to send delegates to the national conference.[4]

Magashule's faction was accused of manipulating the outcome of branch meetings through a variety of dubious means that contravened the ANC's constitution. These included allegedly convening branch meetings in a 'secretive and selective' manner by failing to properly notify all branch members of such meetings, and 'unlawfully' excluding certain ANC members from branch meetings by ensuring that their names did not appear on branch registers.[5] The court found that the applicants had not provided enough evidence to substantiate their allegations. However, later court rulings against the Magashule bloc would confirm that the province's ANC politics was rife with rogue behaviour.

Papi Kganare recalled that in the build-up to Polokwane, his faction wanted the national leadership to intervene in the Free State by helping to ensure that the nomination processes in the various regions were concluded without any funny business. 'Our suggestion was that MPs needed to oversee the process in some districts, or, for instance, that Gauteng's leadership come to oversee the process in the Fezile Dabi district,' he told me.

The request was refused. According to Kganare, the NEC, which could have ensured that voting in the branches and regions occurred in a more transparent and above-board manner, did not wish to interfere. The reason for this, Kganare alleged, was that they were Mbeki supporters who were somehow under the impression that Magashule would back their slate at Polokwane.

'Before Polokwane, [ANC communications head] Smuts Ngonyama came to the Free State to represent the NEC, and he was sure that Magashule would support Mbeki,' Kganare said. 'But we warned him that Ace wouldn't support Mbeki because Mbeki did not make him premier.'

Kganare also said that Essop Pahad, Mbeki's right-hand man, was similarly convinced that Magashule would channel the Free State's support to Mbeki. 'We told him that Ace was not going to support Mbeki, but he was adamant that Ace had promised to endorse Mbeki,' added Kganare.

According to sources close to political developments preceding the Polokwane conference, Magashule's appointment as MEC of sport, arts, culture and recreation in August 2007 was the result of a back-channel agreement orchestrated by the Mbeki camp. 'Mbeki was desperate for the Free State's votes,' said one source. 'He and Essop Pahad came to Bloemfontein to plead for the province's support. That is when Ace was again made MEC.'

This person, a former staffer in Marshoff's office, said the then premier agreed to appoint Magashule 'at Thabo's request' and that there was a 'gentleman's agreement' that the Free State ANC would support Mbeki in exchange for Magashule's appointment as MEC. Marshoff, apparently seeking a second term as premier in 2009, did not want to burn the bridge between her and Mbeki, and therefore agreed to play along.

But Mbeki and his people were gravely mistaken if they thought that they had won the support of Magashule and his followers. At the Free State's provincial nominations conference in late November, Zuma got more than three times the number of votes that Mbeki could muster, despite earlier indications that the winner would be decided by a narrow margin.[6] Zuma had somehow managed to win Magashule's backing.

Kganare said that Magashule could not face Smuts Ngonyama, one of Mbeki's closest allies, after the nominations conference. 'As soon as it was announced that the Free State would endorse Zuma and not Mbeki, Ace disappeared without talking to Smuts,' he told me.

Kganare said that things would have turned out differently if the national leadership had listened to the southern camp's grievances about vote-rigging and other irregularities, seeing as that faction had resolved to back Mbeki. He was not in the least surprised that Magashule threw his weight behind Zuma. 'Ace knew that if Mbeki won, he would never become premier,' Kganare said.

After Zuma thrashed Mbeki at Polokwane, with the Free State's help, Magashule must have reckoned that he had earned his pound of flesh. But there were further opportunities for him to conclusively win over the newly elected ANC president.

After Polokwane, Zuma still faced a mammoth threat in the form of the corruption charges against him emanating from the 1999 Arms Deal. It was a battle that would require considerable monetary resources, a problem for the perpetually broke Zuma.

In July 2008, a month before Zuma was set to appear in the Pietermaritzburg High Court, he attended the Free State's provincial conference in Parys.

After being re-elected as the party's provincial chair, Magashule took to the stage and 'forced' his fellow party members and invited guests, including several businesspeople from the Free State, to make donations to Zuma. 'It is our duty to support the ANC president, both morally and financially,' Magashule told the *Sunday Times* when asked if he was trying to buy Zuma's favour.

The small army of mayors, municipal managers, MECs and business-people in attendance did Magashule proud, donating R52 000 in cash, which was placed in a black leather bag and presented to Zuma on stage, and pledging an additional R1.4 million. The awkward, crude gesture apparently had some senior party members squirming with embarrassment.

Although Zuma refused to say whether Magashule would be the next Free State premier after the incident, judging by subsequent events it did not harm Magashule's chances.[7]

At the end of 2008, Magashule became a key figure in the narrative about Zuma's supposed persecution at the hands of the National Prosecuting Authority (NPA) and the Scorpions, South Africa's former elite corruption-fighting unit.

It was alleged that then Free State Scorpions boss Shadrack Sibiya had wanted to arrest Magashule before the provincial conference in July to prevent him from once again being elected chair. In an instant, Magashule was elevated to the level of fellow martyr in the ongoing battle between the Scorpions, who were accused of pushing a political agenda, and dodgy ANC leaders like Zuma.

'We have been saying that the Scorpions have positioned themselves to persecute leaders of the ANC but nobody listened to us,' then ANC secretary-general Gwede Mantashe told the *Sowetan*. 'There is nothing new about this. We believe they are targeting many more ANC leaders than just Magashule.'[8]

Magashule, who had accusations of corruption hanging over his head long before Zuma, was one of the foremost proponents of disbanding the Scorpions. At the Free State leg of Parliament's series of public hearings on the Scorpions' future, Magashule apparently 'hijacked' proceedings and accused the crime-fighting unit of being prejudiced against black people.[9]

Not long thereafter, Magashule and Zuma got what they desired. In January 2009, the Scorpions were officially disbanded.[10] For a large part of the following decade, shady politicians, government officials and business-people had almost free rein to loot state resources.

It would appear that Magashule had good cause to join Zuma's anti-Scorpions chorus. It can now be revealed that before the unit was disbanded, it was indeed close to arresting Magashule. And contrary to the narrative that the Scorpions were politically motivated, the unit had gathered several solid dockets on Magashule that centred on his transgressions in the Free State.

Sibiya, whom I met in August 2018, confirmed that the Scorpions were investigating Magashule and that they had made good progress in this regard before the unit was dismantled. 'Ace knows about this, he was questioned by the Scorpions on several occasions,' said Sibiya, who now leads the City of Johannesburg's anti-corruption unit.

Other sources familiar with the Scorpions' work provided further details. 'The Scorpions focused on top-level corruption, fraud and other transgressions involving prominent people,' said one former Scorpions insider. 'You might refer to these people as high-flyers or even untouchables. Ace was one of the people we were looking at.'

The Magashule probes were codenamed 'Project Moetapele', which translates to 'Project Leader' in English, the source told me. Some of the issues the Scorpions were probing included Magashule's abuse of state resources at the Glen College of Agriculture. 'Ace was handing out cows, sheep and other livestock to people without following the proper procedures,' confirmed the former Scorpions insider, who also told me that the unit had obtained a search-and-seizure warrant and raided Glen College.

The Scorpions had also been investigating Magashule's possible involvement in the sale of municipal land on the Vaal River near Parys. Marshoff told me that while she was premier, then NPA boss Vusi Pikoli visited her in the Free State. 'Vusi told me that Ace was going to be arrested, and that we needed to be prepared for the political ramifications that this would have in the Free State,' she said.

Of course, the Scorpions were shut down before they could act. 'All of the data and files we had on Ace were handed over to the SAPS [South African Police Service] when we were disbanded,' said the former Scorpions insider.

The Project Moetapele files may well be stashed away in a dusty, unused office somewhere in a SAPS building in Bloemfontein. Or perhaps they were taken to the police's national headquarters in Pretoria. That is, of course, if they were not destroyed.

Magashule received another break in late 2008 with the formation of the Congress of the People. The new opposition party absorbed several key individuals who were formerly members of or aligned to the Free State

ANC's southern (anti-Magashule) faction, including Mosiuoa Lekota and Kganare. Even former Magashule allies who had previously locked horns with Lekota, such as Vax Mayekiso, flocked to the newly formed COPE.[11]

Although the ANC would have to deal with the added scrutiny of a new opposition party, the development subdued the infighting in the province long enough for Magashule to further strengthen his grip.

After one more stop, at the Department of Public Safety and Security in October 2008,[12] Magashule was finally appointed premier of the Free State in May 2009. It would not take long for the money to really start flowing to his family and friends.

But before considering this, we will take an in-depth look at the murder of Noby Ngombane, an event that highlighted the ferocity of the political wrangling between the Free State's rival ANC factions.

7

The assassination
of Noby Ngombane

When Noby Nyovo Ngombane returned to his native Free State in 1998 after a stint abroad, the province was as politically volatile and fractured as it had been since the 1980s. Ace Magashule had become the ANC's chairperson in August of that year, but the province was being run by Premier Ivy Matsepe-Casaburri, the 'outsider' backed by the national leadership of Nelson Mandela and loathed by Magashule and his band of northerners.

Ngombane and his wife, Nokwanda, had spent a few years in Sweden, where he had worked as a programme officer at the International Institute for Democracy and Electoral Assistance. Upon his return to South Africa, he stepped into the Free State's political fray by taking up positions that would inevitably mark him as an enemy in the eyes of the Magashule faction.

Ngombane first served as a special advisor to Matsepe-Casaburri before assuming the same role in the office of Winkie Direko, yet another so-called outsider whom the national leadership had picked to become premier ahead of Magashule. Then, in 2000, the national leadership plucked Ngombane from the proverbial frying pan and dropped him into the fire below by putting him in charge of the ANC's Interim Leadership Committee (ILC). This was the structure put in place after the dissolution of Magashule's PEC amid the unsustainable political volatility and infighting in the Free State.

Nokwanda told me her husband had been somewhat surprised when the Mbeki-led national leadership called him up to help lead the party in the Free State. Ngombane was first and foremost a South African Communist Party (SACP) man, and as such was on the sidelines when it came to the ANC's internal politics.

But his relative detachment from the factional battles probably made him the ideal candidate for the role. Nokwanda said the national leadership viewed her husband as politically neutral, but the Magashule faction was not convinced. 'Noby tried to make the two warring groups reconcile, that is where the hatred [towards him] started,' maintained Nokwanda. She said it was not in the northern camp's best interest to have peace in the province, at least not on any terms set by 'outsiders' who had been 'imposed' on the province by Mbeki and co.

The ILC was mandated with two main tasks: firstly, to ensure that the ANC's branches in the province functioned optimally; thereafter, to organise and oversee a credible provincial elective conference free of allegations and accusations of vote-rigging and other irregularities. As coordinator of the interim structure, Ngombane quickly made some powerful enemies in the Free State, especially among people aligned to Magashule.

In 2001, while Magashule was still serving as an MP in Cape Town, Direko reshuffled the province's executive council and in the process got rid of three MECs who hailed from the north. She replaced them with people from the province's southern region, which obviously angered the Magashule camp. They directed their fury at Ngombane's ILC, which in their view had influenced Direko's decisions.[1]

They saw the reshuffle as a move designed to 'purge' the provincial cabinet 'of supporters of ANC provincial chairperson Ace Magashule', according to a *Mail & Guardian* report.[2] One of the new appointees was Beatrice Marshoff, who became MEC for social development.[3] Although Direko effected the cabinet reshuffle, Marshoff's inclusion in the executive council was 'widely' viewed as having been influenced by Ngombane's ILC.[4] The move was also a precursor to her later replacement of Direko as Free State premier. Ngombane has therefore been described as the man who 'helped' Marshoff 'into the top spot'.[5] This view would later be a key ingredient in the political tension around Ngombane.

Ngombane 'bailed out' of the ILC in 2001, before the provincial conference to be held the following year, recalled his widow. 'He was getting too frustrated,' she explained. 'He had a mandate to build the branches in the province and strike a balance between the two factions, but he could not make any inroads in this regard.'

Ngombane returned to the provincial government, but his days of locking horns with political foes were far from over. He took a job as head of department (HOD) at Economic Development, Tourism and Environmental Affairs, where he clashed with MEC Sakhiwo Belot. According to Nokwanda, appointments were made in Belot's department without following proper processes, and this led to friction. Belot later became a special advisor to Magashule.[6]

A KPMG report highlighted the tension between Ngombane and Belot, and recommended that one or both leave the department.[7] Belot subsequently made way for Benny Malakoane, but the shuffle did not bring the department's problems to an end. In fact, Nokwanda said the fighting between her husband and the new MEC was worse.

Ngombane had by then established himself as an official who respected the rules and laws that govern public bodies, including the Public Service Act and the Public Finance Management Act. He drew Malakoane's ire when he acted swiftly to suspend four of the department's chief directors over financial irregularities.[8] The suspended officials were later reinstated by a court order. At the time, Malakoane had claimed that Ngombane was undermining his authority.[9] 'He had this attitude of "we are here to work",' explained Nokwanda. 'It was not necessarily about cracking down on corruption, but about making sure we give the people what the ANC said it would give people.'

Ngombane's reputation as someone who fought maladministration would continue to swell after Beatrice Marshoff replaced Direko as premier in early 2004. In August of that year, he was appointed head of a newly formed policy coordination unit in the premier's office. It was a powerful position, seeing as he would have Marshoff's ear in matters involving governance and the financial affairs of the province's departments and entities. The appointment was bound to revive the simmering discord between the opposing political camps. Those who had previously blamed Ngombane's ILC for influencing Direko's decision to appoint MECs from the southern faction weren't happy. They saw it as an attempt by Marshoff to promote the man who paved the way for her to become premier. More than ever, Marshoff and Ngombane were viewed as close allies.

Nokwanda, who had been working in Marshoff's office before her husband's arrival, said one of the most drastic early changes that he intended to implement was to centralise decisions around the spending of billions of rands of government funds in his unit's office. For instance, Ngombane wanted his unit to have control over the huge chunks of money allocated to municipalities from the national government's municipal infrastructure grant and the expanded public works programme.

Ngombane's proposed oversight of municipalities' spending no doubt made him enemies within the northern and southern factions, who had apparently both been tapping into municipal resources.

Nokwanda believes the proposed centralisation of municipal spending sealed her husband's fate. 'That is why he is dead,' she said. 'It was about money and not really about politics.'

From Marshoff's vantage point, it appeared as if Magashule's northern faction was more vocal and transparent about their hatred for Ngombane. 'He died because he was close to me. They saw him as their biggest threat,' she told me.

Another issue was a decision by the then premier to move a few HODs to new departments. The reshuffle was intended to improve the functioning of the affected departments, but some of the HODs were unhappy with their redeployment and even took Marshoff to court. The Magashule-led PEC accused the premier of making important governance decisions without consulting the party's provincial leadership.[10]

Nokwanda said her husband was thrust right into the middle of this fracas despite playing no role in the reshuffle. 'They [the northerners] were asking if Noby was running the show. They had somehow gotten the idea that he was behind the reshuffle,' she said.

Towards the end of 2004, the political discord in the province once again became serious enough for the ANC's national leadership to intervene. As previously mentioned, a delegation of ANC leaders, led by Mbeki sidekick Essop Pahad, met with Marshoff and Magashule in Bloemfontein in November.

The northerners wanted Marshoff to resign. They directed much of their anger at Ngombane, she recalled. 'They were saying that Noby was a hatchet man and that he was running things in the province and in the premier's office,' said Marshoff.

A former government leader from the Free State told me, 'I phoned Beatrice [Marshoff] and told her there is a character assassination of Noby, and that she needed to do something about it. I said she needed to publicly condemn the hatred directed at Noby before the character assassination became a real assassination.'

Dennis Bloem, who was still in the ANC at the time, said Ngombane was poised for greatness. 'Noby was this blue-eyed boy and favourite of Luthuli House. There was talk that he was going to take over as premier after Marshoff,' he recalled.

The tension spilled over into 2005. 'There was going to be a cabinet reshuffle, and Ace was going to be removed. It was imminent,' said Nokwanda. Magashule had become MEC for agriculture the previous year, but his antics at the department had put him in line to be chopped from Marshoff's cabinet.

Marshoff met with Magashule and some of his allies on Monday 21 March. Those present from the northern faction included Magashule's right-hand man Pat Matosa, ANC provincial treasurer Mxolisi Dukwana and Casca Mokitlane, a Magashule backer who later joined COPE before eventually rejoining the ANC. Some of the NEC members whom the ANC had deployed to the Free State were also in attendance.

Ngombane's name kept cropping up. The group was apparently highly upset about his perceived influence over the premier. 'Casca was the biggest talker, he spoke the most, but Pat Matosa and Dukwana also weighed in,' Marshoff recalled. 'Ace just sat quietly. He did not say much.'

According to the former premier, she refused to apologise for employing Ngombane in her office. 'Afterwards I asked Noby what he had done to make those people hate him so much,' Marshoff said. 'He told me I shouldn't worry about them, I shouldn't break my head over those people.'

But Nokwanda said her husband became worried and paranoid. 'He would say that "they" wanted to kill him, that he had a gut feeling he was going to be killed,' she told me.

There were calls from both sides of the political divide for Ngombane to be removed, so Nokwanda could never pinpoint exactly who 'they' were when her husband spoke about the danger he was facing. 'He said it was like he was taking money away from them [because of the financial restructuring he wanted to implement],' his wife explained. 'If there was one thing that was banding them together, it was the idea that Noby was a problem and that he needed to go.'

The Ngombanes lived in a spacious home at the end of a cul-de-sac in the upmarket Bloemfontein suburb of Hillsboro.

On the evening of Tuesday 22 March 2005, the family was enjoying a quiet evening. Noby Ngombane had arrived home at about 18:30. When Nokwanda got there a little later, she found several of her relatives at the house. Her husband had invited her brother Bongani and her sister Tantaswa, along with two of her cousins, Vuyokazi and Siphumle, to watch a movie with him. 'Noby wanted to watch a DVD, so he called all of them,' recalled Nokwanda. 'He was not good with electronic devices, so he needed someone to help him with the DVD player.'

After giving her husband some takeaway chicken from a nearby Nando's, Nokwanda, Ngombane and the others started watching *Ray*, a biopic about the American musician Ray Charles. One of the movie's early scenes shows the funeral of Charles's brother, who drowned when he was a child. In the scene, Charles's mother flings herself on the casket of the dead boy and cries and screams in front of the other mourners. This got Ngombane talking about his own death. 'Noby said that if he died we shouldn't have such a dramatic funeral for him,' remembered Nokwanda.

They carried on watching the movie, but a little while later Tantaswa noticed a car in the driveway in front of the house. Ngombane went outside to inspect. Zandile, his and Nokwanda's five-year-old daughter, went after him. 'I saw him go outside,' said Nokwanda. 'The next thing we heard gunshots: two shots, then a brief pause, then more shots fired quickly after each other.' Those inside the house ducked for cover.

When the shooting stopped, Nokwanda moved towards the front door. She saw little Zandile coming back into the house. Then she saw her husband, who was lying face down. He had made it past the door and into the kitchen, but now he was not moving.

Nokwanda screamed and called her brother to come and help her, after which she called the police's 10111 emergency line from a cordless phone. Bongani also phoned the police from his cellphone.

When the emergency services did not arrive quickly enough for their liking, Ngombane's panic-stricken wife and her family decided to get him to a hospital themselves. 'Noby weighed 90 kilograms and he was 1.8 metres tall, but we dragged and pushed him until we got him into my car,' Nokwanda recalled. 'We drove to the Mediclinic and got there within five minutes.'

Ngombane, who had been hit by at least two bullets, was rushed into surgery. One of the bullets had pierced his aorta, so he was suffering from profuse internal bleeding. The surgeons opened his chest to find the source of the bleeding and to try to repair the damage, but it was too late.

Ngombane was declared dead at around 21:30, about an hour after arriving at the hospital. He was thirty-nine years old. The cause of death was given as 'gunshots to the chest and stomach' in the official record.

Premier Beatrice Marshoff rushed to the hospital as soon as she heard about the shooting, but her right-hand man was already dead by the time she got there.

Soon after Ngombane was pronounced dead, the police arrived at the hospital. 'They interviewed me. They were quite forceful, so I asked them if I should get a lawyer,' said Nokwanda. When she returned home, a second set of police officers came to talk to her. 'It was a very long night,' she recalled.

The police were thorough in their questioning of the shocked widow, but it would later dawn on Nokwanda that they had omitted to perform some key tasks that were not only standard practice, but also crucial for any murder investigation. 'A contact in the police later told me that the first thing cops have to do at a crime scene where somebody was shot is test any potential suspects' hands for gunpowder residue,' she told me. 'The police never did this on me or on any of the others who were at the house.'

A week later, Ngombane was buried in Bloemfontein. In front of hundreds of mourners who had come to pay their last respects to the slain official, Nokwanda said her husband's murder was a hit linked to his work in the politically volatile province. 'Let us not beat around the bush when it is said that this murder is a mystery whose motives are unclear,' she declared. 'We are talking about a political killing.'[11]

Marshoff was more reserved, saying they needed to give the authorities room to probe the murder. She said she felt it was insensitive to speculate about the motivation behind Ngombane's death.[12] But if Marshoff did not believe that the murder was politically motivated then, she would soon receive information that would make her seriously entertain the possibility.

What follows is Marshoff's account of her interactions with an intelligence operative who brought her some troubling news not long after Ngombane's death. Marshoff would later tell this tale under oath at a judicial inquiry into the murder. Mysteriously, all of the court documents related to the inquiry seem to have disappeared. At the time, this evidence was heard behind closed doors, so the details about her encounters with the spook are revealed here for the first time, with her consent.

'After Noby's funeral a comrade came to see me,' Marshoff told me in August 2018. 'He was working with the National Intelligence Agency [NIA, which would later be absorbed into the new State Security Agency] and he said he wanted to share something very sensitive with me.'

He told her that he had obtained sensitive information about Ngombane's death during his intelligence-gathering work; that this information pointed to the possible involvement of politicians; and that he had known Ngombane from the struggle days and was keen to get to the bottom of the murder. 'He told me that the police will never find Noby's killer,' she recalled.

According to the spook, the assassin had been provided with a gun, a car and money. There had also been a getaway driver who had waited for the shooter and then driven off with him as soon as the deed was done. In other words, the murder had been a well-planned and well-executed hit.

The NIA agent told Marshoff that the killer and his getaway driver had driven away from the scene of the crime but had stopped the car not far from the cul-de-sac's entrance, where they got into a second car that had been waiting for them. The first car was then driven away by someone else, while the shooter and the getaway driver left in the second car. 'He told me that the two men [the shooter and the driver] drove to Bethlehem, where the murder weapon was thrown into the Saulspoort Dam,' said Marshoff.

There was more. The intelligence operative also told Marshoff that there was a plan under way to frame someone for the murder so that the public's attention would be diverted from claims of a political hit.

The spook said he could not go to the police with the information, because they were part of the cover-up. But he wanted to pursue the matter. To do this, he needed resources. 'He asked for a car that couldn't be traced to him and for some money, and he said he needed a couple of days,' recalled Marshoff.

Given the potential danger of being linked to a sensitive, off-the-books operation, Marshoff got one of her staffers to rent a car for the spook in such a way that it could not be traced back to the premier's office. Marshoff also gave him about R500.

True to his word, the NIA agent returned two or three days later. He told Marshoff that he had managed to track down the getaway driver somewhere in Bethlehem, and that the murder weapon had indeed been thrown into the Saulspoort Dam. But the getaway driver was too afraid for his life to come forward and testify about what had happened, seeing as he knew that the authorities were in on the conspiracy.

The spook also told Marshoff that he had informed some very senior people about what he had learnt, but that they appeared to be unwilling to take the matter seriously. He alleged to have met with or spoken to NIA boss Billy Masetlha, safety and security minister Charles Nqakula and national police commissioner Jackie Selebi.

Before taking leave of Marshoff for the last time, the spook again claimed that there would soon be a scapegoat for the murder. This would form part of a high-level cover-up to protect the real culprits, he told her.

During this time, another curious thing happened. Magashule apparently told at least two people that he was worried he might be held accountable for murder. 'I met with Ace soon after Noby's death,' said one former Magashule confidant. 'He told me he was really concerned that he would get arrested for conspiracy to commit murder.'

A second former confidant also told me that Magashule had expressed fears that he might be arrested. But he need not have worried. As if on cue, less than two weeks after the shooting, *City Press* published a story that pointed to Nokwanda as the main suspect.[13] 'The widow of slain Free State government official Noby Ngombane made enquiries about insurance benefits [in the event of Ngombane's death] 10 days before her husband was shot and killed,' the newspaper reported.

From the article's content, it seems obvious that the paper got its information from the police, as it deals with details of the investigation. Another 'major twist' in the matter was that Nokwanda had apparently refused to cooperate with detectives, reported *City Press*.

The report was an early indication that the authorities had shifted the focus of their investigation onto Nokwanda. It would be a probe fraught with shoddy police work and dubious conduct by some of the cops involved, and it would culminate in an embarrassing failed attempt to prosecute a grieving widow and her family.

In late July 2005, the police made their first move by arresting Nokwanda's brother Bongani and her cousin Siphumle. The authorities stated that Nokwanda was also due to be in custody soon.[14] They insisted that their investigation showed no sign of a political motive behind Ngombane's killing. One can only speculate as to the thoroughness of the probe that informed this conclusion.

'We have now ruled out a political motive to this murder due to overwhelming evidence against the current suspects,' a SAPS spokesperson told the media.[15] Police commissioner Jackie Selebi also weighed in on the matter, affirming the police's findings and stating that all the 'evidence' pointed to Nokwanda and her family. 'We have double-checked and we have triple-checked all the facts,' Selebi told the public. 'The investigation has been thorough.'[16]

I spoke to several sources who were in Magashule's inner circle at the time. It seems Selebi's claim could not have been further from the truth. 'The police did not make any attempt to determine whether Noby's death was linked to the province's politics,' one source told me. 'Given the animosity between Noby and prominent ANC members, all of us should have been suspects and we should at least have been questioned. But we weren't. It would have been easy for the police to go through us one by one to see if anyone was somehow linked to the murder. But there simply was no such probe.'

Two other former members of the so-called northern faction confirmed that they also had not been questioned. Despite the obvious tensions between Ngombane and senior political figures, the police for some reason did not even bother to include politics as a possible motive for the murder. Of the three former Magashule allies I spoke to, two told me they were certain the order to kill Ngombane was politically motivated. The third said it was 'highly probable' that this was the case.

'The local SAPS had already been captured by the political machinery at that time. I believe any attempt to investigate the real cause of the murder was killed from within the police's ranks, and there was a deliberate plan to make Noby's wife the scapegoat,' alleged one of my sources.

It would take a few months before the public would learn how underwhelming the police's so-called evidence had in fact been.

Nokwanda was arrested along with Vuyokazi and Tantaswa mere days after Bongani and Siphumle. All five were charged with Ngombane's murder. Amid the arrests, the police fed the media with sensational information that purported to show why Nokwanda wanted her husband dead. Another *City Press* report, published the day before she was due to appear in court, claimed that her husband's life had been insured for R20 million and that Nokwanda was due to receive this massive payout in August.[17] Again, the paper's information clearly came from someone in the SAPS.

Nokwanda said this was hogwash. 'Noby wanted to take out life insurance because he was scared and paranoid,' she told me. 'He got a quote, but he never got the policy. He consulted with a financial advisor in January

2005, but he only got insurance for our house.' If the police did indeed source evidence that Nokwanda was due to receive millions from her husband's life insurance, the NPA curiously omitted this detail in the charge sheet it filed only a few months later.

The same *City Press* article unintentionally highlighted just how flimsy the 'evidence' on which the police based their decision to go after Nokwanda was: 'It is understood that her conduct after her husband's death led police to consider her as the prime suspect. She broke with common tradition, firstly by addressing mourners at the funeral ... secondly she threw a lavish party to mark the end of her mourning period, which was four months in comparison to the average 12 months.'[18]

Although the police had arrested Nokwanda and her relatives, it soon became apparent that the state did not have much of a case against them. By September, the NPA had not yet formally charged the five suspects. '[The state] is working full-time and uninterrupted to get the case trial ready,' prosecutor Jannie Botha told the magistrate while arguing for a second postponement.[19] The matter was postponed to December.

The police, meanwhile, went on a wild and at times bizarre goose chase while Nokwanda and her co-accused were out on bail. In October, they exhumed Ngombane's body after allegedly receiving information that suggested Nokwanda had hid the gun that killed him in the coffin. A police spokesperson said there had been 'reasonable grounds [to believe] that the murder weapon had been concealed in the body or coffin of the deceased'. A thorough search of the coffin and an X-ray of the body, however, revealed no firearm.[20]

Despite having no solid evidence, the state eventually charged the five accused with murder, obstruction of justice, and possession of an unlicensed firearm and ammunition. According to the charge sheet, the state's main piece of evidence was a recording of Nokwanda's emergency call to 10111 after the shooting. 'According to the recording in the SAPS' possession accused number 5 [Bongani] is being told to stop, after which a shot goes off,' read the charge sheet. If it were not for this recording, the 'true facts would never have come to light', the state maintained.

Nokwanda said that while she was on the line with the 10111 operator, she had frantically screamed and called out for her brother to come and help her. She had also smacked Ngombane on his back a couple of times to try to revive him. These were the sounds that could be heard on the recording and which the state claimed were gunshots. 'A Xhosa translator translated the recording of me and claimed that I had told Bongani to stop, which was not the case,' said Nokwanda.

The NPA's decision to use the recording as its main piece of evidence would prove to be a huge mistake. Not only was it insufficient to get a conviction, but it also drew attention to the fact that the police's probe had the markings of a cover-up.

In March 2006, the state again asked the court for a postponement after having allegedly obtained 'sensitive' information that it said it needed to follow up on. 'The information is of an essential nature that justifies further investigation,' state prosecutor Andre du Toit told the court.[21] A source with insight into the state's case told me that Du Toit was probably referring to a letter received from a prisoner who claimed to have shot Ngombane.

According to later media reports, Bhekisa Andreas Sibisi, who was serving a twenty-seven-year sentence for murder and robbery at Ncome Prison near Vryheid, 'confessed' that Nokwanda had offered him R120 000 to kill her husband. He claimed that while being held at Barberton Prison in Mpumalanga, he was 'secretly released on March 21 2005 under the pretext that he was admitted to hospital'. He was then driven through the night to Bloemfontein, where he was introduced to Nokwanda and her sister. He claimed to have shot Ngombane 'after Nokwanda opened the door and gave the go-ahead'.[22]

Sibisi's claim could only be described as wild and outlandish. For starters, Ngombane was shot outside, as clearly indicated by the yellow chalk marks made by the police where they found the bullet casings in the driveway.[23] The NPA eventually agreed, indicating that an investigation had found Sibisi's claim contained 'no substance'.[24] In September 2007, the NPA formally withdrew all charges against the five accused.

It was an embarrassing U-turn. After a cocksure stance that had been echoed by Selebi, the NPA now said its *prima facie* case against the accused was too weak to pursue. 'After consultation with the witnesses and further investigation we came to the conclusion that there was no reasonable chance of a successful prosecution,' Du Toit told the press.[25]

An NPA insider told me that the police's investigation had been weak from the outset, but that there was massive pressure to prosecute somebody. 'Everybody wanted the NPA to prosecute,' he recalled.

When Du Toit announced that the case against Nokwanda and her co-accused would be withdrawn, he added that the police would continue their investigation and that a judicial inquiry would be held into the matter.[26] The inquiry kicked off in the Bloemfontein Magistrate's Court in late April 2008 and was presided over by Magistrate Dawn Soomaroo.

The most shocking revelation to surface at the inquiry related to the police's handling of the recordings of the phone calls made on the night of the murder. 'An overseas sound expert, who initially testified that a recording of the 10111 call had some distinct sound which could possibly be gunshots in the background, later conceded the opposite after listening to another recording made at the same time,' reported the *Mail & Guardian* in its coverage of the inquiry.[27]

The first recording was of Nokwanda's 10111 call from the cordless phone. The second was of her brother Bongani's cellphone call to the police. This second recording was much clearer, and it was apparent that the sounds in the background were not gunshots, but the investigating officers for some reason failed to give it to the expert from abroad. In other words, the police had withheld crucial evidence from one of the state's key witnesses.

The inquiry also heard from Advocate Willem Edeling, who had represented Nokwanda during the criminal trial. He alleged that the police had tortured Bongani in order to extract a confession.[28]

Nokwanda told me about the curious nature of their arrest and Bongani's alleged torture. 'We were arrested by SAPS members from Queenstown [in the Eastern Cape] and not by the police in Bloemfontein,' she said. According to Nokwanda, before they were charged, the police 'smuggled' Bongani out of the Free State and took him to East London, where he was tortured.

Bongani had detailed his alleged abduction and torture in an affidavit made in 2005. He claimed under oath that the Eastern Cape police had stripped him naked, poured water over him and given him electric shocks.[29] At the time, the police had strongly denied the allegations.

The testimony before the inquiry about the police's conduct, especially with regards to the audio recordings, was compelling enough to raise the spectre of a far-reaching political conspiracy. But that was not the most sensitive testimony made before Soomaroo.

During cross-examination by the state advocate, Nokwanda was asked to elaborate on who she thought her late husband's political enemies had been. She was hesitant to respond, saying that she 'knew the politics' in the province and feared for her and her children's safety. Soomaroo decided that Nokwanda should provide such information in camera.[30]

Then, about midway through the inquiry, Edeling applied to have a second witness testify behind closed doors. This was Marshoff, and her testimony included the story she told me about the NIA agent.

The Soomaroo inquiry wrapped up towards the end of May 2008. It effectively slammed the eagerness with which the police and the NPA had arrested and prosecuted Nokwanda and her relatives. 'Nokwanda, Bongani, Tantaswa, Vuyokazi and Siphumle were not directly or indirectly involved in the murder of Noby,' Soomaroo concluded. Although the inquiry did not come close to identifying those responsible for the murder, Soomaroo found that the evidence given in camera pointed to a 'further route' that required exploration.[31]

Perhaps unsurprisingly, there is no evidence to suggest that the NPA or any law-enforcement agency heeded Soomaroo's instruction. In fact, all indications are that forces in the law-enforcement and justice environments acted to further cover up the matter after the inquiry.

In early 2018, Nokwanda set out to retrieve the inquiry's records from the Bloemfontein Magistrate's Court. She had long entertained the possibility of suing the state for wrongful prosecution, and she wanted the records for this purpose. But her efforts would be fruitless. She showed me emails from Department of Justice officials claiming that the inquiry file had 'disappeared'.

I went to the Magistrate's Court in September 2018 to try to retrieve the documents, but had no better luck. A court official in the records department told me that plenty of people had come looking for the file before me, and that it was indeed missing.

When I asked how it was possible that the court could lose such important documents, the official simply shrugged. Then he told me something even more concerning. Officials from the Hawks had come to the court in early 2018 to draw the file. When they too were told that it had gone missing, one of the Hawks told the court official that the police case file had also disappeared.

The matter was originally registered at Bloemfontein's Bayswater Police

Station under case number 116-03-05. When the Hawks went to retrieve the file from the Bayswater station, they found that it contained documents from a completely unrelated case. Someone had clearly replaced Ngombane's case records with those of another matter.

I managed to corroborate what the court official was told with sources in the Hawks: the records from the 2008 inquiry are gone; so too is the case file opened by the SAPS after the murder in early 2005.

This does not mean that those behind Ngombane's untimely death will never be apprehended. The mysterious NIA agent is still out there. It is also possible that the hitman or his getaway driver, or both, are still alive and well. A proper police investigation, unhampered by any meddling, may yet uncover the truth about a murder that has the markings of a top-level political hit.

PART III

THE R1-BILLION
HOUSING SPLURGE

8

'Bring your people'

When Ace Magashule became Free State premier in 2009, he almost immediately began meddling in the affairs of the provincial departments with the largest budgets. One of those was the Free State Department of Human Settlements (FSHS), which is primarily tasked with providing low-cost housing to the province's poorest citizens.[1] The FSHS became the site of such rampant looting by the Magashule capture network that it deservedly takes up a comparatively large portion of this book.

Let's start with the province's R1-billion Reconstruction and Development Programme (RDP) scandal from around 2010. This sordid saga is underpinned by a toxic combination of mismanagement and corruption, and Magashule's fingerprints are all over it.

Earlier media reports exposed the involvement of a few politically connected individuals. But Magashule's cronies escaped scrutiny and his own role in engineering this financial disaster remained under wraps, thanks to the department's well-orchestrated management of the scandal's fallout, which included selective legal proceedings that deliberately shielded Magashule's friends and associates from exposure and financial liability. Most alarmingly, it appears Magashule may have directly participated in a wide-ranging cover-up to suppress the true facts by roping in a private forensic firm owned by a former government spy boss to 'investigate' the saga. This firm allegedly took hold of key documents and evidence, and subsequently prevented the Special Investigating Unit (SIU), which had also been tasked with probing the issue, from accessing these important materials. As a result, the public was kept in the dark about Magashule and his cronies' apparent involvement in one of the largest low-cost housing scandals this country has ever seen.

For the first time, this book exposes how scores of politically connected people benefited from a R1-billion spending frenzy that left in its wake hundreds of unfinished or poorly constructed RDP houses. Some of Magashule's closest associates pocketed money without completing their projects. And that is just the tip of the iceberg.

While studying the 2010 contracts, I stumbled upon records that detail the full, shocking extent of the capture and rot at the provincial Department of Human Settlements during Magashule's reign as premier. In a period of nearly a decade, the FSHS channelled contracts for new houses worth more than R2 billion to a band of businesspeople linked to or associated with Magashule. There is also evidence to suggest that he punished former political allies who had abandoned his camp by stopping the flow of RDP contracts to companies owned by or linked to them. In effect, a picture emerges that Magashule determined the direction of the department's money flows by acting as its de facto boss.

From a taxpayer's perspective, the Free State's low-cost housing programmes under the Magashule administration should elicit great anger. Many of the preferred contractors failed to deliver houses. Others constructed houses replete with shoddy workmanship and substandard materials. In the worst instances, houses collapsed or were of such poor quality that they needed to be demolished and rebuilt by other contractors.

Among this coterie of cronies were politicians who once sided with Magashule in the ANC's factional battles, former business partners, colleagues in the provincial government and local legislature, and friends from his hometown. Even his daughter later tapped into the scheme.

This wholesale capture of the province's housing budget was achieved by staffing the FSHS with people who could be trusted to act on Magashule's orders. Current and former department insiders attested to a government environment in which the premier loomed in the background to ensure that his friends and associates got the most lucrative housing contracts. 'Ace has spoken,' one former department staffer was told by his superior when he queried a 2012 contract awarded to a known Magashule ally without a tender process.

The premier's meddling, detailed in subsequent chapters of this book, appears to have forced department officials to override or ignore the rules and laws that govern how the state should spend its money. This reckless disregard for prescribed procurement standards is reflected in reports by the auditor-general, which show that the department incurred irregular expenditure totalling a jaw-dropping R7 billion in the nine years that Magashule ruled over the Free State.[2]

To put this into context, in 2013/14 the Gauteng Department of Human

Settlements spent R4.2 billion, of which R461 million, or roughly 10 per cent, was found to be irregular.[3] In the same year, the much smaller FSHS spent about R1.5 billion, but managed to rack up irregular expenditure of R857 million, or 57 per cent of total spend.[4]

And 2013/14 was a relatively good year. In some financial years, as much as 80 (2015/16) and even 90 per cent (2011/12) of the department's expenditure was classified as irregular by the auditor-general.[5] The main culprits appeared to be contracts for housing projects that were awarded without following proper procurement processes. Year after year, the AG highlighted this troubling phenomenon, but the department made no effort to rectify the situation, as evidenced by its consistently ludicrous irregular-expenditure figures.

Irregular expenditure on dodgy contracts could possibly be forgiven if the department had fulfilled its mandate of delivering decent housing. But that was simply not the case. While Magashule's associates, friends and family stuffed their pockets, the province completely missed its housing targets. Today, thousands of incomplete or poorly built RDP houses are strewn all over the Free State. It is a horrific legacy for a politician who has branded himself as a champion of the poor.

So how did it all begin? Shortly after being sworn in as Free State premier on 6 May 2009, Magashule announced with great fanfare that his administration would build 'bigger and better' houses. These houses would be 50 square metres in size, he promised, an improvement on the 40 square metres previously specified for RDP houses.[6] The man who would help him roll out this new strategy was Mosebenzi Zwane, the freshly appointed MEC for human settlements.[7] While at the time it seemed that Magashule was driven by noble intentions, the benefit of hindsight has led several sources, including current and former department insiders, to view the development in a different light.

When Magashule announced his plan to build bigger houses, the department had already finalised its planning for the following financial year. It had appointed about ninety contractors, who would altogether build roughly 16 000 houses, a former senior staffer told me. However, these builders had been appointed in accordance with the old 40-square-metre specifications. The sources I spoke to claim Magashule insisted that the department find new contractors to build the bigger houses, sidelining many of the original contractors.

'The first batch of contractors had already done their bill of quantities based on the old 40-square-metre specifications, and they had signed contracts with the department,' explained the former FSHS official.

With Magashule's new mandate, the department simply failed to honour these contracts. Some of the contractors felt aggrieved enough to take the province to court, but the premier soldiered on. 'Ace told us that people should take him to court if they wanted to; he was going to appoint new contractors,' said my source.

This former official now believes Magashule's call for bigger houses was a ploy to get rid of the original contractors so that a new batch of politically connected businesspeople could benefit from RDP projects. An analysis of the list of new contractors certainly supports this view.

A member of Magashule's erstwhile executive council recalls an even more troubling event. 'Ace called a lot of us together and told us there was going to be this huge series of housing contracts, so we needed to bring "our people" into the mix,' claimed this politician.

According to court papers,[8] in early 2010 the FSHS initiated a fresh tender process based on the new specifications. When the tender closed in April, the department had received bids from 361 contractors. However, amid all the uncertainty over the new specifications, the department was unable to award any contracts before the tender's validity period lapsed. At the end of July, the department's bid adjudication committee met to discuss the contracts.

At this stage, the FSHS was facing disaster. It was already midway into the second quarter of the financial year, and the department had spent virtually none of its allocation from the national fiscus. If the province could not spend its money, the new premier's administration would come under serious fire from the national government, which could lay claim to any unspent money the province had received through conditional grants. An affidavit filed in court explains: 'If a conditional allocation has not been spent by the end of the financial year, it reverts to and must be repaid to the National Revenue Fund, unless the National Treasury is satisfied that the unspent allocation has been committed to identifiable projects.'[9]

Over and above the R1.3 billion the department had received from National Treasury to build 'sustainable human settlements', it had another R120 million that had rolled over from the previous financial year. Magashule risked having R1.42 billion taken away from his province because of the FSHS's inability to spend its allocation.

'If you don't build houses and spend money during the first two quarters of the financial year, it is pretty much a lost cause,' explained another former FSHS staffer. 'December and January are known as dead months in the construction sector because of the holidays, so you're not going to catch up during that time.'

As the tender had now lapsed, the department seemingly had no way to appoint a large group of contractors in a short space of time so that it could spend its budget. At the July meeting, the bid adjudication committee therefore resolved to cancel the tender and instead draw up a database of service providers made up of 'but not limited to' those who had submitted bids for the lapsed tender.[10] The database could therefore include companies that had not even submitted bids in the first round.

This was not the only problem. Of the 361 companies that did submit bids, 252 either had bid compliance issues, such as not possessing a valid tax clearance certificate, or had failed to 'meet the minimum functionality threshold'.[11] In other words, they were simply not capable of delivering on large projects. Despite these shortcomings, the department loaded all 361 companies onto its database, along with a few that had not even tendered. Many of them would go on to clinch lucrative contracts to build RDP houses.

Explaining how fraught the process was, one former department official claimed Magashule was the central figure in the saga. 'We were asked to load batches of new companies onto the database, but many of them didn't even have proper NHBRC [National Home Builders Registration Council] papers or the correct CIDB [Construction Industry Development Board] grading, and many of these companies' finances weren't in order,' this source said. 'The technical committee raised these compliance issues with the department's bosses, but they were ignored.' The source alleged that the head of department, Mpho Mokoena, made it clear where his orders were coming from: 'Mokoena told us that Ace had instructed him to work with these people [the new contractors who were found to be non-compliant], that we needed to help them become compliant.'

There were also more overt signs of Magashule's early meddling in the department's affairs. In 2009, he launched his now infamous Operation Hlasela (Operation Attack), supposedly aimed at eradicating poverty and improving service delivery in all spheres of government. But critics say

Operation Hlasela was abused for party-political purposes.[12] Indeed, the public protector would later confirm that it 'conflated' the functions of the provincial government with the interests of the ANC.[13]

Through Operation Hlasela, which was run out of the premier's office, Magashule exerted control over departments like the FSHS, whose 2016/17 annual report contains a vague explanation of the programme: 'This [Operation Hlasela] is a specific provincial programme focusing on integrated service delivery. All the department's activities are coordinated to ensure integrated human settlements.'[14]

But back to the RDP houses. By October, the FSHS was still woefully behind on its expenditure targets, even after appointing new companies from its dubious database. Tokyo Sexwale, the national minister of human settlements, notified the department that it had spent less than 10 per cent of its allocation.[15]

Losing the unspent money to national government was only one concern. If this were to happen, the FSHS also risked losing out on future grants from the national budget. 'Typically, where a province has failed to spend its conditional allocation, (e.g. for a housing or education project) … the funds will in future years be allocated to other provinces which have a good track record in spending on the relevant housing or education project,' the aforementioned court affidavit explains.[16]

Having more than R1 billion taken away from the provincial government would also have put lethal political ammunition in the hands of Magashule's enemies. They would have been able to accuse his administration of incompetence and maladministration barely a quarter of the way into his first term as premier.

One such political foe was Sexwale. The national housing minister had played a key role in helping Jacob Zuma become ANC president at the Polokwane conference in 2007. For this, Sexwale had been rewarded with a place in Zuma's cabinet. But by 2010, the tectonic plates beneath the perpetually divided ruling party were moving once again. The ANC's 2012 national conference lay in the not-too-distant future, and Sexwale was already being associated with campaigns and factions that sought to unseat Zuma and his allies.[17] 'Sexwale wanted Ace to fail. He wanted the Free State to pay back the money it couldn't spend to make Ace look weak and incapable,' said a source with insight into the Free State's RDP debacle.

To avoid any embarrassment or political damage, the department had to spend its money as quickly as it could. To this end, it developed an expenditure recovery plan (ERP) to fast-track payments to a new batch of contractors.[18] The ERP was, it seems, masterminded by Magashule's office and enforced by Zwane, but neither man would ever be held accountable for the financial disaster that followed.

With the initiation of the ERP, the money sluices were now well and truly open in the Free State. This sudden profligacy attracted all manner of connected contractors, some of them closely linked to Magashule. One was Rachelle Els, a businesswoman and, according to several sources, a 'close friend' from his hometown. Most concerningly, Els and Magashule were once business partners, or at least intended to be. Company records list Magashule and Els as co-directors in an entity called National Pride Trading 456, which was established in mid-2007, about two years before Magashule became premier. It has since been deregistered. A subsequent chapter details the contracts awarded to Els.

'Ace literally ensured that people got allocated RDP projects,' said one former FSHS insider. 'He would meet with someone like Rachelle Els over the weekend, then on the following Monday we were told that we needed to award 50 or 100 houses to Els's company.'

Several FSHS sources told me there were 'zero tender processes' followed for any of these contracts. They claimed that, through Operation Hlasela, Magashule would hand-pick contractors like Els and ensure that their companies were given RDP contracts. In later court proceedings, the department itself would label the contracts signed in late 2010 and early 2011 a 'fraudulent scheme'.[19]

When the national department and National Treasury got wind of the FSHS's radical expenditure drive, they warned that the ERP was a bad idea. Their main concerns were that the department intended making large advance payments to companies before any work had been done and that the new contracts were signed without following proper procurement processes. They urged the FSHS not to proceed with the ERP, but it pressed ahead anyway.[20]

Between November 2010 and March 2011, the final months of the financial year, the FSHS hastily splurged more than R1 billion, or 90 per cent of its entire budget, on payments to companies appointed for new RDP projects. These projects, awarded to more than 100 contractors, were supposed to have delivered nearly 15 000 houses.[21] Together with contracts signed earlier in 2010, the department now had to deliver around 21 000 houses at a cost of just under R1.5 billion.[22] It was a massive undertaking, and it would soon become evident that the department had bitten off more than it could chew.

The plan could have worked if the department had been capable of monitoring the rapid increase in expenditure. However, what ended up happening was that the FSHS simply emptied its coffers at an alarming rate without putting in place the necessary checks and balances to ensure that the new contractors actually delivered. Of the more than R1 billion the department spent in the last five months of the financial year, over R600 million was paid to materials suppliers,[23] and about R500 million was paid to building contractors.

According to one of my sources, the ERP was not necessarily a bad idea. Some of the materials suppliers, such as brick manufacturers, required advance payments to keep operating during the weeks in December and January when they would ordinarily have closed shop. The problem was that the department was completely incapable of monitoring the situation to determine which of the materials suppliers had delivered their goods and which of the contractors were building their houses.

When FSHS inspectors did go out to select sites, they found that some of the contractors and materials suppliers had been cheating to increase their profit margins. 'The contracts with the department stipulate that houses need to be built with SABS [South African Bureau of Standards]-approved materials,' my source told me. 'But either the contractors or the materials suppliers, or both, were cutting corners by using cheaper, low-quality materials. That is why some houses in the province started falling apart after two years.' In some instances, contractors had run out of money halfway through their projects. Others had simply not built any houses whatsoever.

At the end of the 2010/11 financial year, after the aggressive expenditure drive had come to a close, the FSHS had still failed to spend R260 million. This money was subsequently reapportioned by national government.[24] It did not reflect well on Magashule's administration, but it was a hell of a lot better than having to pay back more than R1 billion.

From the perspective of the province's would-be recipients of low-cost housing, however, there was little cause for celebration. Some communities witnessed RDP projects grinding to a halt right in front of their eyes as the inexperienced contractors started running into financial trouble. 'There

were young, new contractors who had never built a single house before,'
one former FSHS official said. 'Now they suddenly had a R17-million contract to build 200 houses. Some of them took their first payments from
the department and bought fancy cars. Others went to the Durban July
and partied like there was no tomorrow.'

Some department staffers knew that the situation would inevitably
explode into the open. The first sign of trouble came in early 2011, before
the financial year-end. In February, Magashule reshuffled his executive
council. He sent Zwane to the Department of Agriculture and Rural Development. Mamiki Qabathe, who would later become the speaker of the
provincial legislature, replaced Zwane at human settlements.[25]

The move could be interpreted in a variety of ways. One source, a
former Magashule ally, said the premier was angry with Zwane because
of the R260 million in unspent housing money that the province had lost
out on. But perhaps that had merely provided Magashule with an excuse
to move Zwane to a department in which his friends from Saxonwold, the
Guptas, would soon require a man on the inside. After all, the infamous
Vrede dairy project would be initiated in 2012, not long after Zwane became
MEC for agriculture, as described in Chapter 14. More likely, however,
is that Magashule needed to parachute his henchmen out of the FSHS
before any probes into the housing contracts commenced.

Sources familiar with the saga revealed some astonishing information
that seems to support this theory. When Zwane left human settlements
for agriculture, he took with him two of the department's most senior
financial officials, Seipati Dlamini, the chief financial officer for the cooperative governance and traditional affairs segment of the department, and
Mmuso Tsoametsi, the CFO for human settlements.

Dlamini became CFO at agriculture under Zwane, where she got herself tangled up in the Vrede dairy mess. She was arrested and charged over
the matter along with agriculture HOD Peter Thabethe in early 2018.[26]
Tsoametsi became a deputy director-general at agriculture.[27]

Mpho Mokoena, the HOD for human settlements at the time of the
R1-billion spending spree, was also quietly moved to another job. He
became head of human settlements at the Mangaung metro municipality.

Sources close to the matter say those four officials – Zwane, Dlamini,
Tsoametsi and Mokoena – should have answered for the debacle at the
FSHS. 'They were the ones who were getting the instructions from higher

up to pay the companies and they were the ones who had the power inside the department to make sure the payments went through,' said one former insider. 'There is no way that a provincial department can spend R1 billion without the approval or involvement of its MEC, HOD and financial heads.'

The FSHS's inability to build houses, meanwhile, was starting to cause unrest and tension in some parts of the province. One tragic day in April 2011, Andries Tatane, a resident of the eastern Free State town of Ficksburg, was shot dead by police during a violent service-delivery protest. He quickly became a martyr of sorts in the intermittent battle between government authorities and some of the country's poorest communities. One of the issues Tatane and his fellow protesters were angry about was the shortage of decent housing in their area.[28]

In July, police were again called in to disperse angry protesters, this time in the eastern Free State township of Tshiame. They too were angry about government's failure to deliver low-cost housing.[29] And in Bethulie, frustrated residents showed a *Sowetan* reporter a site where a contractor had left behind houses without roofs, windows or doors.[30]

In early 2012, Magashule again subjected his executive council to a round of musical chairs. The MEC for economic development, Mxolisi Dukwana, a former Magashule ally, had to go. Dukwana had abandoned the Magashule fold and planned to challenge him for the position of provincial chair as a member of the so-called Regime Change group.[31] Led by Mpho Ramakatsa, the Regime Change faction later protested Magashule's re-election as ANC provincial chair by taking the matter to the courts.[32]

Magashule duly fired Dukwana and replaced him with Mamiki Qabathe.[33] The vacant job at human settlements was then given to Olly Mlamleli, who would remain in that position until she became mayor of Mangaung in late 2016. Mlamleli had been close to Magashule since at least 2008. She had worked for him when he was an MEC in Beatrice Marshoff's administration.[34]

The department also got a new HOD in the form of Nthimotse 'Tim' Mokhesi, a former senior official in the Maluti-a-Phofung local municipality in the eastern Free State. Mokhesi served on the board of directors of Maluti-a-Phofung's water utility, where he rubbed shoulders with fellow director Glen Netshivhodza,[35] a businessman from Parys and a close confidant of Magashule. Two of Netshivhodza's companies were among the scores of contractors who benefited from the big RDP splurge of 2010.

Several sources, including department insiders and other government officials, former Magashule allies and some FSHS contractors, all say Mokhesi became the premier's right-hand man in the department. Under Mlamleli and Mokhesi's stewardship, the FSHS would become the site of even more egregious looting involving Magashule, his associates and his direct family.

But first they had to help clean up the fallout from their new department's R1-billion mess. They deftly began tackling the problem in a manner that made it appear as if they truly wanted to get to the bottom of the fiasco.

In July 2012, Mlamleli told the pro-Magashule newspaper *The Weekly* that six department officials linked to the scam had been suspended. The six suspended officials had allegedly made unlawful prepayments to some of the companies involved in the scheme and had manipulated the department's individual subsidy system to make sure the companies got paid, according to the news report. Department officials had also done very few inspections to make sure that the contractors were actually building houses. In her 'exclusive' interview with the publication, Mlamleli vowed to 'root out corruption' at her new posting.[36] In a subsequent annual report, the department explained that there had been 'collusion between employees and suppliers and overriding of internal controls and the department's information systems'.[37]

But according to my sources, the six suspended officials were just scapegoats. 'Those are all people on the level of director or chief director,' said one. 'They reported to the MEC, the HOD and the CFOs, so it made no sense that they alone were made out to be the masterminds. Some of them may have been guilty of some wrongdoing, but they couldn't be held accountable alone.' But Zwane and Mokoena, former MEC and HOD respectively, were of course safely tucked away in other spheres of government by then. So too was Dlamini, the former CFO.

Around this time, the auditor-general also probed the debacle and confirmed that houses that had been uploaded onto the department's housing subsidy system (HSS) could not be physically verified.[38] In other words, some of the contractors had been paid for houses that were never built. Others had started their respective projects but then abandoned them, leaving scores of unfinished houses all over the Free State.[39]

Magashule and Mlamleli met with senior department officials in April

2012 'to discuss the fact that contractors appointed to construct the ... houses were simply not performing', this according to an affidavit to which Mokhesi would later depose.[40] 'At the meeting, it emerged that the contractors' failure to perform under their contracts was largely caused by the fact that materials had not been delivered to them by the suppliers,' Mokhesi stated.

The FSHS, it seemed, had decided at an early stage that it would apportion most of the blame to the suppliers of building materials, despite the fact that the department's primary contractual relationship had been with the builders. This would create an opportunity for Magashule's associates and other politically connected beneficiaries to escape scrutiny and avoid being held financially accountable.

The department subsequently appointed Open Water, a private forensic auditing firm, to probe the matter. It also appointed two private engineering firms to determine the scale of the wastage. Considering the earlier probe by the AG and the involvement of the National Urban Reconstruction and Housing Agency (NURCHA), an arm of the national Department of Human Settlements, there was no shortage of investigations into the saga.

The Special Investigating Unit had also been on the scene since early 2012. While briefing Parliament's portfolio committee on housing in August 2012, Sexwale said that the SIU had been tasked with probing the Free State contracts under 'Special Presidential Proclamation No. 35',[41] which called for a wide-ranging investigation into fraud and corruption involving the national and provincial housing departments and local authorities.[42] Sexwale also told the committee that the Free State's housing debacle involved irregular expenditure of at least R500 million.[43] Later, in court filings, the department itself indicated that about R500 million of taxpayers' money had been flushed down the toilet.[44]

'No stone will be left unturned in our drive to arrive at the centre of any housing related questionable financial misconduct,' Sexwale vowed before the committee. 'This is disheartening because this is poor people's money. I will be taking this issue to the Cabinet.'[45] He even suggested that the provincial department could be placed under administration in accordance with Section 100 of the Constitution. With only months to go before the ANC convened in Mangaung for its national conference, Sexwale's statement was a barely veiled attack on Magashule and his provincial administration.

But it would be his final say on the matter. Sexwale's bid to become the ANC's deputy president at the party's fifty-third national conference was a complete failure. He did not even make it onto the eighty-member NEC.[46] Zuma axed him as housing minister not long thereafter.[47]

9

Fall guys and fat cats

Magashule must have been relieved that Sexwale was no longer around to scrutinise his province's housing projects.

In 2013, Olly Mlamleli and Tim Mokhesi began legal proceedings to try to recover a significant chunk of the misspent fortune. The FSHS served summonses on 22 of the more than 100 companies involved in the saga. These companies, mostly materials suppliers, had altogether received R631 million throughout the 2010/11 and 2011/12 financial years.[1] In court papers, the department maintained that the suppliers had benefited from 'unjust enrichment', and it wanted them to pay back the money.[2]

It was a curious strategy. Going after the materials suppliers was all well and good if the department could prove that they received money without supplying any materials. But it made no sense that the department chose not to pursue the contractors as well. After all, the contractors had received more than R500 million among them, and the department was already on record saying that these companies were at least as guilty as the materials suppliers when it came to the non-delivery of houses.

Mokhesi's later affidavit summed up the scale of the fiasco:

When the department awarded the construction contracts, it split particular housing sites amongst different contractors – for example, several contractors would be appointed to build houses in a particular township, with each contractor responsible for a particular number of houses in that township.

It was therefore difficult, if indeed possible at all, to determine which contractor had been responsible for what. The difficulties were exacerbated because, in a single township, there were various results – some houses may be completed; others partly completed; others not built at all or barely started; and where construction work had been done, it was often faulty.[3]

Mokhesi also bemoaned the fact that none of the contractors or suppliers had kept proper records of their projects, as stipulated in their agreements with the department. 'The contractors' paperwork was either totally inadequate or simply did not exist,' he said. 'Nor have the material suppliers themselves ever provided proper reports to the department.'

Yet, for some reason, Mokhesi and his department targeted only a select batch of materials suppliers to try to recover some of the money.

The FSHS finally dismissed five of the six suspended officials in June 2015.[4] Other heads would roll later, bringing to eleven the number of officials the department fired. Yet, despite the department's insistence that the officials had been solely responsible for the 'unlawful and fraudulent scheme',[5] it failed to lay criminal charges against any of them.

Mokhesi would later allege that Mokoena, the former HOD, had been 'directly responsible' for the payments.[6] Yet he was not among those who were dismissed. Instead, Mokoena got a plum job as head of human settlements at the Mangaung metro.[7] Of Zwane, Dlamini and Tsoametsi there was no mention. Corney Twala, another top official, also dodged the bullet of dismissal. He was absorbed by the provincial Department of Social Development, where he became a senior manager.[8] So, not only did the department fail to lay charges against the alleged culprits, but the province and the local metro also provided some of them with a safety net.

The axed officials, however, were not so lucky. I spoke to one of them. This person provided me with a troubling account of events that preceded their dismissal. This account is supported by documents filed in arbitration proceedings and by corroboration from other sources. The arbitration matter, instituted by five of the dismissed FSHS staffers, was still ongoing at the time of writing.

When Sexwale first became aware of the R1-billion fiasco, he desperately wanted to bring Magashule to book. That is why he insisted that the SIU probe the matter. The unit's investigation formed part of a wider SIU probe into RDP projects in provincial departments and municipalities all over South Africa. Their work on the Free State contracts, however, was allegedly severely hampered and eventually derailed by the involvement of Open Water, the forensic outfit appointed by the department to investigate the matter in mid-2012.

Although the firm was technically contracted by the FSHS, several sources told me that the order to appoint it came from Magashule himself. They maintained that Magashule had a close relationship with Open Water's chairman, Reavell 'Ricky' Nkondo, a former spy boss at the National Intelligence Agency.

The premier's official diary, obtained through a Promotion of Access to Information Act (PAIA) request, confirms that there was contact between Magashule and Nkondo after Open Water was appointed by the FSHS. In one instance, Magashule met Nkondo for a 'private meeting' at Free State House, the premier's official residence, one evening in mid-July 2013.

I asked Peet Pieterse, Open Water's CEO, about his partner's meetings with Magashule. He replied: 'Mr Nkondo cannot recall the private meeting with Mr. Magashule but agrees that he did meet with the Premier on occasion. We generally briefed the Premier on investigations during ExCo meetings, in the same manner and meetings where other forensic auditors provided feedback on investigations.' The purpose of the 'private meeting' at Magashule's residence therefore remains a mystery.

A member of one of Magashule's earlier executive councils told me Open Water had been brought into the Free State by Magashule shortly after he became premier in 2009. 'The province needed to verify its payroll system, and Ace told us to use Open Water,' said the source. From that point onwards, the firm acted like 'cleaners' when it came to the Magashule administration's shadiest contracts, this person alleged. 'They covered up a lot of things, but they also did some good work,' claimed the source.

Pieterse denied that they were pulled into the Free State by Magashule. The firm was previously known as Ramathe Fivaz and had been present in the province since 2001, he said. He took exception to Open Water being referred to as Magashule's 'cleaners'. In his defence of the firm, he made a rather curious remark. 'We were probably rather Mr Magashule's henchmen than cleaners and we were not well liked as our appointment resulted in employees and office bearers being dismissed and/or criminally charged,' Pieterse contended in a written response. He said he could 'categorically' state that Magashule 'never once asked [Open Water] to manipulate any findings or omit any evidence from [their] reports'.

But the perceptions of an unusually close relationship between the firm and the then premier prevailed. One of my sources told me Open Water's chairman, Nkondo, married Rooksana Moola, a staffer in Magashule's administration, after the firm started working in the Free State.

Pieterse insisted that this presented no problems whatsoever. 'Mr. Magashule's administration was vast and she [Moola] did not work in close proximity to Mr. Magashule, or even in his office, and therefore the insinuation that they married as a consequence of Mr. Nkondo being that close to Mr. Magashule is not only mischievous but devoid of fact or truth.'

If there is anything to say about Nkondo, it is that his career as a government spook was seemingly eventful. In 1997, then Pan Africanist Congress (PAC) politician Patricia de Lille included Nkondo's name on a list of former ANC underground operatives who had allegedly acted as double agents for the old apartheid government.[9] The ANC denied the existence of such a list. His name also surfaced during the 2003 Hefer Commission of Inquiry into allegations that NIA spooks had spied on National Director of Public Prosecutions (NDPP) Bulelani Ngcuka. Nkondo was portrayed as a functionary of the Zuma camp in the highly politicised 'spy wars' of the early 2000s.[10]

After Open Water's appointment by the FSHS, the SIU's Free State branch was apparently strong-armed out of the probe.

A source in the law-enforcement environment with insight into the matter claimed that at one point the SIU was asked to stop its investigation. 'The SIU was told to stop working on the Free State contracts,' he told me. 'I don't know where that order came from, but it must have been from a very senior political office.'

Another source, an SIU insider, said Open Water effectively blocked the SIU's investigative efforts. 'We were told by the department that Open Water took computers, documents and other records,' this source said. 'When we asked for certain documents, Open Water would tell us they didn't have it.'

Contrary to normal investigative procedure, Open Water also allegedly failed to compile a record of what exactly they had taken from the department. This added to the SIU's headaches. 'When we asked for a certain document or contract and Open Water said they didn't have it, there was no record of what they had taken to determine if they were being honest with us,' said my SIU source.

Most alarmingly, the Open Water team allegedly took some documents related to the R1-billion splurge to Magashule's office. 'All the documents were taken to Ace's office on the fourth floor [of the Lebohang Building in downtown Bloemfontein],' claimed one current FSHS insider.

Pieterse denied all of this. 'We kept detailed inventories of each document removed from the department as well as the documentation and electronic data returned.' He said he knew nothing about documents that may have been taken to Magashule's office. 'The investigation relied on a vast number of records and to remove certain records to "take" to the Office of the Premier would serve no purpose to influence the outcome of the investigation,' Pieterse maintained.

The Open Water CEO said the firm had 'never obstructed or prevented any investigative agency in performing their work and has always and will always co-operate with such agencies, which was also the situation in the FS housing matter.'

However, the tone of his response made it clear that there had indeed been friction between Open Water and the SIU. 'The SIU was appointed approximately a year before Open Water was appointed and one would expect that after such an extended period they would have collected the documentation required. When we were appointed they made little progress,' said Pieterse.

An SIU investigator had asked Open Water for the firm's mandate for its investigation, but Open Water refused to comply. 'I respectfully advised him that he held no proclamation to subpoena me for the information, whereafter no further requests for any documentation were received from the SIU,' said Pieterse.

The strangest thing about Pieterse's response was that he tried to convince me that Open Water and the SIU had been tasked to probe entirely different matters. 'My understanding was that the SIU was mandated to investigate the development and delivery of low-cost housing at the time for the period ended July 2010.' The Free State's R1-billion RDP splurge only occurred at the end of that year. 'It is therefore obvious that we investigated different matters and therefore we could not have restricted the SIU or any other law enforcement agency in performing their work,' maintained Pieterse.

But it wasn't 'obvious' at all.

The SIU, in a formal response, made it clear that it had probed the same advance payments Open Water investigated. 'The investigation pertaining to the unauthorised payments of advances by the Free State Department of Human Settlement[s] regarding the 2010/2011 and 2011/2012 financial years is finalised. The findings and recommendations are contained in a report addressed to the Office of Presidency, who acknowledged receipt of the said report on 2 October 2015,' the SIU said in a letter it sent me in October 2018.

Even FSHS HOD Tim Mokhesi confirmed the SIU had been on the scene. 'The prepayments matter relating to material suppliers were investigated by the Special Investigation Unit (SIU),' he said in a written response.

Considering Open Water's alleged meddling, one can't help but wonder how thorough the SIU report was.

The SIU also told me that it had referred three matters to the National Prosecuting Authority for criminal prosecution. The NPA 'in turn referred [the three cases] to the Hawks for finalisation'. But that was more than three years ago. It appears as if these cases were added to the mountain of investigations that ground to a halt once the Hawks got hold of them during Zuma's years in power.

Open Water started its investigation on 19 June 2012 and submitted a preliminary report a mere ten days later. It was on the basis of this report that the department suspended and later dismissed eleven officials.[11]

But Open Water's methodology apparently left much to be desired. My source within the group of axed officials claimed that the investigators did not even bother to interview any of the alleged culprits. 'The Open Water guys came to the department, took our gadgets [computers and other electronic equipment] and then told us to leave the premises,' said the former official. 'They never spoke to us to collect our side of the story.'

The firm and some of its key executives have been accused of employing similar tactics elsewhere. A *Sunday Independent* report from 2017 detailed how an Open Water report had implicated a local logistics company in a supposedly dodgy deal with South African Airways Technical. It had then emerged that Open Water had not interviewed the implicated company's managing director before it concluded its probe.[12]

A 2016 report by amaBhungane highlighted further concerns over forensic work by Pieterse and Open Water, this time involving the Council for Scientific and Industrial Research (CSIR) and its then CEO, Sibusiso Sibisi.[13]

Pieterse's forensic work was also severely criticised by a judge in the Eastern Cape High Court in 2005. A forensic report compiled by Pieterse formed the basis of a fraud case against three senior officials from the Eastern Cape Development Corporation (EDC).[14] Mcebisi Jonas, the EDC's then CEO, was among the accused.[15] The fraud charges were viewed as being part of a political witch-hunt, and Jonas and his co-accused were eventually acquitted.[16] In his ruling, Judge Dayalin Chetty said Pieterse's report showed 'a complete lack of objectivity', was 'severely wanting' and displayed an 'erroneous interpretation of the applicable legislation', according to a *Mail & Guardian* report.[17] The newspaper seemingly directly quoted from the judgment, but Pieterse claimed the publication got it wrong. 'The Eastern Cape matter was my first encounter with the influence of politics and the media on reality,' he told me. 'I have no doubt that in a different time or a different province the outcome of the trial would have been different.'

Meanwhile, after the FSHS officials were suspended, they naturally demanded to see Open Water's report. They wanted to see for themselves how the probe had concluded that they were the guilty parties. 'We wrote to them [Open Water] and asked for the report, but they never got back to us,' claimed one of the axed officials. Some of the suppliers implicated in the FSHS's legal proceedings would later have similar problems, the owner of one such business told me.

Frustrated, the suspended officials turned to the SIU in Bloemfontein. 'We asked the SIU if we could see the Open Water report or any of the documents that supposedly proved we were guilty,' my source explained. 'He told us Open Water took all the department's records.' Even the SIU failed to obtain the Open Water report, my unit source told me. Pieterse claimed the SIU never asked for the Open Water report.

Five of the axed FSHS officials, meanwhile, decided to fight back. They instituted arbitration proceedings against the department in which they challenged the outcome of their internal disciplinary hearing. Their filings[18] laid bare the alleged involvement of Magashule's office and the roles played by Zwane and his fellow department bosses in the most fundamental decisions that led to the R1-billion RDP splurge.

'They [the axed officials] simply fell victim to a modern government contagion – i.e. that the powers that be go about their functions in certain ways (whether lawfully or motivated by malfeasance), implement what is decided in higher structures, and when the actions go wrong some subordinate is sacrificed at the altar of the true culprits,' their legal counsel contended.

Drawing on heaps of documents and records, their submission alleged that 'the scheme' was orchestrated by Magashule's office and implemented by the likes of Zwane, Mokoena and Dlamini: 'It cannot be overstated that this entire model and the operation of the scheme ... emanates from the office of the Premier and employees in the Department responsible for legal compliance.'

The cornerstone of the ERP, namely the contracts between the FSHS and the various contractors, was in fact sanctioned by Magashule's own office, the axed officials argued. 'The chairperson [of the disciplinary proceedings] forgot that the State Law Advisors were asked – at the offices of the Premier – to advise on the drafting of the contracts.'

Their counsel added that the ERP 'was thoroughly researched, contracts drafted and the "OK" given by inter alia Mr Tsoametsi, Mr Taka [the FSHS's deputy director for legal services], the State Law Advisor and Mr Bertus Venter at the Premier's office'.

The officials argued that if they had been implicated in an unlawful scheme, it was because they were acting on orders from higher up. 'The applicants never took the decision to implement the advance payment system,' reads their submission. '[This] was introduced through a decision taken by the Member of the Executive Council [Zwane], the Head of the Department [Mokoena] and the Chief Financial Officer [Dlamini].'

As mentioned earlier, these arbitration proceedings are ongoing. But it seems almost certain that Magashule and some of his key henchmen, including Zwane, orchestrated and executed the plan that resulted in the FSHS emptying its coffers in record time.

The court application that included Mokhesi's affidavit was lodged in late 2016. The department sought to have the Bloemfontein High Court review and set aside its contracts with 106 companies: 85 building contractors and 21 materials suppliers. In terms of trying to retrieve some of the misspent money, however, the department instituted action proceedings against just 22 of the companies in an attempt to recover R631 million. Surprisingly, these included all 21 materials suppliers and only one building contractor. The department was clearly targeting the materials suppliers.[19]

One of the owners of a materials supplier from which the department sought to recover money told the *Sunday Times* that the department's legal bid was a 'façade' and a 'smoke screen'. The R1-billion expenditure drive had been marred by fraud, the businessman said. According to him, the department had merely cited the 106 respondents to convince the SIU that it was doing something about the looting. He lamented the fact that the department had chosen to try to recover money from the materials suppliers only, seeing as some of them had delivered the goods for which they had been paid.[20] 'What about those suppliers and contractors who were paid in advance but are not listed as respondents? Why are they being protected?' the businessman wanted to know.

It sounded to me like the department's selective legal bid to recover some of the money was a cover-up. I obtained documents and records pertaining to the department's expenditure during that period and proceeded to analyse them. It was a classic exercise in following the money, and the results were frightening. I began to realise why Magashule may have wanted to take control of the investigative process.

There were several materials suppliers and contractors, who collectively received a fortune as part of the R1-billion ERP, who were seemingly overlooked in the department's legal proceedings. Some of them were closely linked to Magashule. We'll start with a few materials suppliers who managed to slip under the radar.

In 2011, while human settlements agency NURCHA was probing the matter, an email was sent to several companies that had received advance payments for materials. The email, of which I obtained a copy, contained the names of all 21 suppliers against whom the FSHS had instituted action proceedings to recover the R631 million. However, also included in the email were the names of an additional five companies not mentioned in the department's court filings. These companies had collectively received more than R35 million in 2010/11 alone, according to records from the department's housing subsidy system.

One such supplier was Friedshelf 863. When I looked at its records at the Companies and Intellectual Property Commission (CIPC), I found the name of one of Magashule's oldest and most trusted pals. Hantsi Matseke (née Mayeza), a fellow Parys local whose relationship with Magashule goes back to their Hillbrow days, registered the company in 2007. Its name was later changed to Maono Construction, and it features elsewhere in this book. Matseke also registered a joint venture (JV) with a company called Ubuhlebethu Property Developments in October 2010. In other words, the JV was established just in time for the FSHS's splurge. The

JV subsequently scored a contract to build 271 houses in Bohlokong out-side Bethlehem. This project was awarded to Matseke and her partner as part of Operation Hlasela, the premier's development programme.

Matseke became chairperson of the Free State Development Corpor-ation in July 2012. As we will see in later chapters, this state-owned entity has been very kind to Magashule's daughter, Thoko Malembe, who also later became Matseke's business partner.

Although the NURCHA email listed Friedshelf 863 as a supplier, the department's HSS refers to the company as a 'contractor/builder'. The HSS shows that Matseke's company received a small fortune from the department. In 2010/11, it was paid just under R6 million. In the following financial year, it received R38 million. By 2014, Friedshelf 863 had pock-eted altogether R52 million from the FSHS. The JV, meanwhile, earned just over R23 million for the Bohlokong project.

Matseke said her company should not have been included in the email regarding NURCHA's probe into the advance payments. She said Friedshelf 863 had been paid as both a supplier and contractor, but didn't receive any money in advance. Her company was not 'implicated by the findings of the investigation', she said.

The HSS suggests that Friedshelf 863 and its JV partner left behind incomplete houses at the Bohlokong project. Matseke said the JV finished all but seven of the houses it was supposed to deliver. This was due to 'beneficiary management challenges'.

After being rebranded as Maono Construction, Matseke's firm began to soar in the Free State. Its contracts from the FSHS alone in the period after 2013 were worth more than R150 million, according to the HSS. In total, Maono bagged more than R500 million in contracts from the FSHS and other departments in Magashule's provincial government.

Matseke did not take kindly to my questions about her relationship with Magashule. 'I find this line of question[ing] unacceptable, extremely offen-sive and hurtful as it creates an innuendo that my companies get contracts as a result of certain perceived relationships. In short, this is degrading, sex-ist and undermining to black business women in this country,' she said. She denied that Magashule played a role in contracts awarded to her companies.

Despite Friedshelf 863 having featured in the NURCHA probe, as sug-gested by the leaked email, the department chose not to list the company in its court bid, thus shielding Magashule's chum. Worse still, there were suppliers who received money in the 2010/11 splurge that did not even feature in the NURCHA investigation, let alone the department's later legal proceedings. The payments to these companies are reflected in the HSS.

One such company that drew my attention was Robs Bricks. The database showed that it had received exactly R7 million, a figure that stood out like a sore thumb among the hundreds of payments. It is highly unlikely that any supplier would have provided materials valued at such a precisely round figure.

The company's CIPC records confirmed that my suspicions were justified. Like the JV between Friedshelf 863 and Ubuhlebethu, Robs Bricks had been registered just in time for the department's 2010/11 spending spree. And its sole director was Mohlouoa 'Blacky' Seoe, one of Magashule's former business partners.

Seoe has another company – Robs Investment Holdings – which benefited from the FSHS's largesse to a much greater extent than Robs Bricks. What's more, the HSS shows that its success correlates exactly with Magashule's tenure as premier. Between 2010 and 2017, Robs Investment Holdings netted almost R90 million from the department. Like its sister entity, it was not mentioned in the FSHS's court application.

A 2013 progress report on some of the department's projects sheds light on Robs Investment Holdings' poor performance. During the R1-billion splurge of 2010, Seoe's company clinched contracts to build 400 houses in the former homeland of QwaQwa and in the town of Kestell. By February 2013, it had completed only 187 units. According to the report, Robs Investment Holdings had experienced problems with sourcing materials. At the Kestell site, some of the would-be beneficiaries had become so tired of waiting that they had started to construct their own houses.[21]

Like Matseke, Seoe is also linked to Magashule and his daughter Thoko through business dealings. Magashule was once a director in Sambal Investments, another of Seoe's companies. And I identified at least one property transaction between one of Thoko's trusts and a company owned by Seoe. This deal, incidentally, went down in Kestell. Moreover, when I was working on an investigative piece for News24 in 2017, I found CCTV footage showing Magashule, Thoko and Seoe, along with some others, inspecting a Shell fuel station in QwaQwa. Thoko later scored this property in a dodgy deal involving the FDC, the entity chaired by fellow RDP contractor Hantsi Matseke.[22]

One of the FSHS insiders I spoke to said the department deliberately excluded Seoe's companies from the court application. 'He got advance payments and his two projects were never finished, but he didn't get sued due to his close proximity to Magashule and Mokhesi,' said this source.

Peet Pieterse, meanwhile, denied that Open Water had overlooked companies owned by Matseke and Seoe. Robs Investment Holdings and Friedshelf 863 featured in the Open Water report, he insisted. However, I had asked him about Robs Bricks, not Robs Investment Holdings, seeing as the prior company had received the strangely round figure of exactly R7 million for materials. Pieterse did not indicate whether this entity featured in the Open Water report.

I asked Pieterse why some of the entities included in the Open Water report had apparently been excluded from the FSHS's legal proceedings against contractors and materials suppliers. He said Open Water did not have a say in determining who the FSHS ended up suing.

'It may be that the entities did fulfil their obligations in terms of their agreement[s] with the Department by constructing all the houses, which may therefore cause the advance payments to be of no consequence in civil proceedings had the Department received value for money in terms of the enrichment principal,' said Pieterse.

A proper analysis of the HSS reveals scores more companies with strong political connections, many of them owned by people close to Magashule's inner circle.

The entity with perhaps the funniest name must be Mob Business, a closed corporation that was registered in 2002 by Moreki Moroka, the wife of lawyer and long-time Magashule associate Kenosi Moroka. Magashule and Kenosi were previously co-directors in two companies.

A 2009 *Mail & Guardian* report detailed how Kenosi Moroka allegedly tried to extract a R2-million bribe from a businessman who needed the approval of the Free State Gambling Board for a deal involving the transfer of shares in a casino company. It was alleged that the lawyer had acted on Magashule's behalf.[23]

Sources who attended gatherings or meetings with Magashule alleged that Moroka is something of a benefactor to the former premier. 'I've been to meetings with Ace and some of his associates where we racked up large bills,' said one individual. 'Kenosi would sometimes pull out big wads of cash and settle the bill.' Moroka strongly denied this. 'Our client has never been in any meeting where Mr Magashule and some of his political allies held meetings where our client had to settle restaurant bills,' his law firm said on his behalf.

Moroka should also be familiar with Mokhesi, under whose watch the FSHS drove legal proceedings in relation to the R1-billion RDP splurge. Moroka and Mokhesi have served together on the board of Centlec (SOC) Ltd, the local state-owned power distributor, since 2013.[24] Incidentally, Seoe has also done a stint as a Centlec director.[25]

Moreki Moroka seemingly hit the jackpot when Magashule became premier in 2009. Mob Business pocketed more than R50 million in revenue from the FSHS between 2009 and 2018, according to the HSS. This included a payment of just over R5 million in 2010/11 to build houses in Bloemfontein. In that same year, Moreki and Mosidi Motsemme, the mother of two of Magashule's children, bought properties within walking distance of each other in the same upmarket residential estate on the outskirts of Bloemfontein. Motsemme is known in Free State ANC circles as Magashule's 'Bloemfontein wife'.

Moroka denied that her business's successes could be attributed to perceived political connections. 'The libellous disinformation that seeks to link the operations of Mob Business to the tenure of Mr Magashule as the Premier of the Free State Province are, to say the least, preposterous and malicious,' said her lawyers.

According to the FSHS's 2013 progress report, Mob Business left behind 100 unfinished houses in Bloemfontein. 'Contractor not on site for four months,' reads the report. 'Recommend to terminate.'[26] Although Mob Business was listed as a respondent in the FSHS court bid, it was not among the companies against which the department instituted action proceedings to recover money.

Moreki Moroka insisted that her company did finish all its houses in Bloemfontein. 'As further testimony to [the] absence of malperformance, the Department duly paid the retention fee to our client, which would not be paid in the event [that] there was defective performance present,' claimed her lawyers.

10

Rewarding friends
and punishing foes

While poring over Tim Mokhesi's affidavit and the FSHS's court application, I noticed something interesting.

As mentioned previously, there were 106 respondents in the department's 2016 court application, including the 22 companies from which the department sought to recover R631 million. Of the 106 respondents, 93 are closed corporations or private companies. The remaining respondents are natural persons listed in their capacity as trustees of trusts that received money from the department.

Relying on the court papers, the *Sunday Times* had revealed in January 2017 that former SABC chief operating officer Hlaudi Motsoeneng and the wife of sport minister Fikile Mbalula were among those listed as respondents.[1] Motsoeneng and Mbalula, who would become minister of police in March of that year, both hailed from the Free State. Motsoeneng and Mbalula's wife, Nozuko, were both members of a trust that apparently scored contracts worth about R38 million to build 450 houses in Virginia and Bloemfontein respectively, the newspaper reported. But the houses were never finished.

When asked for comment, Motsoeneng simply stated that he had 'no interest' in the issue. Nozuko denied that she had been involved. 'I'm very angry,' she told the *Daily News*. 'I'm seeking legal advice on how to clear my name in this regard. I'm being labelled a fraudster. I feel my name has been abused.'[2]

The inclusion of Nozuko Mbalula's name in the court application is interesting in light of her husband's strained relationship with Magashule. The beef goes back to 2012, when Mbalula aligned himself with the Free State ANC's Regime Change group. This faction sought first to unseat Magashule as provincial chair before backing the anti-Zuma slate at the

Mangaung conference at the end of that year.[3] The group ultimately failed, and the movement fizzled out in 2013.

Nevertheless, the hostility between Magashule and Mbalula continued to build well into 2017. Not long after his move to the police portfolio, Mbalula took aim at Magashule in one of his famously belligerent tweets. 'Ace Magashule is a definite no no no, the man will finish what is remaining of our movement. He will kill it,' Mbalula tweeted in June 2017, after it became clear that the premier would run for the position of ANC secretary-general at the end of that year. Mbalula's animosity was probably heightened by the recent court action implicating his wife in the Free State housing scandal.

I have always suspected that the inclusion of Nozuko Mbalula's name in the court papers was an attempt by the Magashule administration to settle a political score with her husband. My theory is supported by further compelling indications that the department used its court application to help fight Magashule's battles.

Of the 93 corporate structures listed as respondents, the department included the names of the managers or owners of only four. Of the four people named, three can be linked to political squabbles with Magashule. While the four entities are listed as respondents, they are, however, not among the companies from which the department sought to recover money.

Listed next to one another, as the 17th and 18th respondents respectively, are Clear Creek Trading 115 and Makana Women Construction. According to the court papers, Clear Creek Trading is in the 'care of Petrus Zanemvula Matosa' and Makana Women Construction is in the 'care of Mpho Ramakatsa'. According to the HSS, Clear Creek Trading received more than R2 million in 2011. Coincidentally, Matosa and a few co-directors registered the company in June 2009, a month after Magashule was sworn in as premier. Makana Women Construction has to date earned more than R20 million from the FSHS. This includes payments totalling almost R10 million during the time of the department's big expenditure drive.

What is relevant to this narrative is that Matosa and Ramakatsa both crossed swords with Magashule around this time.

Matosa, a former ANC provincial chairperson and erstwhile member of Magashule's inner circle, had begun to drift away from his former ally in around 2009. Ramakatsa was a leader of the so-called Regime Change group, which locked horns with the Magashule faction in an acrimonious battle for power in the province. Ramakatsa had also orchestrated the court battle that ended in an embarrassing legal lashing for the Magashule camp in late 2012. The Constitutional Court had ruled that the Free State's provincial elective conference held in mid-2012, and where Magashule was re-elected as chairperson, had been fraught with irregularities. The Provincial Executive Committee had therefore been elected unlawfully, the court found.[4]

As a result, the national leadership had dissolved the PEC and scheduled another elective conference for May 2013.[5] It looked as if Ramakatsa was going to challenge Magashule for the position of provincial boss, with Matosa on his slate vying for the position of secretary.[6] But the Regime Change group suffered a major blow when Ramakatsa's branch was barred from participating in the conference.[7]

Ramakatsa later claimed that the second conference, which again re-elected Magashule and his cohorts, was as riddled with irregularities as the previous one.[8] But instead of mounting a fresh legal challenge, Ramakatsa joined the Economic Freedom Fighters (EFF). Matosa, for his part, faded into political oblivion. As far as their companies were concerned, someone behind the scenes ensured that the provincial government's money taps were closed to them for good. Makana Women Construction and Clear Creek Trading received their last payments from the FSHS in the 2012/13 financial year, according to the HSS.

I had a chat with Matosa in late 2018. He said the RDP splurge amounted to 'fiscal dumping', but that the companies targeted in Mokhesi's court application were 'dolphins' while the 'sharks' were let off the hook. As for his own company, Matosa maintained that he was only paid for work that he had completed and for which he had submitted claims. 'Clear Creek got a contract to build 200 houses in Brandfort,' he told me. 'It rained heavily for about four months during that time, so we could only finish about 100 houses before the contract period lapsed. But we were only paid for the houses we completed.'

He felt that he had been targeted in the lawsuit for political reasons. 'They tried to destroy me and Mbalula, through his wife, by listing us in the court papers,' he said.

The third significant person listed in the department's court application is Maggie Nthatisi, wife of Gregory Nthatisi, a former Umkhonto we Sizwe member who later served alongside Magashule in the 1994 provincial cabinet appointed by Mosiuoa Lekota.[9] Sources familiar with

Free State politics told me that Nthatisi played a crucial role in helping Magashule become provincial chair at the 2002 elective conference.

In the 2000s, the Nthatisis started doing brisk business with the Free State government, especially in the low-cost housing sector. The HSS shows that four companies managed by or linked to them have over the years earned revenue of about R400 million from the FSHS. This includes payments of about R23 million in 2010/11, the year in which the department's 'fraudulent scheme' was rolled out.

But, like Mbalula, Gregory Nthatisi was associated with the 2012 Regime Change movement, with the de facto mouthpiece for the Magashule administration, *The Weekly*, going so far as to call him the 'face' of the campaign. For someone who had so richly benefited from government contracts, Nthatisi had some harsh words for the Magashule regime. 'This move … in its nature is aimed at stopping the abuse of power, patronage, corrupt practices at the level of the ANC and state power,' he said.[10]

Nthatisi's 'betrayal' coincided with a dramatic turn in fortune for his and his wife's low-cost housing empire. The FSHS's financial data perfectly encapsulates how their businesses suffered the same fate as those of Matosa and Ramakatsa in the wake of the unsuccessful attempt to oust Magashule and his allies.

In the 2011/12 financial year, just before the Regime Change challengers mounted their attack, the four Nthatisi businesses earned a healthy R25 million in revenue from the FSHS. But by the following financial year, their revenue was down to just under R4 million. And in 2014, the companies collectively earned a paltry R800 000. After that, they did not receive a single cent from the department ever again.

The data correlates with anecdotal evidence that Magashule abused his power as premier to financially reward politically connected contractors who stayed loyal to him, while punishing those who somehow betrayed him. 'If Ace felt that you had stabbed him in the back, he made sure that you never again got contracts from whichever department you had been working with,' said a former close associate of Magashule.

Mokhesi said it was 'not true' that he and the FSHS had used the court application to target Magashule's political foes.

Another major beneficiary of low-cost housing contracts in the Magashule era is soccer-club owner turned construction mogul Mike Mokoena, whose company Tshwara Thebe Construction, or TTC, received contracts from the FSHS worth R310 million between 2012 and 2018. While TTC was one of the 106 respondents in the department's court application, it was not sued to return some of its earnings.

Mokoena is best known as the owner and chairman of the Free State Stars, a professional soccer team based in Bethlehem in the eastern Free State. His career as a tenderpreneur appears to have taken off in 2002, when a collection of companies he co-owned with various family members clinched tenders from the provincial departments of social welfare and education to deliver food parcels, textbooks and stationery.[11]

Mokoena has no qualms about being labelled a tenderpreneur. 'My life is to tender,' he told the *Sunday Times* in 2010. 'I apply for tenders, that's my lifestyle. I've got guys dealing with tenders full time. I'm not ashamed to say that's my lifestyle.'[12]

Magashule seemingly viewed himself as the source of the largesse bestowed on companies like TTC, and he apparently demanded reciprocity from the likes of Mokoena.

One source, a member of the Free State business fraternity, attended a gathering of about fifty contractors at Magashule's office in Bloemfontein in early 2014, before that year's general election. Magashule had invited his favourite friends from the business sector to ask them for a special favour. 'Ace told us we needed to make financial contributions to the ANC for the upcoming elections,' this source told me. 'He said the ANC had been good to our companies, and that he would close the money taps if we didn't support the ANC.'

The businesspeople were asked to each pledge an amount. It was reminiscent of the Free State ANC provincial conference in 2008, when Magashule demanded that party members and invited guests donate towards Zuma's legal fees. According to my source at the 2014 gathering, Mokoena was among those who made the largest pledges to the ANC.

Mokoena said he wouldn't comment on 'alleged rumours' and would only respond to 'factual allegations made by identified persons'.

One 'identified person' was willing to discuss allegedly dubious dealings between Mokoena and Magashule. Mxolisi Dukwana, a former Free State MEC, told me Mokoena once 'pledged' to donate R1 million to the ANC. This was before the Regime Change bloc's failed attempt in 2012 to topple Magashule and his allies. As the ruling party's then treasurer in the Free State, Dukwana was tasked with managing and collecting such contributions. 'The money was to be paid in two instalments of R500 000. The next thing I knew Ace had collected the first R500 000 himself. Mike did later pay the second R500 000 to the ANC, but the money Ace took did not come to the ANC,' alleged Dukwana.

Mokoena strongly denied the allegation. 'The information at your disposal is false and incorrect. I did not pledge the amount of R1 million at any relevant time nor is it true that R500 000 was collected by Mr. Magashule himself or any other person for that matter,' he said.

Dukwana remained resolute. 'If Mr. Mokoena wants to create an impression that I had imagined things about his pledge to the ANC he is making a big mistake.'

Further careful analysis of the companies listed in the FSHS's court papers and on the HSS reveals that the spouses and children of some of Magashule's senior colleagues in the provincial government and the local legislature also benefited from housing contracts. Subsequent progress reports have highlighted problems with the work of each one of these entities.

People First Construction, Moyakhe Trading, Phahama Development Trust and Jore Construction were all listed as respondents in the court application, but were not sued to recover money. Collectively, these companies received payments totalling over R40 million during Magashule's reign as premier. Unlike the entities owned by or linked to Magashule's political enemies, the names of the directors of these businesses are not revealed in the court papers.

CIPC records show that People First Construction's sole director is Tankiso Morule, wife of Playfair Morule, a long-serving Magashule ally. Morule himself was once a director of the company.

Playfair Morule has held several senior political and executive positions in the Free State, including MEC for finance, and for safety and security. He later became the ANC's chief whip in the provincial legislature under Magashule's stewardship. A guilty conviction on a charge of culpable homicide following a hit-and-run incident did not stop him from becoming the mayor of Bloemfontein in 2008.[13]

In 2013, at the height of the Gupta shadow state's rule over South Africa, Morule was appointed as South Africa's high commissioner to

India.[14] And in early 2018, then public enterprises minister and suspected Gupta backer Lynne Brown apparently tried to have Morule appointed as chairperson of Eskom.[15]

Morule's wife, meanwhile, has reaped the benefits of being a building contractor employed by the Free State provincial government. People First has received almost R140 million from the FSHS to date, according to the HSS. The same records suggest that People First is among the contractors guilty of leaving behind incomplete houses. Of the 200 RDP units this company was appointed to build in 2010, 87 were incomplete in 2013, according to one progress report. People First apparently abandoned the project because of delays in getting paid by the department.[16]

Moyanda Mohai, the wife of another former chief whip turned MEC, has also been on the receiving end of lucrative contracts. She is married to Seiso Mohai, who served as Magashule's MEC for finance from 2009 to 2013.[17] Her company, Moyakhe Trading, has to date received more than R18 million from the FSHS, mostly in the period after Magashule became premier.

Moyakhe Trading got a contract to build 300 houses in Bloemfontein in 2010. By 2013, only 132 houses had been completed. A progress report lists 'cashflow problems' among the reasons for the contractor's inability to complete the project on time.[18]

By the look of things, the Free State legislature was the place to be if you wanted your family members to clinch RDP contracts. The husband of the late Mantsheng 'Ouma' Tsopo, a former speaker of the provincial legislature, got in on the action too. Sandile Tsopo is a trustee of the Phahama Development Trust, which over the years earned revenue of about R36 million from the FSHS. This includes payments made during the big splurge of 2010.

Tsopo was convicted in 2007 on fraud charges related to dodgy contracts from the Free State Department of Education, which his late wife once headed.[19] This clearly had no impact on Phahama's ability to score provincial contracts after Magashule took over as premier.

Along with Hlaudi Motsoeneng and Nozuko Mbalula, Sandile Tsopo was one of the few connected individuals exposed by the media in relation to the 2010 splurge. He told *Volksblad* in 2017 that he had been appointed to build 600 houses in Matjhabeng (Welkom), but that he had completed only 200. He claimed that the project ground to a halt after his materials supplier died, and maintained that he had only received payment for work done and for which Phahama had invoiced the department.[20]

Ouma Tsopo's predecessor as speaker, Moeketsi Sesele, was a member of the Free State's pro-Magashule northern faction. His daughter Masedi is the director of Jore Construction, which received payments of more than R10 million for RDP houses between 2010 and 2014. Jore has perhaps the worst performance record of the four entities linked to politicians in the legislature. Appointed to build 400 houses in Thaba 'Nchu near Bloemfontein in 2010, nearly three years later it had completed only 84 units.[21] Most worryingly, the lives of the occupants of some of these houses were literally in danger. One of the completed houses collapsed in 2013, and inspectors refused to accept a further fourteen finished houses 'due to poor mortar mix'.[22]

Thutela Bogolo Trading Enterprise was also on the receiving end of large RDP contracts. This is the company owned by Rachelle Els, Magashule's buddy from Parys. Thanks to her powerful friend, Els seemingly established a small RDP empire. Thutela Bogolo earned more than R110 million from the FSHS between 2010 and 2017, including R35 million paid out during the department's problematic expenditure drive in 2010, according to the HSS. Els claimed the department's records were incorrect and that her company had received much less than that.

Department records suggest that many of Els's construction contracts came to her directly from Magashule by way of Operation Hlasela, the premier's controversial development programme. Of the more than 1 600 houses she was allocated to build in 2010 in the towns of Kroonstad, Steynsrus, Oranjeville and Koppies, 510 were given to her through Operation Hlasela.

By early 2013, only 240 of the houses allocated to Thutela Bogolo had been finished.[23] Els admitted that it had taken years to complete some of her houses, but she blamed administrative and financial problems at the FSHS for the delays. She was adamant that all of her construction work had been of the highest quality.

As with other RDP contractors, there were rumours of an unusually close bond between Magashule and Els.

The former premier's official diary confirms that there was contact between the two during his incumbency. For example, in August 2011 Els met with Magashule at his office in Bloemfontein. This was right in the middle of a financial year in which Thutela Bogolo earned R21 million from the FSHS, according to the HSS.

Several sources have claimed that Magashule often visited Els at her home in Parys and sometimes even spent the night. His diary contains details that suggest this may be true. On the weekend of 20 and 21 October 2012, for example, Magashule's diary shows consecutive 'private visit[s]' at 'Roshelle's Place Parys' [sic].

Els told me Magashule sometimes spent the night at a guesthouse in Parys owned by her daughter. 'Everyone in Parys knows him, so he needed a place to stay over where people wouldn't be able to bother him,' she said. Magashule apparently paid for his accommodation.

There is also the matter of an overseas trip that Els, Magashule and other Free State officials embarked on in 2010. My sources told me the then premier went to the USA in that year, and that contractors like Els helped foot the bill.

Els admitted that she went to the USA with Magashule. She denied that she had bankrolled the entire trip, but indicated that she'd had to pay money into a bank account to help fund the journey. Magashule was going to accept some award from an American institution, according to Els. When it turned out that he needed to pay for the accolade, he decided not to accept it. But the trip continued regardless. Els denied that the trip had been a way of showing her gratitude to Magashule for her company's RDP contracts.

In May 2012, the FSHS named Els 'Best Contractor of the Year for the role her company, Thutela Bogolo ... played in helping the department meet its objective of building sustainable houses for the poor', according to The Weekly, which covered the occasion.[24]

The Govan Mbeki Awards, in which Els was honoured, were hosted by human settlements MEC Olly Mlamleli, who was 'flanked' by Magashule, the newspaper reported. At the ceremony, Els described how she got ahead in the RDP business: 'I approached the [Mangaung metro] municipality and spoke with the mayor Thabo Manyoni and I offered to help the government build better RDP houses. He then linked me with the Free State premier, who subsequently gave me the opportunity to build one of the show houses that formed part of the government's building projects.'

'I would like to thank Mr Magashule for believing in me and for giving me a chance to showcase what I think every human being should have – a decent house,' she said in her acceptance speech.

I spoke to Manyoni who denied 'linking' Els with Magashule. 'She knew Ace and Hantsi [Matseke] long before me!' he protested.

Els's comments, no doubt unintentionally, confirmed the long-held suspicion that Magashule directly influenced the awarding of tenders in his provincial departments. Instead of obtaining contracts through a competitive bidding process or even through lobbying the department itself, Els seemed to be affirming that one had to win Magashule's approval to get a foot in the door.

Or maybe it simply came down to good-neighbourliness. As mentioned earlier, businessman Glen Netshivhodza was another Parys local and Magashule confidant who scored big during the housing department's R1-billion spending spree. Incidentally, Magashule's wife, Seipati, is in business with Netshivhodza's wife. Seipati and Elsie Netshivhodza are listed as co-directors of a company called Kumba Civils.

In March 2013, Netshivhodza was appointed chairperson of the Free State Tourism Authority, a troubled provincial government entity that later merged with the provincial gambling board and liquor authority.[25] Sources familiar with developments say that, as with nearly all major moves in his government, Magashule was behind Netshivhodza's appointment to the tourism authority.

Netshivhodza's two companies – Ithuteng Consultancy and Harakisha Building Construction – together pocketed more than R30 million from the FSHS, about R20 million of which was received during the first two financial years of Magashule's reign as premier.

Like some of the other connected contractors, Netshivhodza apparently failed to complete his houses. For instance, Harakisha was appointed in 2010 to build 400 houses in QwaQwa. By 2013, the company had not finished a single one of these units, according to a progress report. The FSHS was left with no choice but to terminate the contract. The project was then taken over by TTC, the company owned by soccer boss Mike Mokoena.[26]

This apparent inability to finish projects seems to be a common trait among the contractors from Magashule's circle.

The final contractors worth singling out are owned by businessmen Madoda Khoba and Tlale Mokgadi, both alleged to be close to Magashule.

Khoba is based in the former homeland of QwaQwa and is said to be one of Magashule's closest friends in this part of the province. His two companies, Group Two Trading Enterprise and Group YWO Trading Enterprise, earned an impressive R210 million in revenue from the FSHS between 2009 and early 2018, coinciding exactly with Magashule's rule as premier.

There is documentary proof that Khoba may have dished out bribes to clear certain regulatory obstacles. Records from a court case in the North Gauteng High Court detail how he allegedly paid an official of the Construction Industry Development Board R6 000 to get a higher CIDB grading in 2007. A higher grading would have allowed Khoba's companies to bid for more lucrative government tenders, such as the ones he clinched in the Free State.[27]

Mokgadi's company, E'tsho Civils, is one of the private firms the FSHS appointed to draw up a report following the R1-billion debacle in 2010. But it has been doing well on the construction side of things too. Between 2011 and 2017, E'tsho Civils netted a cool R150 million in revenue from the department, the HSS shows.

A few of my sources told me that Mokgadi and Magashule 'travel the world together'. I found some evidence of this in the IgoFiles, the leaked documents I unpack in Part VII. A document from the premier's office shows that in early 2014 Mokgadi flew to Cuba with Magashule.

There is overwhelming evidence that a large slice of the pie in the Free State housing department's big splurge was gobbled up by contractors who either had tangible links to Magashule or were said to be close to him. In fact, R250 million was channelled to ten such companies in the two years between 2010 and 2012 alone. This included large payments to the likes of Blacky Seoe (a former business partner), Hantsi Matseke (a close friend from Parys) and Moreki Moroka (wife of a long-time lawyer pal).

But this was just the start of a process that would eventually see a mountain of money shift to people in Magashule's inner circle. These contractors, along with a few others who got in on the action only after the R1-billion splurge, altogether received a staggering R2 billion in revenue from the FSHS during the nine years of Magashule's reign as premier.

His daughter, Thoko Malembe, started scoring FSHS contracts in November 2013. Unital Holdings, the company in which she is a 30 per cent shareholder, received contracts worth more than R150 million from the department for the failed Vogelfontein housing project outside Bethlehem. My work on this story for *News24* revealed that Magashule's office influenced the awarding of the contract, and that he visited the site in person after Unital was appointed.[28] Magashule denied influencing the awarding of the contract, but failed to or refused to comment on his daughter's stake in the company.

Despite clear indications that contractors linked to Magashule are among the worst culprits when it comes to failed, delayed or substandard RDP projects, these companies were excluded from the FSHS's attempts to recover wasted money.

In July 2015, the Democratic Alliance asked the department to provide figures on incomplete houses to the provincial legislature's portfolio committee on public works, infrastructure, roads, transport and human settlements. Mokhesi came back with a truly shocking number – there were almost 11 000 incomplete houses all over the province, the HOD admitted.[29] Another submission to the portfolio committee in 2018 failed to put a figure on the total number of incomplete houses, but it confirmed that the problem had not been resolved and that projects awarded to politically connected contractors during 2010 had still not been completed.[30]

The man who should be held accountable for this mess is Ace Magashule. As evidenced by the myriad examples unpacked in this chapter, Magashule clearly loomed large in the province's allocation of housing contracts during his time as premier. This allowed him to dish out RDP contracts worth billions of rands to friends, family members, former business partners and other associates. Many of these contractors were completely unprepared for large RDP projects and consequently contributed to the scourge of unfinished houses that still affects poor people in the Free State today.

The fact that the auditor-general identified R7 billion in irregular expenditure at the FSHS during Magashule's time in office shows that there is much more to uncover. Furthermore, Open Water's handling of the 2010 contracts and the apparent derailing of the SIU investigation points to a massive cover-up that would have required the involvement of senior politicians.

So far, not a single top-level government leader has been held to account for one of the largest low-cost housing debacles in South African history.

PART IV

IRON FIST

11

Regime unchanged

As premier of the Free State, Ace Magashule presided over the provincial government's financial affairs with a despot's flair for centralisation. Former and current MECs, erstwhile confidants, senior and mid-level officials, and businesspeople in the province all attest to a frightening executive environment in which 'the fourth floor', a reference to the premier's office, controlled every stream, brook and tributary of the Free State's cash flows. 'There wasn't a contract in the Free State that Ace didn't know about. Whether it was for supplying toilet paper to municipalities or building roads for the province, he had a say in which contractors got the work,' claimed one of Magashule's closest former allies.

In some instances, the premier's office sought to formalise its iron grip on pockets of the province's budget, with disastrous effect. A plan initiated in 2010 to consolidate the Free State's entire government advertising spend in Magashule's office drew the ire of National Treasury and culminated in a forensic report that recommended criminal investigations (see Chapter 12).[1]

Operation Hlasela is another case in point. Magashule seemingly used his so-called development programme to impose himself on procurement decisions at the Free State Department of Human Settlements. And Operation Hlasela ensnared the expenditure policies at the province's other big spenders, including the departments of public works,[2] and police, roads and transport.[3] As we have seen, the former premier took a hands-on approach to the appointment of key officials in every sphere of government. From mayors, municipal managers and directors at municipalities to MECs, heads of department and directors at provincial departments, Magashule apparently had the final say when positions with even the faintest financial function needed to be filled.

A growing number of former and current political insiders are now willing to talk about Magashule's ruthless rule in his home province, but their claims are not new. As far back as 2013, Mpho Ramakatsa, one of the few ANC members who dared challenge the Magashule bloc's political hegemony, warned about the then premier's behaviour. 'There is no single municipality in the Free State that is independent of Magashule's influence,' Ramakatsa told the *Mail & Guardian* in May that year. 'He appoints everybody from heads of department to a cleaner. Those that do not toe the line are taken out [fired]. He has also centralised procurement in his office precisely to control the economy of the Free State. This makes him indispensable to a lot of people.'[4]

By all accounts, Magashule enforced a pervasive and smothering degree of authority over government affairs. To maintain his alleged capture of the provincial government, he needed to remain equally powerful in his guise as leader of the ANC in the Free State. He clung to the position of provincial chairperson for a record number of years, and seemed proud to be known as the ANC's 'longest-serving provincial chairman'.[5] He ascribed his prolonged occupation of the ANC's top spot in the province to the broad support the party's branches supposedly lavished upon him. 'I will always respect the branches of the ANC. I have never imposed myself as a leader. The branches have always nominated me. I will be elected unopposed at the provincial conference next month,' a confident Magashule told the *Sowetan* ahead of the 2012 provincial conference.[6] His prediction turned out to be 100 per cent correct.

His victories at so many successive provincial conferences inevitably convinced commentators and journalists that he enjoyed near-universal support in the Free State. Over the years, the media consistently reported on his 'popularity in the province',[7] and described him as 'popular at grassroots level'.[8] And so a myth was perpetuated that Magashule remained in power because he had authentic and widespread support from the 300-odd ANC branches in his home province.[9] However, there is ample evidence to the effect that Magashule and his allies at least partly assured their political domination through dirty tricks. Developments that unfolded soon after the ANC's 2012 provincial conference especially suggested that the provincial leadership had virtually no respect for the party's most fundamental democratic processes.

Two scathing court judgments, a tiny trove of leaked documents and myriad source accounts enabled me to piece together the astonishing story of how Magashule and his cohorts obliterated the ANC's branch-based system of participatory democracy to prolong their faction's reign. As previously mentioned, opponents of the former premier and his allies were subjected to all manner of irregularities to keep them away from provincial conferences. A majority of South Africa's highest court found that ANC members at many of the province's branches were effectively disenfranchised.[10] As a result, the voices and votes of those who sought to bring about political change in the province were discounted at the very conferences where the Magashule bloc emerged as victors. In some instances, would-be challengers were neutered through intimidation and even violence.[11]

All of this relates to the stick end of Magashule's political scheming. But he and his allies wielded plenty of carrots too. Branch members who stayed on their side were treated to luxury accommodation and other perks during provincial conferences. To fund this largesse, Magashule leaned on companies that got contracts from his provincial government. This practice seems to reaffirm the view that Magashule captured his province's finances in order to benefit from revenues earned by various contractors, whether for personal gain or political survival.

Magashule's conduct in his dual role as provincial premier and party chairperson is indicative of someone who harboured equal disregard for both spheres of power. As we have seen, as premier he oversaw a provincial administration that bent, broke or bulldozed over the clearly defined laws and prescripts that are meant to ensure proper procurement. In this regard, the auditor-general's reports on the Free State alone provide ample evidence. As ANC chairperson, Magashule led a party apparatus that consistently decimated the century-old liberation movement's proud tradition of participatory democracy.

There are strong indications that Magashule had no qualms about getting his hands dirty to help keep his bloc in power. In March 2011, the Free State ANC's Winburg branch held a branch general meeting at the local town hall.[12] The municipal elections were just two months away and the branch had to nominate its candidates for councillors. Magashule was present to chair the meeting, which soon turned violent amid fierce contestation between two nominees from opposing camps. It was later alleged that Magashule had insisted on a candidate who did not enjoy the branch's support. Branch member Joel Maleka, who supported the rival candidate, told this story to the media:

I was one of the people who were going to the stage to vote and supporters of [Kgotso] Segamme [the candidate Magashule allegedly preferred] were blocking our way to the stage. When we asked to pass, we were told that we would not be allowed to vote for our chosen councillor. The next thing I felt someone pulling my shirt and trying to strangle me. I looked up and it was the premier himself. He ended up pushing me down to the ground. The premier grabbed my right arm and shook me. Then he ordered his bodyguards to arrest us.[13]

The *Sowetan* reported that Magashule had allegedly 'slapped and kicked' Maleka and fellow branch member Mzwanele Moletsane.[14]

Magashule did not deny that he was involved in the disturbance, but claimed that he merely played the role of peacemaker. 'I was chairing that meeting but I did not beat them up,' he told reporters. 'I was just separating them because they were about to start a fight. The truth will come out in court. Let the police investigate. The people who were there will be my witnesses. Politics is a dirty game.'[15]

Maleka and Moletsane laid charges of assault against the premier, but later withdrew them. Brigadier Sam Makhele, a spokesperson for the SAPS in the province, confirmed this. I got hold of Maleka, who told me that he and Moletsane withdrew their complaints after 'sorting things out' with Magashule. He did not want to provide further details on the matter.

Dennis Bloem, the former long-serving ANC member from the Free State who later joined COPE, sketched a disconcerting picture of Magashule's alleged improprieties when it came to the ruling party's meetings and conferences in the period before he became premier. Bloem, who jumped ship in 2009, claimed that Magashule effectively bought his way to the top of the ANC's Free State hierarchy. 'That man was not scared to produce money at ANC conferences,' he told me when we spoke about Magashule's rise in the party's ranks. 'We saw him with cash, and this made some delegates very uncomfortable. But others were brought to conferences in buses that stopped at KFC or Nando's. Some of these delegates were also put up in nice hotels or guesthouses, away from other party members. This was all done to buy their support.'

Even some of Magashule's closest former allies admitted that the party's democratic processes had been a farce. One of them made a startling admission during an interview in mid-2018. 'I helped Ace to swing conferences and branches for years,' this former PEC member and MEC told me. 'We bought members. The capture started at the branches and then spread to the regional conferences and finally the provincial conferences. Everything mentioned during those court cases was true.'

We will get to those legal proceedings in a bit, but first let us unpack some of the financial transactions that seem to prove that Magashule indeed squeezed cash out of contractors to book certain party members into comfortable hotels and guesthouses during provincial conferences.

I spoke to a businessman whose firm secured contracts worth more than R50 million from the provincial government during Magashule's time as premier. In early 2012, this person needed to meet with the premier about his company's work in the Free State. He told me that Mamorena Mosala, the office manager at the ANC's head office in Bloemfontein, facilitated the meeting. Email exchanges between him and Mosala seemingly confirm this. For the pleasure of meeting with Magashule, the businessman was allegedly required to make a donation to the ANC. To this end, Mosala sent him the account and branch numbers for the party's 'salary acc[ount]' at FNB. He duly paid his donation into the account and thanked Mosala for setting up the meeting, to which she responded: 'Thank you. Always remember I am just a phone call away should you need anything from him [Magashule].'

But it was the premier, or at least the party he headed, that needed something from the businessman first. A day before the ANC's 2012 provincial conference in Parys, my source transferred R200 000 to the hotel and conference centre that was due to host the gathering. He showed me the proof of payment. According to him, Magashule himself had issued the instruction to pay the hotel. The businessman claimed Mosala had 'coordinated' the transaction.

As mentioned previously and elaborated on below, the 2012 conference ended up being declared unlawful. The Magashule-led PEC was forced to convene a new conference in May the following year. Once again, Magashule allegedly asked the businessman to provide financial support. The 2013 conference was held in Welkom, and my source transferred just under R100 000 to a few guesthouses in and around town to accommodate conference delegates. He provided me with proof of payment for these transactions.

* * *

In late 2011 there were murmurs of a possible attempt by fed-up ANC members in the Free State to dismantle the hegemony of chairman Ace Magashule and his cohort.[16] What apparently started as a band of disaffected party members in the Motheo region grew into a fully fledged faction which became known as the Regime Change group. The challengers not only aimed to unseat the Magashule bloc in the Free State, but they also planned to oppose Jacob Zuma's reign as party president at the next national conference in Mangaung by backing then president Kgalema Motlanthe instead.

Far from being mere upstarts and opportunists, the Regime Changers included former provincial chairperson Pat Matosa, MEC and provincial treasurer Mxolisi Dukwana, provincial secretary Sibongile Besani, then national sport minister Fikile Mbalula, and former MK member and Free State MEC Gregory Nthatisi.

In April 2012, about two months before the provincial conference was scheduled to take place in Parys, an unnamed ANC leader sympathetic to the Regime Change cause told the *Mail & Guardian* why the chairperson had to go. 'There is rampant corruption in many government departments and in the form of the Hlasela Fund, which is not a policy of the ANC but a vehicle to enrich Magashule and his cronies,' the newspaper quoted the senior ANC member as saying. 'There is patronage and we have seen a skewed distribution of government work in favour of those close to the chosen one.'[17] Magashule framed such criticism as mere political campaigning by the Regime Change group. 'There is no patronage,' he told the *Sunday Independent*. 'It is people who are too ambitious who say this ... I don't have time for ambitious people.'[18]

The Regime Changers campaigned hard and were convinced that they would unseat Magashule and his allies. Across the province, the party's members attended branch general meetings, where it was decided which delegates each branch would send to the provincial conference. This is the very foundation of the ANC's internal democratic process, but there was trouble on the horizon. The Regime Changers were confident that they enjoyed the support of branches in four of the Free State ANC's five regions.[19] However, they underestimated the lengths their opponents were willing to go to in order to quell the anti-Magashule movement.

About a month before the conference, provincial secretary Besani sent letters to then national secretary-general Gwede Mantashe, some members of the ANC's NEC deployed to the province, and the Magashule-led PEC in which he highlighted 'material irregularities' that had occurred when the Free State's branches chose their delegates for the upcoming conference. Among the problems listed were widespread 'manipulation of the membership numbers in specific branches'; 'exclusion of bona fide delegates'; and 'the establishment of parallel structures and the decision to allow and sanction the participation at the provincial conference of "delegates" from parallel structures'.[20] These complaints, along with other grievances, would form the basis of the Regime Change group's soon-to-be-launched legal bid.

According to the ANC's Membership Audit Guidelines, the membership lists compiled at the branch general meetings had to be subjected to pre-audits by the PEC or by each region's Regional Executive Committee. After that, the National Audit Team had to determine which of the branches were in good standing before verifying how many paid-up and legitimate members each branch had. This was a vital process. Once the National Audit Team confirmed that a branch had been 'constitutionally launched', that branch could send its paid-up and verified members to the provincial conference.[21] The Regime Changers claimed that their branches had not been given the opportunity to 'query the audit findings, in breach of the audit guidelines', according to court papers they later filed.

Despite these grievances, the provincial conference went ahead on 22 June. Besani, Dukwana and other branch members affected by the alleged irregularities did not attend. Unsurprisingly, the Magashule bloc emerged victorious. Magashule was re-elected provincial chairperson, while his allies filled nearly all the other top PEC positions. The dubiously constituted conference then turned into a pro-Zuma festival. In defiance of an NEC resolution prohibiting party members from endorsing candidates for the upcoming national conference until the nomination processes opened in October, Magashule openly announced his support for Zuma. In fact, the conference could easily have been mistaken for a Zuma campaign gathering. Delegates carried placards warning 'Hands-off our President Jacob Msholozi Zuma',[22] and the stage was decorated with large posters bearing the president's face.[23]

When Magashule was later asked to comment on the complaints of his opponents in the province, he pleaded innocence. 'The audit of branches is the terrain of the national office through the ANC secretary general [Mantashe]. Ditto the provincial conference is also the terrain of national [leadership],' he told the *Mail & Guardian*.[24] But the validity of these audits would soon come under fire. In late August, with the Mangaung conference drawing near, Mpho Ramakatsa, a former MK soldier, and five other party members from branches across the Free State launched an application in the Bloemfontein High Court. While the court papers did not expressly identify the applicants as members of the Regime Change group, some media reports branded Ramakatsa as one of the faction's central figures alongside Dukwana and Besani.[25] Magashule and the rest of his PEC, along with the ANC's national leadership, were listed as the respondents.

The applicants wanted the latest Magashule-led PEC to be disbanded. They argued that the processes leading up to the Parys conference had been 'manipulated and abused', and that the 'principle of fair political play was flagrantly undermined', while 'the election was not free and fair'. They also wanted the court to overturn the national ANC leadership's recognition of the PEC as a 'lawful, authentic and representative leadership structure'. In late October, Bloemfontein High Court judge Mojalefa Rampai ruled against Ramakatsa and his fellow applicants. But his judgment was based solely on 'fatal procedural defects and irregularities' in the application itself. Rampai did not rule on the 'substantive merits' of the case, namely the alleged irregularities at the branch meetings.[26]

The six disgruntled party members insisted on having a court pronounce on the alleged irregularities. They therefore took the matter to the Constitutional Court. This allowed them to present to the country's most senior judges a detailed, branch-by-branch breakdown of the underhanded tactics that had prevented some party members from attending the elective conference.

At the Fidel Castro branch in the Motheo region, for example, 'a properly elected chairperson and branch secretary' requested that they be allowed to 'participate in the audit process' and 'complained about the creation of a parallel branch to theirs'.[27] According to the court papers, Magashule's PEC simply ignored the request and never gave them an opportunity to review the audit. The Constitutional Court judges were not impressed with the PEC's reason for doing so:

> The respondents' answer to this allegation is that an audit could not be carried out because members of the 'regime change group' seemingly

wanted their own membership file audited. One thing is clear, no audit was conducted nor is it suggested that members of the *Fidel Castro* branch are not entitled to have their membership numbers audited only because they support the so-called regime change. In our view, the members of the *Fidel Castro* branch were entitled to have their membership audited to assess their good standing and failure to do so amounts to conduct inconsistent with the Membership Audit Guidelines and is thus an irregularity.[28]

Ramakatsa belonged to the Joyce Boom branch, also situated in the Motheo region. On 6 May 2012, this branch held a 'legitimate' and 'quorate' meeting where delegates were 'properly elected to represent the branch at regional and provincial conferences'. The branch also nominated some of its members to be elected to the PEC. Despite submitting a report to the PEC that set out in 'remarkable detail' the credentials of the elected deployees and the branch's legitimacy, the PEC simply barred the branch from attending the provincial conference. Magashule and his fellow respondents tried to convince the court that the meeting in May 'never took place'. Again, the judges dismissed this response. 'Other than the bare denial, the respondents do not furnish even the slightest evidence that the meeting did not take place,' they noted. The court found that the respondents 'in effect disenfranchised members of a branch in good standing', an action that was also 'inconsistent' with South Africa's Constitution.[29]

Members of at least four branches in the Thabo Mofutsanyana region were also found to have been 'disenfranchised' by being denied 'representation at the provincial conference', this time due to a disconcerting dereliction of duty by certain members of the ANC NEC. In the months before the provincial conference, the National Audit Team determined that several branches in this region had to rerun their elective processes because of alleged irregularities. NEC members who formed part of the National Audit Team were supposed to oversee fresh elections at the affected branches; however, they failed to pitch up at the branch meetings, which meant the elections could not take place. As a result, several branch members in this region could not attend the provincial conference. Bizarrely, despite the fact that there were no fresh elections, the affected branches were somehow still represented in Parys by mystery 'delegates'.[30]

The court papers revealed that the provincial conference was attended by many more of these supposed 'delegates' who had no business being there. Members of the Lovemore Koto branch in the town of Petrusburg, which forms part of the Xhariep region, were denied an opportunity to view the preliminary and final audit reports on the delegates to be sent to the conference. Lovemore Koto and two other branches in this region were also eventually represented by mystery delegates. 'There is no denial that no preliminary audit report was presented to these branches. Nor do the respondents deal with the serious allegation that the provincial conference was attended by delegates who were not duly elected by the branches concerned,' the court found.[31]

Magashule and his fellow respondents sought to convince the court that not a single 'branch delegate not authorised to do so attended the provincial conference' and that no 'branch delegate entitled to attend was denied the opportunity to do so'. But the Constitutional Court judges found these 'bare denials' unconvincing and 'generic'. 'This is particularly so because where ... the appellants adduce facts which support the categories of irregularities, region by region, they are not seriously disputed,' they said. They set aside the Bloemfontein High Court's earlier ruling and declared the Parys conference and its decisions and resolutions unlawful and invalid.[32]

The Constitutional Court reached its decision on 14 December 2012, two days before the ANC's national conference was due to get under way in Mangaung. As a result, the NEC barred the PEC from voting at the conference, but Magashule was allowed to attend in his capacity as a member of the NEC.[33] Furthermore, the court's 'declaration of invalidity' only applied to the provincial conference.[34] Mantashe explained to the media that Free State branch delegates could still attend the national conference, seeing as the processes through which they had been elected were overseen by the party's electoral commission and not by the Magashule-led PEC.[35] This undoubtedly helped ensure the Zuma slate's victory at Mangaung, but there were also suspicions that the membership numbers in pro-Zuma provinces such as the Free State, KwaZulu-Natal and Mpumalanga had been 'rigged' in order to send more delegates to the conference.[36] The Free State's ANC membership figures, as reflected in an organisational report presented by Mantashe at the conference, certainly made for very interesting reading. Before the Polokwane conference in 2007, the province had

61 000 members. In January 2012, the figure stood at 76 334. By that June, there were 121 074 members, which means the party somehow recruited almost 45 000 new Free State members in just six months.[37]

The Constitutional Court decided that either the NEC or the national conference needed to fix the dual problems of the discredited Free State provincial conference and the disbanded PEC.[38] During an NEC meeting on the sidelines at Mangaung, the ANC's national leadership appointed a task team of twenty people to organise a fresh provincial conference. But it appeared as if the deck was stacked against the Regime Change faction. The task team included Magashule, social development MEC Sisi Ntombela and a bunch of other party figures aligned to Magashule's camp. Besani was one of the few task-team members who stood outside the fold. From Ramakatsa's viewpoint, the national leadership had put in charge the very people who were behind the irregularities criticised by the Constitutional Court. Ramakatsa contended that he and his fellow applicants were not consulted when the task team was formed.[39]

The follow-up Free State conference was held at Phakisa Freeway, the motor-racing circuit in Welkom, over a weekend in May 2013. Ramakatsa and the Regime Change group again boycotted the event.[40] They were adamant that the same 'mistakes and irregularities' that caused the Constitutional Court to declare the previous year's conference in Parys unlawful had preceded the latest gathering.[41] With no Regime Change challengers present to spoil the party, Magashule again became chairperson, while some of his closest allies were elected unopposed to top spots on the PEC. Mosebenzi Zwane, who still enjoyed relative obscurity, became the ANC's Free State treasurer.[42]

Then deputy president Cyril Ramaphosa, who had popped in to address the conference, seemingly chose to side with the Magashule bloc with regards to the Regime Changers' successful Constitutional Court challenge the previous year. 'Whilst we respect the rights to legal recourse of any individual, including ANC members, the emerging of a culture of taking the organisation to court *must* be discouraged and it *must* come to an end,' Ramaphosa told an appreciative audience of Magashule backers.[43] He failed to recognise the fact that Ramakatsa's group only took the ANC to court after they had first submitted their grievances to the party's top national and provincial leadership structures.[44]

In the weeks after the Welkom conference, Ramakatsa vowed to again fight the latest outcome in the courts.[45] 'I wonder whether comrade Ace and those who conspire with him to wreck the ANC sleep well at night. For them the ANC is merely a vehicle for self-enrichment,' he told *Volksblad*.[46] It would be one of his last public utterances as an ANC member. Instead of continuing his legal battle against the Magashule faction, Ramakatsa turned his back on the ANC. In July 2013, he was introduced as the national coordinator for Julius Malema's newly established Economic Freedom Fighters.[47] Thus ended one of the strongest challenges ever to Magashule's hegemony. The Regime Change movement faded into oblivion and the chairman and his allies were again free to rule the ANC roost in the province, at least for the following four years.

The Constitutional Court's judgment did not inspire those implicated in dubious political practices to mend their ways. In 2017, Magashule and his allies again received a lashing in court following complaints about their conduct. This is unpacked in Chapter 29.

12

Fourth estate capture

State capture is most efficiently curtailed by a free and independent media. The ideal environment for raiding the public purse is therefore one in which the fourth estate – the press – does not function optimally. Under Ace Magashule's watch, the Free State government moulded the province's media landscape into a friendlier and more forgiving space by propping up allies in the industry and effectively suppressing critical publications.

Local journalists who exposed Magashule's skeletons were threatened and intimidated, but the province's foremost critical media voices were ultimately muzzled using what appears to have been a deliberate financial strategy. Millions of rands in taxpayers' money were channelled to blatantly obsequious media platforms while simultaneously withheld from those that refused to toe the line.

A calculated plan to capture the province's collective budgets for advertising, communication, printing and related services began to take shape a year into Magashule's first term as premier. Up until then, the Free State's provincial departments were responsible for managing their own budgets for media and communications services. But in March 2010, Wisani Ngobeni, the chief director of communication in the Free State premier's office and Magashule's long-time spin doctor, compiled a report that paved the way for the centralisation of the separate departments' media budgets.[1]

Instead of creating a new entity to oversee expenditure, Ngobeni proposed that the premier's office become the 'implementing agent' for these services. 'The current process of [placing] advertisement[s] in the media is time consuming and makes it impossible for departments to advertise on short notice,' Ngobeni explained in his report. Centralising to the premier's office would 'enable Departments to buy media space without the administrative burden of obtaining quotations,' he argued.[2]

In April 2010, the province's executive council 'resolved to centralise the communication services of all the provincial departments in line with the turnaround strategy for communication', according to a damning report by National Treasury concluded in early 2013.[3]

A prevailing story told by those with insight into the workings of Magashule's Free State is that 'the fourth floor', a reference to the premier's office in the Lebohang government building in Bloemfontein, always had the final say in how the various departments spent their budgets. In most instances, the control Magashule and his colleagues exerted over these cash flows was through informal arrangements. The 2010 'turnaround strategy' for media services, however, formalised Magashule's capture of this segment of the province's expenditure.

The premier's office now wielded an extremely powerful weapon. It could determine how the province's entire media budget would be spent. While it was bound to favour people close to Magashule, more import- antly it could also withhold vital advertising revenue from media outlets that were possibly viewed as too critical and too independent.

The provincial government's new 'implementing agent' for media ser- vices was quick to flex its procurement powers. In April 2010, Magashule's office issued tenders for 'public information', 'media bulk buying services', 'printing and distribution services' and the 'provision of event management services'.[4] One of the benefactors of this set of contracts was business- man Setumo 'Tumi' Ntsele, whose company, Letlaka Communications, was appointed as the exclusive printer and distributor of provincial newsletters in August 2010.[5] Letlaka also clinched a contract to provide the province with event management services.[6]

The Treasury report found that the establishment of a centralised 'implementing' unit for media services within the premier's office was unlawful, and that the contracts awarded to Letlaka were therefore also in breach of the relevant legislation. According to the report, 'all of the other Provincial Departments, which purported to appoint the Premier's Office as their implementing agent, based on the direction of the Premier's Office, also contravened the applicable Legislative Framework'.[7]

The Treasury investigators called for 'a more in-depth investigation into Letlaka's business in order to determine whether or not there may be financial misconduct, which may lead to criminal charges'.[8] There seemed to have been some solid grounds for their suspicions. Dan Kgothule, a former MEC for sport, arts and culture in the Free State, later claimed that Ntsele had tried to bribe him with a 30 per cent share in Letlaka in exchange for advertising his department in Letlaka's publications.[9]

Addressing the National Council of Provinces in November 2013, then finance minister Pravin Gordhan discussed the report's findings. 'The report confirmed the existence of financial misconduct and elaborated on the nature and extent thereof, as well as the responsible parties within the department of the premier,' he said. 'Details were provided in the report together with the recommendation that the department of the premier should lay criminal charges with the SAPS against the implicated parties.'[10]

Magashule's office took no such action. Instead, the premier claimed ignorance of the Treasury report. 'The Premier is not aware of any recommendations which were made to the effect that criminal charges should be instituted against any official following the so-called Letlaka investigation,' he wrote in a reply to Roy Jankielsohn, the DA's leader in the Free State provincial legislature.[11]

Ntsele's printing and event management contracts were just the start of his lucrative relationship with Magashule's government. In 2011, a consortium headed by the businessman won a controversial tender to design and develop websites for various provincial departments, municipalities and state-owned entities in the Free State. The contract was reportedly worth a staggering R120 million.[12] The project was later suspended amid a public outcry over the exorbitant costs, but Ntsele and his partners nevertheless bagged at least R48 million.[13] According to one report, the province spent as much as R95 million on the websites, although it is not clear whether this entire amount was paid to Ntsele's consortium.[14]

Several tech experts have described the project as a gigantic rip-off, seeing as the web pages were built on simple WordPress templates that required little design work.[15] There has been no shortage of calls for the police to probe the deal, but such requests have apparently fallen on deaf ears. I conducted a small probe of my own, and I did not have to dig all that deep to unearth some red flags. The consortium that won the website contract consisted of Cherry Online-Design, of which Ntsele is the sole director, Ikamva ICT and Jagganaut Trading and Projects. The latter company's sole director is Kenneth Thandiwe Mpembe, who, according to company records, hails from the northern Free State town of Sasolburg. Mpembe also happens to have business links to Magashule's son, Tshepiso. Mpembe and Tshepiso were co-directors of BMMW Liquor Trading and

Projects, as well as of a shelf company called Friedshelf 1076, company records revealed.

Apart from the website debacle, Ntsele is also known for being the owner of *The Weekly*, a provincial newspaper that forms part of his Letlaka group. After the centralised media unit was established in Magashule's office, *The Weekly* became one of the foremost benefactors of government advertising revenue, along with the Gupta-owned *The New Age*. In its 2013 report, Treasury noted that '*The Weekly* seems to be funded almost solely by the Free State government, in particular the Department of the Premier, as very little commercial advertising could be identified'.[16] In exchange for such favourable treatment, *The Weekly* seemingly transformed itself into Magashule's personal mouthpiece.

The newspaper was distributed for free and could be picked up at the offices of all major government departments, municipalities and other state organs in the province, among other distribution points. The fact that the publication was readily available to most government officials and employees made it a powerful tool of influence within the province's hallways of power. An assessment of *The Weekly*'s reportage over a period of about six years allowed me to conclude that Ntsele's publication indeed amounted to little more than a propaganda machine for Magashule and his political allies. When *The Weekly* was not singing the premier's praises, it was attacking his political foes. Magashule's would-be challengers from 2012's Regime Change group, other adversaries and even rival media publications all landed in *The Weekly*'s crosshairs. In the process, the publication consistently ran afoul of journalistic ethics and best practice.

Here is perhaps the most shocking example of the paper's questionable reportage. In March 2011, the *Sowetan* broke the story about Magashule's alleged assault of two ANC branch members in Winburg, as referred to in the previous chapter.[17] More than a year later, in May 2012, *The Weekly* published a story under the headline 'Ace plot revealed'.[18] The report opened with a quote from Joel Maleka and Mzwanele Moletsane, the two men who had laid charges of assault against Magashule following the alleged fisticuffs. 'We are sorry, we did not want to open a case, and we love our chairman [Magashule],' they told the paper during 'an exclusive interview'. Maleka and Moletsane apparently admitted to *The Weekly* that 'they were promised jobs and money if they acted against the ANC provincial chairperson'.[19] The article continues:

An investigation conducted by *The Weekly* then established that the allegations by the two were nothing but a conspiracy aimed at tainting Magashule's reputation. This was after several high profile sources who were present at the meeting confirmed that Magashule never assaulted the duo as per media reports … The two have now realised that the senior ANC leaders who offered them bribes were sworn enemies of Magashule who wanted to use the incident to embarrass him.[20]

The article did not reveal the names of the 'senior ANC leaders' behind the alleged plot, but it included this little afterthought: 'They [Maleka and Moletsane] made it clear that no one pressured them to spill the beans to *The Weekly* about the plot.'[21]

It would have been a fantastic scoop, if only it were true.

I managed to get hold of Maleka in August 2018. He told me that he was never involved in a plot to smear Magashule's reputation. He was also adamant that the alleged fracas at the branch meeting did happen. Most troublingly, Maleka claimed that he had not spoken to *The Weekly* at all. He was reluctant to discuss the issue, but said he could only remember at the time having talked to either the *Sunday World* or the *Sunday Sun*. According to Maleka, he and Moletsane withdrew their complaints against Magashule after discussions with the premier. 'We sorted things out, everything is fine now,' he told me. He did not want to provide further details on how the matter was resolved.

I asked Ntsele whether his newspaper had fabricated the 'plot'. He did not respond to any of my queries about his business dealings in the Free State or his alleged friendship with the former premier.

Another early 'scoop' by *The Weekly* was a front-page lead in late 2011 that detailed an alleged plot to 'assassinate' Magashule.[22] The story was wafer-thin in terms of its sourcing and it lacked concrete evidence that a plot really existed. It was also strangely reminiscent of similar claims that had been circulated about Jacob Zuma since at least 2007.[23] Zuma and his allies propagated such claims to great effect to paint the former president as a victim and thereby bolster his support at key moments in his scandal-ridden career as a politician.

Then, in early 2012, as the ANC was starting to prepare for that year's elective conference in Mangaung, Ntsele's newspaper followed up with a report headed 'Inside regime change war room'. The piece outlined a series of dubious tactics used by the Regime Change faction in an attempt to get rid of Magashule and Zuma. Yet one of their main sources was Magashule himself, a fact *The Weekly* was astonishingly candid about:

> After months of painstaking investigations and extensive interviews with ANC branch members and chairperson [Magashule], *The Weekly* can reveal the diabolical and delusional modus operandi employed by the Regime Change in its endeavour to dislodge the current leadership from the state and party hegemony.[24]

Furthermore, according to the paper, Magashule was not only the target of an assassination plot, he was also the victim of an elaborate smear campaign designed to tie his name to political assassinations:

> *The Weekly* has been reliably informed by provincial intelligence sources about plots being hatched to eliminate prominent political rivals of the current provincial ANC leadership. The aim is to use such assassinations to win public sympathy, and smear and discredit the current provincial leadership, especially Ace Magashule.[25]

At the time, the Mangaung metro was wracked by service-delivery protests in the Thaba 'Nchu and Botshabelo areas outside Bloemfontein. In its report, *The Weekly* claimed that the Regime Change group had hijacked the residents' legitimate grievances to 'embarrass and discredit the incumbent provincial leaders'.[26]

As the Free State provincial conference drew closer, *The Weekly*'s reports on the Regime Change faction became wilder and more unbelievable. 'Terror campaign unmasked,' screamed one of its headlines from May 2012. In the article, the newspaper claimed it had obtained a report compiled by the party's Mangaung region 'authenticating allegations of a nefarious plot involving violence, intimidation, and formation of illegitimate ANC branches by Regime Change leaders and members'. *The Weekly* insisted that the document corroborated its earlier revelations about the Regime Change group's 'war room strategy'. One of the paper's main sources for the article, apart from the Mangaung region report, was 'a key lobbyist close to the Magashule re-election campaign'.[27]

Sometimes the propaganda carried by *The Weekly* was laughably obvious. In November 2011, the paper published a letter from Steve Nale, who hailed from Magashule's hometown of Parys. Nale was angry with other media outlets' 'unfounded attacks' on the premier. He scoffed at the corruption allegations that swirled around Magashule's administration and described the premier as a champion of the poor. 'We will need a space bigger than this to showcase Free State government's achievement under the leadership of Magashule,' he wrote. '[W]herever you go many of our people views [sic] him as a saviour ... I never said a saint ... but a true embodiment of the aspirations of our people.'[28]

On closer inspection, Nale was not a random member of the public. In fact, he was the spokesperson for the Ngwathe local municipality in Parys, where Magashule's wife was a senior manager. The Weekly did not disclose this information, at least not in the letter's online version.

There are even more comical examples of The Weekly's pro-Magashule propaganda. In March 2015, it ran an 'Open letter to Ace Magashule' from Tiisetso Makhele. 'I greet you in the name of the organisation you lead, the ANC, and on behalf of the people of the Free State,' the letter began. 'Like the biblical Moses, you won people's hearts behind your vision of [Operation] Hlasela ... Premier Magashule, I am proud to have a leader like you. As a Free State citizen, I have confidence that under your watch and leadership, the people of our province are safe.' Later, Makhele remarked: 'I know that many will question my intention in writing this open letter. In fact, I know that some will even accuse me of attempting to solicit benefits from you ... If you happen to read this piece, by some accident, please know that I ask of you no favour.' He concluded his love letter by imploring, 'Mr Premier, please live long, for the benefit of our people.'[29]

At the time, Makhele, a regular columnist for The Weekly since at least 2012, was working at the Free State branch of the South African Local Government Association (SALGA). A few months after The Weekly published his open letter, Makhele was appointed as Magashule's new spokesperson, replacing Makalo Mohale, who was moved to the Free State Department of Human Settlements.[30] Makhele, who stayed on as the spokesperson for current Free State premier Sisi Ntombela, says his appointment was in no way influenced by the open letter. 'My deployment at [the] Premier's office was a decision of the ANC, not of the former Premier,' he insisted.

While The Weekly kept up its flattering and uncritical reporting on Magashule and his administration, a few of the province's other news outlets remained committed to holding the premier to account. Because Ntsele seemingly formed part of Magashule's capture network, the Letlaka group and its affiliated entities inevitably featured in rival publications' news reports. In response, *The Weekly* sometimes lashed out at its competitors in 'exposés' of its own, but these reports fell well short of the South African Press Code's benchmarks for acceptable journalism.

In November 2017, the Afrikaans daily *Volksblad* revealed that Magashule's government had splurged R95 million on the contentious website contract that had been awarded to Ntsele's consortium in 2011.[31] A few weeks later, *The Weekly* retaliated with street posters and a front-page report that cast *Volksblad* in an unflattering light. 'Volksblad covert agenda exposed,' read the posters. The newspaper claimed that *Volksblad* was running a 'cloak and dagger smear campaign' aimed at discrediting and embarrassing Magashule, his administration and some of the black-owned businesses with which the province did business, including Ntsele's companies.[32] *The Weekly* seemed to be accusing *Volksblad* of racism. 'According to investigations carried out by this newspaper it has emerged that very senior white officials in the office of the Premier, under the pretext of being loyal to him, are intercepting government information and passing it on to *Volksblad* newspaper,' the article claimed.[33] *Volksblad* submitted a complaint to the Press Ombudsman, who found that *The Weekly* had no facts to substantiate its story and was thus ordered to apologise to *Volksblad*.[34]

The Weekly's most significant media battle occurred much earlier, however. In 2011, Zimbabwean-born journalist-turned-media-entrepreneur Basildon Peta launched the now defunct *Free State Times*. 'I was the main publisher in Lesotho, but I wanted to expand to South Africa,' Peta told me during an interview in late 2018. 'The Free State was the logical starting point to do so.' He felt that the province's media offering left ample space for a new publication. *Volksblad* was doing great work in terms of holding the Magashule administration to account, but it only catered for Afrikaans readers.

After assembling a team of journalists and setting up shop in Bloemfontein, the first edition of the *Free State Times* hit the streets in April 2011. The publication was unflinchingly independent and critical right from the start. 'Our very first front-page story ran under the headline "Premier Magashule under fire",' Peta recalled. 'It detailed alleged irregularities involving the premier. In the months thereafter, we published story after story about

Ace and his [alleged] corruption.' The *Free State Times* tackled a series of government deals with companies and businesspeople who were allegedly close to Magashule, including Ntsele's contentious website contract. Peta's paper also investigated and wrote about the Magashule bloc's dubious political manoeuvring within the ANC's provincial structures.

'We had been following the story of how legitimate [ANC] branches were sidelined, how Ace was elected as chairperson through [alleged] cheating, how delegates were [allegedly] paid off,' Peta told me. 'We published many reports on the branch-level manipulation that ensured Ace's continued power.' These hard-hitting reports soon earned the *Free State Times* a reputation as an uncompromising newspaper dedicated to exposing corruption in the province. This translated into promising circulation figures for a young publication.

'We sold 15 000 copies of one edition in which we exposed a government contract that had been awarded to a businessman with links to Ace,' said Peta. 'The circulation began to increase at a steady rate.' The publication also became a preferred channel for government officials and other individuals who wanted to tell their stories about problems in the Magashule-led government. 'On some days, the reception area was full of people who wanted to share information about corruption,' Peta explained.

Given the *Free State Times*'s reporting on the website contract, it did not surprise Peta when Ntsele's *The Weekly* began to attack his newspaper. *The Weekly*'s 'Letters to the Editor' section was routinely used for this purpose. Nale, in his letter, accused the *Free State Times* of 'perpetuat[ing] a sinister agenda that projects Magashule as corrupt'.[35] Another letter claimed that the *Free State Times* was controlled by 'Regime Change handlers', without providing a shred of evidence.[36]

It was not long before such sentiments gained traction within the ANC's formal structures. In March 2012, *The Weekly* reported that 'ANC Youth League leaders have declared war against *Free State Times*, accusing the newspaper of waging an anti-ANC agenda'. The article quoted ANC Youth League Fezile Dabi regional secretary Phindile Motha as saying that her organisation supported the ANC's controversial call for the establishment of a media tribunal, and that the *Free State Times* would be the first publication to appear before it. 'We should seriously begin to probe as to who is funding this paper and its agenda,' Motha told *The Weekly*. 'In asking we should remember the info scandal of 1979 and we will certainly be guided to find answers.'[37] She seemed unaware of the irony of her comments. The so-called information or Muldergate scandal involved the misappropriation of apartheid state funds for covert propaganda projects. In the Free State's case, it was *The Weekly* that was being propped up with government funding, not the *Free State Times*.

The hostility was not confined to *The Weekly*'s pages. According to Peta, *Free State Times* reporters and staffers were exposed to intimidation and threats when they attended government press briefings and other events. 'I once received a phone call from someone who told me I should go back to Zimbabwe,' Peta told me. 'Before he hung up, he asked me if I remembered what had happened to Noby Ngombane.'

But the biggest threat to the *Free State Times*'s continued existence was financial in nature. Peta told me Magashule effectively placed 'an embargo' on state advertising in his newspaper. It is something that clearly still irks him. 'If we had received a fraction of *The New Age*'s government advertising revenue, we would have been fine,' he said. 'It is simply unethical for bureaucrats to punish newspapers for criticising government.'

From the outset, Peta was less than optimistic about his gutsy publication's chances of securing much revenue from Magashule's government. Given the newspaper's promising circulation figures, however, he had thought that the *Free State Times* would secure enough advertising income from the private sector. Things were not that simple. Peta and his colleagues were told that large companies and other businesses operating in the Free State had been pressured into boycotting his newspaper. 'Potential clients told our advertising team that people from government had asked them not to support us,' Peta claimed. 'These companies were afraid of losing out on business with the provincial government, so they complied.'

A former advertising agent at the *Free State Times* told me the same story. This source gave me the name of a large retailer in Bloemfontein that initially agreed to advertise in the *Free State Times* but later backed out for alleged 'political reasons'. I asked the retailer for comment. It admitted that it had placed one advertisement in the *Free State Times* before terminating its relationship with the new publication, but maintained that this was for purely commercial reasons. 'We didn't get much traction after our once-off advertisement and therefore decided not to make use of it again,' the retailer maintained.

Peta cited other companies that, according to him, boycotted the *Free State Times* because of alleged pressure from Magashule's administration. These included cellphone network giants and other major South African companies. Regardless of the reasons for these businesses not wanting to advertise in the *Free State Times*, the dual snub from the private and public sectors soon pushed the newspaper towards the brink of bankruptcy. Peta had started the *Free State Times* with a cash injection from a foreign investor, and he needed to keep up with the loan repayments. He also had to protect his employees' jobs. In the end, he decided to do a deal with the devil, in a manner of speaking. One of his friends knew Ntsele. This person suggested that instead of closing down the *Free State Times*, Peta could enter into a partnership with Letlaka.

'I did what a responsible publisher and businessman needed to do,' Peta told me. In early 2013, he agreed to sell a controlling stake in his newspaper to Ntsele's Letlaka.[38] After that, government advertising revenue apparently started to roll in. But this money came at a great cost. 'When we went into bed with Letlaka, we had to change the newspaper's editorial policy,' Peta explained. 'We could no longer do stories that could be seen as being anti-Ace. It wasn't a question of being pro-ANC, we had to be pro-Ace.' Gone were the days of the *Free State Times*'s corruption exposés. The newspaper's reports on Magashule and his administration instead began to look remarkably like *The Weekly*'s. For instance, in December 2013, the *Free State Times* ran two stories that depicted Magashule as a good leader ('Hlasela has done wonders' and 'Premier orders jobs for widows').[39]

However, the marriage between the *Free State Times* and Letlaka did not last long. In 2014, Ntsele pulled out of the agreement after a series of disputes with Peta over how the business should be run. Peta once again had full control of his newspaper, but it was too late to save it. 'Ntsele was the conduit for the government advertising revenue,' Peta said. 'After he left, we again had no revenue.' The newspaper that once shone a light on corruption in the province finally closed for good in 2015.

Volksblad was apparently also subjected to an advertising boycott of sorts by Magashule's administration. Gert Coetzee, the newspaper's editor, told me they experienced a decline in government ad spend after Magashule became premier. Like Peta, Coetzee was critical of the provincial government's strong financial support of *The Weekly*. 'It's not much different from the National Party's info scandal, only nowadays it is done openly, and it doesn't come across as a scandal any more,' he quipped.

The Weekly was not the only media outlet that seemingly received advertising revenue in exchange for favourable coverage of the Magashule administration. As will be shown in the following chapter, the Guptas' *The New Age* earned a significant portion of its advertising income from the Free State provincial government. I spoke to two former journalists about their experiences at the Guptas' publication. Both were adamant that Magashule had a direct line to the Guptas and that this relationship influenced the newspaper's reportage.

Cathy Dlodlo, who now heads up radio station OFM's newsroom, was one of *The New Age*'s early staffers after the Guptas launched the paper in 2010. Like most South Africans, Dlodlo at that stage had little knowledge of the wealthy brothers and their state-capture plans. She therefore tackled her job at *The New Age* as she would have done at any other publication. With her knack for investigative reporting, Dlodlo wrote stories that cast Magashule's government in a bad light. 'For example, I would get the auditor-general's report on the province's horrific finances and write about that,' Dlodlo told me.

This quickly got her in hot water with the newspaper's powerful owners. 'I was asked to tone down my negative reports on Ace and the province,' she said. 'The request first came from someone lower down. But then Atul Gupta came through to Bloemfontein one day and spoke to me directly. He asked me to stop writing such stories, but I refused.' The Guptas then tried to fire her for insubordination. Dlodlo took *The New Age* to court and won the case. The High Court in Bloemfontein ordered the Gupta-owned publication to pay out the remainder of her salary,[40] after which Dlodlo left the paper for good.

Another former *The New Age* reporter, who asked to remain anonymous, claimed that Magashule sometimes directly determined which stories or events would be included in the publication's news diary. 'I literally had to follow Ace around and create positive coverage on him,' this journalist told me. 'For instance, when he opened houses as part of Operation Hlasela, I needed to be there. He sometimes phoned me directly to tell me where I had to be.'

Magashule's influence apparently also extended to the public broad-caster. Thuso Motaung, a presenter at the SABC's Lesedi FM radio station, which reaches over three million listeners, is said to have been close to Magashule. According to my sources, Motaung often praised the former premier on air. As we will see in Chapter 21, Motaung travelled to Cuba with Magashule in early 2015.

One former SABC reporter claimed that Magashule also influenced the public broadcaster's news diary for the region. Magashule allegedly instructed then SABC COO Hlaudi Motsoeneng to make a key appointment at the SABC's regional office in the Free State. The source claimed the appointee ensured that Magashule received very good coverage. 'On some days we had environmental issues or other stories on our diary, but, after Ace or one of his MECs called, the whole diary would change. We then instead had to run after the politicians and cover their events,' claimed the former SABC staffer.

Magashule's grip on *The New Age*, *The Weekly* and the SABC's local office ensured that a sizeable portion of the province's population saw, read or heard only sanitised reports of his and his administration's conduct.

A younger Ace Magashule (right) with Thabo Manyoni, who later became mayor of the Mangaung (Bloemfontein) metro. The source who gave me the picture suggested it was taken at some point circa 1990, after Magashule had returned from a short stint in exile in Zambia and Tanzania.

Large commemorative vases in Tumahole, the township near Parys where Ace Magashule grew up, bear the names of erstwhile struggle heroes who hailed from the area. Stompie Seipei, perhaps Tumahole's most famous son, was brutally murdered in Soweto in 1989.

Left: This picture of Ace Magashule may have been taken at some point between 1997 and 2002, when he served as a member of Parliament in Cape Town. Magashule was effectively 'banished' to Cape Town amid the never-ending squabbles between the Free State ANC's rival factions.

© Felix Dlangamandla

© Gallo Images / City Press / Leon Sadiki

Magashule at an NEC meeting in Midrand in late 2008, one of the last NEC gatherings before he became premier. A year before, Magashule had helped Jacob Zuma rise to power at Polokwane. Zuma seemingly rewarded Magashule by appointing him premier, a position Magashule had viewed as rightfully his since the 1990s.

Magashule (centre), Jacob Zuma (right) and other politicians and businesspeople about to release white doves during an unveiling ceremony in 2012 for the statue of Nelson Mandela on Naval Hill in Bloemfontein. Less than a week after this photo was taken, the ANC re-elected Zuma as its president at the Mangaung conference, which all but guaranteed that Magashule would stay on as premier of the Free State.

Thoko Malembe, Ace Magashule's daughter, with Thato Magashule, one of his sons. Malembe was involved in several suspicious government deals in the Free State. Thato Magashule worked for politically connected Durban businessman Vivian Reddy's company, Edison Power Group. Malembe posted this picture to her Instagram account in 2014.

Magashule's daughter Thoko Malembe has greatly benefited from a R150-million low-cost housing project in an area called Vogelfontein outside the town of Bethlehem. Magashule has denied that he influenced the contract, but he was seemingly involved right from the start. This picture, taken in early 2013, shows Magashule and a group of government officials at the site for the new houses. Peering over the then premier's shoulder is Jianliang Li, Malembe's business partner.

This now deserted fuel station in Phuthaditjhaba (QwaQwa) in the eastern Free State was once a thriving business that provided much-needed employment in the area. However, after a dubious property deal involving Ace Magashule's daughter and the Free State Development Corporation, the business closed down. Many of its former employees were left without an income. The business remains closed at the time of writing.

The Free State's Department of Police, Roads and Transport dished out vehicles and equipment for road maintenance to emerging small businesses in the Free State. These companies also received lucrative contracts. However, in 2015 and 2016, companies owned by family members of Ace Magashule and other top politicians were included in the programme, apparently to the exclusion of contractors without political links.

Igo Mpambani, a businessman linked to Magashule, grew up in Welkom in the Free State. Leaked emails and documents detailing some of Mpambani's business dealings, which I refer to as the IgoFiles, contain perhaps some of the most compelling information to date regarding Magashule's alleged involvement in corrupt government deals. (Supplied)

This piece of land in Tumahole near Parys was earmarked for a low-cost housing project. The Free State Department of Human Settlements paid millions of rands to a company owned by Igo Mpambani for designing certain elements of the project. Today, the field is still empty, save for litter strewn all over it, and there are no signs of a pending housing development.

© Michael Butler, *Sandton Chronicle*

On Tuesday 22 June 2017, Igo Mpambani was gunned down in broad daylight while driving his Bentley Continental GT on Sandton's Bowling Avenue. Police found almost R1 million in cash in the car. At the time of his death, Mpambani was involved in several projects funded by the Free State provincial government, including a contentious R255-million 'asbestos audit'. Documents and correspondences in the IgoFiles suggest Magashule benefited financially from Mpambani's contracts.

Then state security minister David Mahlobo, Ace Magashule and outgoing ANC president Jacob Zuma in earnest discussion at the ANC conference at Nasrec in December 2017.

Divided we stand: The ANC's latest Top Six, as elected at the party's Nasrec conference. From left to right are Jessie Duarte (deputy secretary-general), Ace Magashule (secretary-general), Gwede Mantashe (chairperson), Cyril Ramaphosa (president), David Mabuza (deputy president) and Paul Mashatile (treasurer-general). Continued tensions between rival power blocs, especially those loyal to either Ramaphosa or his predecessor, Jacob Zuma, suggest the party remains as fractured as ever. Ace Magashule is a key figure in this ongoing political tug-of-war.

The Weekly newspaper, based in Bloemfontein, was widely viewed as a mouthpiece for Ace Magashule and his political allies. The publication's favourable reportage seemingly did not end when Magashule vacated his office in the Free State to take up his position as ANC SG at Luthuli House in Johannesburg. The stack of newspapers was photographed outside the offices of *The Weekly*'s holding company in July 2018. The poster pictured here was on lamp posts in Bloemfontein in September 2018.

I met this man wearing an ANC T-shirt at a problem-ridden low-cost housing development outside the town of Vrede. His grandmother has been waiting for about three years for her house to be built on the concrete slab in the background. It is among scores of empty slabs in the area. Sources familiar with this project claimed that former president Jacob Zuma had received a 'thank-you fee' from contractors appointed by then premier Ace Magashule's provincial government to build the houses.

© Felix Dlangamandla

Ace Magashule outside Luthuli House in February 2018. Chris Ackeer, the man in the yellow shirt, has been at Magashule's side since his days as premier of the Free State

LUTHULI HOUSE, JOHANNESBURG

ZUMA RECALLED Magashule: We'll decide on process after response

BREAKING NEWS
'WE HAVE DECIDED TO RECALL PRES ZUMA'

End of an era: In February 2018, SG Ace Magashule announced that the ANC had decided to recall Jacob Zuma as head of the party. Given Magashule's allegiance to Zuma, this must have been an awkward task for him. Zuma resigned as president of South Africa a few days later. These developments had grave implications for alleged state captors associated with Zuma and Magashule. This picture shows the broadcast of Magashule's announcement on the Gupta-owned news channel ANN7. ANN7 closed down later in 2018, along with other businesses owned by the Gupta brothers.

PART V

ALL THE PRESIDENT'S PALS

13

Tea with Atul

The ANC's 2012 elective conference in Mangaung reinforced the political dominance that President Jacob Zuma and his clique first established at Polokwane five years earlier. Buoyed by a 75 per cent backing from the party's internal electorate, the Zuma faction cruised into a fresh five-year governance cycle with renewed self-assurance. This unwavering confidence fuelled the audacity with which the president's predatory associates in the business world started to loot the public purse. The next half-decade would see the Zuma-centred state-capture project mature before reaching its terrible climax. In the process, South Africa would experience some of its darkest moments.

Ace Magashule and his provincial government were at the centre of this depressing epoch. Directly after Mangaung, Magashule initiated the formation of what would become the most significant political power bloc during Zuma's second term as party leader. He first teamed up with the North West ANC chairperson, Supra Mahumapelo,[1] who became that province's premier not long thereafter. Mpumalanga strongman and premier David Mabuza joined later, and by 2015 the term 'premier league' began to appear in reports on this influential coalition. Political insiders in the Free State told me that Magashule was the 'architect' of this formation. Some of these sources moved very close to the premier during this period.

The premier league rallied behind Zuma and ensured that the scandal-ridden president survived attempts by frustrated members of the party's NEC to oust him.[2] This manoeuvring was political in nature, but there were equally important financial dealings in play. If the business representatives in Zuma's shadow state were to continue benefiting from dodgy government contracts, he needed to stay in power. His continued rule also ensured that the National Prosecuting Authority, the Hawks and other supposed bulwarks against the looting of state resources remained paralysed by the poison of political interference.

In this toxic environment, the Free State became one of the foremost sites of capture. For years, Magashule's own patronage networks had operated mostly independently from role-players outside the Free State. But around 2012, the Guptas and other businesspeople linked to Zuma began to infiltrate the province in earnest. Magashule evidently had no qualms about his boss's friends feasting on Free State contracts along with his own associates. In fact, synergy and aligned interests were the order of the day. The nexus between Zuma, Magashule and the Guptas is a case in point.

One warm Saturday morning in late 2013, Ace Magashule knocked on the door of Thabo Manyoni's Bloemfontein residence.

The arrival of the Free State premier at the home of the city's mayor might ordinarily have drawn a fair amount of attention. But these were not ordinary circumstances. There were no bodyguards, no escort vehicles and none of the flashing lights that usually announce the arrival of top-level politicians like Magashule. The only clue that the visitor was someone important was the black, government-owned BMW SUV he was driving. The premier seemingly did not want any witnesses.

Manyoni had no clue why he had been asked to accompany his boss on a trip, he told me in an interview in mid-2018. Magashule had merely told him to be ready to travel to Gauteng for an important meeting. Perhaps the mayor thought he was going to be taken to Luthuli House, the ANC's headquarters in downtown Johannesburg.

As they progressed northwards on the N1 highway, Magashule and Manyoni mostly talked shop. The 2014 national and provincial elections were around the corner, and both men would be required to help convince the bulk of the Free State's nearly 1.5 million registered voters[3] to once again gift their inky crosses to the ruling party. There was also the issue of the lists the party needed to compile of candidates it would send to the provincial legislature and the National Assembly after the elections. It was issues such as these that dominated the conversation during the four-hour drive, leaving Manyoni without any hints as to where they were going.

When they arrived at Johannesburg's southern edge, Magashule steered the BMW X5 past the exits that led to the city's CBD. Manyoni could now rule out Luthuli House as a possible destination. The premier instead continued driving up the M1, the national highway's four-lane tributary that snakes through the city's affluent, forested core.

Before they reached the point further north where the two highways again merge, Magashule took an off-ramp. The black BMW now cruised westward on one of the area's wider, tree-lined roads. After a couple of turns, the premier and the mayor entered Saxonwold, a suburb where the top-floor windows of double-storey homes peeked over tall gates and walls.

Magashule slowed as they reached a particularly large property. It was protected by a white, spiked fence perched atop an already imposing wall. This concrete bulwark stretched down the road for what seemed like hundreds of metres.

The premier turned the car onto a short, cobblestone driveway with a black gate. There was a guardhouse and several guards standing around, but the black SUV was promptly allowed onto the property. It seemed to Manyoni as if his boss had been there before.

They parked, and Magashule led the mayor up some steps and into the main entrance of one of the garish mansions that cluttered the expansive property. A male servant directed them to a sitting room with comfortable sofas. He also offered them tea, small cakes and cookies, a gesture that lent itself to what Manyoni perceived as a laid-back, informal atmosphere. But his comfort was short-lived.

They had not waited long before a chubby character with black hair and a moustache made his entrance. Manyoni thought he recognised the man's face. Before the mayor could figure out if he had seen the man before, Magashule introduced him as Atul Gupta. 'This is the person you will be working with,' Magashule told their host after giving Manyoni a brief introduction.

The mayor did not know what that was supposed to mean, but his bafflement quickly gave way to disbelief as Magashule and Atul got into the details of a plan that had clearly been in the making for some time.

Magashule explained that he would vacate his position as Free State premier not long after the elections. Apparently, he was due to be included in President Jacob Zuma's cabinet as the new national minister of communications. This was an important portfolio to Atul and his family, given their ventures in broadcasting and print media.

The plan was for Manyoni to become the new premier of the Free State. Atul told Manyoni that he viewed the province as an important partner in his family's businesses. He also boasted about the power and influence his family wielded within the ruling party and within Zuma's government.

The Guptas donated a lot of money to the ANC, he said, including generous donations to the party's coffers in the Free State.

In fact, the Guptas could 'invest' R400 million in a plan to bring Bloemfontein's decommissioned coal-fired power station back to life. Some of this money could then be channelled towards the ruling party for the upcoming elections, Atul said.

Their host's swagger swelled as he continued to talk. 'If we call any cabinet minister right now, he or she will be here in an hour,' he boasted.

Then came one of the not-so-subtle threats that the Guptas would later become notorious for issuing during such conversations. 'We have files on cabinet ministers and other politicians in the basement,' Atul told Manyoni.

The implication of this remark was not lost on the mayor. Government officials who refused to work with the powerful family would be dealt with by having their darkest secrets revealed to the world. All Manyoni had to do was 'work with them' once he became premier, Atul said.

One of the projects in the metro that the Guptas had their eyes on was the R11-billion business and residential node that was going up near Bloemfontein's airport, Manyoni was told.[4]

The family also desired more advertising revenue from Free State government departments and municipalities for their newspaper, *The New Age*. When Manyoni told him that these entities did not really have big advertising budgets, Atul responded: 'It isn't really about the money, it is about power.'

Magashule chipped in now and then in an effort to persuade Manyoni to warm up to their host. It must have been obvious to him and Atul that the mayor was horrified.

When the premier excused himself to go to the bathroom, Atul told Manyoni that his 'body language' betrayed a lack of enthusiasm. 'It doesn't look like you want to work with us,' he observed.

Given Manyoni's apparent unwillingness to play along, conversation soon fizzled – but not before Atul made one last attempt to persuade him to join their ranks. He produced a large A4 envelope stuffed with cash and handed it to the mayor. This was for 'organisational work', Atul told him. A shocked Manyoni quickly handed the envelope to Magashule. He wanted no part in their murky dealings.

Magashule and Manyoni then took their leave and drove back to Bloemfontein.

About a month later, however, the pair was back in Saxonwold. Magashule had again driven Manyoni up the N1 in his black BMW X5 to the family's compound, where Atul Gupta tried to 'court' the mayor for a second time.

Magashule once again laid out the plan for Manyoni to succeed him as premier. 'Ace said he looked forward to me taking over as premier, because then he wouldn't have to deal with the province's problems any more,' Manyoni told me.

But Manyoni once again disappointed them with his lack of enthusiasm for the plan. After this second visit, no further attempts were made to try to lure him into the Guptas' state-capture network, Manyoni said.

The former mayor now believes that his unwillingness to work with the Guptas led to his political demise. The events that followed certainly suggest this may be true.

After the elections in 2014, Zuma did install a new minister of communications. However, it was Faith Muthambi and not Magashule who replaced Yunus Carrim in the portfolio.

Manyoni thinks he may have 'ruined' the grand plan to include Magashule in Zuma's cabinet with his negative responses at Saxonwold. Having no one they could trust to take over as premier in the Free State meant that Magashule had to stay where he was.

Despite the failure of what appeared to have been plan A, Muthambi proved to be a most helpful communications minister as far as the Guptas were concerned. The so-called #GuptaLeaks, a series of leaked emails and documents from servers of Gupta-owned companies, later revealed that she had emailed important documents relating to the broadcasting industry to one of the family's known lieutenants.[5]

Manyoni's relationship with Magashule, meanwhile, started to deteriorate in 2014 and throughout the following year.

In June 2016, as the ANC was preparing for that year's local government elections, the party gave Manyoni the boot as Mangaung's mayor. After a meeting of its NEC, it announced the names of several 'mayoral candidates' for the upcoming elections.[6] It was the first time ever that the ANC released such a list.

The would-be mayor for Mangaung was Olly Mlamleli, a staunch Magashule ally. According to Manyoni, he was led to believe that he would simply swop places with Mlamleli, who at that point served as the Free

State's MEC for cooperative governance, traditional affairs and human settlements. Manyoni was told that the NEC, the party's highest authority between elective conferences, had sanctioned the decision. Given his background as chairperson of the South African Local Government Association, the intended move made sense to him.

But it was not to be. Instead, Manyoni was sent to Parliament in Cape Town and social development MEC Sisi Ntombela was moved into Mlamleli's former position in October 2016. Ntombela, who is also considered a close ally of Magashule, succeeded the latter as premier in 2018.

Manyoni saw this as a plan devised by Zuma to move him into a far less visible and influential political position. If indeed the case, it did not go unnoticed by Zuma's fellow NEC members.

When Manyoni later attended an NEC meeting in his capacity as SALGA's chairperson, ANC secretary-general Gwede Mantashe asked him why he had not become the MEC for cooperative governance. It had been an NEC decision, after all. Manyoni said an irate Mantashe confronted Magashule over the matter. The latter, of course, simply defended himself by saying that Zuma wanted Manyoni in Parliament.

The former mayor's stint as an MP in Cape Town officially started in September 2016.[7] But it would be a temporary arrangement. According to Manyoni, the distance between the Mother City and Bloemfontein did not stop Magashule from making his life difficult.

At that stage, Manyoni was still the Free State ANC's deputy chairperson, and as such was required to attend meetings of the party's PEC. These were usually scheduled for Mondays to allow PEC members who were also MPs to attend committee meetings in Parliament, which usually took place between Tuesday and Friday. But Magashule started to call PEC meetings on Tuesdays, Manyoni said. This obviously put him in a bind, seeing as he was torn between his duties as an MP and his position as a senior party leader in his home province.

By May 2017, Manyoni had had enough. He resigned as an MP after just eight months in the National Assembly. To this day, he believes that his political fate was sealed after those two awkward meetings with Atul Gupta. His account of this saga is one of the most compelling indications that Magashule participated in and actively abetted the shadowy parallel state that the Gupta family ran from their fortified seat in Saxonwold.

It seems Manyoni was not the only Free State official who was dragged to the Gupta compound by Magashule. In October 2018, news broke that Magashule and Mxolisi Dukwana, the former MEC for economic development, had allegedly visited Saxonwold in 2011.[8] In a so-called Anton Piller application submitted to the Bloemfontein High Court, Dukwana claimed that the Guptas had tried to strong-arm him into approving a R140-million property development project backed by the Free State government. He also claimed that the Guptas had offered to pay him R2 million a month for ten years if he signed off on the deal, and that all of this occurred in Magashule's presence.[9] Magashule said Dukwana's claims were 'not only baseless and malicious, but [were] also based on fabrications'.[10] Dukwana was due to testify about his alleged trip to Saxonwold at the Zondo Commission of Inquiry into allegations of state capture. At the time of writing, he had not yet appeared at the inquiry.

Documents in the #GuptaLeaks show that Magashule became increasingly prominent within the Guptas' social circles after he became premier. In November 2010, the family sent an invitation to 'Ace Magashule and partner' to attend their annual Diwali celebrations at the Saxonwold residence. It is not clear whether Magashule attended that year's event, but sources confirm that they saw him at at least one such Gupta Diwali celebration.

There are further indications of contact between Magashule and the Guptas early in his first term as premier. In January 2011, Gupta staffer Joleen Roux negotiated with a car rental company for a chauffeur-driven sedan. Apparently someone from the Gupta family or their clique was set to visit their powerful friend in the Free State.

'Can you see if there is anything available for us on Friday. We are actually waiting to get confirmation from the premier of free state office to confirm appointment,' Roux wrote in her email to the rental company.

By 2015, at the pinnacle of their capture of the state, the Guptas viewed Magashule as one of their most important allies in government. This is seen in those #GuptaLeaks related to the 2015 edition of Gupta-owned news channel ANN7's South African of the Year Awards. One document shows that Magashule was to be seated at the event with Hlaudi Motsoeneng, Faith Muthambi and Mosebenzi Zwane. The document refers to the group as the 'A team'.

We know that the Guptas did not cosy up to political leaders like Magashule for the purpose of making friends. To them, every new connection in government represented a fresh business opportunity. The Free State premier was no exception.

This is best illustrated by another document from the #GuptaLeaks. In June 2011, Santosh Choubey, a Gupta associate best known for his involvement with Sahara Computers, created an Excel spreadsheet titled 'Copy of Free State Schools'. It is a record of hundreds of government schools, Further Education and Training (FET) colleges, libraries and provincial departments that 'subscribed' to some or other Gupta-provided product or service around that time.

The document does not explicitly state the nature of the subscriptions, but I had a hunch. So I phoned a few of the schools and libraries listed. They all confirmed my suspicions: that they received copies of the now defunct *The New Age* newspaper. 'We received a small heap of *The New Age* newspapers every morning, but nobody really read them,' said one employee at a municipal library somewhere in the Fezile Dabi district municipality. 'They were mostly just left on a heap.'

The document, it would seem, is a blueprint for one of the Guptas' early coups. *The New Age* first hit the shelves in December 2010. By June the following year, it was distributing over 4 000 subscriber copies a day to those government entities listed in the spreadsheet.

The document shows that more than 1 300 copies of *The New Age* were delivered to hundreds of primary schools, high schools and FET colleges all over the province each morning. Just over 1 000 copies a day were sent to provincial government departments and municipalities, of which the Office of the Premier was the single largest subscriber. A further 1 770 copies a day were delivered to 177 libraries that fell under the custodianship of the Free State Department of Sport, Arts, Culture and Recreation.

The New Age never subjected itself to an audit of its circulation figures by the Audit Bureau of Circulations (ABC), so in order to put these subscription figures into perspective, one has to dig a little deeper and do a bit of educated guesswork.

Each year, a non-profit organisation called the South African Audience Research Foundation releases the All Media and Products Survey (AMPS), which includes detailed information on the public's consumption of newspapers. According to the AMPS data for 2011, each issue of *The New Age* had an average readership figure of 39 000 in the paper's first year in existence.[11]

Readership figures do not equate to actual physical copies. It is generally accepted that more than one person reads each copy of any given edition or issue. In South Africa, on average, one newspaper is shared by roughly seven people.[12]

Based on the AMPS readership figure of 39 000, and considering the reader-to-newspaper ratio of 7:1, *The New Age* distributed about 5 600 copies per issue in 2011. According to the average readership figure, this would suggest that the 4 200 subscriber copies sent to schools, colleges, libraries and government departments in the Free State constituted about 75 per cent of all copies sold.

Under Magashule, the Free State government appears to have been the first major tax-funded dumping ground for *The New Age*. It must have been a considerable source of stability for a new publication entering an industry that faced serious financial constraints. It leaves one wondering whether the Guptas would have been able to launch the newspaper at all had it not been for their close ties to the premier.

The bulk of any newspaper's revenue, however, does not come from its cover price. It comes from selling advertising space. Magashule's government also contributed generously in this regard. It is rather telling that one of the few full-page advertisements in *The New Age*'s pre-launch 'Heritage Day special edition' in September 2010 promoted 'the rate of service delivery by the Free State government'.[13]

A review of advertisements in *The New Age* in March 2011 revealed that, after state-owned telecommunications company Telkom, the Free State government was the paper's most frequent advertiser.[14] In 2016, the provincial government spent just shy of R4 million on advertisements in *The New Age*, amounting to half of its advertising budget for print media.[15]

The #GuptaLeaks offer further insight into the business dealings between the newspaper and Magashule's government. In January 2015, *The New Age* boss Nazeem Howa emailed an Excel spreadsheet to Rajesh 'Tony' Gupta and Kopung Ralikontsane, the director-general in the premier's office. It was a list of 'Free State debtors', presumably for advertising services. The spreadsheet gives a good idea of which Free State departments spent the most money on advertisements in the Guptas' newspaper. Of the R5 million owed to *The New Age* at the time, Magashule's office owed almost R3 million. The Department of Police, Roads and Transport and the Ngwathe local municipality, which encompasses Magashule's home-town of Parys, were among the other big spenders listed.

Money also flowed from Free State government departments to the Guptas for other media-related services. The #GuptaLeaks include a state-ment from Infinity Media Networks for services provided to the 'Free State provincial government' in 2014. It lists four separate invoices that add up to R4.4 million. Infinity was the holding company of ANN7, the twenty-four-hour news channel launched by the Guptas in 2013. The statement does not say what services were provided; the only clue is the recipient's address, Bophelo House in the Bloemfontein CBD, which, I discovered, is occupied by the Free State Department of Health.

I asked the department if it had ever been invoiced by Infinity. According to one of its finance officials, the Free State Department of Health paid Infinity an amount of R220 000 in 2014 for 'media services'. When I asked the department to elaborate on the nature of the services provided, a spokesperson said it was for a 'media breakfast networking session with provincial service delivery partners … held in Welkom'.

In September 2018, the Zondo Commission of Inquiry heard evidence from a National Treasury official who confirmed that Magashule's Free State had made a hugely disproportionate contribution to the Guptas' media empire. Jan Gilliland's data showed that the province had poured nearly R80 million into *The New Age* and Infinity Media Networks between 2011 and mid-2018. By comparison, KwaZulu-Natal, Jacob Zuma's home province and the second-biggest spender, spent just R25 million on media services from the two companies.[16]

Magashule's official diary shows the amount of direct contact he had with *The New Age* bosses. In May 2013, for instance, he had the following appointment scheduled for two different days: 'Meeting with NEW AGE (Ms [sic] Nazeem Howa & Mr Ricky Naidoo)'. Howa, who is definitely not a woman, was the newspaper's CEO and Naidoo was its politics editor before he later became editor-in-chief. And in early July 2013, Magashule had this engagement in his schedule: 'Premier meets The New Age'. All three of these meetings took place at the premier's office in Bloemfontein, according to the diary.

The Guptas seemingly used Magashule's Free State as a testing labora-tory for their state-capture schemes, which involved more than just their media ventures. Mediosa, a Gupta-linked supplier of high-tech mobile medical units, achieved notoriety mostly due to reports of dodgy contracts in Premier Supra Mahumapelo's North West province. According to *City Press*, the North West health department awarded the company a contract worth R180 million in early 2017 for mobile units that were superfluous to the province's needs. This included an upfront prepayment of R30 million.[17]

But Mediosa's operations were, in fact, first rolled out in the Free State. Cureva, as Mediosa was known before it changed its name, signed a memorandum of understanding with the Free State Department of Health in 2015. The two parties then signed a contract in early 2016 for the provision of primary healthcare services in rural areas at a cost of R954 per patient, the same rate Mediosa later offered North West. Documents in the #GuptaLeaks reveal that Cureva/Mediosa would forward R650 of each per patient payment to what appeared to be Gupta front companies in Dubai. By March 2018, the Free State health department had splurged R25 million on the Gupta-linked firm's services.[18]

A source from the Free State Department of Health provided shocking details on how Mediosa ripped off taxpayers. This government healthcare worker was based in the eastern Free State's Maluti-a-Phofung local municipality, one of the early pilot sites for the mobile units. 'Mediosa's staff would come into our hospital and take pills, other medicines and basic consumables like bandages,' he told me.

In other words, the company's mobile clinics were leeching off government facilities in the areas it was servicing. This would partly explain how Mediosa could afford to ship the bulk of its revenues to Gupta-linked companies abroad.

More terrifying, the Free State and North West were just the starting points for the scheme. Another document from the #GuptaLeaks shows that Mediosa intended rolling out its services in nearly all of South Africa's nine provinces. By doing so, the firm projected that it would rake in revenues of about R1 billion a year. But the national roll-out of the Mediosa scheme was seemingly halted by the changing political landscape and the concurrent demise of the Gupta family's business empire in South Africa.

14

A family of fixers

The Vrede dairy scandal remains perhaps the most glaring example of the callous manner in which the Guptas and their accomplices in government captured state projects that were meant to uplift poor South Africans. Court documents filed over the matter later suggested Magashule had been involved in the scandal right from the outset.

In February 2012, the then relatively obscure MEC for agriculture and rural development in the Free State, Mosebenzi Zwane, delivered his department's budget vote address in the province's legislature in Bloemfontein. Zwane had not been in this role for too long, having been parachuted out of the provincial Department of Human Settlements following 2010's R1-billion RDP advance payments fiasco, as unpacked in Part III.

Zwane stated that his department would embark on a 'multi-year mega public and private partnership business concept' to help initiate 'income generation through farming in the rural areas of the province' and, ultimately, to support 'black economic empowerment'.[1] The initiative (initially) had a budget of more than R131 million, said Zwane, and it would include a dairy hub in the Thabo Mofutsanyana district municipality in the eastern Free State.[2] 'With this investment we want to break the back of unemployment, poverty and food insecurity,' Zwane declared.[3]

Less than four months later, Zwane's department signed a contract with a little-known company called Estina. The latter was appointed as the 'implementing agent' for a dairy project in the small town of Vrede, Zwane's very own hometown. According to the agreement, Estina was required to provide a 'capital investment' of R228 million, while the provincial department would pour up to R342 million into the venture over a period of three years.[4] The project's main beneficiaries were supposed to have been eighty emerging dairy farmers that were to be identified by the department. According to the original agreement, one of Estina's main responsibilities was to set up an 'Agri-BEE company' for the venture. The emerging farmers were going to get a 51 per cent stake in this 'Agri-BEE company', while the remaining shares were to be transferred to Estina.[5]

It sounded like just the kind of plan the country needed to solve its unemployment problem, but it wasn't that simple. In May 2013, when many South Africans were still outraged by the story that a private jet carrying Gupta wedding guests had been allowed to land at Air Force Base Waterkloof, *Volksblad* newspaper revealed links between the Free State dairy venture and the controversial family from Saxonwold. Linkway Trading, a company strongly associated with the Guptas, had been one of the project's consultants, and Atul Gupta himself attended meetings during the project's planning phase, *Volksblad* reported.[6]

Despite further scrutiny from media outlets, opposition parties and civil society bodies, Magashule's provincial government kept pouring huge sums of money into Estina's bank account. Most alarmingly, the intended beneficiaries from Vrede later said they were never uplifted by the project,[7] while the dairy farm seemingly went to ruin due to mismanagement.[8]

Then came 2017's #GuptaLeaks bombshell: according to leaked emails and documents, the Guptas had allegedly funnelled more than R80 million of Estina's earnings from the dairy venture through a series of shell companies in the United Arab Emirates (UAE).[9] Of this fortune, R30 million had made its way back to South Africa to help settle the bills for their niece's lavish wedding at Sun City in 2013.

In the end, the Free State government paid Estina a whopping R334 million,[10] seemingly with little to show for it.

After Cyril Ramaphosa's victory at the ANC's elective conference at Nasrec in December 2017, the Hawks and the NPA began to move on the Estina scandal. There were raids in early 2018 at the Gupta estate in Saxonwold, at the provincial Department of Agriculture in Bloemfontein and even at Magashule's office. The Hawks arrested a group of Gupta associates, including their nephew, Varun, and three former provincial officials. But in December 2018 the NPA provisionally withdrew its charges against the eight accused. It seemed like a lack of cooperation from Indian and UAE authorities had made it impossible for the NPA to prove that the Guptas had orchestrated an elaborate cross-border money-laundering operation with the proceeds of the dairy project.[11] It remains to be seen if anyone will be convicted over the matter.

The legal proceedings may have ground to a halt, but not before one of the myriad court filings implicated Magashule as an apparent early role-player in the Vrede project. An affidavit filed by Peter Thabethe, the Department of Agriculture's former HOD and one of the Vrede accused, included a very interesting titbit. He claimed Ashok Narayan, a known Gupta associate, had acted as an 'advisor' to Magashule during early 2012, when plans for the dairy project were being put together. He also claimed that Magashule had approved a trip to India that Thabethe and Narayan embarked on in order to do research for the dairy.[12] In other words, the then premier had been intimately involved in the planning process for the controversial project, at least according to the affidavit.

In January 2018, soon after becoming secretary-general of the ruling party, Ace Magashule faced a small army of journalists for the first time in his new role. The purpose of the event was to brief the public on the outcomes of the party's first NEC meeting of the year, but the topic inevitably turned to the Guptas. After all, it was in Magashule's Free State where some of the worst Gupta-linked looting had occurred, such as the Vrede dairy scandal.

Magashule didn't say a word about his alleged role in the failed venture. 'Because we have … adopted the resolution that we must fight corruption, this is what is happening. We are saying whenever there is corruption, the law must take its place, whether it is with Vrede dairy or any other thing … So let's leave that matter. It's with the NPA, it's with the law enforcers. Whatever happens, we are actually reiterating the stance of the ANC, that we need to fight corruption wherever it rears its head.'

Magashule faced another line of questioning at the press conference. Like his boss Jacob Zuma, he had a son, Tshepiso, who worked for the Guptas, but he denied there was anything wrong with this. 'It has never been a secret,' he said. 'When I became premier he was working for the Guptas, it was not a secret, you knew as the media.'[13]

But claiming that he had been transparent about Tshepiso's role in the Gupta business empire was disingenuous. The media and public only became aware of the dubious tasks Tshepiso performed for the Guptas thanks to the #GuptaLeaks, not because the premier had been candid about what his son was doing for the controversial family.

Magashule also conveniently left out the fact that it was not just Tshepiso who was working for the Guptas. Several members of the Magashule family had been doing the Guptas' bidding, including the premier himself, as evidenced by the meetings he allegedly facilitated between Atul Gupta, Thabo Manyoni and Mxolisi Dukwana.

Tshepiso, the eldest of Magashule's sons with his wife Seipati, started working for the Guptas in November 2010, about a year and a half after his father was sworn in as premier of the Free State. He would have been about twenty-seven years old.

A spreadsheet in the #GuptaLeaks shows that Tshepiso worked as a consultant for Mabengela Investments, an entity in the Guptas' stable of companies. Duduzane Zuma was a shareholder and director of Mabengela; therefore Tshepiso would have worked alongside the president's son.

In 2012, Tshepiso earned a basic salary of just under R60 000 a month, according to the spreadsheet. Although not quite as generous as the R100 000 a month that Zuma Jnr earned at that point, for a twenty-eight-year-old it was not bad.

Tshepiso proved to be a very useful link between his father and the Guptas. The #GuptaLeaks illustrate his role as a conduit for information between the premier's administration, the ruling party and Saxonwold.

In July 2014, Magashule's chief of staff, Janet Kay, emailed the following request to Moipone Ngomane, the deputy director for international relations in the Office of the Premier: 'Tshepiso Magashule, the Premier's son has requested the Premier's itinerary whilst in India. I am not sure whether it's confidential. If not, please forward to him at [Tshepiso's email address].' Tshepiso was copied in on the email.

Ngomane responded to Kay as follows: 'We do not have the itinerary, at the time of departure the itinerary within India was not available from the Embassy.' Tshepiso forwarded this response to Tony Gupta.

Correspondence in the #GuptaLeaks shows that Tshepiso was not the only one carrying messages between Magashule and the Guptas. A day before the general election in May 2014, Mosidi Motsemme sent Tshepiso an email with a list of names and cellphone numbers for hundreds of 'FS ANC party agents'. 'It will be appreciated if air time amounting to R120 per person could be loaded today, 06 may 2014,' Motsemme wrote, adding that the request was 'as per directive of the FS ANC chairperson'. At the time, Magashule was still chair. The email was also forwarded to Kabelo Nthongoa, who then passed it on to Tony Gupta.

One media report on this exchange referred to Motsemme as 'an employee at the Free State provincial legislature'.[14] While correct, it is not the full picture. As previously mentioned, Motsemme, who is described as Magashule's 'Bloemfontein wife' in ANC circles, is the mother of two of his children. Magashule is also linked to an upmarket property in Bloemfontein's Woodlands estate owned by Motsemme. In 2015, *Volksblad* reported that the structure was allegedly in breach of building regulations.[15] The property is registered in Motsemme's name, but Magashule for some reason told the newspaper that he was the owner and that he had funded it through a bank loan.[16]

Meanwhile, none of the media reports gave further details about Nthongoa, the person who forwarded the 'directive' regarding the airtime to Tony Gupta. Some digging revealed that she is Magashule's daughter-in-law, having married Tshepiso in 2014. According to consumer trace records, Tshepiso and Nthongoa reside at an address in Avonwold Road, Saxonwold. The house is about a kilometre away from the Gupta compound and is owned by Confident Concept, one of the Gupta family's property-holding companies.

Further investigation revealed that Magashule used this property to meet up with the Gupta brothers. A source who did business with the Free State government said he was once asked to meet the premier at a residence in Saxonwold. I showed him a picture of the house in Avonwold Road and he confirmed that it was the place. When my source got there, Magashule was with a man who looked vaguely familiar. He would later realise that it was Atul Gupta.

The meeting took place in September 2015, shortly before Free State agriculture MEC Mosebenzi Zwane was appointed as the new minister of mineral resources in Zuma's cabinet. My source said Magashule and Atul discussed Zwane's imminent promotion. Apparently Magashule wanted Atul to bring certain issues concerning the appointment to Zuma's attention. 'I asked Ace why he doesn't just tell Zuma directly,' my source told me. 'He said the Guptas have more influence with Zuma than he did.'

As a national minister, Zwane went on to become one of the most prolific functionaries in the Guptas' shadow state. All indications are that he abused his position as mining minister to help the Guptas buy the Optimum Coal Mine, one of their biggest cash cows thanks to lucrative coal-supply contracts with Eskom. And when the Guptas' empire started to unravel, Zwane threatened to punish the country's major banks after they decided to close the family's accounts.

Zwane's appointment as mining minister was, it seems, facilitated by several connected businesspeople from the Free State who acted as messengers between the Guptas and Magashule. As one example, shortly before Zwane's unexpected appointment, his CV was forwarded to Tony Gupta by France Oupa Mokoena,[17] a businessman from Zwane's hometown of Vrede. One of Mokoena's companies, Koena Property Developers, had pocketed R25 million through housing contracts during Zwane's short stint as MEC for human settlements.

To say that Zwane served the Guptas well in his position at the Free State Department of Agriculture and Rural Development would be a gross understatement. As we have seen, as MEC he oversaw plans for the establishment of the Gupta-linked dairy farm in Vrede. It would have made sense for the family to elevate Zwane to the national cabinet.

And Zwane was just one example of the small band of former Free State officials from Magashule's administration with whom the Guptas chose to staff their state-capture project. As mentioned previously, when Zwane moved from human settlements to agriculture, he took with him Seipati Dlamini, who had been CFO for the cooperative governance and traditional affairs segment of the provincial housing department. In her new role as CFO for agriculture, Dlamini was involved in putting together the Vrede dairy farm project. When Zwane moved to the Department of Mineral Resources, she once again went with him. This time she was appointed as deputy director-general for mineral regulation.[18] The Vrede scheme later came back to bite her when she was arrested and charged over the matter.

In March 2017, Zwane appointed Thabo Mokoena as the mining department's new director-general, a powerful position that partly entails approving or rejecting applications for mining licences. Mokoena was no doubt well acquainted with Magashule. After all, he had been the municipal manager in Magashule's hometown of Parys from 2011 to 2013.[19] Mokoena's conduct at the Department of Mineral Resources suggests that he was as eager as Zwane to further the Guptas' interests. For instance, he fired an official for serving non-compliance notices on Gupta-owned collieries in Mpumalanga.[20]

Richard Seleke is another former Free State government official who was later called upon to serve in the Guptas' state-capture enterprise. He was the HOD at the Free State Department of Economic Development, Tourism and Environmental Affairs when he was appointed to the Transnet board in late 2014.[21] At the time, Zwane was the MEC for this department, his last posting in Magashule's executive council (apart from a brief return to agriculture) before his promotion to Zuma's cabinet. Transnet has, of course, been at the centre of the Gupta narrative.

In 2015, Seleke was appointed as director-general of the Department of Public Enterprises, the custodian of state-owned entities (SOEs) such as Transnet and Eskom. Emails in the #GuptaLeaks reveal that about six months beforehand, his résumé was sent to Duduzane Zuma from a mysterious email account with the alias 'Business Man'. Judging by the email's content, it appeared as if Seleke was behind the account. 'Evening sir please find attached my CV and supporting documents,' Business Man wrote to Zuma Jnr.[22]

More disturbingly, this same account was used to forward confidential information about certain SOEs to the Guptas.[23] Seleke denied all knowledge of the emails, but in October 2018 he stepped down as director-general amid the ongoing probes into his relationship with the controversial family.[24]

There is plenty of evidence that the Guptas also roped in Magashule's mates for their state-capture project. In 2011, the SABC made the fateful decision to appoint Hlaudi Motsoeneng as its acting chief operating officer. Despite unresolved problems with his qualifications, he was later appointed to the position permanently.

Motsoeneng, who is known to enjoy a close relationship with Magashule, grew up in QwaQwa in the eastern Free State.[25] He started his career as a journalist and presenter at Radio Sesotho, which later became the popular radio station Lesedi FM. In the mid-1990s, Motsoeneng moved from his rural hometown to Bloemfontein to work at Lesedi FM's new headquarters, where he soon ingratiated himself with the province's top politicians.

At the time, Magashule's northern camp was still involved in a fierce political battle to gain control of the Free State. Motsoeneng and some of his radio colleagues apparently sided with the Magashule bloc and provided them with a platform on Lesedi FM. 'They gave Ace airtime when he had that fight with Terror Lekota,' Mahlomola Majake, a former Free State ANC insider, told News24 in 2016. 'With their constant coverage they helped push Ace into power.'[26]

Upon being appointed to his powerful position in the SABC, Motsoeneng almost immediately entered into a costly subscription agreement for *The New Age* to be delivered daily to SABC personnel. By all accounts, the staff were not interested in reading the Guptas' newspaper, and complained about the wasteful expenditure.[27]

Motsoeneng also sought to help the Guptas by broadcasting *The New Age* (TNA) Business Briefings for free on SABC2.[28] Magashule and his provincial administration made regular use of this propaganda platform. One of the earliest TNA Business Briefings was broadcast from Ilanga Estate, an upmarket events venue outside Bloemfontein, in May 2012. The guest speaker was President Jacob Zuma.

After that, the business breakfast circus rolled into the Free State at least once a year. In December 2013, the event was held at the Barnard Molokoane High School in Magashule's hometown of Parys, according to his official diary. Magashule would use these briefings to 'unpack' his State of the Province addresses.[29]

In August 2015, public enterprises minister Lynne Brown installed Hantsi Matseke at the state-owned diamond company Alexkor as its new chairperson. A #GuptaLeaks report later revealed links between known Gupta associates and a company that had been appointed by Alexkor to market its diamonds.[30] The #GuptaLeaks also revealed that the powerful family once wanted Matseke to be appointed to the board of the South African National Roads Agency (SANRAL).[31] As mentioned previously, Matseke is one of Magashule's oldest friends from Parys. She is also in business with Magashule's daughter Thoko, and her company Friedshelf 863 benefited from the Free State housing saga of 2010. 'I have no relationship, whether personal or business, with any member of the Gupta family,' Matseke told me. She said her CV was in the public domain and was therefore accessible to anyone. 'Accordingly, I have no control over comments made by third parties, including the Gupta family, about my suitability for positions.'

In early 2018, before her own sacking as minister of public enterprises and in an apparent last-ditch effort to ensure some continuance of the Gupta capture project in the Ramaphosa era, Lynne Brown tried to have Playfair Morule appointed as Eskom's new chairperson.[32] As previously mentioned, Morule, South Africa's former high commissioner to India, is a long-serving Magashule ally. His wife, Tankiso, was among the band of connected businesspeople who secured lucrative housing contracts during Magashule's reign as premier.

There is overwhelming evidence that Magashule, his administration, his family and some of his closest friends formed key cogs in the Guptas' state-capture machinery. Under his watch as premier, the Free State pumped almost R440 million into the Guptas' coffers through the Vrede dairy farm deal, the controversial mobile clinics and payments to the family's media entities.

The Guptas plundered his home province, and it is inconceivable that Magashule played no part in it. After all, he was 'advised' on the Vrede dairy project by Ashok Narayan, one of the family's most trusted lieutenants.[33] And he personally met with *The New Age* bosses when the Free State was committing to ever-larger subscriptions of the newspaper. He allegedly took Mangaung's mayor and at least one MEC to Saxonwold for clandestine meetings with Atul Gupta. His son Tshepiso lives in a house owned by the Guptas and located a stone's throw from the former shadow state's main seat of power, a property that Magashule himself used as his Johannesburg base on at least one occasion. Furthermore, his son, his daughter-in-law and the mother of his children served as conduits for the flow of information to and from his shady friends in Saxonwold.

And finally, some of the most prominent figures in the Guptas' shadow state hailed from the Free State. Some of these people first served in Magashule's provincial government. Others were in his inner circle years before the Guptas required their help.

In light of all this, if one had to identify the foremost enabler of the Guptas' dodgy dealings in South Africa, it would be difficult to choose between Jacob Zuma and Ace Magashule.

15

Reddy to rumble

The Guptas were not the only connected businesspeople from the Zuma fold who raked in government contracts in Magashule's backyard. Enter the Reddy family. Durban-based energy tycoon Vivian Reddy is the founder of the Edison Power Group (EPG), which is probably best known for a contentious R1-billion electricity smart-meter tender it secured from the City of Johannesburg's power distributor, City Power, in 2012.[1] Reddy's son, Shantan, is Edison's deputy chairman.

Vivian Reddy has never been coy about his relationship with the ANC and Zuma. He once openly admitted that he had lent Zuma money to help pay for his Nkandla homestead.[2] When I asked if he had also donated money to the ruling party, an Edison spokesperson responded as follows: 'Mr Reddy has supported the ANC since the 80's and will never stop doing so as it's the organization that fought for our freedom and dignity.' This financial support was in no way related to the tenders Reddy's companies have clinched from the ANC-led government, insisted the spokesperson. 'Mr Reddy has publicly stated that his support for the ANC is uncon-ditional and he requires nothing in return. Ninety per cent of Mr Reddy's various business interests are in the private sector.'

The first indications of contact between Reddy and Magashule surfaced as far back as 2009. In that year, the *Mail & Guardian* reported on a court case in which it was alleged that Reddy had facilitated a meeting between businessman Bongani Biyela and Magashule. Reddy had also attended the meeting. According to the report, Biyela was trying to sell his company's stake in a casino in Welkom, but the Free State's gambling authorities appar-ently blocked the transaction. When the parties later met in Bloemfontein, the report continued, Biyela was asked to pay a 'bribe' into the account of Magashule's long-time lawyer friend Kenosi Moroka, allegedly in exchange for the then premier's support for the casino deal. At the time, Magashule, Moroka and Reddy all denied any impropriety.[3] 'The entire allegation was hogwash and part of the politics playing at that time,' an Edison spokesperson told me in December 2018. 'Mr Reddy was not "familiar" with Mr Magasule in 2009.'

If Reddy and Magashule were not well acquainted back then, they certainly became close later. When Reddy turned sixty in early 2013, the Free State premier was among the politicians and other VIPs who attended the businessman's birthday bash in Durban.[4]

And they clearly remained in touch after Reddy's party. Few people know this, but Reddy absorbed one of Magashule's children into his business empire, just as the Guptas had done with the former premier's eldest son, Tshepiso. Tshepiso's younger brother, Thato, worked for Edison Power, the crown jewel in Reddy's business empire. I picked up this titbit from sources who had once been close to Magashule's family, and it was confirmed by records I consulted. Edison confirmed that Thato had worked there, but the company denied that this in any way influenced its work in the public sector. 'Thato Magashule was partly involved in our Africa operation,' the company informed me. 'He was not involved in any of our activities in SA due to our corporate governance policy and to avoid any perception of perceived political influence.'

Magashule senior's diary, which I obtained through a Promotion of Access to Information Act application, revealed that he met Reddy in Cape Town for a 'private lunch' at the time of the ANC's 103rd birthday celebrations in January 2015. Edison said it was 'normal' for Reddy to host people on the day before the party's birthday. On this occasion, forty people from all over South Africa and two international guests attended Reddy's 'luncheon' in Cape Town, the company told me. 'There was at no time any business discussions whatsoever with anyone. It was a celebration.' Edison maintained that Magashule's diary incorrectly described the gathering. 'This was not a "private lunch" but a private function,' the company said.

During this time, Reddy's son Shantan got involved in some business activities with Magashule's daughter Thoko Malembe. In February 2015, a month after Reddy's 'function', Shantan registered a company called SVR Group. Thoko became a director in SVR two months later. 'This company was established with eight directors for a venture that did not get off the ground,' said Yuri Mohan, one of Shantan's business partners. 'All of the directors except Shantan Reddy resigned. We are unaware that Thoko Malembe is Ace Magashule's daughter.'

Whatever they may say, by around 2015 there was an undeniable level of familiarity between the Reddys and the Magashules. It serves as the backdrop to a troubling series of government contracts worth a neat R230 million awarded to one of Shantan Reddy's companies.

In February 2015, coincidentally the same month in which Shantan founded the SVR Group, the Free State Provincial Treasury awarded a R60-million contract to Central Lake Trading 149, of which Shantan Reddy is the sole director. This company trades under the name Empire Technology. It was tasked to provide the province with software that would help it manage its database of suppliers. It was known as the Free State Supplier Management System, or the FSSMS.

The contract was first advertised in *The New Age* newspaper in May 2014, according to a written response from the Free State Provincial Treasury. The department received bids from four IT firms, but it seems only Empire Technology ever stood a chance. 'Other than Empire Technology, all the other bidders did not meet the minimum score for the functionality and were therefore disqualified,' read the response. At least one of the disqualified firms has contested this assertion. 'I can guarantee that we met the minimum score. We were never informed that we didn't meet the minimum functionality score; we were simply told that we weren't successful,' the owner of one of the three losing bidders told me. The auditor-general also questioned the contract and found that it was irregular. Government departments and entities are legally required to procure IT-related goods and services through the State Information Technology Agency (SITA), but the Free State Treasury had circumvented the agency when it appointed Empire Technology, the AG found.[5]

As it turned out, Empire Technology's Free State boon was just a stepping stone to an even fatter purse. In September 2016, the *Mail & Guardian* revealed that Empire Technology had clinched a R171-million contract linked to South Africa's controversial proposed nuclear energy programme. The national Department of Energy had appointed Empire Technology to supply an IT 'management system' for the nuclear build programme.[6] Shantan Reddy's latest success could be traced all the way back to the Free State. Instead of opening a new tender process, the Department of Energy had 'piggybacked' on the Free State contract by exploiting a loophole in South Africa's procurement laws that allows state departments to transfer certain contracts between them.[7] In Chapter 21, I explain how this process works.

In this case, there were serious problems with the manner in which the transferral had been executed, the *Mail & Guardian* revealed in a follow-up report.[8] When government entities or departments share contracts, the contract values need to be roughly the same. In this instance, the value of Empire Technology's contract from the Department of Energy was almost triple that of the Free State contract. The scope of work and duration of the respective contracts also differed too greatly to qualify for a lawful transferral, National Treasury later warned the Department of Energy in a letter.[9] The AG subsequently found that Empire Technology's contract from the energy department had also been irregular, just like that of its project in the Free State.[10] Empire Technology's nuclear contract was halted in January 2017, but by then the company had already pocketed almost R100 million.[11] This was on top of the R60 million that Empire Technology had secured from the Free State government shortly before.

According to the *Mail & Guardian*'s second report, a key player in the Department of Energy's efforts to piggyback on Empire Technology's Free State contract had been Thabane Zulu, the department's director-general. After Empire Technology won the Free State bid, Zulu approached Yuri Mohan, Shantan Reddy's partner in Empire Technology, requesting the company's 'approval' for the transfer.[12] Empire Technology naturally had no objections. In December 2015, Mohan told Zulu that the company would accept the latest contract.

Zulu's involvement immediately piqued my interest. As I explain in Part VII, he played a key role in another controversial contract transferral involving a R255-million asbestos audit from the Free State Department of Human Settlements. Zulu was director-general of the national Department of Human Settlements before being moved to energy.

Regarding Empire Technology's two successive IT contracts, the circumstances and sequence of events were curious. Without the Free State contract, the company would not have been able to clinch the even larger national contract, as orchestrated by Zulu. Why didn't the Department of Energy run its own tender process? And how did Zulu find out about Empire Technology's contract from the Free State Provincial Treasury in the first place?

I put these questions to Zulu and the Department of Energy, but did not get much of an answer. 'The matter of Empire Technology is under investigation by the Office of the Public Protector,' the energy department informed me. 'Therefore, it is the Department's view to allow the Public Protector to conclude her investigation without prejudicing any information under investigation.'

I could not help but wonder whether the Reddy family's ties to Magashule and two of his children somehow played a role in the first of the two contracts awarded to Empire Technology, namely the R60-million contract from the Free State Provincial Treasury. When I asked the treasury if this was the case, the answer was a simple 'no'. Empire Technology said it was insulted by the suggestion. 'We are not aware of any role that the premier played in the award[ing] of this contract,' Mohan told me. 'We deny the offensive allegation that the alleged friendship [between Vivian Reddy and Ace Magashule] influenced [our] business success in the Free State.'

Vivian Reddy seemed especially keen to put distance between him and his son's company. After the *Mail & Guardian* first reported on Empire Technology's R171-million nuclear contract, Reddy took the newspaper to the Press Ombudsman. He took umbrage at being mentioned in a report about his son's activities. The Press Ombudsman's appeals panel eventually decided that the *Mail & Guardian* only needed to revise its headline. Instead of saying 'Zuma pals clinch first nuclear deal', in reference to both Vivian and Shantan, the headline should have mentioned only one 'Zuma pal', namely Shantan.[13]

But I subsequently found plenty of proof that Edison and Empire Technology were closely linked. On their respective websites, both companies list the same address in Umhlanga for their KwaZulu-Natal offices. For its Gauteng office, Empire Technology lists an address on Sandton's bustling 5th Street. When I went looking for their premises, I found the name 'Edison Power Group' on the office building's shiny exterior. And when I phoned Edison's Sandton office and asked a receptionist if I could speak to Shantan Reddy, she told me he was out, but that she would take a message. There's more. Shantan and Yuri Mohan attended the 2015 edition of the Association of Municipal Electricity Utilities' annual conference, according to a list of delegates.[14] At the time of the event, Empire Technology had already secured its R60-million contract from the Free State government. However, according to the delegates list, Reddy and Mohan attended the conference as representatives of 'Edison Power Group'. Finally, when I approached Mohan for comment in late 2018, he asked me to send him queries via email. 'Send it to yuri@edison ...,' he began, before quickly correcting himself and giving me his email address at Empire Technology. Curious, I copied the emails to the Edison address, and they seemed to go through.

When I asked Vivian Reddy about the close links between Empire Technology and Edison, his spokesperson, Brian Mpono, responded rather aggressively. 'Your unsubstantiated malicious false allegations are considered hostile and offensive,' he huffed. 'Empire and Edison Power Group are two separate entities. Vivian Reddy is not involved in any manner whatsoever with Empire Technology.' He said Edison and Empire did not share an office in Umhlanga, but failed to explain why the two companies listed the same address on their websites. He did, however, admit that Shantan's partner in Empire Technology was linked to Edison. 'Yuri Mohan does some consulting work for Edison Power,' Mpono told me.

'Both companies are independent entities and there is no cross-shareholding whatsoever and they operate in different ambits of business,' Mohan concurred.

I got the distinct impression that Edison and Vivian Reddy did not want me sniffing around Shantan's work in the Free State. When I first sent him queries, Mpono was quick to fire off this warning: '[Vivian Reddy] is very principled and does not hesitate to report misrepresentations and false perceptions created by the media to the Press Ombudsman and in some cases [he has] even sued.'

Then something strange happened. In response to my queries about the apparent links between Edison and Empire Technology, Mpono made this claim: 'Mr Reddy is currently in litigation with the *Mail & Guardian* for defamation so this issue is sub judice.' But I later learnt this was not the case. The *Mail & Guardian* said they were not being sued by either Vivian Reddy or Edison. Mpono subsequently claimed that there had been a mix-up; Edison was in fact suing *City Press*, not the *Mail & Guardian*. This was over a report on Edison's City Power smart-meter contract in Johannesburg, an entirely different matter.

I continued digging and recalled an explosive newspaper report from September 2018. The *Sunday Times* had revealed that Magashule, Zuma and a host of other ANC figures opposed to President Cyril Ramaphosa had held a series of clandestine meetings in Durban. The purpose of these gatherings was to plan a fightback against Ramaphosa and his allies, the newspaper reported. Magashule, former South African Airways chairperson

Dudu Myeni and former North West premier Supra Mahumapelo alleg-edly attended one of the meetings at Durban's Beverly Hills hotel. When the gathering broke up, some of the alleged conspirators got into two Mercedes-Benzes, one of which belonged to Dudu Myeni's son, Thalente. (He features in the next chapter.) The other car apparently belonged to the son of a well-known Durban businessman, the newspaper reported. ANC leaders who spoke to the *Sunday Times* claimed the clandestine 'plot' and related activities were being funded by 'tenderpreneurs' who had benefited from government contracts during Zuma's time as president.[15]

The newspaper did not divulge the name of the latter individual, but I later got some interesting information from Qaanitah Hunter, one of the *Sunday Times* journalists who broke the story. The other Mercedes belonged to a company owned by Shantan Reddy, she told me. When the story was published, the *Sunday Times* could not get hold of him for comment, so they left out his name. Hunter gave me the car's registration details. The Mercedes had been registered to Central Lake Trading 149, or Empire Technology, the very company that so richly benefited from consecutive contracts from the Free State Provincial Treasury and the national Department of Energy. Empire Technology's Mercedes was a white 2016-model SUV, which meant it had been purchased after the company secured the two government contracts.

'Our instructions are to deny that Mr. S Reddy of our client [Empire Technology] had any knowledge of the alleged meeting at the Beverly Hills Hotel and furthermore, we have been instructed to place on record that Mr S. Reddy was out of the Republic at the time of the alleged meet-ing,' Empire Technology's lawyer told me in a letter. He strongly denied any suggestion that Empire Technology or Shantan Reddy were involved in funding the meeting or any other 'political projects'.

But the alleged Durban plot was just the tip of the iceberg. My sources, including a former colleague of Magashule in the Free State's executive council, described a disconcerting level of familiarity between the former premier and Shantan Reddy. It is a relationship that apparently goes back several years. One source recalled that the businessman once drove to the Free State in 2012 to meet with Magashule on the sidelines of a lekgotla for executive council members and mayors. 'We were meeting at the Philip Saunders Resort outside Bloemfontein. Shantan and Ace held a private meeting,' said the source, who had been privy to parts of the talks between

Magashule and Reddy. The source claimed the meeting had been about a tender with a government entity that Reddy had apparently lost out on. Reddy maintained this never happened. 'Insofar as you allege that you have been informed of a private meeting held between Mr. S. Reddy and Mr. Magashule, in and during 2012, our instructions are to deny that such a private meeting occurred,' said Reddy's lawyer.

In late 2018, I received even more intriguing information regarding alleged meetings between Shantan Reddy and Magashule. Two sources with direct knowledge of the Reddy family's business dealings, whom I interviewed independently of one another, alleged that Magashule was a regular visitor to Edison and Empire Technology's offices in Sandton throughout 2015. Both sources claimed that they had on several occasions witnessed with their own eyes how Magashule had walked out of the office building, and they were both able to recollect striking details about these alleged visits.

At the time, Empire and Edison occupied the first floor of a building near the Michelangelo Towers hotel at Sandton's Nelson Mandela Square. Edison only later moved to its current address on 5th Street. The Signature Hotel now occupies the building that housed their former offices. One of my sources was able to provide me with a floor plan for Edison and Empire's old offices, including the exact location of the offices of Shantan, Yuri Mohan and the fifteen-odd other employees who worked with them in that building. This source showed me in which office Magashule and Shantan usually met. He said he could not remember exactly how many times Magashule came to Empire and Edison's offices, seeing as it had been a 'regular occurrence'. The source claimed Magashule and his driver frequently left the building carrying large bags.

My second source corroborated the story about the bags. He claimed he had bumped into Magashule at Empire's Sandton offices on two occasions in late 2015, about a month apart. He showed me where Magashule's driver had parked the car in which they had arrived, near the entrance to the basement parking on the northern side of Nelson Mandela Square. 'When they were done meeting with Shantan, Ace and the driver would walk out of the building carrying large travel bags. They put the bags in the back of their car. All of this was done very openly and casually,' said this source.

I had a look at Magashule's diary. It was interesting to note that, compared to previous years, he more frequently attended unspecified meetings in Johannesburg in 2015. I excluded meetings in Johannesburg for which his diary indicated a specific purpose or destination, such as 'Luthuli House' or 'AU Summit'. (His stop at the AU Summit in Sandton, coincidentally, occurred in December 2015 and was followed by a 'family visit' in 'Saxon world', according to the diary.) In 2013, Magashule attended only one unspecified meeting in Johannesburg, according to his diary. This increased to two in 2014, both in January. In 2015, the year in which my sources claimed to have often seen Magashule at Shantan's Sandton offices, the premier had no less than five unspecified meetings in 'Sandton' or 'Jhb', the diary indicated.

Shantan Reddy's company strongly denied my sources' claims. 'Any suggestion that a visit by any ANC or Government official to our client's offices [occurred], be it in Johannesburg or Durban, in relation to business dealings, is specifically denied on the basis that our client and/or its Directors have never engaged any ANC or Government officials in regards to its business, all such business of our client having been done and secured through a rigorous and compliant public process,' said Empire Technology's lawyer, adding that the allegations were 'malicious' and 'outrageous'.

Edison's lawyers also strongly denied the allegations regarding Magashule's visits to the Sandton offices and said they were 'nothing more than scandalous and malicious rumour-mongering'.

16

Zuma's Vrede 'thank-you fee'

If one were to map the Gupta family's state-capture exploits, the tiny Free State town of Vrede would feature as a prominent point of interest, along with Dubai, Saharanpur, Saxonwold, Sun City and their former coal mines in Mpumalanga.

The Vrede dairy scandal is one of the most notorious examples of how state resources were allegedly plundered by friends of Jacob Zuma and his ally in the Free State, Ace Magashule. But Vrede also fell prey to another, previously unknown scandal, one that appears to bear Magashule's and Zuma's fingerprints. In this chapter, I reveal how more than R220 million in taxpayers' money was earmarked for a disaster-ridden housing development on the town's outskirts. A band of politically connected contractors were appointed to build 1000 houses for some of Vrede's poorest inhabitants, yet five years after the project began, less than 200 houses were finished. But of greater concern was the fact that, while digging up information on this deal, I began to hear rumours that one of the contractors had channelled a R2-million 'thank-you fee' to Zuma. At first, I didn't make much of this, but information I would later obtain made me pause.

The saga took place while the public and the media were focused on the infamous dairy scandal playing out around the corner from the housing project. As usual, some of the country's most destitute citizens paid the price for what appears to have been a toxic combination of mismanagement, incompetence and possible corruption.

The saga begins in Jacob Zuma's home province of KwaZulu-Natal, where, in 2010, a company called Khaya Readykit started doing work for government.[1] Khaya Readykit specialises in alternative building technologies (ABT). It has a patent on special timber wall panels that are manufactured in factories and then transported to building sites, where they are erected on top of concrete foundations, and covered with a bind-ing agent and a few layers of plaster. According to the company's website, this method allows it to finish new structures much faster than traditional building contractors can. In addition, the buildings are allegedly just as durable as houses with brick walls, but cheaper to put together.[2] The technique can be used for low-cost housing, clinics and classrooms.

Khaya Readykit's promise of cheaper, better structures caught the attention of officials in KwaZulu-Natal. To navigate the province's highly politicised construction environment, the company hired a 'contracts agent' for its work with government.[3] Considering the function this person was required to perform, however, he could be described as a 'fixer' of sorts. This role was assigned to businessman Vikash Narsai, who appears to have operated on the periphery of Zuma's circle.

Narsai's company, VNA Consulting, brands itself as a 'multi-disciplinary professional services consultancy' in South Africa's 'built environment'.[4] VNA is also unabashedly pro-ANC. In 2012, the company bought a full-page advert in the Progressive Business Forum's magazine, *Progressive Leader*. Next to an image of the ANC flag superimposed onto a map of South Africa, Narsai congratulates the party on its 100th birthday, saying that VNA is 'a proud supporter of the African National Congress ideology'.[5]

Narsai featured vaguely in the Arms Deal mess. He was listed as witness number 136 in the state's list of witnesses for the matter.[6] During a meeting with him in 2018, Narsai told me he had been dragged into the Arms Deal probe as a result of VNA's involvement with the Development Africa Trust, set up by Vivian Reddy, the businessman we met in the previous chapter. In his judgment in the Schabir Shaik trial, Judge Hilary Squires found that money from French arms supplier Thales was flushed through Reddy's trust and ultimately used to help pay for the first upgrades to Zuma's Nkandla homestead in the early 2000s.[7]

But Narsai was adamant that his company had nothing to do with Zuma's Arms Deal shenanigans or the Nkandla upgrades. He told me that VNA had worked alongside Reddy's trust on King Goodwill Zwelithini's palace, and that the Scorpions investigators had mistakenly identified VNA as a role-player in Zuma's Arms Deal payments. The Scorpions had been 'off the mark', Narsai told me.

More than a decade later, however, VNA did become involved with Zuma and a construction project near Nkandla. Between 2010 and 2012, Narsai seems to have delivered in his role as a 'contracts agent' for Khaya

Readykit. The company clinched contracts to build thirty early childhood development (ECD) centres for the KwaZulu-Natal provincial government.[8] But it would turn out to be a cursed deal for Khaya Readykit.

In an anonymous letter to a community newspaper in 2017, one of the company's directors later explained what happened. 'We were being set up by the KZN [KwaZulu-Natal] contracts agent [Narsai] who directed that the healthy profit [from the ECD centre contracts] be spent delivering free houses to ANC beneficiaries around KZN including eventually 15 of them at Nkandla,' this person alleged.[9] A source familiar with the matter agreed with this interpretation. 'Narsai motivated for this by saying that Khaya Readykit would get much bigger contracts as a result of the houses we donated,' the source told me. Narsai denied that he or VNA ever made such promises. He also denied having a close relationship with Zuma, although he admitted that VNA had worked on projects for one of the former president's organisations. 'VNA was not involved in the donation of houses prior to 2013 to the Jacob Zuma Foundation as Khaya [Readykit] was already working with the then ANC Youth League in the Province of KZN,' Narsai claimed in an email. 'VNA's involvement with the Jacob Zuma foundation only started in June 2014 when Khaya Readykit was approached and I was the person that was introduced to the Foundation by the owner [of Khaya Readykit].'

During an earlier interview, the businessman admitted that he had been involved in Khaya Readykit's decision to donate houses in KwaZulu-Natal, but he said the figures were lower than the fifteen mentioned in the newspaper article. 'We donated four houses to the Zuma foundation, and only one of them was at Nkandla. The rest were all over the province,' he told me.

Video footage on the Government Communication and Information System YouTube channel shows Zuma handing over one of Khaya Readykit's houses to a beneficiary at Nkandla in August 2013. Flanked by then social development minister Bathabile Dlamini and a small army of politicians, businessmen and bodyguards, Zuma can be seen cutting a ribbon wrapped around one of the houses before taking an appreciative beneficiary inside her new abode. The president then claims that the Sizakele MaKhumalo Zuma Foundation, a charitable entity headed by his first wife, funded the project.[10]

We now know that the houses were sponsored by Khaya Readykit, which seemingly made the donation in the hope of winning bigger government contracts. The donation could not have come at a better time, as Zuma was at the centre of a political firestorm over the state's latest upgrades to his homestead. What better way to placate supporters in his immediate surroundings than to give them new houses?

About 300 kilometres from Nkandla, residents of the eastern Free State town of Vrede were looking forward to receiving new houses of their own. In August 2013, the same month in which Zuma handed over the houses built by Khaya Readykit in Natal, the council of the Phumelela local municipality, which includes Vrede, approved a layout plan for 1700 new residential erven on the town's outskirts in order to house people from the nearby Thembalihle township.[11] What the poor township residents did not know was that powerful politicians were allegedly concocting plans to capture the budget for this new development. Their hopes of becoming homeowners would eventually be dashed by the very leaders who were supposed to have looked after their interests.

At this stage, the Free State provincial government was already pouring money into the Vrede dairy project, just a stone's throw away from the proposed housing development. The Gupta-linked dairy venture had by then begun to attract some media attention,[12] but the scheming around the nearby low-cost housing project remained under wraps.

A source from the construction industry who was intimately involved in the project alleged that Zuma and Magashule were pulling the strings. This source, who attended meetings with Magashule, said he was shocked by the premier's brazenness. 'Ace met with me and told me that the old man [Zuma] was behind the Vrede houses,' he claimed. 'He told me Zuma needed money and that we therefore needed to get the project going.'

This source explained how the 'corrupt scheme', as he called it, was put together. 'From the outset the Vrede project was a means to take money out of the national Department of Human Settlements,' he told me in 2018. 'To avoid governance issues, the Free State province was identified as a safe haven to facilitate this. An amount was transferred to the province from which transactions would be made. This included a "thank-you fee" to Zuma.' This was the first time I heard the phrase 'thank-you fee' in connection with the Vrede RDP project, but it wouldn't be the last.

Current and former FSHS insiders became suspicious when companies from KwaZulu-Natal, and not the Free State, were contracted for the project. The department appointed Tekeweni Civils, an outfit from Durban, as the main contractor, with Narsai's VNA acting as its consultant. Tekeweni and VNA then subcontracted Khaya Readykit, seeing as government wanted the houses to be built using ABT methods. All of this was done without a tender process. 'The contract was awarded by our department, but it was on a directive from the national Department of Human Settlements. We started to refer to it as Zuma's houses,' one FSHS insider told me. The letter from the anonymous Khaya Readykit director seemingly also confirmed the president's involvement in the Vrede housing project. Zuma 'arranged' the project, this person claimed.[13] Yet another FSHS source alleged that after a meeting between Zuma and Magashule in 2013, department officials were informed that the province would invest in a new low-cost housing development in Vrede.

The FSHS denied that Zuma and Magashule planned the project, but admitted that the contract was awarded without a tender process. In its written response to me, the FSHS said the contract had not needed to go out on tender because the project formed part of the national department's Enhanced People's Housing Process (EPHP). The EPHP programme allows for beneficiaries of low-cost housing to determine who the contractors should be, the FSHS explained. 'In this case consultation with [the] beneficiaries was conducted and they chose the Alternative Building Technology to be used for their houses resulting in the appointment of said contractors,' the department told me.

I visited Vrede in November 2018, and the residents I spoke to claimed they were not consulted. 'We just heard the province was going to build houses for us; we didn't know how the contractors were appointed,' said one Vrede local.

Narsai said the national Department of Human Settlements brought VNA in for the Vrede project in late 2013 because of its earlier work with Khaya Readykit. This confirmed what I had already been told, namely that the project's origins were in national government and not at provincial level.

But there was a potential hitch. As we saw in Part III, the national government in the past took back money for housing projects that the FSHS had been unable to spend. If this were to happen again, the Vrede development risked running out of money.

Faced with a housing department that could not spend its budget, the Magashule administration needed to find new ways to keep its claws in the province's housing allocation, maintained my sources. If the FSHS could transfer its unspent money to third-party entities tasked with housing-related projects, the national government would not be able to reapportion large chunks of the province's housing budget.

The FSHS's annual reports contain clues as to how the alleged plan was rolled out. In the 2012/13 financial year, the department transferred over R200 million of its unspent grant money to the Housing Development Agency, the Social Housing Regulatory Authority and two private funds for housing-related projects.[14] In other words, instead of forfeiting its unspent housing grant to national government, the department chose to transfer the monies to third parties. These entities were supposed to use this money for projects related to housing. The total amount the FSHS transferred to third-party entities more than tripled to R620 million in the following financial year.[15] This time, some of the largest transfers were made to entities whose principals and other officials were said to be close to Magashule. Bloem Water, for instance, received R230 million to 'expedite the delivery of water and sanitation services to [housing] beneficiaries within [the] Free State'.[16] The chair of Bloem Water, Bernard Tefetso Phitsane, is a former business partner of Magashule and his son Tshepiso.[17]

Phitsane also sat on the board of the Free State Development Corporation, along with two other known Magashule associates: Thoko Malembe's business partner Hantsi Matseke, who was appointed FDC board chair in 2012;[18] and Magashule's former business partner Blacky Seoe. At the end of 2013, Ikhraam Osman became the entity's new CEO. Osman had worked under Magashule when the latter was still an MEC. In fact, sources told me that Osman was among the five officials at Magashule's Department of Economic Affairs and Tourism who were suspended in 1996 by then premier Mosiuoa Lekota over allegations of dodgy financial dealings.[19]

Like Bloem Water, the FDC received some of the FSHS's unspent funds. In late 2013, the provincial government approved the transfer of up to R100 million from the housing department to the FDC 'to facilitate the pilot implementation of alternative building technology (ABT) in a people's housing process (PHP) project in Thembalihle Ext 4, Vrede', according to a government gazette from March 2014. The FDC was to act as 'account administrator' for the construction of 1000 subsidised houses in the eastern Free State town.[20] This was all part of the plan. 'Paying the money to the FDC was a much safer bet, seeing as Ace was very close to the FDC's leadership,' one of my sources alleged.

The department subsequently transferred just over R50 million to the FDC in 2013/14,[21] and another R12 million the following financial year.[22] For some inexplicable reason, in its 2013/14 annual report the department stated that the money was meant for the 'procurement of land'.[23] Yet an earlier township planning report confirmed that the site for the proposed houses was situated on a portion of the farm Krynaauwslust, which belonged to the local municipality.[24] Therefore, there appears to have been no need to procure any land for the proposed development. Another portion of the same farm was later controversially leased to the Gupta-linked Estina for Vrede's disastrous dairy venture.

Meanwhile, the auditor-general picked up that all was not well with the department's strategy of transferring unspent grant money to third-party entities such as the FDC and Bloem Water. 'The transfer of a portion of the human settlement development grant (HSDG) to the receiving entity was not made in accordance with section 16(2) of DORA [Division of Revenue Act], as the payment schedule was not approved by Treasury,' read the AG's 2013/14 report on the department.[25] It is not clear which 'receiving entity' was being referred to. The AG also bemoaned the fact that the department had failed to surrender unspent conditional grant monies that National Treasury had forbidden it to keep. Nevertheless, the FDC now sat with a sizeable chunk of the province's housing funds. If the FDC had received the money in an unlawful manner, it would be a long and arduous journey for national government to retrieve it.

In early 2014, the Vrede housing project kicked into gear. After the official site handover in January, work commenced in May that year.[26] By October, less than six months into the project, the first signs of trouble surfaced. The FDC had paid Tekeweni, the contractor from KwaZulu-Natal, just over R40 million in three instalments, including an 'EPHP advance' payment in April.[27] Narsai told me the advance payment amounted to about R17 million and that it was used for materials and other expenses related to the project.

But there seemed to be very little progress on site. In a letter addressed to the director-general of the national Department of Human Settlements, dated November 2014, Narsai highlighted problems that were hampering the project. They mostly related to what appeared to have been a total lack of planning on behalf of the local municipality and the Free State provincial government. The province's list of beneficiaries for the project was in tatters, and so Tekeweni and VNA did not really know who they were building the houses for, Narsai wrote. There was also no electricity supply to the site, and the water supply was insufficient. All of this severely affected the small factory Khaya Readykit had opened on site to manufacture their prefabricated timber wall panels, explained Narsai in his letter. The manufacturing process and construction on site had to be kept going with power generators and water tanks. Even if the houses could all be finished under such undesirable circumstances, the contractor would not be able to connect them to services, he warned the director-general. It appeared as if the local authorities and the provincial government had done virtually no planning before they started spending money on the project.

This was because immense political pressure was brought to bear so that illicit funds could begin flowing to the political beneficiaries of the scheme, said one of my sources.

By June 2015, only five houses had been finished, according to a progress report. 'The current rate of progress is still of great concern as the contractor will never be able to complete the expected 800–1000 houses within the 18–24 months construction period,' warned the report.[28] This was despite the fact that the FDC had by now spent almost R60 million on the project, according to its annual reports. Tekeweni and VNA had been on site for more than a year, but the end was nowhere in sight. The main reasons for the severe delays included the late delivery of materials, a lack of fuel and a breakdown of the manufacturing plant, the report found. Furthermore, many of the houses that were still being finished had 'external and internal cracks ... on the walls'.[29] By October 2015, only 136 houses were finished.[30] The project was in serious peril, as all 1000 units should have been completed at this point.

The Vrede dairy project had by now become a national scandal, but it was the housing debacle that threatened to boil over and spark serious unrest in the normally quiet town. When the completed houses could not be connected to water or electricity, the local community protested and stole most of the tiled roofs.[31]

A follow-up progress report found that cash-flow problems also contributed to the debacle. 'Spending to date not a true reflection of work done,' read this report. It found that 'actual progress' was 'sitting at 10%

and the project has passed its completion date'. The report recommended a new completion date of 31 March 2016.[32] Some of the role-players involved in the project now started to panic. Based on Khaya Readykit's original quotes, the less than 200 completed houses should have cost about R18 million. As mentioned earlier, the FDC had by now splurged almost R60 million on the project. People started to wonder where the rest of the money had gone.

A series of emails between some of the people working on the project, sent in October 2015, raised some serious concerns. One individual alleged that the funds for the project had dried up because Narsai's VNA had stolen the initial upfront payment from the FDC. 'The Vrede contract seems to be a textbook case for how not to undertake a housing contract in South Africa,' fumed the email's author. The source who gave me the emails also alleged VNA had channelled a 'thank-you fee' to Zuma using some of the proceeds of the FDC's upfront payment. This was the second time I was told about a 'thank-you fee', by an independent source.

Narsai strongly denied this. He said all the money Tekeweni and VNA received could be accounted for. But why were there less than 200 completed houses, I asked him. Narsai said VNA and Tekeweni had to spend much more money on preparing the sites for the houses than they had anticipated. The local council was supposed to provide platformed sites for each house, along with roads, water and electricity. Narsai explained that this was not done. 'The scope of works changed completely,' he told me. Tekeweni and VNA had to fork out much more money on work other than building the houses, he claimed. Originally, the project was expected to cost R100 million, but due to the added expenses it was going to cost taxpayers almost R240 million, according to a progress report VNA compiled in February 2015.[33]

One of my sources who worked on the project contested Narsai's claims. 'The contractor teams were bloated with various team members to justify the exorbitant fees they were charging,' he told me. In other words, VNA and Tekeweni were allegedly pocketing large fees instead of spending most of the money on the project. 'These allegations are strongly refuted by VNA,' Narsai said. There had been a 'fixed cost' for the houses' top structures, and it was impossible to exceed this cost seeing as it formed part of the bill of quantities, he claimed.

VNA's project-management fee also seemed exorbitant. According to

Narsai, VNA's original fee was valued at 15 per cent of the project's initial estimated cost, which came to R100 million. The company's fee, including VAT, therefore amounted to just over R17 million, he told me. This did not include Tekeweni's fees. A professional in the construction industry told me that project-management fees should range between 3 and 5 per cent of the total project cost. Another South African project-management firm charges between 6 and 9 per cent, according to its website.[34] Narsai was adamant that VNA's fees were not excessive. In fact, he claimed VNA had spent more than R20 million on the project and therefore actually suffered a loss.

Selvan Moodley, Tekeweni Civils' co-owner, also denied that his firm had been overpaid. Moodley told me Tekeweni spent a lot more money than anticipated on earthworks, servicing the sites and related tasks.

But I was handed an explosive set of documents that seem to explain why VNA might have needed to charge an apparently inflated fee. These papers also support my sources' claims about Zuma's 'thank-you fee' from VNA. A closed corporation called Premier Attraction 1016 received R2 million from Narsai's VNA in the 2015/16 financial year, according to its financial records. Premier Attraction had invoiced VNA for 'consulting services' in June 2015, and Narsai's company paid the R2-million fee at some point before the financial year ended in March 2016, right in the middle of the Vrede housing project. According to the invoice, Premier Attraction had done work for VNA relating to a 'Mpumalanga development'. In November 2018, I asked Narsai whether VNA had done any work in Mpumalanga. At the time, I did not mention the invoice from Premier Attraction. Narsai said VNA had only worked as a 'sub-consultant' in Mpumalanga between 2003 and 2005. He would later tell me a different story.

The man behind Premier Attraction is Thalente Myeni, the son of staunch Zuma ally Dudu Myeni. Thalente Myeni and a band of politically connected businessmen were shareholders in a consortium that won a huge contract worth R51 billion to supply new commuter carriages to the Passenger Rail Agency of South Africa (PRASA). Dimadox, the company Myeni used for his stake in the PRASA deal, was supposedly located at Zuma's house in Forest Town, Johannesburg, according to the company's registration records. In 2005, the Scorpions raided this property during their probe into Zuma's involvement in the Arms Deal.[35]

There have long been rumours that Zuma and Myeni's mother were in a romantic relationship. Both have denied this.[36] But the documents detailing Thalente Myeni's financial affairs suggest there is a close link between the Zumas and the Myenis. Thalente once submitted a 'change of bank details' form to the South African Revenue Service (SARS). One section of the form required the 'personal details of person providing proof of residential address'. Myeni provided the name and contact details of Duduzile Zuma, Duduzane Zuma's twin. Next to 'relationship to tax-payer', Myeni wrote 'cousin'.

When I first researched Myeni's involvement in the PRASA deal, sources claimed he was fronting for Zuma. The latest documents I obtained suggest he was using some of his income from 'consulting' work – possibly including his payments from VNA – for the benefit of Zuma's family. A bill for legal work done for Duduzile by a Johannesburg law firm was addressed to and apparently paid by Myeni in early 2016, according to the documents.

VNA's R2-million payment to Premier Attraction at the time of the Vrede housing project, coupled with Myeni's apparent ties to Zuma's family, suggested my sources might have been onto something. Could tax-payers' money have been extracted from the Free State's coffers in order to benefit the then president?

I finally confronted Narsai with Premier Attraction's invoice in early 2019. He strongly denied that VNA had channelled a 'thank-you fee' to Zuma, or that his firm had paid any politically exposed persons in rela-tion to the Vrede project or any other projects. He admitted that VNA had paid Premier Attraction R2 million, but he said it had been for 'consult-ing services' related to a construction project in Bethal in Mpumalanga. Myeni's company apparently acted as the 'development manager'. 'Premier Attraction 1016 and by virtue Thalente Myeni was never involved in the Vrede ABT project,' Narsai said.

As mentioned earlier, Narsai initially claimed VNA had not done any work in Mpumalanga since 2005. When I asked him why he had changed his tune only after I asked him about the R2-million payment to Myeni's company, he told me the following: 'You were not expressly clear about what work we did in Mpumalanga as I understood that you were request-ing whether we had undertaken work directly for Provincial Government. The work [in Mpumalanga] I refer to is for a Private Developer hence I responded accordingly.'

In a follow-up email, Narsai claimed VNA had paid Myeni's company to take over the Mpumalanga development. He also said that he had first been introduced to Thalente by Dudu Myeni, the latter's mother and Zuma's 'friend'.

Meanwhile, Thalente Myeni's apparent involvement in the alleged Durban 'plot' meetings in September 2018 raised further questions about how he had been spending some of his earnings from 'consulting services'. As mentioned in the previous chapter, a Mercedes owned by Myeni was one of the vehicles allegedly used to collect Magashule, his mother, Dudu, and other 'conspirators' after one of the gatherings at a Durban hotel.[37] Another Mercedes allegedly spotted on the scene belonged to Empire Technology, the company owned by Shantan Reddy, who later claimed that he was not in South Africa at the time.

Given the fact that Reddy's Empire Technology had directly benefited from a Free State contract and Myeni had been paid on at least one occasion by a contractor to Magashule's erstwhile province, I had to wonder about the links between the various players and the alleged clandestine fightback operation against Ramaphosa. Myeni did not respond to queries, but Reddy strongly denied that he had been involved in any such scheming. In fact, he claimed that he did not know Myeni at all. 'Our client and/or its directors further deny being familiar with, a business associate and/or a partner of Mr. Thalente Myeni, either directly or indirectly,' said Empire Technology's lawyer.

But Shantan Reddy was also the deputy chairperson of his father's Edison Power Group, and I discovered indisputable financial links between Edison Power and Myeni's Premier Attraction 1016. In the 2014/15 financial year, Edison paid Premier Attraction just over R240 000 in three instalments for 'consulting services', according to financial records. Although this was a relatively small amount, the implication of these payments was significant. It cast serious doubt over Shantan Reddy's assertion that he did not know Myeni. Not only were their respective vehicles allegedly spotted outside a Durban hotel at the same time, but Edison, in which Reddy held a senior position, had also made payments to Myeni's company in at least one financial year.

Edison stated that it had paid Premier Attraction about R276 000 'over a period of time' for 'legitimate services'. Myeni's company had been among some forty-five 'emerging subcontracting companies' Edison had paid for doing work on one of its many projects, said Edison's lawyer.

However, Vivian and Shantan Reddy apparently had no clue that Premier Attraction's principal was Thalente Myeni, or that their 'emerging subcontractor' was the son of Dudu Myeni. 'The directors and/or senior executives of Edison Power are not involved in such appointments. No one was aware of who the principal of Premier Attraction was or indeed who his parents were,' claimed Edison.

Back in Vrede, five years after Tekeweni and VNA first began work there, only 166 houses had been finished and occupied by November 2018, according to a written response from the FSHS. In early 2017, Tekeweni had pulled out of the project and the department had appointed Maono Construction, again without a tender process, to build the remaining 834 homes. FDC chairperson Hantsi Matseke owns Maono.

In her budget vote speech in March 2017, human settlements MEC Sisi Ntombela discussed the Vrede housing project. Considering that it had already dragged on for more than three years, her speech was laughable. 'Madame Speaker, as part of our efforts to speed up construction and improve on quality while addressing environmental concerns, we are exploring alternative building technology,' she told the provincial legislature. 'The advantage of this technology is faster completion of houses which would enable us to address the backlog quicker.'[38]

Maono Construction's appointment presented another potential problem. The FDC, which acted as the Vrede project's account administrator and implementing agent, would be paying Maono. In other words, the state-owned entity Matseke chaired would be paying millions to her own private company. Neither the FDC nor Matseke nor the FSHS viewed this as a conflict of interest. 'All PHP projects are paid for by the FDC on behalf of the Department of Human Settlements. This is why the previous contractors and Maono would be paid by the FDC,' Matseke told me. 'This relationship between the Department of Human Settlements and the FDC cannot be changed simply because Maono has now been appointed to the project.' She further claimed that she only interacted with the FDC 'at board level' and did not have any 'operational responsibilities'. 'In compliance with the applicable requirements, I declared Maono's PHP appointment to the FDC board and no conflict of interest was raised by the FDC board,' she insisted.

Matseke told me that the project was still not finished due to 'various challenges'. Even though Maono was appointed in 2017, site handover only took place in March 2018. Some of the challenges included a lack of water at the site and problems with the beneficiary lists, she explained. These were the same problems that had been raised in progress reports in 2014 and 2015 by VNA. Matseke said Maono was 'scheduled to complete the project within the allocated time frame of three years'. In other words, the housing project launched in 2014 would be finished in 2020, if everything went well.

A provincial government gazette from February 2018 announced that the FSHS would channel a further R156 million through the FDC for the purpose of completing the Vrede project.[39] Including the previous payments made to Tekeweni and VNA, the project cost had now ballooned to at least R220 million. The province seemed to be pouring more and more taxpayers' money into a project that it was incapable of finishing.

During a visit to the site in December 2018, I met a young man who lived in a shack with his grandmother. Their makeshift home was erected right next to a concrete platform on which the grandmother's ABT home should have been built years before. All around them, people lived in shacks next to identical concrete squares. 'My grandmother was added to the beneficiary list in 2015, so she has been waiting for three years,' the young man told me. Ironically, he was wearing a bright yellow ANC T-shirt bearing Jacob Zuma's grinning face. I recalled something the former president had said on more than one occasion about the ANC's continued rule over South Africa.[40] Standing in a field littered with shacks and bare concrete slabs, baking under the Free State's merciless sun, I struggled to remember his exact words. 'The people of Vrede will wait for their new houses until Jesus Christ returns.' Was that it? It sounded about right.

PART VI

DADDY'S GIRL

17

The R9-million freebie

Since coming to power, the ANC has consistently promised to tackle South Africa's alarmingly high unemployment rate. President Cyril Ramaphosa renewed the ANC's vows regarding job creation at the party's 2019 election manifesto launch in Durban. Considering some of the characters who shared the stage with him at this event, the declaration was a farce. Not only has the ANC government continuously failed to make meaningful inroads into reducing unemployment, but some of its top leaders have actively destroyed existing jobs through their questionable conduct.

Secretary-general Ace Magashule is one such leader. As premier of the Free State, Magashule seemingly had a hand in ensuring that the Free State Development Corporation effectively sold his daughter, Thoko Malembe, a property that was once the site of a thriving business. In the process, Thoko pocketed R8.9 million. The deal ultimately destroyed the business and cost its employees their jobs and livelihoods.

Thoko has been at the centre of some of the most egregious examples of Magashule's alleged state-capture schemes. As mentioned in Chapter 3, she only met her father relatively late in life. Her mother had followed Magashule into exile in Tanzania, where she gave birth in 1990. Magashule later returned to South Africa without them and they apparently lost touch. Thoko was reunited with her biological father in 2011. Ironically, it was Ramaphosa who played a key role in getting them back together. When I first started looking into Thoko's business dealings in the Free State, sources familiar with the matter told me that her stepfather – a man with a few political connections of his own – asked Ramaphosa to facilitate a reunion, which he duly did. Ramaphosa's people have never contested this version of events. 'This is a private matter and it would not be appropriate for the deputy president to comment,' his spokesperson told me in January 2018, shortly before Ramaphosa became president of South Africa.

Magashule and Thoko have been equally coy about their relationship.

Thoko at first denied that Magashule was her father. 'I have no relationship with the guy,' she told me in early 2018, while Magashule's spokesperson said he would not 'entertain any questions on the private affairs of the premier'. Shortly after *News24* published an article I wrote about Thoko's dealings with her father's administration, another report appeared in the *Bloemfontein Courant* detailing how she had benefited from alleged tender maladministration and tender rigging.[1] Magashule lashed out at the media. 'They will say this one or that one has a lot of work – so what?' he asked during his final State of the Province Address in February 2018. 'There are processes of procurement, so I as premier, believe in radical economic transformation. I will not be bullied into not supporting black business because of all these allegations of corruption against me.'[2]

His remarks contained an apparent contradiction. On the one hand, Magashule was adamant that people such as Thoko won government contracts through proper procurement processes. On the other hand, he seemed to suggest that businesses like Thoko's won contracts because of his support. He had inadvertently acknowledged his power and influence within the province's procurement environment.

Before I dig into some of Thoko's many government deals, allow me to comment on the privacy issue. The spokespeople for both Magashule and Ramaphosa insisted that the then premier's relationship with his daughter was a 'private' matter. I believe that this argument cannot be upheld in the face of strong indications that their relationship, to a large extent, revolved around dubious deals involving public funds and assets.

I have also been asked why people like Thoko should not be allowed to do business with government. When it can be shown that their dealings are free of nepotism and corruption, there should be no reason to prohibit family members of public servants from dealing with the state. Thoko was well within her rights to do business with government provided her powerful father remained at a distance. But he did not, and all indications are that her success was largely attributable to Magashule's meddling.

While studying at the University of Johannesburg (UJ), Thoko did an internship at a Free State provincial government contractor. Sources alleged that Magashule 'forced' the company to take her on board. According to one of her social media accounts, Thoko graduated from UJ with an honours degree in logistics management in June 2014. Posing next to her in her graduation photo was Thato Magashule, the premier's younger son.

Before her graduation, Thoko co-founded Botlokwa Holdings with Joy Hlongwane, a relative of Fana Hlongwane, one of the controversial figures at the centre of the Arms Deal saga. According to sources, Thoko told Joy that she would secure work for their nascent company in the Free State. The earliest documented indication that she made good on her promise can be found in the Ngwathe local municipality's 2013/14 annual report. According to this, the municipality seated in Magashule's hometown of Parys paid Botlokwa Holdings R2.1 million for 'protective clothing' for municipal employees.[3]

At some point, Botlokwa teamed up with Maono Construction, the company owned by FDC chairperson and fellow Parys local Hantsi Matseke. According to its website, Maono Construction secured contracts worth more than R500 million from the Free State government while Magashule was premier. These included the RDP projects mentioned in Part III. Matseke told me that Botlokwa became Maono's 'enterprise development' partner, but secured revenues of only about R2 million through the partnership. Matseke, however, was also present on the fringes of the property deal unpacked in this chapter.

In early 2014, Ikhraam Osman, who had worked with Magashule at the Free State Department of Economic Affairs and Tourism in the 1990s, was appointed CEO of the FDC. Sources claim that Osman, along with Matseke and a few other FDC officials, abetted Magashule's capture of the state-owned entity's purse.

The FDC, which has a mandate to grow and support the Free State's economy, partners with a wide range of businesses all over the province. One such business was a Shell fuel station in the eastern Free State town of Phuthaditjhaba, the former capital of the QwaQwa homeland. The FDC owned the land on which the petrol station was situated, and the petrol station's owner rented the site from the FDC. It was a thriving business, according to sources familiar with the saga. It employed about sixty-five petrol attendants, shop assistants, cleaners and other staff, who in turn fed many more mouths in a corner of the province where unemployment and poverty are about as bad as it gets.

In June 2014, the petrol station's owner received notice from the FDC that it intended to cancel the lease agreement for the site. In October, the

FDC applied for an eviction order at the High Court in Bloemfontein. One afternoon in December, while the eviction matter was still being heard, a convoy of SUVs and luxury sedans arrived at the petrol station. Footage from the business's security cameras captured the day's events.

Thoko Malembe alighted first from one of the SUVs. She walked over to one of two BMWs that formed part of the convoy and got in. She emerged after about a minute, followed by Magashule and a guard or aide who held an umbrella over his head. They were joined by about five other men. Sources identified Vish Maharaj, an FDC board member, and Mohlouoa 'Blacky' Seoe, a former FDC chairperson and one of Magashule's old business associates, among them. The group walked around the petrol station as if inspecting it, before reconvening near the fuel pumps, where they stood for about five minutes, apparently locked in earnest discussion. The group then broke up and left the site in their respective vehicles. Some of the petrol station's former employees recalled the visit and agreed that it appeared as if the visitors were doing an inspection. It was after this that rumours began to circulate among the staff that Magashule wanted to buy the business for his daughter.

In June 2015, the Bloemfontein High Court ruled that the FDC could ask its tenant to vacate the site if it wanted to, seeing as the original lease agreement had lapsed. The petrol station's owners tried to fight the ruling, but they eventually relented in May 2016. The business was shut later that year and all the employees immediately lost their jobs.

Shell's corporate head office, meanwhile, learnt that the FDC planned to sell the property. Seeing as it had supplied fuel to the business's previous owner, the company naturally had an interest in the matter. According to a written reply from Shell to my inquiries, they were told that the FDC wanted to sell the site to 'progress black female land ownership in the Free State'. When Shell entered the negotiations, the FDC indicated that it was considering selling the property to an entity called the MMAT Trust. Thoko Malembe happens to be the sole trustee of the MMAT Trust, which she registered at the Bloemfontein master's office in 2016. Shell, who told me it had no idea Magashule's daughter was behind the MMAT Trust, supported the deal. 'It is in line with our transformation agenda to progress black female business ownership,' the company said.

According to deeds office records, the FDC sold the property to the MMAT Trust in April 2016. But it was not a straightforward transaction.

Instead of having to put up her own money or secure a bank loan, Thoko effectively scored the property for free while simultaneously pocketing R8.9 million. A notarial lease agreement filed at the deeds office explains how it worked: Shell agreed to pay the MMAT Trust R11.5 million as an 'upfront rental' to lease the site for fifteen years. 'On receipt of the upfront rental CDH [Cliffe Dekker Hofmeyr, the notary attorneys for the lease deal] shall issue a guarantee of R2 600 000.00 in favour of … the attorneys attending to the registration of the transfer of the property into the name of the Lessor [MMAT Trust],' stated the lease agreement. 'The guarantee will be made payable on the simultaneous registration of the transfer of the Property into the name of the Lessor and this Lease.' The agreement also stipulated that 'the balance of the upfront rental will be paid to the Lessor on Registration'. In other words, when the property was finally registered to the MMAT Trust in early 2017, Shell effectively gave Thoko the money to buy the property from the FDC, plus an R8.9-million windfall that went straight into her trust's account. Thanks to the FDC's willingness to sell the property to the MMAT Trust and Shell's concomitant involvement, Magashule's daughter became a millionaire with the stroke of a pen.

It was a strange deal, but Shell maintained that it made good business sense. The upfront rental worked out to about R64 000 a month, which, they told me, was 'below market value'. Shell intended to appoint a new franchisee to operate the petrol station, but it first had to upgrade the site. The new landlady, Thoko Malembe, would not have to fork out a cent for these upgrades. According to the notarial lease agreement, Shell would be responsible for these expenses. The fuel giant told me it had submitted building plans to the local municipal council and was awaiting approval. 'Once the site is up and running it will create jobs in the area, potentially more jobs than previously, as we intend to put in a full shop offer that was not at the site,' one of Shell's executives promised in January 2018. 'This will employ more cashiers, merchandisers, bakery staff, back office [staff] etc.'

More than two years after the property was effectively gifted to the premier's daughter, the site remains abandoned. A few days after the ANC's 2019 election manifesto launch in Durban, I checked in with one of the previous petrol attendants who had lost his job. 'There is still nothing happening there, no building or upgrades,' he told me. 'Ace destroyed our lives.'

Thoko is the only winner to have emerged from the transaction. Even the FDC has suffered a financial loss. The SOE had held an 18 per cent share in the former operator's business, which earned it a slice of the petrol station's profits. It had also received a monthly rental fee of about R30 000 before the business was closed down. After the deal with Thoko, these income streams dried up.

I asked several sources familiar with the FDC's dealings how this could have happened. They all pointed to Magashule. 'This is just one example of Ace's grip on the FDC,' said a former MEC and erstwhile Magashule ally. 'He appointed its board members and executives and made sure the money flowed in the right direction.' Two other sources who had insight into the deal with Thoko claimed Magashule influenced the transaction. 'When the FDC's handling of this deal was questioned internally, FDC staff were told to keep out of it, seeing as the big man was behind it,' alleged one of them, in reference to Magashule.

My sources also claimed that Matseke and Osman, the FDC's chairperson and CEO respectively, had deliberately furthered Magashule's interests. 'Ace placed those two at the FDC for exactly this reason,' said one. Tiisetso Makhele, Magashule's spokesperson at the time, denied the allegation. 'The premier has not exerted any pressure on any FDC official to do or not do anything,' he insisted. Osman echoed this sentiment. 'Management was never put under pressure by anybody and certainly not [by] the premier,' the FDC chief executive told me.

In a written response, Matseke admitted that she knew 'Mr Magashule and his daughter Ms. Thoko Malembe … on a personal basis', but strongly denied any impropriety. 'FDC board members get appointed in accordance with the FDC Act and by the MEC responsible,' she stated in response to my questions about Magashule's alleged role in high-level appointments. Allegations that she had influenced the property deal with Thoko were 'baseless', she insisted. 'I, in my capacity as the chairperson of the FDC, only interact with the FDC at board level and therefore have no ability to influence any operational transactions.'

None of the implicated parties, however, were able to provide me with a sound reason as to why Magashule visited the property along with his daughter and FDC officials just before negotiations to sell the site to Thoko's trust began. Thoko herself has only provided me with broad comments and remarks. 'Everyone has freedom of trade. U can call it whatever u want, that's ur view,' she said in a text message after I asked her if her dealings amounted to corruption or nepotism.

Shell conducted an investigation into the matter after my article appeared on *News24* in January 2018. 'To date the investigation has not demonstrated any awareness of the landlord's political affiliation from Shell's side,' one of the company's executives told me. As for the petrol station's former employees and their families, they are all eagerly waiting for the business to one day reopen its doors. Until such time, they remain mostly unemployed, their prospects further curtailed by Ace Magashule's version of 'radical economic transformation'.

18

Vogelfontein

Thoko Malembe's reunion with her powerful father seemingly brought her great joy and a sense of belonging. 'Theres no greater feeling like being reunited with ur family, knowing who u are n where u come from,' she wrote on her Facebook page in June 2011. The reunion certainly seems to have set her on a path towards wealth and success. When she finished her degree in logistics management in 2013, she was spared the trouble of having to look for a job. She was just twenty-three years old when her newly established companies started clinching contracts from the Free State provincial government led by her father.

One particularly troubling project would ultimately net one of her businesses government contracts worth R150 million. This story centres on a failed low-cost housing development on the outskirts of Bethlehem in the eastern Free State. As with the Shell fuel station debacle, Ace Magashule's shadow again loomed over the deal.

In early 2012, Magashule and human settlements MEC Olly Mlamleli visited Bethlehem's Selahliwe informal settlement. They promised residents living in shacks that the provincial government would soon launch a new development nearby and that they would all be moved to proper houses.[1] The premier and the MEC were back in Bethlehem in April the following year, but this time their visit was a low-key affair. Photos of the gathering show Magashule, Mlamleli and other government officials meeting with a Chinese businessman at a tract of open land officially known as Baken Park. Bethlehem locals call the area Vogelfontein. According to sources familiar with the matter, Magashule introduced the Chinese businessman, whom he referred to as Mr Lee, as the property developer who had been appointed by government to build houses at Vogelfontein for Selahliwe's shack dwellers.

Mr Lee was in fact Jianliang Li, a Chinese–South African businessman based in Johannesburg. A month after meeting with Magashule at

Vogelfontein, Li co-founded a company called Unital Holdings. His co-director was none other than Thoko Malembe. Unital's company records contain an interesting piece of information: for her residential address, Thoko listed the Gupta-owned property in Saxonwold where Tshepiso Magashule had lived and where her father sometimes met with contacts. Registration documents submitted by Unital to the National Home Builders Registration Council confirm that Thoko was also a shareholder in the company. She owned 30 per cent, while Li held the remaining stake.

Magashule and his allies in government apparently tried their best to conceal the fact that his daughter would benefit from the Vogelfontein contract. In a presentation on the Free State's housing projects, human settlements HOD Tim Mokhesi listed Unital as '100% Chinese-owned'.

Magashule and some MECs returned to Vogelfontein in November 2013 to formally launch the RDP project with a small sod-turning ceremony. The *Eastern Free State Express* covered the event. 'We don't want to build a "kasi" township here – we want to build a human settlement,' Magashule told the local newspaper. 'We should have schools, recreational places, community halls and many others.'[2] The Selahliwe community was elated.

In the same month, the FSHS awarded a contract worth almost R64 million to Unital to build 500 RDP houses. There was no tender process. The FSHS later told me that Unital had been appointed as a 'sub-contractor' to VNA Consulting, the department's 'implementing agent' for select housing projects. When I pointed out that Unital had a contract with the FSHS itself, according to the department's own records, I heard nothing further.

The apparent lack of a proper procurement process was not the only problem. Unital was awarded the large contract just six months after it was established. Neither Li nor Thoko had any apparent experience as a construction contractor and they seemed woefully unprepared for a project of this scope. Being a new company, Unital had a Construction Industry Development Board grading of 1, the lowest possible score. Although CIDB gradings do not apply to government tenders for housing projects, these scores serve as a good indication of a company's capabilities and experience.

By October 2014, it was apparent that Unital was not up to the task. The *Eastern Free State Express* reported that Unital's subcontractors had downed tools because Li had not been paying them.[3] The involvement of Magashule's daughter, however, remained under wraps.

Despite the problems on site, the FSHS continued to lavish contracts on Unital. In August 2015, the company clinched a R78-million contract to build a further 500 houses at Vogelfontein. In April 2017, it received R9 million to build 50 more. In total, Unital was awarded contracts worth R150 million to deliver 1 050 RDP houses at Vogelfontein, all without having to submit a single tender. But getting the contract is the easy part. Completing the project is an entirely different matter. Given Unital's inexperience, it should come as no surprise that the Vogelfontein development counts among the province's many unfinished RDP projects.

There is some confusion as to how many houses Thoko's company actually completed. In response to my queries in early 2018, the FSHS initially said that it had thus far paid R67.5 million to Unital for 630 finished houses. But the department later sent me an updated figure – there were in fact only 568 completed houses. The R67.5 million correlates with the housing subsidy system's records. The fact that Unital did not receive the full R150 million confirms that the company did not finish its work. Neither the FSHS nor Unital was able to explain why.

Inundated with complaints from Vogelfontein's new residents, the local branch of the Democratic Alliance conducted an investigation and compiled a report in September 2017.[4] According to the report, there were fewer than 200 finished houses, many of which appeared to have been built with substandard materials and showed poor workmanship. The biggest problem, however, was that the entire development had been left without water, sewerage and electricity. As a result, many residents were forced to build dangerous pit toilets. Others simply relieved themselves in a nearby stream, causing considerable health risks. Because the area had no basic services, some of the completed houses were left unoccupied, which resulted in them being vandalised or used by local teenagers as drug dens. In short, Magashule's vision of a fully serviced 'human settlement' had turned into an underserviced 'kasi'.

I visited Vogelfontein in March 2018 to see for myself. The DA report was no exaggeration, and they were not the only political party alarmed by the situation. A group of local SACP members showed me around and pointed out some of the problems. In one section of the development, open trenches were the only indication that the contractor had at some point considered installing sewerage and water pipes. One beneficiary who had decided to move into his new home regardless told me it had not been built well. 'When it rains, it leaks into my house,' he said. 'Some of us go up a nearby hill to relieve ourselves because there aren't any working toilets.'

The lack of basic services was not merely the result of bad project management. Further investigation revealed that Magashule's apparent meddling was the root cause of the terrible conditions in which the people of Vogelfontein now lived. Long before Unital arrived on the scene, the Dihlabeng local municipality appointed a firm from Gauteng to oversee a mixed housing development at Vogelfontein. The company, Emendo Project Managers and Planners, was appointed as a turnkey developer, which meant it was tasked with providing bulk services and other infra-structure along with new houses. Emendo was making good progress with some of the work. It had provided water and sewerage to some of the sites, and was in the process of constructing a sewage pump station.

In late 2013, a few months after Magashule met with Jianliang Li at Vogelfontein, one of Emendo's subcontractors, Dam Civils, which had started on the design and construction of the new neighbourhood's road network, was suddenly halted in its tracks. Busa Molatseli, Dihlabeng's municipal manager, informed Emendo and Dam Civils that the local council could not approve their plans for the roads and houses. In fact, Emendo was to abandon all its activities at Vogelfontein. Baffled by the municipality's sudden change of heart, one of Emendo's directors asked to meet with Molatseli. During the meeting, it became clear who was behind the municipality's unwillingness to cooperate with the turnkey developer. '[Dihlabeng municipality's] justification for its action was that ... the honourable Ace Magashule had instructed it to no longer cooperate with the defendant (Emendo) on the project,' read court papers later filed by Emendo in an ongoing legal battle over the matter.

Sources who were involved in the saga told me that, in 2014, Magashule's office began to strong-arm the municipality into cutting ties with Emendo, signed agreements notwithstanding. These sources were able to provide me with specific details about Magashule's meddling, including the dates, venues and attendees of meetings in which the matter was discussed. At one meeting, Magashule told the MEC for human settlements, Olly Mlamleli, the director-general in the Office of the Premier, Kopung Ralikontsane, and the HOD in the Free State Department of Cooperative Governance and Traditional Affairs, Mokete Duma, that Dihlabeng's contract with Emendo was unlawful and needed to be terminated.

When I first reported on this issue in early 2018, Magashule's office admitted to being involved in the Vogelfontein affair. It said it had advised the Dihlabeng municipality to boot Emendo off the project. 'It appeared that the contracts concluded with Emendo were irregular, and as such, it should be reviewed and set aside by a competent court,' I was told. 'The office of the premier did not instruct the municipality, but gave legal advice.' This seemed a bit strange. At the time, almost 90 per cent of the Free State's municipalities were guilty of irregular expenditure, according to an auditor-general's report.[5] Why was Magashule seemingly taking a special interest in this particular contract?

Over the next few years, the provincial government and the Dihlabeng municipality worked together to get rid of the incumbent developer. The wheels of the alleged scheme turned slowly, but once they were put in motion, Emendo's fate was all but sealed. In November 2015, the FSHS sent the municipality a letter urging it to institute legal proceedings against Emendo.[6] During a Dihlabeng council meeting on 25 November 2016, it was resolved that the municipality would 'approach the High Court regarding the appointment of Emendo in order to nullify the agreement with Emendo on the land availability and development framework'.[7]

While all of this was playing out, Thoko and her partner were being paid millions by Magashule's government. At the same time, the work on Vogelfontein's sewer network and related infrastructure ground to a halt. Emendo, meanwhile, was not willing to back down without a fight. The company complained to the national minister of human settlements, Lindiwe Sisulu, who contacted Magashule.

In September 2016, Magashule, Mokhesi, Molatseli, and other officials and stakeholders met with Emendo. The meeting's minutes highlight Magashule's involvement in the Vogelfontein saga. 'Free State exco cabinet led by Premier Ace Magashule took the resolution to take over the project … from the Dihlabeng local municipality,' Mokhesi said, according to the minutes. He also said Emendo had been urged to 'walk away from the project'. Furthermore, Mokhesi stated that his department had 'appointed another Contractor to build 1 000 RDP [houses] on the project and funding was made available to them'. That would be Unital. Emendo's representative wanted more information on the department's 'Chinese' contractor and the processes through which it had been appointed. According to the minutes, Mokhesi and Molatseli remained mum.

On 'legal advice' from Magashule's office, the Dihlabeng municipality finally lodged a legal bid at the Bloemfontein High Court in January 2017 for its agreement with Emendo to be declared void.[8] That case is ongoing.

A document from the national Department of Human Settlements' Housing Development Agency (HDA) provides a clue as to why Magashule may have wanted to get rid of Emendo. In 2016, while the premier's office and the local municipality were busy fighting with the incumbent turnkey developer, the HDA compiled a 'fact sheet' for the Vogelfontein development. According to the document, the HDA envisaged that Vogelfontein would be developed into a whole new town with more than 5000 housing units. The total project value, which included the new houses and related infrastructure, would come to almost R4 billion.[9] Considering his connections with businesspeople in the construction industry, including his own daughter, it is not difficult to imagine why Magashule would have wanted full control of this potential revenue stream.

When I first wrote about this issue for News24 in March 2018, Magashule denied that he had helped Thoko's company clinch the RDP contracts from the FSHS. 'The honourable premier is not at all involved in the awarding of tenders or any related processes,' his office told me. 'The honourable premier was therefore not involved in the appointment of the service provider with regards to the Bethlehem RDP project.'

It was the same kind of broad denial that his office routinely dished up when confronted with allegations of corruption. The circumstances that led to the Vogelfontein mess, however, make it extremely difficult to take this denial at face value. After all, Magashule was physically present at the very first site meeting with Thoko's Chinese business partner. In this sense, the Vogelfontein saga resembled the Shell fuel station debacle. In both instances, the premier was at the proverbial scene of the crime right before his administration effected decisions that enriched his daughter. Most tellingly, it was Magashule who had flexed his executive muscles to make sure the incumbent contractor got taken off the project.

Even if Thoko's Unital somehow won the contracts without any meddling from her father, the fiasco remains a terrible blight on Magashule's legacy. In 2012, Selahliwe's shack-dwelling residents enthusiastically bought into his promises of a fully serviced neighbourhood. While his daughter's company made millions, these people are now left with substandard houses and no water, flushing toilets or electricity.

19

Paved with gold

No chronicle of Ace Magashule's contentious career as premier of the Free State would be complete without mentioning the province's Department of Police, Roads and Transport (DPRT). A host of sources ranging from former and current top provincial officials to department insiders claim that the DPRT was at the centre of Magashule's alleged capture scheme.

Like the Department of Human Settlements and its R1-billion housing debacle, the DPRT became embroiled in a massive scandal almost immediately after Magashule took office in 2009. In 2010, the department dished out contracts to a value of about R4 billion for the rehabilitation of twenty-three roads in the province.[1] There was at least one Johannesburg Stock Exchange (JSE)–listed construction giant among the lucky contractors. According to sources familiar with the matter, some of the usual Free State businesspeople linked to the premier also got in on the action. National Treasury eventually got wind of the deal and, after an investigation, found that the DPRT had made 'illegal and unfunded contractual commitments' to the construction companies.[2] In an early blow to the new premier, the DPRT was placed under administration by national government as a result of the Treasury investigation.[3] One source who had been privy to the probe told me that investigators had identified apparent kickbacks paid to government officials by some of the contractors. He said the matter had been referred to the Hawks, but the case somehow died an early death.

If Treasury's intervention ensured cleaner governance at the department, it was temporary. By the 2017/18 financial year, the DPRT was again in the auditor-general's bad books. With irregular expenditure sitting at R650 million and unauthorised expenditure at about R240 million – mostly resulting from dodgy contracts – the department received a qualified audit opinion.[4] While the auditor-general's findings are shocking, the figures do not betray the brazenness with which departments such as the DPRT were apparently captured in order to enrich Magashule's friends and family.

One DPRT insider explained how the alleged capture scheme was carried out. 'Ace ensured people from Ngwathe and other northern municipalities were appointed as supply chain management and financial officials at our department,' said this source. He gave me names of officials from the Ngwathe local municipality (which includes Parys), who had been moved to the DPRT. They included Norman Selai, Ngwathe's former municipal manager, and Makalo Mohale, a former Ngwathe procurement official and ANC Youth League chairperson in the Free State. Selai became a chief director at the DPRT, said my source, but more importantly, he became the chairperson of the department's bid adjudication committee and later the chair of the bid evaluation committee (BEC). Mohale, who once served as Magashule's spokesperson,[5] was appointed as a supply chain manager, according to my source. He was later moved to the FSHS.

Both officials were therefore involved in appointing contractors. 'That is how they gained control of the whole tender process,' my source claimed. 'The evaluation committee identifies [would-be contractors] and makes sure the company that provides kickbacks is in the lead before the BEC's recommendation goes to the bid adjudication committee. The supply chain manager then ratifies the decision and ensures the department makes prepayments to the contractors.' My source further claimed that Magashule's departure from the Free State did not affect the status quo. 'Ace is still in charge of the departments,' he told me.

And Mohale and Selai did not act alone at the DPRT. 'I can count at least fifteen senior managers in critical [financial] positions who come from Parys or from elsewhere in the Fezile Dabi region,' said the department insider. Sandile Msibi, another alleged Magashule associate, became the department head in 2011. My sources claimed that for years Msibi acted as Magashule's lieutenant in the DPRT, just as Tim Mokhesi had done at the FSHS. Msibi died suddenly in December 2017 from an unknown illness.[6] At his funeral, Magashule described his fallen comrade as the 'best HOD in the history of the administration'. He then shocked mourners by claiming that the forces of 'white monopoly capital' had poisoned Msibi because he had refused to give contracts to such companies. 'We are in danger of being murdered,' Magashule claimed. 'Once you touch the nerve of white monopoly capital, you will never survive.' While justifying his theory, Magashule once again let slip that his administration gave out contracts on the basis of considerations other than those prescribed by the Public Finance Management Act and related laws and regulations. Msibi 'diverted tenders away from white-owned firms to benefit blacks', Magashule said.[7] No department head should be able to unilaterally 'divert' contracts in any particular direction.

There is another theory doing the rounds in the Free State's political circles regarding Msibi's death. It gained traction after an amaBhungane report published in *City Press* in March 2018 revealed that Msibi had somehow amassed properties worth a staggering R25 million before his untimely death.[8] The properties were mostly held in his trust's name, and almost all of them had been bought after he became HOD. Most tellingly, Msibi had managed to buy the properties without bank loans. This, according to some of my sources, was proof that he had received kickbacks. 'There is no other way to explain this,' said one former MEC. 'He was a senior government official, yes, but where in the world would he have gotten that much money through legal means?' According to the amaBhungane report, the Hawks had opened a 'commercial crime inquiry' into Msibi in early 2016.[9] The alternate theory suggests that Msibi's death was somehow linked to the Hawks probe. 'There were very senior ANC people in this province who were getting nervous about what might be revealed through an investigation into Msibi's assets,' one politician in the province told me. 'There was even talk that he was going to cooperate with the authorities. Remember, if he had been taking bribes, he certainly hadn't done so alone.'

So far, no one has been able to unearth evidence linking Msibi's death to a political conspiracy. However, there are plenty of concrete facts outside the realm of rumour that detail how Magashule's family benefited from his alleged capture of the DPRT. It would appear that a once-noble initiative to help emerging contractors in the province find their feet was turned into a cash cow for people closely linked to the then premier.

The DPRT's Contractor Development Programme (CDP) was launched in 2008. Emerging businesses in the construction industry could apply to become beneficiaries. The department would assist them with training and skills development, after which they would be given small contracts to help them gain experience. The contracts were mostly for road maintenance, grass cutting and related projects.[10] Thanks to the CDP, emerging contractors from all over the Free State had an opportunity to gain valuable experience and earn much-needed revenues to get their businesses going. Other provincial departments ran similar initiatives, but the province's expenditure on the DPRT's CDP alone was by no means insignificant. In Magashule's nine years as premier, the Free State spent almost R2 billion on CDP contracts and other costs related to the programme.[11]

The 2013/14 auditor-general's report on the DPRT unwittingly revealed when Magashule seemingly began to take an interest in the CDP. In that year, 'the Premier requested an independent consulting firm to conduct an investigation at the department relating to the verification of Contractor Development Program (CDP) Contractors,' read the report. Ironically, 'the investigation was initiated based on irregularities and allegations of misconduct and corruption on the part of certain employees of the department'.[12] Later developments suggest that Magashule intervened for entirely different reasons.

In 2015, the DPRT expanded the CDP to include new emerging con-tractors, the names of which were subsequently announced in an April 2016 government tender bulletin. Of the thirty-three new CDP companies, thirty-one hailed from the area around Parys. '[The] Fezile Dabi region was overlooked in previous years,' the department later claimed in a presenta-tion document on its development programme.[13]

I started to research the new CDP companies for an article in the *Daily Maverick*, and could scarcely believe to what extent the programme had been transformed into a feeding trough for relatives of the province's politi-cal elite. Among the new contractors were Botlokwa Holdings, owned by Thoko Malembe; ME Construction, owned by Ezekiel Magashule, the then premier's younger brother; MDBS Trading, owned by S'busiso and Duduza Ntombela, the sons of current Free State premier Sisi Ntombela; Juda in Zion Trading, owned by Katleho Mochela, the daughter of Parys mayor Joey Mochela; and 4Ever Friends Trading, founded by Moshe Tladi, the late ANC regional secretary for the Fezile Dabi region.[14] Of the thirty-three new contractors, at least ten were directly linked to either Magashule, his political allies or his former business associates.

Some of the companies were absorbed into the CDP itself, which would have enabled them to become subcontractors on lucrative road maintenance projects, while others were given contracts for grass cutting and related services. A select few got the best of both worlds. Botlokwa, for example, was included in the CDP and secured contracts for 'grass cutting', 'fleet branding services' and to 'supply, deliver and install emergency response and law enforcement vehicle accessories'.[15] It is not clear how much money Botlokwa and the other connected companies received through the CDP and related contracts, but sources in the department allege that it amounted to millions.

Furthermore, some of these new contractors were not even based in the Fezile Dabi district. According to information at my disposal, Thoko spent her time between Bloemfontein and Johannesburg. Duduza Ntombela worked at the provincial Department of Social Development in Bloemfontein. His younger brother, S'busiso, apparently lived in Johannesburg. None of the three responded to queries about their involvement in the CDP.

The DPRT predictably denied that the premier's family members and their fellow CDP beneficiaries were appointed through dubious means. 'We hereby wish to advise you that the Department of Police, Roads and Transport has followed due processes in terms of Supply Chain Management as required for the appointment of contractors in the Contractor Development Programme,' it told me.[16]

Apart from lucrative contracts, the DPRT also gave the connected companies Ford Ranger bakkies, trailers and grass-cutting equipment free of charge. Previous CDP beneficiaries were not as fortunate. The department told me that the vehicles and equipment had cost taxpayers R11 million, but the figure seemed a little low. After my story on the scandal broke in the *Daily Maverick*, a local DA councillor told *Volksblad* that some of the bakkies were seen all over Parys and that a few of them had been fitted with tinted windows and shiny 'mag' wheels.[17] It was unclear how many of these vehicles were actually being used for grass cutting and other road maintenance projects.

The worst part of the CDP scandal is that it came at great cost to a group of emerging contractors in the Free State with no political connections. When I first researched the matter, I spoke to a few contractors who had been included in the CDP initially. They told me that their contracts from the DPRT dried up when Thoko Malembe, Ezekiel Magashule and the other connected businesspeople were pushed into the programme. By early 2019, the situation had not changed. 'The department does not want to hear us out,' said one dejected former CDP beneficiary. 'If you want to get anywhere in this province, you have to be connected to Ace.'

PART VII

THE IGOFILES

20

Enter Igo

Long before he became involved in Ace Magashule's circle, Phikolomzi Ignatius Mpambani was something of a local hero in the northern Free State town of Welkom.

Mpambani matriculated from St Dominic's College, a private school, in 1997.[1] It was a difficult time for Welkom – the gold-mining sector that had for decades been the lifeblood of the town's economy was in serious decline.[2] But Igo, as his friends and family affectionately called him, was destined to do greater things.

He did well in school. Some of those who knew him described him as gifted and brilliant. In 1999, he left the province's ailing gold-mining mecca after clinching a scholarship to study at Texas Southern University in Houston. He first obtained a bachelor's degree in finance and economics before completing his MBA in accounting and finance in 2004.[3]

On his return to South Africa in the mid-2000s with two sought-after qualifications, Mpambani got a job as an investment banker at the Johannesburg office of the international banking group Standard Chartered.[4] He apparently harboured much bigger ambitions, however, and was with the bank for less than a year.

During his stint at Standard Chartered, Mpambani put together the first Beach on the Track New Year's Eve festival, an annual event held at Phakisa Freeway, a motor-racing circuit just outside Welkom. At its pinnacle, the festival attracted thousands of partygoers and boasted impressive line-ups of local and international DJs and other entertainers.

'The concept was created to provide upwardly mobile and working class individuals with the opportunity to enjoy the festive season in grand style without spending a fortune,' Mpambani told the *Sowetan* in 2010.[5] Nevertheless, Beach on the Track catered for those with thicker wallets too. At the 2013 edition, socialites and celebrities such as Kenny Kunene and Boity Thulo partied to the music of rap group Teargas while the VIP crowd sipped on Moët champagne and Belvedere vodka.[6]

By this time, Mpambani had established himself as a fixture in the Free State's tender scene. He first got into business with fellow Welkom local Sechaba Mogoera in around 2006, and the duo soon made headway in the highly politicised business environment.

Mpambani was made co-director of two of Mogoera's companies – Sechaba Group and Sechaba Solutions. Soon, both were clinching construction tenders in and around Welkom. According to a source who knew Mpambani and Mogoera, the two young businessmen fostered or consolidated valuable political connections in the Free State during this period.

One such connection was Mathabo Leeto, the then mayor of Matjhabeng local municipality, which includes Welkom. According to my sources, Leeto, who later became the Free State MEC for sport, arts, culture and recreation under Magashule's premiership, had a long-standing relationship with Mpambani's family. She was apparently close to Mpambani's mother, who for many years worked as a nurse in Welkom. The two women also shared a background as political activists during the struggle.

Incidentally, Leeto has had corruption charges and investigations hanging over her head since her time as mayor. She was charged for allegedly accepting bribes related to tenders awarded by the Matjhabeng municipality between 2007 and 2009.[7] When the charges were withdrawn in late 2016, then premier Magashule released a statement welcoming the development and claiming, incorrectly, that Leeto had been found not guilty.[8] Leeto was charged again in February 2018,[9] only for the NPA to back down later that year.[10]

It was from Leeto's Matjhabeng municipality that Mpambani and Mogoera scored some of their earliest projects as tenderpreneurs, according to my sources. But they soon started to extend their reach. One court record from a civil case in the Free State mentions the involvement of Mpambani and Sechaba Solutions in a 2007 project to construct a sewerage network for the Hoopstad municipality.[11] Sechaba Solutions also got a foot in the door at the provincial Department of Human Settlements in 2008, when it got a small contract worth around R2 million.[12]

Their fortunes improved dramatically, however, after Magashule became Free State premier. In the 2009/10 financial year, Sechaba Solutions' earnings from the FSHS climbed from R2 million to R13 million thanks to a contract to construct subsidised houses in Bultfontein, a small town some seventy-five kilometres from Welkom.[13]

Two sources who knew the businessmen well told me that Mogoera and Mpambani became acquainted with Magashule shortly before he became premier in 2009. One of these sources said Mogoera 'supported' Magashule in those early days. This alleged support sometimes took the form of paying for buses whenever Magashule organised political rallies in the province, claimed the source.

My sources also said that Mogoera had a falling-out with Magashule not long after the latter came to power. 'There was an exodus of people in Mogoera and Mpambani's circle to Gauteng because Ace had closed their money taps,' said one. FSHS records seem to support this claim. In the 2008/09 and 2009/10 financial years, Sechaba Solutions earned R15 million from the housing department, but in 2010/11 its earnings dwindled to a meagre R56 000. After that, Sechaba Solutions did not do business with the department again.[14] But according to my sources, only Mogoera remained persona non grata. Magashule later welcomed Mpambani back into his Free State fold.

According to a third source, Mpambani became close to Glen Netshivhodza, the Parys businessman who is also one of Magashule's closest associates. As mentioned previously, Netshivhodza was appointed chairperson of the Free State Tourism Authority in 2013. The entity fell under the provincial Department of Economic Affairs and Tourism, the same department Magashule had led under Lekota in the mid-1990s. (It was later rebranded as the Department of Economic, Small Business Development, Tourism and Environmental Affairs.)

Around the time of Netshivhodza's appointment as chair of the tourism authority, the entity began pouring substantial amounts of taxpayers' money into Mpambani's Beach on the Track parties. The authority, which received between R30 million and R50 million from its parent department each year, confirmed in its annual reports that the Beach on the Track festival was one of the events it 'successfully held and supported'.[15] The reports do not specify how much the entity made available to Beach on the Track, but one source familiar with the deal says the tourism authority contributed about R10 million annually.

The cooperation between Mpambani and Mogoera, meanwhile, came to an end in around 2012. Mpambani, now back in Magashule's favour, needed new entities through which he could continue to do business in the Free State. In 2012, he co-founded Diamond Hill Trading 71 with Kato

Motsoeneng, a former municipal manager in the province's Tswelopele and Mohokare local municipalities. Motsoeneng's last stint as a municipal manager had ended under suspicious circumstances in late 2010, when he resigned from the Mohokare municipality, based in the southern Free State town of Zastron, amid a graft investigation commissioned by the Department of Cooperative Governance and Traditional Affairs.[16] Like Mpambani, Motsoeneng was said to be close to Magashule.

Mpambani next registered 605 Consulting Solutions in July 2014. His wife, Michelle, would later become a director of this venture. Although he was still involved in the Beach on the Track event and other business projects in the Free State, Mpambani and Michelle chose to settle in Johannesburg. He was ready for the big league.

It was in 2014 that Mpambani and a coterie of businesspeople, politicians and government officials apparently began to mastermind the looting of more than R250 million from the Free State government's coffers. Based on several records, timelines and interviews with sources, it seems clear that Magashule became a key figure in this saga. The leaked documents and emails I refer to as the IgoFiles especially fuel suspicions that the then premier was closely linked to Mpambani and that he had benefited from the asbestos audit.

21

Plunder plot

Ace Magashule and six of his closest associates from the Free State landed in Havana, Cuba, just before 1 p.m. on Wednesday 28 January 2015. With the final leg of their draining journey from Johannesburg now over, the group no doubt looked forward to some downtime in the Cuban capital.

Accompanying the Free State premier were businessman Tlale Mokgadi, Lesedi FM presenter Thuso Motaung, Free State ANC secretary William Bulwane, provincial MEC for police, roads and transport Sam Mashinini, and two other government officials. According to an official government briefing document, they formed part of a forty-nine-person delegation that consisted of provincial government officials, the mayors of select Free State towns, MECs and businesspeople.[1] The same document outlined the purposes of the trip, which included an opportunity to 'strengthen relations with [Cuba's] Matanzas Province', 'political education', a 'visit to our [South African medical] students' and a 'tour of Cuba'. The trip lasted a total of two weeks and was funded by taxpayers.

In keeping with the ruling ANC's enduring inability to separate state and party functions, the aforementioned briefing document highlighted elements of that year's ANC January 8th Statement as further justification for the trip. These included the ANC's decision to 'consolidate and strengthen existing party-to-party relations with like-minded sister parties all over the world', and 'solidarity with Palestine; Western Sahara and Cuba'.

The then MEC for human settlements, Olly Mlamleli, was also part of the delegation. She had come to Cuba to interview and recruit thirty Cuban engineers for deployment in Bloemfontein and other municipalities in the province. This initiative would later draw widespread criticism after it came to light that the cost of employing and accommodating the Cuban engineers over a period of three years would wipe out R110 million from the provincial fiscus.[2] Moreover, according to news reports, the engineers could not speak English well, and most of them apparently did not do much work once they arrived at the various municipalities.[3]

The businesspeople accompanying Magashule, meanwhile, were supposedly present as part of a joint effort by the Cuban province of Matanzas and South Africa's Free State province to 'facilitate and promote economic and commercial links between businessmen and enterprises of the respective provinces, thus contributing to the development of this important sector between the two countries'.[4]

One businessman not named in the official briefing document but who was present in Cuba at the same time as the South African delegation was Igo Mpambani. Documents in the IgoFiles show that he arrived in Cuba just two hours after Magashule and his fellow travellers from the Free State. His presence was not a coincidence and he was certainly not in Havana to enjoy a Caribbean holiday. The purpose of Mpambani's visit was to process the first invoices for a R255-million contract from Magashule's provincial government for auditing houses with asbestos roofs.

How this asbestos auditing contract came about is pertinent to this story.

In 2013, the national Department of Human Settlements advertised a bid for the appointment of a panel of companies to assist the Gauteng housing department and municipalities with 'planning and implementation support'. The companies were referred to as professional resource teams (PRTs).[5] One of the companies subsequently appointed to the panel was Johannesburg-based Blackhead Consulting, which in April 2014 received a letter of notification from the national department's director-general, Thabane Zulu. 'As you are aware, the services to [be] executed will be needs based and on an "instruction to perform work" (IPW) basis. Appointment to a departmental panel is for a period of three years,' Zulu wrote to Edwin Sodi, Blackhead Consulting's CEO.[6]

Like many of the characters in this saga, Zulu has a colourful past. In 2007, he crashed his Range Rover in Pietermaritzburg after being followed by a mysterious car with blue lights. When the police arrived on the scene, they found almost R50 000 in his boot.[7] Zulu at the time claimed the money was his own and there was nothing irregular about it. In 2010, he was appointed director-general for human settlements. According to a report in the *Sunday Independent*, he formed part of the South African

Social Security Agency's bid adjudication committee that in 2011 approved a R10-billion bid from the controversial Cash Paymaster Services to administer social grants. The report alleged that Zulu had received a 'bribe' of R1.4 million in relation to the contract. He strongly denied the allegation.[8]

Blackhead's IPW from Zulu, meanwhile, allowed the company to be appointed by the Gauteng Department of Human Settlements in accordance with a needs-based model. In other words, the department could appoint Blackhead whenever it needed its services without each time having to advertise a fresh tender. The bid process that led to Blackhead's appointment was questionable from the start. Why, for example, did the national department administer a tender process for service providers to do work for the provincial department? The latter has its own procurement unit to appoint contractors through its own supply-chain management processes.

Blackhead ended up raking in hundreds of millions of rands thanks to contracts from the Gauteng housing department, which included those it had received as part of the panel of PRTs, as well as work it had secured at an earlier stage. According to an article in *Sunday World* in 2015, Blackhead won contracts worth nearly R700 million to build low-cost houses all over Gauteng. Thanks to these deals, Sodi became a very wealthy man, and he certainly knew how to enjoy his riches. The *Sunday World* article listed a Rolls-Royce Wraith, a Lamborghini, a Ferrari, a McLaren, a BMW X6 and an Aston Martin as being among the tenderpreneur's four-wheeled indulgences.[9]

Several sources familiar with Sodi told me that his company's lucrative involvement with the Gauteng housing department was a result of his close relationship with Nomvula Mokonyane, who served as premier of Gauteng from 2009 until 2014, when she became national minister for water and sanitation. Mokonyane's stint in this department, which lasted until January 2018, has been the subject of countless news reports about dodgy deals involving contractors linked to her.

Sodi apparently continued to benefit from his alleged relationship with Mokonyane after she became minister. In 2016, *City Press* reported on a R500-million contract that Blackhead Consulting secured from the Department of Water and Sanitation for work on a dam near Tzaneen in Limpopo. Sodi and Mokonyane were 'allegedly close friends', the newspaper reported.[10] In 2017, the auditor-general classified at least one of

Blackhead's contracts from Mokonyane's department as irregular.[11] Sodi said any claims that his company had scored contracts because of his alleged friendship with Mokonyane were 'without substance'.

Meanwhile, Blackhead's appointment to the Gauteng Department of Human Settlements' panel of PRTs put it on a path that led straight to the coffers of the Free State provincial government. Presumably having set his sights on that province, Sodi probably knew that he would need someone with good connections in the Free State if he were to clinch contracts there. Igo Mpambani, the Welkom local whose Beach on the Track parties and other business dealings had given him access to the province's social and political circles, must have seemed like the perfect fit.

A shareholders' agreement between Sodi's Blackhead Consulting and Mpambani's 605 Consulting Solutions highlights the value that the latter's political connections in the Free State and other provinces brought to the table. 'It is recorded that Ignatius Mpambani has an existing relationship with the provincial governments of the Free State, Northern Cape, North-West and Eastern Cape. 605 Consulting hereby undertakes to procure contracts in relation to consulting engineering and project management from the various clients,' reads the agreement. The fact that Mpambani could allegedly 'procure' government contracts is a glaring red flag.

A letter from Sodi's lawyer to Mpambani, sent in September 2016 after the two men had an almost inevitable falling-out over the Free State asbestos auditing contract, further elaborated on Mpambani's expected role in the whole affair, summarising the joint-venture agreement between their companies as follows: 'Blackhead [Consulting] and Diamond [Hill] would jointly submit a tender in respect of the asbestos eradication programme – Free State ... Diamond [Hill] would attend to all necessary tasks in order to maximize Blackhead's opportunity of being appointed as a service provider.' That the document does not elaborate on the 'necessary tasks' Mpambani was expected to perform is another red flag.

The paper trail of Sodi's and Mpambani's efforts to secure the R255-million asbestos auditing contract from the Free State provincial government leads back to May 2014, when a letter bearing the logos of Blackhead Consulting and Diamond Hill Trading 71 landed in the Free State Department of Human Settlements' mailbox. It was a formal request from the companies to be appointed by the department for the 'assessment [and] audit of houses roofed using asbestos material', and, following the completion of the audit, the 'handling and disposal of asbestos sheets to an approved, designated disposal site'.[12]

According to the letter, Blackhead and Diamond Hill intended to form a joint-venture entity for the project. They put forward some good arguments for why the department should appoint them. 'An informal study in the Free State province has indicated that the asbestos sheets in a large number of old township houses have deteriorated to great extents with cracks and breakages that most likely release dust particles into the air which is the very cause of asbestos associated diseases,' read the proposal. For its 'door-to-door assessment' of houses with asbestos roofs, Blackhead and Diamond Hill would charge the department R1 350 per house. They would then charge a further R32 760 per house once the project reached the 'removal and disposal' phase. All of this would be undertaken on a 'risk basis', meaning the FSHS would not need to pay a cent. 'Diamond Hill/Blackhead Consulting will identify and secure funds on behalf of the Free State Provincial Government for the above costs,' according to the letter. No indication is given of where Sodi and Mpambani intended to source the money.

To avoid having to go through a time-consuming tender process, the parties involved made use of a loophole in the legislation that governs the state's procurement of goods and services. The Public Finance Management Act (PFMA) stipulates that organs of state must appoint contractors through 'a system which is fair, equitable, transparent, competitive and cost-effective'. This includes running open and competitive tender processes whenever state bodies need to appoint new service providers or suppliers. The Treasury Regulations of 2001, which apply to the PFMA, however, provide for a variety of circumstances under which government entities or departments may deviate from an open and competitive bidding process.

Treasury Regulation 16A6.6, for instance, states: 'The accounting officer or accounting authority may, on behalf of the department ... participate in any contract arranged by means of a competitive bidding process by any other organ of state, subject to the written approval of such organ of state and the relevant contractors.' The clause effectively allows one government body to piggyback on the tender process of another. For example, the transport department would technically be allowed to use the services of a company that has already been appointed through a competitive bidding process by the public works department. The provision has since been fine-tuned by the courts, which have found that the goods or services must be the same, as must the contract price.[13] What this means is that, without a bidding process, the transport department now cannot appoint company X to supply it with computers worth R100 million on the back of a tender granted by the public works department for toilet paper worth R1 million. In this hypothetical scenario, both the price and the type of the goods vary too greatly to qualify for a deviation from the PFMA.

The FSHS made use of Treasury Regulation 16A6.6 to appoint the joint venture between Blackhead and Diamond Hill. In July 2014, FSHS HOD Tim Mokhesi wrote a letter to Margaret-Ann Diedricks, who was acting HOD in Gauteng's human settlements department, seeking her approval for the appointment of the Blackhead/Diamond Hill joint venture by his department in line with Treasury Regulation 16A6.6.[14] (More than one source has described Mokhesi, whom we met in previous chapters, as Ace Magashule's henchman in the FSHS.) Diedricks, who would be redeployed to the national Department of Water and Sanitation as director-general later that year after being 'headhunted' by Nomvula Mokonyane,[15] wasted no time writing back to Mokhesi: 'I hereby confirm my decision taken on 21 July 2014 that the Gauteng Department of Human Settlements granted approval in terms of Treasury Regulation 16A6.6 for the Free State Department of Human Settlements to participate in the contract arranged by means of a competitive bidding process from the database of the Gauteng Department of Human Settlements for Professional Resource Teams where Blackhead Consulting (Pty) Ltd was appointed from.'[16]

Thabane Zulu, director-general in the national department, wrote a letter to Mokhesi a few weeks later in which he confirmed Diedricks's decision: the FSHS could appoint Blackhead without a tender process, based on the company's earlier appointment in Gauteng.[17] Zulu, coincidentally, also played a key role in the transferral of Shantan Reddy's R60-million Free State IT contract to the national Department of Energy, as discussed in Chapter 15. He left the Department of Human Settlements in October 2015 to become the Department of Energy's director general. Zulu said he was sure he had handled the transferral of the asbestos audit contract in a lawful manner. 'In all probabilities, I would have handled the matter within the legal framework provided in law in handling a matter of this nature. I have always considered legal compliance on all matters during my period at the said department, as part of my sole responsibility as the accounting officer at the time.'

With their path now all but cleared, Sodi and Mpambani must have felt quite certain that they would secure the contract, for on 10 August 2014 they finally put pen to paper to formalise the joint-venture agreement between Blackhead and Diamond Hill. 'The parties to this agreement will tender for the asbestos-related works jointly,' read the signed document.[18] It was curious wording to include in the agreement, seeing as there would never be a tender process thanks to Treasury Regulation 16A6.6.

On 1 October 2014, Sodi and Mpambani received formal word of their appointment from Mokhesi. 'After due consultation with the Department of Human Settlements – Gauteng Province and concurrent approval by Free State Provincial Treasury it is with great pleasure to announce that you have been duly appointed ... as a Professional Resource Team to assist the Free State Department of Human Settlements in eradicating asbestos in the Free State province,' read the HOD's letter. 'The department wishes to advise that your company has been exclusively appointed for the audit and assessment of asbestos, handling of hazardous material, removal and disposal of asbestos-contaminated rubble and replacement with SABS approved materials in the Free State Province.' As an appointment by a government entity is confirmation that the state will pay, it now appeared that the Free State would foot the bill for the project, despite earlier promises from Sodi and Mpambani that they would source funding.

Mokhesi next had his department enter into a service level agreement with Blackhead and Diamond Hill. Finally, in December 2014, Sodi and Mpambani received an IPW document signed by Mokhesi, in which they were instructed to 'audit, assess and GPS all pre-1994 government housing units in the province at a rate of R850 vat exclusive per unit up to a maximum of 300 000 units (R255m vat exclusive, hereinafter to be referred to as the total project cost)'. There must have been negotiations between the parties after the initial proposal for Diamond Hill and Blackhead to be paid R850 per house as opposed to the R1 350 they had requested. In the greater scheme of things, this would turn out to be a near negligible victory for taxpayers.

A senior FSHS official explained to me why the structure of the deal amounted to a gigantic rip-off: 'The audit was not necessary in the first place, but let's say it had to be done. Why did we agree to pay them [the Blackhead–Diamond Hill joint venture] for a fixed number of houses that they were going to assess? They should only have been paid for the ones where they identified asbestos roofs, not each one they looked at. The fact that they were going to get paid for a predetermined number of houses tells me these guys had come up with R255 million as the target amount for this scam.'

Besides this obvious issue, there were several other problems with the contract and the way in which it was obtained. Firstly, it is always concerning when companies submit unsolicited requests for work to government. This is exactly what Mpambani and Sodi did when they first wrote to the FSHS in May 2014. It was through similar uninvited approaches that the Gupta-linked consultancy firm McKinsey and its local partners, first Regiments and then Trillian, bagged multibillion-rand advisory contracts from Eskom.[19]

Secondly, there is the IPW signed by Mokhesi. In this document, the FSHS agreed to pay R51 million 'on commencement' of the project.[20] In other words, Blackhead and Diamond Hill were due to receive a large amount of money up front, long before they submitted anything of value to the department. South Africa has a long history of such problematic upfront payments made to politically connected contractors. For example, in 2016 Eskom made a 'prepayment' of just under R660 million to Tegeta Exploration and Resources, one of the Gupta family's mining entities. Then public protector Thuli Madonsela found that the transaction may have amounted to fraud,[21] and a National Treasury report released in November 2018 called for criminal investigations into this and other matters involving the Guptas and the state-owned power utility.[22]

The manner in which Mpambani and Sodi received the IPW is also suspicious. Emails contained in the IgoFiles show that John Matlakala, a director in the FSHS's supply-chain management division, emailed the IPW from his work account to his private Gmail account on 3 December 2015. He then forwarded the document from his Gmail to Mpambani and Sodi about ten minutes later, cc'ing Mokhesi's private Yahoo account on the email. It would appear that Matlakala wanted to avoid leaving any trace of communication between him, Mpambani and Sodi on the department's server. Department insiders describe Matlakala as being 'very close' to Mokhesi and Magashule. The FSHS said there was nothing sinister about the fact that Mokhesi and the other officials used private email accounts. 'At the time, the department had problems with the [IT] network, making it difficult to send emails, hence we tended to use Gmail or other private emails.' Curiously, Matlakala had seemingly not experienced any such difficulties when he sent the IPW from his work account to his private email.

A third problem is encountered when comparing Blackhead's contract in Gauteng to the one in the Free State. As mentioned earlier, a deviation from the PFMA in terms of Treasury Regulation 16A6.6 requires that the contract price be more or less the same. I managed to find an IPW from the Gauteng department that confirms Blackhead was appointed for a 'specialist study' on asbestos roofs in the Ekurhuleni metro municipality in March 2014. But this project had a value of only R148 million, R107 million less than the Free State contract.

The fourth major problem is that in Gauteng, the asbestos contract related to the appointment of Blackhead Consulting only. For the Free State contract, Blackhead had teamed up with a new player, namely Mpambani's Diamond Hill. There is no mention in the Treasury Regulations that it is permissible for a government department to appoint a completely new corporate structure, in this case a joint venture between two companies, when invoking Regulation 16A6.6. In this regard, the FSHS had the following to say: 'Blackhead was the lead contractor with Diamond Hill as a supporting partner. However, the substance of the service had not changed with the inclusion of Diamond Hill.' The documents I obtained pointed to the contrary. As far as the contract was concerned, Diamond Hill and Blackhead were clearly equal partners in a joint venture. What's more, the joint venture's fees from the FSHS would be paid into a bank account controlled by Diamond Hill's Mpambani and not by Blackhead or Sodi, as we will come to see.

The fifth and biggest problem with the contract was just how much money Blackhead and Diamond Hill were set to make. The formal letter of appointment and the subsequent service level agreement indicated that the joint venture was appointed not only for the audit and assessment of asbestos roofs, but also for the subsequent handling, removal and disposal of the asbestos-contaminated sheets, as well as their replacement with 'SABS approved materials'. Recall that in their unsolicited request for the work, Blackhead and Diamond Hill indicated that they would charge R32 760 per house once the project reached the 'removal and disposal' phase. The eventual asbestos audit report found that 36 303 houses out of the 300 000 assessed had asbestos roofs. The joint venture therefore had the potential to make another R1.2 billion from the contract. Together with the R255 million for the audit and assessment, Blackhead and Diamond Hill stood to clinch contracts worth more than R1.4 billion without ever submitting a tender.

While it never got that far, I do not doubt for a second that those involved in the scheme intended to drain the full amount from the department. In the IPW received in December 2014, the instruction to perform the audit and assessment work is given as 'IPW 001' and is referred to as 'phase 1'. It seems quite reasonable to infer that 'IPW 002' or 'phase 2', namely the removal and replacement of the asbestos sheets, would have followed.

In early 2015, the Democratic Alliance in the Free State learnt about the R255-million asbestos auditing contract and subsequently launched court proceedings to halt what it viewed as a flagrant heist of state resources. It was probably this scrutiny that prevented the roll-out of the scheme's even more lucrative second phase.

Finally, the sequence in which Mokhesi and the FSHS sent key documents to the joint venture raises further suspicion. In early 2015, Blackhead–Diamond Hill submitted the final audit report to the FSHS. In the report, they indicated that they had 'commenced with the audit from the 17th of November 2014'. Yet Mokhesi only signed the IPW on 2 December, which in any case stated that the 'commencement period for the appointment will be effective from 01 December 2014'.[23] This meant that Blackhead and Diamond Hill had begun work on the asbestos audit two weeks before they received the instruction from the department to commence with the project.

Most professionals, civil servants and politicians in South Africa take a break between the end of December and the first weeks of January, but those involved in what became the asbestos heist were especially busy during the holiday period of late 2014 and early 2015.

According to documents contained in the IgoFiles, on 22 December 2014 the FSHS transferred R20 million to an FNB business account that had been jointly opened in the names of Blackhead Consulting and Diamond Hill Trading 71. This payment represented a deviation from the initial plan. As mentioned earlier, the IPW signed by Mokhesi promised an upfront payment of R51 million, payable on 1 December. Several sources explained to me that the department's finance office was completely caught off guard by the new contract Mokhesi suddenly brought to the table. 'There was no business plan or budget for this asbestos thing we were now hearing about,' a current FSHS staffer told me. 'We asked the HOD where we were going to get the money to pay for this thing.' As an unforeseen expense, the R51-million prepayment was simply too large to pay out all at once. The department instead opted to break up the prepayment into smaller amounts, of which the R20 million was the first. This was followed by a second payment of R31 million, which was transferred to the Blackhead–Diamond Hill FNB account on 15 January 2015. The entire haul of more than R200 million was eventually paid out in eight batches.

According to insiders familiar with the saga, some FSHS staffers queried the prepayments. They were concerned that proper procedures were not followed with regards to the appointment and payment of Blackhead and Diamond Hill. At that point, Magashule's alleged involvement in the deal came to the fore. 'Ace worked behind the scenes with Mokhesi and other senior managers to get the asbestos thing going, but his role was revealed when some officials questioned the contract,' alleged one department insider. 'They were told that Ace was behind the contract and that they should stop questioning things if they wanted to keep their jobs.' In response to staffers' concerns over the prepayment, Mokhesi and other senior managers apparently told them that Ace had issued 'political orders' to ensure Blackhead and Diamond Hill got paid.

22

A blueprint for bribes

One of the most damning documents in the IgoFiles is an innocuous-looking Excel spreadsheet titled 'Free State Asbestos'. One cannot imagine that many corrupt tenderpreneurs would be reckless enough to create a document detailing exactly how they intend to share their earnings from government with officials and politicians, yet this spreadsheet appears to be exactly that.

It is not clear whether Mpambani or Sodi created the document, but its creation date – November 2014 – is reflected in the file's metadata. It was later emailed between the two businessmen, and went through various revisions. In essence, it appears to be a blueprint for the distribution of bribes to Magashule and officials from the Gauteng, Free State and national housing departments who played a role in the asbestos auditing contract. Its very existence may explain why Magashule and others wanted the FSHS to pay the Blackhead–Diamond Hill joint venture, despite concerns from mid-level officials that the deal looked suspicious.

Emails contained in the IgoFiles show that Sodi sent a version of this document to Mpambani under the subject line 'Fees Calculation'. Mpambani then altered the document. Later, in March 2015, in a draft email intended for Sodi, Mpambani wrote the following: 'Sho Eddie, please note that payments in yellow are the ones you will take care of and rest, us. As discussed, I have effected the payments in 2 batches. Kindly find attached the updated schedule with minor adjustments.' By this point, Blackhead–Diamond Hill had received its upfront payments worth R51 million.

The spreadsheet, on face value, provides rare insight into how corrupt government deals involving millions of rands are put together. Under the heading 'cost of business', the document lists several names, many of them abbreviated, with the amounts that each was due to receive. A certain 'AM', for instance, was to be paid R10 million. 'TZ' would receive R10 million, while 'TM' would receive R5 million. 'JT' was to get R3 million,

'MEC' R2.5 million and 'OM' R1 million. Those unabbreviated included a company called Mastertrade (to be paid just over R44 million) and an individual called Diedricks (R1 million). The 'total cost of business', reflected on the spreadsheet, amounted to R82.6 million. The 'project value' of R255 million minus this 'total cost of business' left an amount of R172.4 million. This was the profit Blackhead and Diamond Hill would split after settling their expenses – R86.2 million in pure profit each. According to the spreadsheet, the third parties were set to receive their 'fees' in staggered tranches coinciding with payments received from the FSHS in the Blackhead–Diamond Hill joint FNB account. Mpambani's Diamond Hill would be responsible for making most of the payments to third parties, according to the spreadsheet. This may explain why Mpambani did not pay Sodi's company exactly half of each of the first three payments from the FSHS, seeing as he would have needed to settle the third parties' claims first.

I showed the document to a source who had been privy to certain aspects of the asbestos auditing scheme. Working through the spreadsheet, he suggested the initials 'AM' stood for Ace Magashule. The source thought that 'MEC' could be Mathabo Leeto, the former mayor of Matjhabeng and current Free State MEC for sport, arts, culture and recreation. My source explained that Leeto maintained close ties with Mpambani after her tenure as mayor, and that she sometimes acted as a facilitator for some of Mpambani's deals in the Free State. This may have been the reason why she was included in the asbestos auditing scheme, the source suggested. After Mpambani's death, Leeto posted the following comment on Facebook: 'I am so hurt. Igo was like a younger brother to me.'

Leeto sang a different tune after I asked her about her ties to the late businessman. 'There is no relationship between MEC Leeto and Mr Igo Mpambani including his family other than the former being known as a person who grew [up] and stayed in her neighbourhood in Welkom,' said her spokesperson. Leeto denied that she had ever influenced a contract awarded to Mpambani, and she claimed she was unaware of the asbestos audit deal. 'MEC Leeto harbors no knowledge of her name being used in any documents by Igo Mpambani and further denies that she received a payment of R2.5 million from Igo Mpambani.'

A senior ANC figure from the Welkom area told me that the Leeto family was almost certainly involved in the asbestos auditing scheme.

'When that deal was being put together, Mathabo's husband, Lehana, spoke about how he was going to be involved in the project,' said this source. 'He went into quite a lot of detail, like the proposed sites near Welkom and Odendaalsrus where the asbestos roofs would be safely disposed of once the audit was finished.'

Leeto denied this. 'The MEC has established from her husband that the said allegations are devoid of any truth,' said her spokesperson.

The source with whom I shared the spreadsheet suggested that 'TZ', 'OM' and 'Diedricks' were also government officials involved in the asbestos saga, and that 'JT' was most likely retired soccer star Jimmy Tau. I asked this person how Tau had got involved. Apparently, the former Kaizer Chiefs player had represented Nomvula Mokonyane, under whose reign as Gauteng premier Blackhead had first started clinching major government contracts. This sounded a little far-fetched, but I then remembered having seen something about a link between Tau and Mokonyane before. In fact, it was EFF leader Julius Malema who first claimed at a press conference in August 2016 that Tau was one of the younger men with whom Mokonyane was allegedly romantically involved.[1]

The spreadsheet is compelling, but it does not prove that Magashule and the others received their share of the asbestos auditing contract loot. Luckily, further information and documents in the IgoFiles show that Mpambani did indeed make payments in accordance with the spreadsheet's payment schedule. Bank records in the trove of documents reveal that Mpambani channelled payments totalling exactly R19 983 427.16 from the Blackhead–Diamond Hill joint FNB account to several recipients on 23 December 2014. This was a day after the FSHS made the first payment of R20 million.

That exact amount, to the very last cent, appears in the spreadsheet under the heading 'first payment'. According to the spreadsheet, it was the sum of ten separate payments that Mpambani had to make to third parties after Blackhead–Diamond Hill received its first payment from the FSHS. The document lists a payment of almost R13.3 million to Mastertrade; R1 million each to AM, TZ, TM and MEC; R500 000 to Diedricks; R200 000 to OM; R1 million to 'others'; R500 000 to 'Martin'; and R500 000 to Diamond Hill, Mpambani's own company. This all equalled exactly R19 983 427.16. This amount is captured as a 'consolidated payment' in bank records for Blackhead–Diamond Hill's joint FNB account, meaning it is the sum of several payments. According to bank statements in the IgoFiles, Mpambani transferred almost R13.3 million to Mastertrade's FNB account on 23 December, exactly as listed in the spreadsheet. Despite the payment records, Mastertrade's director, Sello 'Sydney' Radebe, flatly denied that his company had received the money. He also denied that he had in any way participated in the asbestos project. Radebe's behaviour only fuelled my suspicions about the entire affair. Mastertrade's company records showed that it was operated from an office in Sandton, but I established that Radebe hails from the eastern Free State. According to his CV, Radebe grew up in Phuthaditjhaba, in QwaQwa. He worked at the QwaQwa Development Corporation, which has since been incorporated into the FDC. A source who worked with Mpambani told me that Radebe was close to then Gauteng ANC chairperson Paul Mashatile.

A noteworthy observation is that Mpambani was in Bloemfontein when he effected these first payments. Records from the Grasmere toll plaza south of Johannesburg and the Brandfort toll plaza near Bloemfontein show that he passed through these points on 23 December. The following day, he withdrew a few thousand rands in cash from an FNB ATM in Bloemfontein's Brandwag suburb. This ATM is located 2.3 kilometres from Free State House, the official residence of the premier. Records show that Mpambani frequently withdrew money from this and other ATMs near Magashule's residence shortly before or after his company received a payment from the FSHS. So often, in fact, that it became a pattern.

On 23 December, Mpambani moved R3.5 million from the joint venture's FNB account to an account held by 605 Consulting Solutions, the company he had registered earlier that year. The next day, Christmas Eve, he paid R1 million from 605 Consulting's account to Kingdom Impact General Trading. The payment was marked as 'Consulting Services Invoice 001'. It was not a once-off payment. On 24 August 2016, just after the FSHS transferred its final payment to the Blackhead–Diamond Hill joint account, one Motsamai Kareli emailed an invoice for R990 000 to Mpambani for 'professional engineering services'. It was made out to 605 Consulting Solutions. That same day, Mpambani transferred R990 000 from 605 Consulting's FNB account to Kingdom Impact. We therefore know for a fact that Mpambani channelled at least R1.9 million to Kingdom Impact in two payments that were made right after Blackhead–Diamond Hill received money from the Free State government.

For those in the business of uncovering corruption, money laundering and other dodgy dealings, terms such as 'consulting services' count among the most common red flags. Paying third parties for vaguely described services such as consulting is one of the ways in which facilitators of bribes channel large payments to venal politicians or officials. And when the third party is unable to provide evidence that it performed any actual work, the alarm bells start to sound.

Kingdom Impact's sole director is a woman named Thulisiwe Kareli. Her husband, Motsamai Kareli, is the founder and senior pastor of the evangelical Empowerment Ministries International church in Bloemfontein. While Thulisiwe is also a pastor and heavily involved in the church, she has held other jobs. I found her name on a 2015 tender document from Centlec, the Mangaung metro municipality's state-owned power distributor. She worked in Centlec's procurement division. At the time, FSHS HOD Tim Mokhesi was a Centlec board member. Other board members included Kenosi Moroka and Blacky Seoe, both former business partners to Magashule.

Empowerment Ministries International can also be linked to Magashule and Mathabo Leeto. According to the former's diary, he delivered a keynote address at an Empowerment Ministries event in November 2012. And in August 2017, Leeto was a speaker at the church's Affluent Women's Conference hosted by Thulisiwe. Sources in the Free State's political circles told me that Magashule kept a few pastors and other religious figures close to him. These clergymen would sometimes include messages of support for his administration in their sermons. One contact, a senior provincial official, told me Motsamai Kareli was one of Magashule's 'favourites'. Kareli denied this. 'I have no connections with Mr Makgashule [sic] or Mr Tim Mokhesi. I doubt they even know me,' he responded when I asked him about it.

This is hard to believe. The Karelis' listed residential address is a property in the upmarket Woodland Hills Wildlife Estate on the outskirts of Bloemfontein. Mosidi Motsemme, Magashule's 'Bloemfontein wife', and Moreki Moroka, wife of Kenosi Moroka, also have houses here. Furthermore, Motsamai Kareli is a director of KICS Holdings. According to the entity's website, one of its clients is E'tsho Civils, the engineering firm owned by Tlale Mokgadi, the businessman who travelled to Cuba with Magashule in January 2015. 'You won't be doing business with E'tsho or Mokgadi without crossing paths with Ace at some point,' one of Magashule's former confidants told me. Kareli later put me in touch with his lawyers, none other than Moroka Attorneys, the firm owned by Centlec board member Kenosi Moroka, Magashule's former business partner and one of his closest associates. A former member of Magashule's provincial cabinet also poured cold water on Kareli's assertion that he did not know the former premier. 'Ace was going to get some award from Kareli's church in around 2012. He couldn't attend that event, so he sent one of his MECs,' this source told me.

I asked the Karelis to explain why Kingdom Impact received almost R2 million from Mpambani for 'professional engineering services' when neither of them are registered with the Engineering Council of South Africa. I also applied to inspect Kingdom Impact's share register. My queries and requests elicited the following response from Moroka Attorneys:

> ... cognizance needs to be given to the type of economy that the country is currently in and as such any financial information of our clients and/ or any individual that is made public, such disclosure opens a person to vulnerability in relation to other negative aspects in our country and these includes [sic] but not limited to crime and other criminal elements and activities that such information can be used in.

That the Karelis are unable or unwilling to explain the nature of the services provided by Kingdom Impact to Mpambani is cause for concern. A simple peek by any law-enforcement agency into the company's bank records would no doubt yield some interesting results.

23

Havana nights

A bagman is a person who collects or distributes illicitly gained money, such as bribes to public officials. Igo Mpambani seemingly became a bagman for Ace Magashule when the first millions from the Free State government began to flow into the Blackhead–Diamond Hill joint bank account.

Sources from the province's political circles, including senior former and current officials, told me that they increasingly saw the Sandton-based businessman in Magashule's company from around January 2015. These sources held varying views on Mpambani's prominence among the tribe of contractors, businesspeople and other moneymen who seemed to orbit around the premier. One current MEC said he knew that Mpambani was somehow linked to Magashule, but that he was under the impression that the young businessman had played second fiddle to Magashule's more established business associates. 'There would always be this group of hangers-on at ExCo meetings and other gatherings. They all vied for Ace's attention, some with more success than others. I always thought Igo was a bit of a wannabe,' this official told me.

One of Magashule's former confidants had a different opinion. 'If Igo was trying to get into Ace's inner circle, he was making good progress,' he told me. This impression is supported by documents in the IgoFiles. In the nearly two years between Blackhead–Diamond Hill's first payment from the FSHS in December 2014 and the final transfer in August 2016, Mpambani was invited by Magashule's office to several distinguished events, including the premier's State of the Province addresses.

But the devil lay in the finer detail. Mpambani's bank records allowed me to build a detailed timeline of when he was spending his money, and where. I compared this dataset to Magashule's official diary. The results were interesting, to say the least. At times, it looked like Mpambani was literally following Magashule around the country. Other documents from the IgoFiles and additional source accounts confirmed that the young tenderpreneur was indeed spending a lot of time with Magashule and even accompanying him on trips abroad.

A case in point is a trip to Cape Town in early January 2015, between the first payment of R20 million from the FSHS to the Blackhead–Diamond Hill joint venture in late December 2014 and the second payment of R31 million on 15 January 2015. On Wednesday 7 January, Magashule flew to Cape Town. According to his diary, he attended an NEC meeting there, met with then social development minister Bathabile Dlamini and enjoyed a 'private lunch' with controversial tender mogul Vivian Reddy. That Saturday, 10 January, Magashule attended the ANC's 103rd birthday celebration at the Cape Town Stadium in Green Point before flying back to Bloemfontein the following day.

Bank records from the IgoFiles show that Mpambani arrived in Cape Town on the Friday before the ANC birthday bash. Using money from the asbestos audit that he had transferred to the 605 Consulting Solutions bank account, that weekend he splashed about R5 000 on booze at a liquor store in Green Point, around the corner from where the ANC festivities were due to take place. He also swiped one of his bank cards at various restaurants in the area.

Magashule was back at work in Bloemfontein on Monday 12 January, according to his diary. On that Thursday, the second instalment of R31 million from the FSHS arrived in the Blackhead–Diamond Hill joint account. Mpambani transferred the entire amount to Diamond Hill's own account, from which he made several large payments for 'loans' and 'consulting services'. He also moved just under R9 million to 605 Consulting, citing 'engineering services' as the reason for the transfer. From 605 Consulting's account, Mpambani made further payments that correlate with the damning 'cost of business' column in the 'Free State Asbestos' Excel spreadsheet. On 20 January, he transferred R1 million to El Jefe Consulting. According to company records, this entity's sole director is Jimmy Tau, the retired Kaizer Chiefs soccer star who was allegedly cut in on the asbestos deal because of his proximity to Nomvula Mokonyane. That the company was only registered in February 2014, shortly before Mpambani and Sodi began putting together the deal, is suspicious. I got hold of Tau in November 2018 to find out why his company received money from Mpambani. He asked me to email him with my queries, which I duly did, but he hasn't got back to me.

After the second payment from the FSHS, Mpambani again travelled to the Free State, where he withdrew large amounts of cash from ATMs all over Bloemfontein and nearby towns. According to his diary, Magashule had several engagements in Welkom and Sasolburg between Monday 19 January and Friday 23 January. Records in the IgoFiles show that Mpambani spent money from the 605 Consulting account on food, liquor and other expenses in these two towns in the same week.

On the Friday, Magashule was in Sasolburg for 'various' executive council activities and Operation Hlasela engagements. That evening, Mpambani used the 605 Consulting bank card at a lodge in Three Rivers, Vereeniging. The lodge is located about twenty-five kilometres from Sasolburg. He spent just under R5 000 at the establishment in two payments. The following day, Mpambani travelled to Gauteng, as evidenced by the fact that he withdrew money from the 605 Consulting account at FNB's Merchant Place branch in Sandton in the afternoon. According to Magashule's diary, he too was travelling to Gauteng that day: 'travel to JHB,' reads the entry for Saturday 24 January.

And so it went. Each time Blackhead–Diamond Hill received money from the FSHS, Mpambani's movements matched those of Magashule. This would continue for the next year and a half, until his death in June 2017.

On Sunday and Monday (25 and 26 January 2015), Magashule attended a two-day ANC NEC lekgotla at the Saint George Hotel in Pretoria. While the NEC gathering was under way, the Free State Development Corporation's company secretary, David Nkaiseng, forwarded to Mpambani the 'briefing documentation' for the Free State delegation's upcoming visit to Cuba. The document bore the emblem of the Office of the Premier.

On Tuesday 27 January, Mpambani printed a company resolution for Diamond Hill at a print shop in Sandton. It read: 'Directors' contribution to the Free State Asbestos project will be paid to the company of their choice.' At 11:10 that morning, Magashule and his six associates boarded South African Airways flight SA222 at O.R. Tambo International Airport, from where they flew to Cuba via São Paulo, Brazil, and Bogotá, Colombia. That same evening, just before 7 p.m., Mpambani boarded an Air France flight that took him to Havana via Paris.

Although Mpambani did not form part of the official Free State delegation, sources who went on the trip said that the businessman was frequently in Magashule's company in Cuba. 'Ace mostly spent time with people from the FDC and his business associates; he didn't really pay much attention to the provincial and municipal officials,' said an employee of a Free State municipality who tagged along. On a few occasions, Magashule and his band of businesspeople joined the government officials for dinner. 'We were all eating at a restaurant in Havana one night when Ace introduced us to this young businessman. It was Igo,' the same source told me. One of Magashule's former staffers confirmed that Mpambani formed part of the premier's group in Cuba. 'I don't know how they knew each other. I met the guy for the first time in Cuba,' this official told me.

The IgoFiles show that Mpambani's visit to Havana was brief. He must have arrived there quite late on Wednesday 28 January. That evening, before 10 p.m. local time, he spent just under R6 000 from the 605 Consulting account at a hotel in Havana. The following day, he paid just under R4 000 for an air ticket that would take him to the Cayman Islands that Sunday. This picturesque archipelago south of Cuba is known for its beautiful beaches, pristine blue water and infamously opaque financial sector. The Cayman Islands ranks third on the Tax Justice Network's 2018 Financial Secrecy Index,[1] meaning it is one of the best places in the world to stash money without being asked difficult questions.

Mpambani landed at the Owen Roberts International Airport in George Town, the Caymans' capital, at 15:25 local time on Sunday 1 February 2015. He checked into the Holiday Inn Resort Grand Cayman later that day. The following evening, he started doing some serious business in the tropical paradise. At just before midnight local time, he sent an email with an attached Word document to the private Gmail account of John Matlakala, the FSHS director who had sent him and Sodi the IPW for the asbestos auditing contract. The document Mpambani sent to Matlakala was an invoice for R76.5 million, marked 'Invoice Number 002'. The following morning, Mpambani sent two more invoices to Matlakala for R20 million and R31 million respectively. Clearly, these were for the two payments the department had already made. In other words, the FSHS paid Blackhead–Diamond Hill R51 million without being invoiced first. This is an indefensible accounting transgression.

According to the contract, the department was supposed to pay Blackhead–Diamond Hill in accordance with the following fee structure:

the full contract amount of R255 million was to be divided into two equal payments of R127.5 million. Blackhead–Diamond Hill was entitled to 40 per cent of R127.5 million as an upfront payment – in other words, R51 million. The remaining 60 per cent of the first payment of R127.5 million, which amounted to R76.5 million, was to be paid as 'progress certificate no. 2', according to the IPW.

The fact that the upfront payment of R51 million had been split clearly confused Matlakala, who now needed to process the invoices Mpambani was sending him from the Caymans. He emailed Mpambani with the following request: 'Kindly forward your documents in PDF format and observe the following: 1. Invoice 001 for R51 [million] must be dated 02 Dec 2014. 2. Invoice 002 for R31 [million] must be dated 12 Jan 2015.' Mpambani tried to clarify. 'Good day Mr. Tlaks, there seems to be a little confusion,' he wrote. 'Invoice 1 was for R51 million but it was paid in 2 parts (R20m in Dec and R31m in January). Therefore I can't make an invoice for R51m (40%) and then another for R31m (part of the same 40%) unless that's what is required for administration purposes.' This must have satisfied Matlakala, as he did not reply.

With the invoices for the first R127.5 million now submitted to Matlakala and R51 million already paid out, Mpambani tended to some banking business. Information from the IgoFiles suggests he met with Jarard Blake, the head of banking and operations at the Caymans' branch of UBS Fund Services. I reached out to Blake to ask him whether Mpambani had been to his bank and, if he had, what he did there. He ignored my queries and later blocked me on Twitter. Blake clearly did not want to talk about the South African businessman.

On 3 February, Mpambani flew back to Cuba. The next day, he returned to Johannesburg via Paris. Three days later, Magashule flew back to South Africa via São Paulo.

It is curious why Mpambani chose to execute so much of the financial admin for the asbestos deal while he was abroad with Magashule. And his sojourn in the Caymans, with its reputation as a great place to hide money, and his probable meeting with UBS, pose tantalising questions about the payment of the directors' contributions outlined in the Diamond Hill company resolution. Thanks to the Caymans' secretive financial sector, we may never know whether Mpambani made payments and, if he did, to whom.

* * *

Mpambani's trip to Cuba suggests that the young businessman had finally established himself as a member of Magashule's inner circle of connected contractors. According to his official diary, the premier's first scheduled engagement after the Cuba trip was at the University of the Witwatersrand in Johannesburg on Monday 9 February. He most likely returned to Bloemfontein later that day, as he had a meeting scheduled there for the following morning. Mpambani drove to Bloemfontein that same Monday, where he withdrew R16 000 from an ATM at the Dynarc Walk shopping centre that evening. The next morning, between 08:07 and 08:11, he withdrew a further R24 000 in separate batches from the Brandwag ATM around the corner from Free State House. According to Magashule's diary, he had a 'private meeting' scheduled at Free State House for 9 a.m.

It may be mere coincidence, but anecdotal evidence suggests that the money Mpambani withdrew went straight to Magashule. A source who worked closely with Mpambani told me that whenever the FSHS made payments to Blackhead–Diamond Hill, the businessman would set off for the Free State to meet with either Magashule or one of his proxies. 'When he went to meet with Ace or one of his people, Igo would sometimes leave Johannesburg with large amounts of cash,' alleged my source.

Mpambani would apparently regularly meet with Chris Ackeer, another Parys local who effectively worked as one of Magashule's aides. Ackeer later joined Magashule at Luthuli House when the latter became ANC secretary-general. 'Igo met with Chris a lot during that time; he told me whenever he went down to meet with him,' my source told me.

I had heard about Ackeer even before I started researching the asbestos auditing contract. Several sources in the Free State close to Magashule alleged that Ackeer was not only like an assistant, but also a fixer of sorts. 'Ace first brought Ackeer into the ANC to try and get more support from coloured voters in the Free State. Then he gradually started to work for Ace. Later, he allegedly started doing Ace's dirty work. He would pick up money for Ace or do other things that Ace couldn't do with the people from his official blue lights security team,' a top politician in the province told me. A second source, a current MEC, agreed: 'Chris and Ricardo [Mettler] did the same kind of things for Ace. They did most of his dirty work.' Mettler, another member of Magashule's security detail, was implicated in the alleged theft of a Pierneef painting worth an estimated R8 million from the Free State premier's office in early 2018, during the time that Magashule was vacating it.[2]

Ackeer strongly denied the allegations. 'I am not the SG's fixer and I don't collect cash from other people on his behalf,' he told me. 'The SG is not my employer. I am a strategic manager for the ANC and I don't report to the SG,' added Ackeer. He said he had not known Mpambani well and only met him 'maybe two or three times' at social events. 'I never took money from him,' he said.

I discussed Mpambani's pattern of withdrawing cash from ATMs near Free State House with three former members of Magashule's inner circle. They were all convinced that the cash went to the then premier. 'This is how Ace operates,' said one. 'A similar thing happened with another FSHS contractor in the Riebeeckstad area. After the businessman got paid by the province, Ace himself collected cash from the guy at an Engen garage.' Another alleged that 'Ace deals in cash. He knows that by doing so it will be very difficult for anyone to catch him red-handed.' Nevertheless, I believe I have established beyond any doubt that the former premier was an active participant in the asbestos auditing scheme, as further detailed in the next chapter.

24

Ace shows his hand

In mid-February 2015, Mpambani received an email from A.K. Manyike on behalf of the Ori Group. The email included the 'final 100% report' for the asbestos audit. The report itself indicates that the audit commenced in November 2014.

Documents in the IgoFiles explain the Ori Group's role in the saga. In August 2014, after it had become clear that the Blackhead–Diamond Hill joint venture would be awarded the asbestos contract, Mpambani and Sodi appointed Mastertrade to compile the audit report. According to the breakdown of fees detailed in the dubious 'Free State Asbestos' Excel spreadsheet, Mastertrade was set to receive R44 million from the joint venture for their services.

At the end of October 2014, Mastertrade's boss, Sello 'Sydney' Radebe, subcontracted a company called Ori Group to perform the audit. Mastertrade promised to pay them just over R21 million. This meant that of the R255 million for the asbestos audit and assessment that the FSHS had agreed to pay Blackhead–Diamond Hill, roughly 90 per cent, or just over R230 million, was unadulterated profit. And who knows how much profit the Ori Group made on the R21 million. It took just three months for them to complete a report that, at fifty-three pages, cost taxpayers nearly R5 million per page.

It gets worse. The audit report's main finding was that just over 36 000 of the 300 000 houses assessed had asbestos roofs. The report included a breakdown of where these houses were situated. I spoke to a source from the auditor-general's office with insight into the project. He said the entire contract was a 'sham'. 'The old houses with asbestos roofs are usually concentrated in the same area in each township, and the municipalities have records of where those houses are located,' he told me. In other words, the asbestos audit was completely unnecessary. A current FSHS staffer agreed. 'The location of houses with asbestos roofs forms part of a dataset for government's discount benefit scheme. Government already sat with this information, so the asbestos audit was not necessary,' this source said.

Also, when the AG's office went over the work submitted by Blackhead and Diamond Hill, it found that many of the houses in the report had been duplicated. 'You would see a picture of house number 20 in a certain township, and, a few pages later, you would again see the same house. This happened with more than one house,' my source in the AG's office told me.

Even if the department could somehow justify the audit, we now know that 'only' R21 million went to the company that did the actual work. This left plenty of cash for all manner of indulgences, including luxury cars. A few weeks after the second payment from the FSHS, Mpambani treated himself to a Bentley Continental GT. It was a second-hand model from a local dealership in Vanderbijlpark, but it nevertheless cost the business-man R1.2 million. Ominously, this is the vehicle he would die in about two years later. Mpambani later bought more luxury vehicles and a string of upmarket properties.

Shortly after Mpambani bought the Bentley, he received an invitation to Magashule's 2015 State of the Province Address, which was scheduled for 24 February. The invitation had been sent by an employee from C-Squared, a controversial events-management company whose owner is said to be close to Magashule.[1] Documents in the IgoFiles show that three days after receiving the invitation, Mpambani withdrew R150 000 from 605 Consulting Solution's account at an FNB branch in Rivonia, near Sandton. At that stage, 605 Consulting had about R2 million left of the nearly R9 million that Mpambani had transferred from the Diamond Hill account the previous month for 'engineering services'. The day before Magashule's speech, Mpambani drove down to Bloemfontein, swiping his Diamond Hill and 605 Consulting bank cards at toll gates and a fuel station along the way. He booked into the Southern Sun hotel, across the road from the FNB ATM in Brandwag near the premier's official residence. The following afternoon, after the State of the Province Address, Mpambani spent money at restaurants and clothing stores in Bloemfontein's Mimosa Mall and elsewhere in the city. He returned to Gauteng the next morning, filling up at an Engen fuel station across the road from his hotel just after 9 a.m. and swiping his bank cards at the series of toll gates between Bloemfontein and Johannesburg.

On 26 March 2015, a third payment of R25 million from the FSHS landed in the Blackhead–Diamond Hill joint account. Once again, Mpambani made several large payments for 'consulting' and 'engineering' services to various entities, including another R500 000 to El Jefe Consulting, former soccer star Jimmy Tau's company. This correlates exactly with the payment schedule set out in the dubious 'Free State Asbestos' Excel spreadsheet, which shows that 'JT' was supposed to get half a million rand after the third instalment of the asbestos payments was received.

The spreadsheet also shows that 'AM' (Ace Magashule?) and 'MEC' (Mathabo Leeto?) were due to receive R1 million and R1.5 million respectively at this time. Mpambani made payments that matched those amounts exactly. For instance, on 28 March, after transferring a 'project management' fee of R2.4 million to Diamond Hill's account, he paid a third party R1 million for 'consulting services'. Unfortunately, the IgoFiles contain a few blind spots with regards to the identity of the beneficiaries of some of these payments.

Shortly before receiving the third FSHS payment, Mpambani emailed an employee at the South African Music Awards (SAMAs) with a special request. 'Please be advised that MEC Mathabo Leeto (Sports, Arts, Culture and Recreation FS) and her husband have expressed a keen interest in attending the SAMA 2015. As this will be a private arrangement and not through her office, I will be attending to her needs and requests,' Mpambani wrote. 'The travelling guests will be 6 in total (excluding the 2 bodyguards) and I will also be part of the guests. Kindly advise how we can arrange for the accreditation for the security detail. Since accommodation has been arranged, please advise on VIP/Executive tickets.'

A few days later, the SAMA employee came back with a quote of just over R4 000 for the tickets. But Mpambani did not immediately settle the invoice. Instead, he waited until 26 March, the day on which Blackhead–Diamond Hill received their third payment from the FSHS. Mpambani apparently made good on his promise to attend to Leeto's needs at the SAMAs. The awards ceremony was held at Sun City on Sunday 19 April. That weekend, Mpambani spent almost R50 000 at The Palace of the Lost City, Sun City's most luxurious hotel. This was all money channelled into 605 Consulting's account from the asbestos contract's third instalment. While these amounts are small in the greater scheme of things, the transactions seemingly showed that Leeto was indeed a recipient of at least some of the asbestos funds, supporting my source's theory that Leeto and 'MEC' are one and the same. Leeto denied that she and her husband attended the SAMAs or that they stayed in The Palace hotel. Her spokesperson said it was a 'blatant lie to tarnish her name'.

Not long after the third instalment was paid, Magashule showed his hand.

Shortly before 10 a.m. on Friday 10 April, Mpambani withdrew R300 000 from 605 Consulting's FNB account at one of the bank's branches in Rivonia. A few days before, he had transferred R7 million of the third FSHS instalment to the 605 Consulting account in two tranches, marking the payments as 'engineering services'. Loaded with cash, Mpambani once again drove to Bloemfontein, where he booked himself into a local guesthouse. At just after 7 p.m. that evening, he received an email from one of Magashule's staffers. 'See below bank details. I just don't have details for Unisa. Will forward as soon as I get them,' Ipeleng Morake, an employee in the premier's office, wrote from her private Gmail account.

The 'below bank details' were contained in an email that had been sent to her earlier that day by Moroadi Cholota, Magashule's personal assistant. Cholota had also used a private Gmail account, but her email to Morake included her job title and contact details at the Free State Office of the Premier. The forwarded email included the bank details for the University of the Free State (UFS), North-West University (NWU) and the Central University of Technology (CUT). Mpambani was instructed to reference certain student numbers when he made the payments. These details must have been discussed with him elsewhere, as the student numbers were not included in Morake's email.

The following morning, after creating payment links to 'UFS', 'NWU' and 'CUT', Mpambani made eight successive payments totalling just over R240 000 from 605 Consulting's account. Each payment was identified by a different student number and labelled 'student bursary dona[tion]'. Shortly thereafter, Cholota emailed Mpambani. 'I received all the proof of payments. Thank you very much and may the good Lord bless u,' she wrote.

I showed this information to a few sources who had insight into Magashule's way of doing business. Apparently his unofficial bursary schemes were an open secret. My sources alleged that Magashule promised to cover the university or college fees of scores of young people in the province. He did not pay these fees himself, but instead directed business-people who had clinched government contracts to do so.

I showed the Excel spreadsheet to some of these sources. They told me something that resonated with what I had repeatedly heard while researching Magashule's dealings. 'Don't just look for money flowing into Magashule's own pockets,' one told me. 'After he had helped you get a contract, he would take his cut in the form of something like a credit facility. In this case, he would have told the asbestos guy when and how to make certain payments until the R10 million was finished.' Another source, a former associate, encouraged me to look out for possible cash payments. 'Ace likes cash, because it doesn't leave much of a trail. He always has lots of cash with him,' alleged this person. The IgoFiles appear to support both these claims.

On 6 May 2015, Cholota emailed Mpambani with another special request. 'Following the discussion with Ipeleng Morake, Premier requested that you pay full amount of R470 000 and the remaining amount of R30 000 to one of the SRC President in Cuba,' she wrote, this time from her official government email account. She included the banking details for Pule Nkate, who is described by *FS News Online* as the 'Student Rep-resentative of South African [Medical] Students in Cuba'.[2] Attached to the email was an invoice for tablet devices valued at R470 000. If Mpambani settled these bills, he did so either in cash or from accounts that do not show up in the IgoFiles.

The FSHS paid a fourth instalment of R15 million to the Blackhead–Diamond Hill joint account on 4 June 2015. Mpambani handled this payment in a now familiar manner. Half of the R15 million was trans-ferred to Sodi's Blackhead Consulting, while the rest was flushed into the accounts of Diamond Hill and 605 Consulting in several payments that ranged from R900 000 to R3 million and that were labelled as 'project management' or 'engineering services' fees. From his company accounts, Mpambani made payments to a range of other parties for 'consulting ser-vices', 'engineering services' and 'loans'. They were mostly rounded figures of as much as R1 million at a time.

Mpambani also sent emails during this period that provided insight into his relationship with Magashule. On 8 June, a representative from China U-Ton Holdings, a Chinese fibre-optics company with a listing on the Hong Kong stock exchange, emailed Mpambani, Free State Development Corporation CEO Ikhraam Osman and David Nkaiseng, the FDC official who had sent Mpambani the details of Magashule's trip to Cuba. 'I must say that it was my great pleasure to know you and I fully enjoyed our meetings and dinner last week,' wrote the China U-Ton representative. 'I have returned to China over the weekend and would like to reiterate our interest in working with FDC ... to construct a fibre optics network.'

Mpambani responded as follows: 'We are excited of the opportunity to partner with a reputable entity as your esteemed organisation. As discussed, we will embark on a trip to China with the Premier of the Free State Province in July and would like to take the opportunity to visit some of the functional [China U-Ton] sites.' While it does not look like this deal ever materialised, the exchange highlighted the fact that Mpambani was involved in the province's business dealings with private companies and showed his continued proximity to Magashule.

The IgoFiles reveal that Mpambani used some of the money from the fourth FSHS payment to sponsor a R40 000 luxury holiday for Chris Ackeer, Magashule's aide and alleged fixer. Documents show that Ackeer and two young women flew to Cape Town, where they stayed in an upmarket apartment at the V&A Waterfront for a couple of nights in early July. The trio racked up huge bills at restaurants and clothing stores, which Mpambani seemingly paid using money from the asbestos audit. Just two days before Ackeer's trip, Mpambani paid himself a 'salary' of R100 000 from the Diamond Hill account. The money was paid into his personal RMB cheque account, from where he seemingly settled Ackeer's holiday expenses. Ackeer denied that Mpambani had paid for any of his holidays.

On 11 August 2015, the FSHS paid a fifth instalment of R36.5 million to the Blackhead–Diamond Hill joint account. Mpambani immediately transferred R12.5 million to Diamond Hill and R1.5 million to 605 Consulting. He then drove from Johannesburg to Bloemfontein, where he booked himself into his usual guesthouse. Magashule's official diary places him in Bloemfontein during this time. An email from Cholota to Mpambani the next day suggests the businessman met with either the premier or one of his representatives. 'Good day. This was the initial request send [sic] to the Premier,' Cholota wrote at around 1 p.m. on 12 August. Included in her email was another sent to Magashule in July that year from Refiloe Mokoena, who was at the time an acting judge in the Bloemfontein and Johannesburg High Courts. 'Dear Premier,' Mokoena had written. 'Herewith please find the necessary documents for purposes of settling my daughter's university account.' Mokoena's daughter had been accepted into Lycoming College in the United States, and she needed about R150 000 to cover the first tranche of fees. On 13 August, the day after Cholota forwarded Mokoena's request to Mpambani, the latter paid US$4 000 (roughly R51 000 at the time) from Diamond Hill's account to help cover the costs. The money was paid into Lycoming College's account. On 18 August, Cholota thanked him in an email for the money. 'Proof of payment received and acknowledged. Thank you very much,' she wrote.

Mokoena's stint as an acting High Court judge came to an end in January 2016.[3] She later became head of legal at the South African Revenue Service, where she played a key role in a VAT scandal involving the Guptas and then SARS boss Tom Moyane.[4] Mokoena was also a member of the new board for state-owned arms manufacturer Denel appointed by then public enterprises minister Lynne Brown in mid-2015. This board later approved questionable deals between Denel and the Gupta-linked company VR Laser, fuelling suspicions that Mokoena and her colleagues had been appointed by the Saxonwold shadow state. It is not clear when or how Mokoena met Magashule.

After contributing to Mokoena's daughter's college fees, Mpambani returned to Johannesburg, where he withdrew R200 000 from 605 Consulting's account at FNB's Merchant Place branch in Sandton. Three days later, he drove back to Bloemfontein, where he spent two nights in a guesthouse. During this time, he withdrew a further R55 000 from FNB ATMs, including R35 000 at the Brandwag ATM around the corner from Free State House. According to his diary, Magashule was in Bloemfontein during Mpambani's latest visit to the city. Furthermore, emails in the IgoFiles show that the premier's office was in contact with the businessman during this time.

Of the R12.5 million Mpambani transferred into Diamond Hill's account on 11 August, only R600 000 remained the following week. Once again, Mpambani had made large payments for things like 'engineering services'. One such payment, for R3.1 million, went to Kato Motsoeneng, the former Tswelopele and Mohokare municipal manager and co-founder with Mpambani of Diamond Hill Trading 71. Over the entire period of the asbestos auditing saga, Mpambani channelled more than R5 million to Motsoeneng or to Katfin Financial Solutions, another of Motsoeneng's companies. Mpambani mostly marked the payments as 'engineering ser-vices', although neither Motsoeneng nor Katfin appears to be registered with engineering bodies.

Sources from the Free State told me Motsoeneng was once a key mover in the province's political circles, until he had a bitter fight with Magashule over tenders. I wanted to ask Motsoeneng about his windfall from Mpam-bani, but he died in 2016. He was forty-six years old. His wife told me that he was hospitalised after a fall and later passed away in a Johannesburg hospital. She did not want to talk about her late husband's dealings.

By late August 2015, Mpambani was increasingly dividing his time between Johannesburg and Bloemfontein. After a short stay in Gauteng, he was back in the Free State on 24 August. This time, he drew R12 000 from the FNB near Magashule's official residence. Again, the premier's diary shows that Magashule was in town that day. Shortly thereafter, Mpambani received another back-channel request from the premier's office.

On 28 August, a Vodacom employee emailed a quotation for 200 electronic tablet devices to Ipeleng Morake. Morake first forwarded the quotation from her official work account to her private Gmail address. From there, she sent it to Mpambani, who quickly settled the bill of R300 000 for the tablets. Morake later told me the devices were for students. It appears that Magashule was again playing Father Christmas with taxpayers' money. When I asked her why she had forwarded the request through her private email account, Morake remained silent.

Mpambani continued to make payments for 'engineering' and 'con-sulting' services. Apart from the larger payments, he made several smaller payments ranging between R100 000 and R300 000. Some of these were made on days when he was in Bloemfontein, or shortly before or after Magashule's staffers contacted him.

25

The ANC's asbestos benefits

One of the most enduring allegations against Magashule is that he ran a bona fide shakedown operation in the Free State. The former premier allegedly made sure that businesspeople who got contracts from provincial departments and municipalities paid their dues to him as soon as they received money from the public purse. Several sources who once worked with Magashule claimed that such dubious funds were intended not only for his own pockets, but also for those of the ANC.

The IgoFiles provide unique insight into how the former premier tapped into the proceeds of the asbestos auditing contract to further his own political agenda and to benefit his party. In what can only be described as a kickback scheme, Mpambani funnelled money that came directly from the province's coffers towards party-political projects. His orders to do so came from Magashule's office.

In November 2015, Magashule's newly appointed spokesperson Tiisetso Makhele joined eighteen fellow Free State compatriots on a three-week jaunt to Cuba. '[T]he ANC Free State Provincial Executive Committee, under the visionary leadership of Comrade Ace Magashule, sent me and 18 other comrades on a political course in the South American island of Cuba,' Makhele later wrote in *The Weekly*.[1] The group of travellers, which according to Makhele became known as 'the Cuban 19', should have thanked South African taxpayers for their lengthy holiday in the Caribbean.

On 28 January 2016, shortly after their return to the Free State, Moroadi Cholota once again emailed Mpambani. 'Good day. Kindly find the below details as discussed telephonically,' she wrote, including the bank details for Astra Travel, a travel agency in Bloemfontein. Her timing was impeccable. Just forty minutes after she sent the email, the FSHS transferred R10 million into the Blackhead–Diamond Hill joint account. This was the sixth payment for the asbestos audit.

The fact that Magashule's personal assistant emailed Mpambani during the exact time frame in which the FSHS paid yet another instalment to Blackhead–Diamond Hill resonates with what I was told by several of the former premier's erstwhile associates and allies. 'Ace kept tabs on all the large and medium-sized payments made by municipalities and provincial departments. He knew exactly when most companies were due to receive money from his government, and he would then very quickly collect his share once the payment had been made,' a former MEC in one of Magashule's earlier executive councils told me.

The following day, Cholota sent Mpambani an invoice for R250 000 from Astra Travel for the 'Cuba delegation'. It was for the group's accommodation abroad. 'Kindly find the attached invoice as discussed. Hope you will find it in order,' she wrote. In this instance, by following the money trail it is possible to see exactly how Mpambani attended to this political request with the proceeds of the asbestos auditing contract. Through a series of complex transactions, the businessman moved the FSHS bounty around in a manner that has all the hallmarks of a classic money-laundering operation.

When the sixth instalment of R10 million landed in Blackhead–Diamond Hill's account, Mpambani immediately transferred about R5 million to Blackhead Consulting. He also put R600 000 into his private RMB account. A couple of days later, he paid over R4 million to 605 Consulting. As soon as the R600 000 landed in the RMB account, Mpambani transferred R400 000 and R160 000 respectively to Diamond Hill. He marked these transfers as 'loans'. He then immediately transferred these amounts from the Diamond Hill account to 605 Consulting, marking them as 'loan–Diamond Hill'. Minutes after the R400 000 'loan' landed in 605 Consulting's account, Mpambani paid R250 000 to Astra Travel to settle the bill for the Cuban 19. He marked the payment as 'Travel–Cuba'.

And the 'loan' of R160 000? About two weeks before the FSHS paid out the sixth instalment, Mpambani received an email from Kemi Akinbohun, a lawyer from Welkom, with the banking details of a non-profit entity called Evolution POT. 'Kindly note that we shall send you a formal acknowledgement of the receipt of the donation when received,' Akinbohun wrote. Two weeks later, after Mpambani had channelled some of the FSHS cash through Diamond Hill and into 605 Consulting's account, he paid R100 000 to Evolution POT, marking it as 'school fees donation'. According to its website, Evolution POT is a foundation established by Mathabo Leeto.

Its objectives include 'capacity building and training', 'moral regeneration', 'healthy living styles' and 'support [for] youth education'. Akinbohun confirmed the donation and said Mpambani's money was used to buy school uniforms for needy children. The donation had not been influenced by MEC Leeto, insisted Akinbohun.

According to accommodation bookings in the IgoFiles, Mpambani was in Bloemfontein when he made the first payment to Evolution POT and settled the travel bill for the Cuban 19.

By now, there was a clearly discernible pattern. No sooner had the FSHS transferred money into the Blackhead–Diamond Hill account than Mpambani would receive requests from Magashule's aides or people linked to politicians like Leeto. He would then move his share of the money into his own company accounts, from where he would make all manner of payments, including settling the requests. Mpambani also started to withdraw ever-larger amounts of cash before or during his trips to Bloemfontein.

The IgoFiles, Magashule's diary and other records allowed me to identify a sequence of events that show how Mpambani channelled even more of the money from the asbestos auditing contract into political projects. On Tuesday 19 January 2016, Magashule met with President Jacob Zuma at the latter's Mahlamba Ndlopfu residence in Pretoria. That same day, ANC spokesperson in the Free State Thabo Meeko tweeted: 'ANC Free State to convene the mother of all marches in defence of President Zuma, on 06 Feb 2016. In Bloem. Details to follow.'

Zuma was in the middle of yet another political storm after his shock appointment, and subsequent reversal, of Des van Rooyen as finance minister a month before. His relationship with the Guptas was also keeping him in the firing line and he needed all the support he could get. The march was scheduled for the week after the FSHS made its sixth payment for the asbestos audit, and Mpambani's money once again came in handy. On Wednesday 3 February, he withdrew half a million rand in cash from the FNB branch in the Sandton City shopping mall. He then drove to the Free State, swiping one of his bank cards at the Grasmere and Vaal toll plazas before later buying petrol at the Engen 1-Stop on the N1 outside Bloemfontein.

While we do not know for sure what the R500 000 was for, the IgoFiles suggest that Mpambani met with someone about the planned Zuma march that same day. The following day, he made three separate payments totalling about R230 000 to three transport companies. He marked the payments as 'bus shuttle services Igo-Cosatu', 'bus shuttle services WL Mangaung' and 'bus service – rally' respectively. He also sent payment notifications to the three transport companies. I spoke to an employee at one of the bus companies, and he confirmed that they had been paid to drive members of the ANC Women's League (WL) to the rally. This person would not disclose where the money had come from. As it happens, MEC Leeto was treasurer of the ANC Women's League in the Free State during this time.

Mpambani would later also make at least one payment to Thabo Meeko, albeit a relatively small one. In November 2016, Mpambani made an eWallet payment of R2 000 to a cellphone number which a simple Google search revealed to be Meeko's.

The February march, meanwhile, was touted as a celebration of the ANC's 104th birthday, but it turned out to be blatant propaganda in support of the party's beleaguered president. A few thousand marchers, wearing mostly yellow ANC T-shirts or green ANC Women's League uniforms, walked through Bloemfontein's streets before gathering at the city's Dr Petrus Molemela Stadium. A news broadcast of the event shows a huge 'Hands Off President Zuma' banner and marchers carrying placards displaying the same message of support.[2] Later, then ANC secretary-general Gwede Mantashe and Magashule addressed the crowd,[3] with Mantashe claiming that reports about the Gupta family's links to top politicians were exaggerated. 'If people have relations with the Guptas it's their business, I don't have a relationship with them, I have no problem with people who have a relation with them,' he said from the podium.[4]

Mpambani had clearly been on Magashule's mind during that week. On the Tuesday before the rally, he received an invitation to the premier's upcoming State of the Province Address. As had happened the previous year, it appears that Mpambani drove down to Bloemfontein specifically for the event on 16 February. Data in the IgoFiles shows that he swiped 605 Consulting's bank card at toll gates en route.

The FSHS transferred the seventh instalment to Blackhead–Diamond Hill on 28 April 2016. It amounted to exactly R15 million. Mpambani transferred half of it to Sodi's Blackhead Consulting and the remaining R7.5 million to 605 Consulting. From the latter account, Mpambani made the usual payments for 'engineering services' and 'professional services'. Less than two weeks later, only about R200 000 of the R7.5 million remained in the 605 Consulting account.

In keeping with the pattern, Mpambani travelled to Bloemfontein frequently after receiving the latest instalment. On Monday 9 May, he withdrew R100 000 in cash from the FNB ATM around the corner from Free State House. He almost certainly had contact with Magashule or someone close to him that week, as evidenced by events. According to his diary, Magashule was at the ANC's Bloemfontein offices on Friday 13 May to prepare for the party's manifesto launch. That same day, Mpambani transferred R50 000 from the 605 Consulting account for 'bus shuttle service'. The ANC's manifesto launch for the upcoming local government elections took place the following day. It was held in Botshabelo, near Bloemfontein, with Zuma as the keynote speaker. Magashule also delivered a speech. Considering the timing of the payment and the fact that Mpambani was in Bloemfontein at the time, it is unlikely that the bus service would have been for anything other than the manifesto launch.

In late July 2016, with the local elections only days away, Mpambani made his most direct financial contribution to the ruling party. He funded this donation with the proceeds of the asbestos auditing contract in a clear example of the ANC's habit of funding itself with money squeezed from state coffers through dodgy contracts. The little scheme worked as follows: By 28 July, 605 Consulting still had a small amount of money left over from the seventh FSHS instalment paid out in April. That day, Mpambani transferred R100 000 from the 605 Consulting account to his FNB Private Wealth cheque account, marking it as 'salary'. Just a few minutes later, he transferred this entire 'salary' from his Private Wealth account to an unknown bank account, flagging it as 'party fundraising'. A subsequent SMS sending-fee notification stated that the payment was for 'ANC Fundraising'.

26

Zizi

One notable problem with the IgoFiles was the fact that they mostly contained bank records, emails and other documents relating to only Igo Mpambani's financial activities. The dealings of Edwin Sodi, Mpambani's partner in the Free State asbestos audit project, therefore remained hidden from view. However, in an attempt to quell my suspicions about Blackhead Consulting's role in the saga, Sodi and his lawyers invited me to inspect the company's bank statements for the period in which the Blackhead–Diamond Hill joint venture received millions of rands from the Free State Department of Human Settlements.

I accepted the invitation. If anything, the exercise further fuelled my doubts over the contract. As mentioned in Chapter 22, one version of the 'cost of business' spreadsheet in the IgoFiles, along with a draft email written by Mpambani, implicated Sodi in suspicious payments. Sodi was to 'take care' of those payments highlighted in yellow, while Mpambani would handle the rest of the amounts detailed in the spreadsheet, according to the email.

Sodi did not deny that he had seen such a spreadsheet, but he seemed to suggest that the version I obtained had been altered. 'The spreadsheet that was prepared does not bear the abbreviations and names asked about,' his lawyers said. They denied that Sodi or his company had made any donations or payments to politically exposed individuals or entities that could reasonably be viewed as 'kickbacks' or 'bribes' related to Blackhead's government contracts.

'Blackhead is a reputable business operating fully within the laws of South Africa, is tax compliant and rejects the allegations that its business has benefitted from any unlawful activity or political connections,' Sodi's lawyers claimed. 'All the contracts that Blackhead has won have been through proper procurement processes. Any other suggestion is simply wrong.' They said they had undertaken a 'complete review' of Blackhead's financial activities. 'It does not disclose payments to any politically connected individuals.'

The lawyers were certain that once I had sight of Blackhead's bank records, I would conclude that Sodi's firm had not made any of the suspicious payments listed in Mpambani's version of the spreadsheet. They were wrong.

On 26 March 2015, the FSHS transferred R25 million to the Blackhead–Diamond Hill joint account, according to bank records in the IgoFiles. This was the third payment. If the spreadsheet were accurate, after receiving a slice of this instalment from the FSHS, Blackhead would have been required to pay altogether R3.2 million to five of the abbreviated third parties listed in the document. The amounts ranged between R300 000 and R1 million. One such payment, at least according to the spreadsheet, was for an amount of exactly R1 million to a certain 'TZ'. One of my sources alleged that 'TZ' was a top-level official at the national Department of Human Settlements who had played a role in transferring the asbestos audit contract to the Free State without a tender process. This official's name is being withheld on legal advice, seeing as the IgoFiles do not contain proof that this person received the money.

But a peek at Blackhead Consulting's bank statements allowed me to establish that Sodi's firm had indeed made at least one payment that matched those listed in the spreadsheet. On 27 March, a day after the R25 million landed in the Blackhead–Diamond Hill joint account, Mpambani transferred almost R20 million to four bank accounts. Of that, R10 million went to Mastertrade, the company owned by Sello Radebe, the former Free State official who evaded my queries about his role in the saga. Mpambani also transferred R6.4 million to two accounts belonging to his other companies. The remaining money, exactly R3.2 million, went into the account of Blackhead Consulting. In other words, Mpambani paid Blackhead the exact amount that Sodi's firm was required to pay five third parties after the third instalment from the FSHS, as detailed in the spreadsheet. On 1 April 2015, just a few days after Mpambani transferred the money, Sodi paid exactly R1 million to an unknown account. The payment was marked as a 'loan'. I could not help but wonder if this was perhaps the payment to 'TZ'. I asked Sodi's lawyers to whom Blackhead had lent money. I also asked them for a loan schedule and loan agreement. This time, they remained mum. Blackhead Consulting also extended a 'loan' of R5 million, among other payments, to another unknown third party. The firm's lawyers ignored my queries over this second loan.

Just before the Blackhead–Diamond Hill joint venture received its third instalment from the FSHS, Sodi made another curious payment. On 24 March, he transferred R250 000 to Bongani More. Blackhead also paid More R100 000 in October the following year. Poring over Blackhead's bank records, the name immediately rang a bell. I later recalled that I had come across a Bongani More during my research into Ace Magashule's student days. Someone had told me that More was a student leader at Fort Hare when Magashule was there. More importantly, More later became a deputy director-general at the Gauteng Department of Human Settlements. This department was Blackhead's first client for an asbestos audit project, and it was from here that Blackhead's services, along with Diamond Hill's, were transferred to the Free State. I wondered if More was one of the many officials Blackhead and Diamond Hill needed to pay off. If not, why did Blackhead pay More R350 000 during the period of the Free State asbestos audit saga? I asked Sodi's lawyers to comment on Blackhead's payments to More, but they sidestepped my questions. More read my WhatsApp message regarding the alleged payments, but he did not reply.

Blackhead also made a series of payments to the ANC. Between September 2015 and February 2016, Sodi's firm transferred R100 000 to someone listed in its bank statements as 'ANC volunteer'. In January 2016, Blackhead paid R150 000 for 'ANC TG funds'. The company also transferred a neat R500 000 for the benefit of 'ANC Gauteng' in July 2016. In all, the ANC and its unnamed 'volunteer' received R750 000 from Blackhead during the time of the asbestos audit. In light of long-standing concerns that the ANC was funding itself through alleged kickbacks from government contracts, I asked Sodi if these payments were in any way related to the Free State contract. One of his lawyers responded as follows: 'My client has made no secret of his membership of and support of the ANC. The fact that my client has made donations to the ANC does not mean that any of the contracts which it has won are tainted by any form of irregularity. All the contracts that Blackhead has obtained have been through an open and transparent tender process.' The last assertion was not quite correct. There had been no tender process for the Free State asbestos audit. As previously explained, Blackhead and Diamond Hill bagged the lucrative contract through the transfer of the original Gauteng contract.

A series of payments made by Blackhead Consulting in 2016 also caught my eye. In the month-long period between late August and late September, Sodi's firm made three payments totalling almost R105 000 to someone listed in its bank records as 'Zizi'. The name had been redacted with a black marker, but whoever did this did not do a very good job. Holding the black blotches to the light, the name 'Zizi' clearly shone through. Asked why the name had been redacted, Sodi's lawyer later said his client had wanted to protect the identities of certain individuals. 'He does not seek to hide any inappropriate payments. Where a name has been redacted this is to protect the privacy and confidentiality of the recipient.'

I could not help but wonder if this was an attempt to cover up payments to Zizi Kodwa, the ANC's then acting national spokesperson and one of the party's most visible members. There was a tangential link between Kodwa and Sodi, so it did not seem entirely implausible. As mentioned in Chapter 21, Blackhead Consulting allegedly started securing contracts from the Gauteng government when Nomvula Mokonyane was still premier of the province. Sources claimed that Sodi and Mokonyane were close, but Sodi denied that his company had secured contracts because of their alleged friendship. Kodwa, meanwhile, became Mokonyane's 'special adviser' in 2013, towards the end of her stint as premier.[1]

I wondered whether Kodwa had perhaps met Sodi during this time and for some reason ended up on Blackhead's payroll. I expressly asked Sodi's lawyer if the 'Zizi' listed in Blackhead's bank statements was the ANC's well-known spin doctor. If it was a different Zizi, could Blackhead indicate who this person was, I asked. He ignored these questions and instead gave me a general response about the need for 'privacy' and 'confidentiality'. I was hoping Kodwa would be willing to engage with me over the matter. After all, the acting ANC spokesperson had taken a vocal stance against corruption, state capture and strange payments from government contractors after revelations about controversial state contractor Bosasa's murky dealings surfaced in early 2019.[2] Former Bosasa executive Angelo Agrizzi's shocking testimony at the Zondo Commission of Inquiry elicited this comment from Kodwa: 'We can't have public servants who are in the pocket of people who are a cartel, who are basically running the country like an underworld, like a mafia.'[3]

I asked Kodwa if he had ever received money from Blackhead Consulting. I also asked him if the alleged payments might have been connected to his former position as Mokonyane's special adviser. Kodwa ignored the question about the alleged payments. His only response came in the form of a WhatsApp message: 'My name is Zizi Kodwa I was never advisor to Minister of Water Affairs Ms Mokonyane, thanks.' I pointed out that there were newspaper reports about his role as Mokonyane's adviser during her term as Gauteng premier, but at this point Kodwa cut all communication with me. I even hounded him for a response on Twitter, but he kept ignoring me. We will have to keep wondering whether some of Blackhead Consulting's proceeds from the Free State asbestos audit or other government contracts ended up in Kodwa's account. If true, it begs the question of why Kodwa received such payments.

Finally, a payment made by Blackhead in late 2015 also drew my attention. On 11 August, the FSHS paid R36.5 million into the Blackhead–Diamond Hill joint account. This was the fifth instalment for the asbestos audit. That same day, Mpambani transferred over R13 million to Blackhead Consulting. About six weeks later, on 18 September, Blackhead paid R400 000 to an unknown account. The transaction was marked 'Parys farm'. The mention of Magashule's hometown naturally sparked my interest. By way of explanation, Sodi told me he owned a farm near Parys. I later checked up on this. There were no records at the Bloemfontein deeds office for a farm owned by Sodi or any of his companies or related entities in that part of the province. When I pointed this out to Sodi's lawyers, they stated the following: 'The purchase of the farm is on an instalment sale basis with transfer to take place on payment of the final instalment. The final instalment has not yet been paid.' I asked for the farm and portion numbers to locate the property, but the lawyers ignored my request.

By allowing me to review Blackhead Consulting's bank statements, Sodi's legal team hoped to convince me that the transaction records in Mpambani's 'cost of business' spreadsheet were incorrect. Their tactic had the opposite effect. Blackhead made at least one payment that correlated with the spreadsheet. Sodi's lawyers then refused to indicate who had been on the receiving end of this transaction. They also failed to disclose details of some of the other payments I flagged, including those made to 'Zizi'. These outflows, along with the confirmed donations to the ANC, only cemented my belief that the Free State's R255-million asbestos audit project was replete with political meddling and possible corruption.

27

The last cash run

The FSHS made the final payment for the asbestos audit in August 2016. It came to a hefty R77.5 million, meaning that the department had now splurged altogether R230 million on the dubious project. Although the full contract cost was R255 million, the remaining R25 million would not be paid out. Sources familiar with the saga told me that the contract had virtually drained the department's coffers, so there was simply no more money to settle the rest of the bill.

When the last payment landed in the Blackhead–Diamond Hill joint account, Mpambani immediately moved the entire amount to 605 Consulting. He next embarked on a spree of intricate transactions that saw him move millions of rands through bank accounts held in his name or in those of his other companies and trusts. In the process, he splashed more than R10 million on upmarket properties, adding to an already impressive portfolio of houses acquired since the first asbestos audit payment. He also used R1 million to settle his vehicle finance for a Range Rover. Apart from this and the Bentley, Mpambani now owned an Aston Martin V8 Vantage, a Porsche Cayenne and a Maserati, all bought with the proceeds of the asbestos audit.

He continued to make large payments for 'consulting services', 'engineering services' and other similarly named expenses. Some of this money ended up in his other accounts, but the recipients of most of these payments remain unknown. It was from this final tranche of money that Mpambani paid R990 000 to Kingdom Impact, the company represented by Kenosi Moroka's law firm.

By early September, nearly the entire R77.5 million had been drained from 605 Consulting's account when Edwin Sodi, Mpambani's partner in the joint venture, came knocking. According to their original agreement, Sodi should have received half of the asbestos audit's proceeds, once all the payments to third parties had been settled. But Mpambani had not shared the final payment with his partner. Sodi fired off an email to Mpambani on 5 September. 'I expect in my account R38 212 500 in the next 24 hours and nothing less,' he fumed. The IgoFiles show that Mpambani had sent Sodi a 'payment recon', a spreadsheet that supposedly justified why he had not paid his partner half of the final R77.5 million. According to the document, the public protector had laid claim to R60 million of the joint venture's earnings from the asbestos audit. In a subsequent court battle, Sodi elaborated on this development.

According to court filings, the two men met in Sandton on 6 September. Mpambani told Sodi that 'he [Mpambani] had been informed by the Free State Department [of Human Settlements] that the Public Protector intended recovering approximately R60 million ... on the basis that the [department] had been "overcharged",' Sodi explained in his affidavit, adding that he had been 'sceptical' about Mpambani's story. He had good cause to feel that way. The public protector does not have a mandate to seize the proceeds of dodgy contracts. Furthermore, in this case, the public protector had not even published a report on the matter. Sodi again asked Mpambani to pay him his half. Later that day, Mpambani transferred just R8 million to Sodi's company. The outstanding R30 million formed the basis of the legal proceedings Sodi would later institute against the executor of Mpambani's estate.

Amid the growing tension between the partners, Mpambani continued making regular cash runs to the Free State. On 17 August, he withdrew R100 000 from an FNB ATM a few kilometres away from where Magashule was attending an executive council meeting. He was back in Bloemfontein three weeks later. This time, he withdrew R150 000 from 605 Consulting's account at the Brandwag ATM near Free State House. According to the premier's official diary, Magashule returned to Bloemfontein later that day after a meeting in KwaZulu-Natal.

On 2 December, Mpambani withdrew R150 000 from an ATM in Welkom, MEC Leeto's hometown. By that time, Magashule was in Hong Kong, having flown there from O.R. Tambo International Airport in late November. In the week after the premier's departure, Mpambani and his wife also flew to Hong Kong. There is nothing in the IgoFiles to suggest that Magashule and Mpambani spent time together in the Far East, as they had done in Cuba nearly two years before, but the timing of their respective trips is curious.

With 2016 nearly at its end and the final payment from the FSHS in the bag, Mpambani's financial activities linked to the asbestos auditing deal seemingly took a break. It is worth reviewing how Mpambani spent some of this money.

In the preceding two years, the FSHS had transferred R230 million in a series of staggered payments to the Blackhead–Diamond Hill joint account. Financial records from the IgoFiles and related documents suggested the joint venture and some of its partners, including Mastertrade, had earned more than R200 million in clean profit from the project. But Mpambani's partner was adamant that the asbestos audit did not amount to a huge rip-off. He refused, however, to tell me how much profit the joint venture had bagged. 'The conclusions you draw about the amount of profit are incorrect and it is not incumbent on the JV to answer questions about its profitability. The assumption that the JV "milked" the taxpayer is wrong and is rejected,' Edwin Sodi said through his lawyers. Mokhesi also denied that the FSHS had massively overpaid Blackhead–Diamond Hill. 'We are not sure about your understanding of the scope and the nature of the work that was done on this issue,' said the HOD.

However, Mpambani's management of the joint-venture account raised too many red flags to ignore. It was clear that he had funnelled much of the huge payments from the FSHS through a complex web of bank accounts opened in his name or in those of his companies. In the process, he bought a small fleet of luxury cars worth millions of rands. He spent even more on upmarket properties bought without bank loans. And he paid tens of millions of rands to unknown accounts belonging to third parties, masking the transfers as 'engineering services' and 'consulting' fees. The timing and value of these payments frequently mirrored the amounts Mpambani and Sodi had seemingly agreed to pay people and companies listed in their 'Free State Asbestos' Excel spreadsheet.

That Magashule's fingerprints were on the deal seems undeniable. In late 2014, when FSHS staffers queried the contract, they were told that Magashule was behind it. When the premier travelled to Cuba in early 2015, Mpambani was right by his side. As we have seen, Mpambani submitted the first invoices to the FSHS during this trip. Later, throughout 2015 and 2016, Mpambani complied with requests from Magashule's office to settle invoices for, among others, the 'Cuban 19', student fees and Refiloe Mokoena's daughter's college tuition. All of this amounted to about R1 million.

Mpambani's contributions to the ruling party, including the bus service and the direct donation in July 2016, came to about R400 000.

MEC Mathabo Leeto's non-profit organisation got at least R100 000. Mpambani also forked out more than R50 000 for her and her entourage's stay at Sun City for the 2015 SAMAs, according to the IgoFiles.

Finally, over the course of two years, Mpambani withdrew almost R3 million from various ATMs and bank tellers each time Blackhead–Diamond Hill received funds from the FSHS. He withdrew most of this cash in Sandton, oftentimes shortly before driving to the Free State. Of the roughly R500 000 he withdrew in Bloemfontein, more than R300 000 came from the FNB ATM around the corner from Magashule's official residence. Magashule's diary, meanwhile, indicates that he was mostly at home when Mpambani made such withdrawals.

When I met one of Mpambani's former business partners in mid-2018, I asked him if there was any reason why Mpambani drove around with large amounts of cash. Did he perhaps need to pay wages? 'There would have been no reason why Igo would have needed to travel with that much cash,' this person told me. 'He was a consultant, not a contractor or project manager. He didn't pay wages or anything like that.'

'So where did all that cash go?' I asked him. He was silent for a while. When he spoke again, he looked worried. 'I think you know the answer, but I am not going to go into details,' he said. 'If I do that, I could end up like Igo.'

No sooner had he received the final payment for the asbestos audit contract than Mpambani set his sights on looting even more money from the FSHS. In June 2016, the department advertised a contract for the 'design and implementation of water and sewer networks in various Districts in the Free State over a period of three (3) years'.[1] This time, Mpambani would use 605 Consulting Solutions to tap into the latest revenue stream, with his wife, Michelle, as his co-director.

The entire process was a farce. By the time the call for bids closed in July 2016, 605 Consulting was not even registered with the Construction Industry Development Board, a prerequisite for securing construction contracts from government. This happened only in November of that year, and Mpambani's company obtained the lowest possible grading. With a CIDB score of just 1, 605 Consulting was woefully underqualified for the multimillion-rand infrastructure design work. No doubt aware of its limitations, 605 Consulting made a presentation to the FSHS in late

August. It vowed to identify specific parts of the project that would be 'sub-contracted to local emerging contractors'.[2]

In January 2017, the department informed 605 Consulting that it had been chosen for the 'design and supervision' of water and sewerage infrastructure projects in several municipalities in the northern Free State, including Tumahole, where Magashule grew up. The letter, signed by HOD Tim Mokhesi, curiously swopped 'implementation', as stipulated in the request for proposals, with 'supervision'. The FSHS no doubt knew that 605 Consulting was by no means capable of implementing large water and sewer networks. The promise to rope in 'emerging contractors' became a fixed requirement of the deal. 'A 30% sub-consulting obligation will apply to this appointment and is to be awarded to an emerging consulting engineering firm agreed upon by the department,' read the letter signed by Mokhesi. In other words, the HOD, or whoever pulled his strings, could nominate the company (or companies) that would benefit from the project.

But before that could happen, Mpambani first had to deliver design reports for the proposed water and sewerage infrastructure. Seeing as neither he nor his wife were engineers, they subcontracted a string of professional firms and qualified people. As always, such expenses would only constitute a fraction of 605 Consulting's revenue, and there would be plenty of fat left over to pass around.

In May 2017, Mpambani submitted preliminary infrastructure design reports for Tumahole and other proposed residential developments in Heilbron and Sasolburg. He also sent off a few invoices for the reports, which included 605 Consulting's 'inception' fees. In all, the FSHS now owed Mpambani a fresh R11 million. And this was only the first round of invoices. By May 2018, 605 Consulting had reaped more than R40 million from the department, according to the housing subsidy system database and related documents.

Mpambani sent these preliminary reports and invoices to the private Gmail account of Freddy Tokwe, an FSHS staffer said to be close to Magashule and Mokhesi. The four preliminary reports looked a lot like copy-and-paste jobs. But that was not the biggest problem. The reports contained the details of the two 'civil engineers' who had been subcontracted to respectively author and review the work. I looked up their names at the Engineering Council of South Africa. Contrary to what was claimed in the reports, neither was a civil engineer: the author was registered as a professional engineering technologist, and the reviewer as a candidate engineering technician.

Getting the first R11 million payment from the FSHS was not all smooth sailing. On Tuesday 20 June, the day he died, Mpambani got an email from a senior official in the FSHS financial department. 'The challenge we have currently is that your company is not on our BAS [Basic Accounting System],' read the email. 'In order for [the] department to process your claims further it must be created with Provincial Treasury.' At just before 10 a.m., Mpambani responded as follows: 'All the required documents you mention have been submitted 2 weeks ago to the office of Mr. Freddy Tokwe. Kindly assist by double-checking…'

It is not clear where Mpambani was when he sent the email. But fifteen minutes later he withdrew half a million rand in cash from a teller at FNB's Benmore branch in Sandton. Although the FSHS had not yet paid 605 Consulting for the infrastructure design reports, there was a fair amount of money in the account. The previous day, Mpambani had transferred R1.1 million from Diamond Hill to 605 Consulting, flagging it as 'Loan–Diamond Hill'. This was leftover cash from the asbestos audit payments.

After sending some additional paperwork regarding the BAS to the FSHS official, likely the last email he would ever write, Mpambani drove to an FNB branch in Woodmead, north of Sandton. Here, at 11:39, he withdrew exactly R499 900. With just R100 shy of a million rand in his Bentley, he headed back towards the Sandton CBD. Less than twenty minutes later, Mpambani's lifeless body sat slumped over the steering wheel of the expensive car. He had been shot dead on Bowling Avenue in full view of at least a dozen bystanders. Reports from the scene show that he had stuffed the R499 900 into a small cooler bag that was found next to him in the car. He had put the other R500 000 in the boot.

More than 400 kilometres to the south, Magashule was meeting with party officials at the ANC's provincial headquarters in downtown Bloemfontein, according to his diary. The premier's schedule at that time was dominated by party-political events. The previous week, police minister and fellow Free State local Fikile Mbalula had publicly attacked Magashule on social media after it became clear that the premier was going to make a run at becoming the ANC's new secretary-general.[3] Magashule had hit back at Mbalula at a Provincial General Council (PGC) meeting in Bloemfontein on the weekend before Mpambani's murder.[4] With about six months left before the ANC's elective conference at Nasrec, Magashule's latest political battle was now really heating up. The premier needed every ounce of support he could find, financially and otherwise. Mpambani, with his riches from the asbestos auditing contract and even more money heading his way thanks to 605 Consulting's latest project, no doubt formed part of Magashule's financial planning for his upcoming battle to become secretary-general. There is good reason to suspect that the R1 million Mpambani withdrew shortly before his death was intended for Magashule.

One of the slain businessman's former associates told me about an interesting development that took place the day before his death. On Monday morning, 19 June, Mpambani apparently received a phone call instructing him to be in Bloemfontein the following day. 'Igo was very secretive about his dealings in the Free State, but he told me he was going to meet with someone from Ace's office. That was the last time I saw him alive,' this source told me.

Back in Bloemfontein on that Monday morning, Magashule had a 'meeting with alliance' at the ANC's Free State headquarters, according to his diary. If the premier or someone in his circle had phoned Mpambani, subsequent developments suggest that the conversation may have been about cash. It was at 11:02 that day that Mpambani transferred the R1.1 million 'loan' from Diamond Hill to 605 Consulting's account. This is the money he would withdraw the following day, before his untimely death.

According to sources familiar with the murder investigation, when the police found the cash in Mpambani's car, they naturally asked his wife and other family members what it was for. 'Michelle and Manny [her brother] told the police that Igo was on his way to Bloemfontein when he was killed,' one source told me. Apparently, they were evasive and vague when the police tried to get more information regarding the money. They simply told the investigators that the cash was for 'business', according to my sources.

I made several attempts throughout 2018 to ask Michelle about her late husband's dealings in the Free State, his involvement with Magashule and the almost R1 million he withdrew on the day of his murder. She evaded all of my efforts to discuss the matter. This hardly came as a surprise, considering how involved she became in 605 Consulting's dubious dealings with the Free State provincial government after her husband's death.

28

'Ace's girls'

In late June and early July 2017, Igo Mpambani's friends, family and business associates attended memorial services held for him in Johannesburg and Welkom. He was finally buried in his family's ancestral homestead in the Eastern Cape. All indications are that his death neither affected 605 Consulting's latest dealings with the FSHS nor deterred the company from continuing to make questionable payments to third parties.

On 6 July, less than a week after Mpambani was laid to rest, the FSHS transferred more than R11 million to 605 Consulting for the preliminary infrastructure design reports. At the end of that month, Michelle, who had taken over her late husband's role as the company's manager, made the usual payments for 'engineering services', 'services rendered' and similar fees. This included a payment of exactly R1.1 million to a company called Kaykaysim Projects. This entity's sole director is Katleho Sothoane, a twenty-five-year-old project-management student at the Central University of Technology. According to her Instagram account, Sothoane also has a qualification from the North-West University's Vaal Triangle Campus. Further payments from 605 Consulting were made to Kaykaysim Projects in August and October 2017, each time shortly after money was received from the FSHS. In all, Sothoane's company earned at least R1.5 million from 605 Consulting. When I visited Kaykaysim Projects in Bloemfontein, I found a near-deserted office with only a receptionist on site. The office, incidentally, is right across the road from Botlokwa Holdings, the company owned by Magashule's daughter Thoko Malembe.

When I later got hold of Sothoane on the phone, she told me that Kaykaysim had 'tendered' to do work for 605 Consulting. I asked her in an email if she could elaborate on the kind of work her company did and how she came to hear about 605 Consulting's water and sewer design projects for the provincial government. My queries went unanswered. Her social media accounts, however, provided valuable information. Apart from professing her support for the ANC on her Facebook page, Sothoane's various social media posts revealed that, like Igo Mpambani, she was in close proximity to Magashule on numerous occasions. I managed to determine this by comparing the location details of her posts to Magashule's diary and to media reports detailing his activities.

For example, on Sunday 30 July 2017, just five days after Kaykaysim received more than R1 million from 605 Consulting, Sothoane posted a picture on Instagram of herself sitting in a camp chair somewhere near Parys. Magashule was due to attend an ANC PEC meeting in his hometown the following morning, according to his diary. In the background of the picture is a VW Golf with a clearly visible number plate. I established that the car belongs to Lerato Mofokeng, an ANC member from Parys who once worked in Magashule's office. Like most of the operators in Magashule's sphere, Mofokeng hails from Tumahole. His Facebook profile reveals the extent of his involvement in ANC activities.

According to sources familiar with the province's political landscape, Mofokeng performed 'political tasks' for Magashule when he worked in the premier's office. He later moved to the Masilonyana local municipality, and in early 2017, he joined the FSHS, just before Kaykaysim became a subcontractor on projects for the department. One source told me that Mofokeng was a 'fixer' for Magashule.

Sothoane's link to Mofokeng was an important discovery. The young businesswoman, who now sat with at least R1 million of FSHS funds channelled to her through the Mpambanis' 605 Consulting, was spending time in the company of one of Magashule's alleged fixers. Politically, this was a crucial period for Magashule. Like Igo Mpambani before her, Sothoane seemed to be ideally positioned to help finance the premier's political campaigns.

Sources who attended a Provincial General Council gathering in Parys in November 2017 alleged that Sothoane had been present on the sidelines. As we'll see in the next chapter, the PGC was apparently called in a last-minute effort to validate the Free State's support of Nkosazana Dlamini-Zuma for the upcoming elective conference at Nasrec.

By the time the PGC commenced, Sothoane was driving around in a sporty white-and-red Mini Cooper, which she had presumably bought with a portion of Kaykaysim's windfall from the FSHS. One contact said she was 'very busy' during that time, driving around Parys in her conspicuous Mini.

I asked Sothoane if she attended the PGC or any other ANC gatherings after her company received money from 605 Consulting. 'Why would I be at that meeting? I don't recall going to any ANC meeting. I don't even have a membership,' she replied in a text message. I also asked about her relationship with Mofokeng, the former staffer in Magashule's office, but she did not respond.

Like the #GuptaLeaks, the IgoFiles have a cut-off point. The documents reflect 605 Consulting's financial dealings only up to and including October 2017. Nevertheless, the company concluded a very interesting transaction that month. On 29 September, the FSHS effected a smaller payment of just over R2 million to 605 Consulting. Over the following few days, Michelle Mpambani, or whoever controlled the company's bank account, made several payments to third parties, including a neat payment of R220 000 to Kaykaysim and just under R500 000 in two tranches to Ramtsilo Trading. This company's directors are Kekeletso and Kedibone Tsiloane, sisters in their twenties who hail from Sasolburg. Unlike Sothoane, the Tsiloane sisters have documented links to Magashule's family. According to company records, they are directors in a non-profit called Yetsang Empowerment Bato. This entity's registered address is in Parys, and one of its other directors is Thato Magashule, the former premier's son.

A source who was previously close to Ace Magashule claimed that he once saw the Tsiloane sisters in Ace Magashule's company at a restaurant in Bloemfontein. 'Those are Ace's girls,' he told me.

Kedibone, the older of the two, told me their company was 'privileged' to have been commissioned as a subcontractor to 605 Consulting following the latter's appointment by the FSHS to connect RDP houses to sewer and water pipes in Sasolburg. When I asked to see proof of the work Ramtsilo Trading had supposedly done, Kedibone referred me to Michelle Mpambani, who did not respond to any of my queries. Kedibone, who defended her company's work for 605 Consulting, remained mum when I queried her and her sister's ties to Magashule's son.

Nearly two years have passed since Mpambani's murder without anyone having been brought to book. When I first tried to get an update on the police's investigation, a SAPS spokesperson told me the matter was being investigated by the Hawks. The Hawks then told me the matter was with the

SAPS. I finally determined that the docket had been passed on to a lieutenant colonel at the Tembisa police station on the outskirts of Johannesburg. The last time I checked, Mpambani's killers were still at large.

PART VIII

TOP SIX FIX

29

Nas(w)rec(k)

Ace Magashule found himself in perhaps the most important battle of his long, conflict-ridden political career in the period leading up to the ANC's December 2017 national conference at Nasrec. The first indications that he would campaign to become the party's new secretary-general surfaced in around June that year.[1] His drive to occupy this position could be viewed as at once a power play *and* a fight for survival. The politically ambitious premier had probably always intended to one day rise to higher stations outside of his home province.

Having cast his lot with the Nkosazana Dlamini-Zuma slate, Magashule fought hard for the faction, but his personal campaign to become secretary-general was much more consequential. Magashule no doubt knew that he needed to make it into the ANC's Top Six if he were to prolong his political life, regardless of whether Dlamini-Zuma prevailed over Cyril Ramaphosa or not. With the latter's promises of a 'new dawn' in South Africa, an all-out defeat for the Dlamini-Zuma slate could have been the end of the road for Magashule. Developments after Ramaphosa's victory gave a good indication of what his fate might have been had he not squeezed himself into the Top Six. The new ANC president was quick to pounce on one of Magashule's old 'premier league' buddies, North West premier Supra Mahumapelo, after violent protests in his province called for him to step down. With pressure from Ramaphosa, Mahumapelo took 'early retirement' in May 2018.[2]

Becoming secretary-general therefore offered Magashule a chance to secure one of the party's most powerful positions and, more importantly, to avoid being swept into political oblivion by the brooms of change Ramaphosa threatened to wield. With such high stakes, it is no wonder the political machinery that propped up Magashule's rule in the Free State kicked into overdrive in the months before Nasrec. The intense campaign was accompanied by the same sort of mischief that came under fire in the

Constitutional Court's ruling in 2012. This latest wave of unscrupulous political manoeuvring would also eventually be subjected to a legal lashing.

The earliest and most prominent objection to Magashule's bid for secretary-general came from fellow Free State local Fikile Mbalula. After the ANC Youth League and the Umkhonto we Sizwe Military Veterans Association (MKMVA) announced their support for Magashule in mid-2017, Mbalula posted his tweet that Magashule was 'a definite no no no' and that he would 'finish what is remaining of our movement. He will kill it.'[3] Magashule retaliated at a Provincial General Council meeting in Bloemfontein,[4] but his squabbles with national party figures like Mbalula were of secondary concern. It was in his home province that Magashule needed to lay the foundation for his ascent to the party's Top Six. But his path was strewn with obstacles. In fact, as Nasrec drew closer, it appeared at times as if the wheels were coming off.

In November, a group of disgruntled ANC members sought to stop the very processes that would see Magashule nominated by the Free State for his preferred position. The dissatisfied party members took Magashule, in his capacity as provincial chair, and his PEC to court.[5] The ANC in the Free State was due to hold a provincial conference on the first weekend of December, but the applicants wanted to prohibit the gathering from taking place. They argued that a series of branch general meetings (BGMs) and biannual meetings in four of the Free State's regions, held between August and November, had been replete with irregularities.

The BGMs were extremely important, as it was during these meetings that branch members nominated their preferred candidates for the ANC's NEC and Top Six. These decisions would then be consolidated and affirmed at the provincial conference scheduled to take place just before the national gathering at Nasrec. The branch meetings also determined which party members would attend both conferences. In a particularly hefty court application of nearly 1 000 pages, the twenty-six dissatisfied party members laid bare the astonishing level of skulduggery that still prevailed in the party's provincial structures. This time around, some of Magashule's closest political associates were fingered as the alleged perpetrators of blatantly undemocratic and unlawful acts that barred certain branch members from participating in the nomination processes.

It is worth delving into some of the myriad examples cited in the court documents. In late October 2017, one of the party's branches in the

Lejweleputswa district municipality (Welkom and surrounds) held its BGM. Sizwe Mbalo, the provincial legislature's deputy speaker and a staunch Magashule ally,[6] attended the meeting as a representative of the Magashule-led PEC. He was supposed to merely observe the proceedings, but he did much more than that. According to the court filings, Mbalo arrived with a 'pre-signed attendance register'. Some of the branch's legitimate members were not listed on this form and therefore could not vote for their preferred candidates. 'Despite the fact that the meeting was never formally quorate, nominations were accepted. Mrs Nkosazana Dlamini-Zuma was nominated as a candidate, which nomination was accepted without counting the votes. Another member nominated Mr Cyril Ramaphosa, but that nomination was completely ignored by the chairperson. Tempers consequently flared and a violent altercation broke out.'[7]

Another Magashule ally did something similar at a BGM in Koffiefontein, located in the province's Xhariep region. This meeting was attended by provincial spokesperson and PEC 'deployee' Thabo Meeko. 'During the counting of the votes for the presidential candidates the said deployee deliberately distorted the figures in favour of one presidential candidate [Dlamini-Zuma],' read the court application. There was also meddling from a senior provincial party leader at Ward 1 in the Xhariep region. Thandiwe Reachable, mayor of the Letsemeng local municipality (Koffiefontein) and one of Magashule's fellow PEC members, 'chaired the [branch] meeting in clear violation of the guidelines which specifically states that the [PEC] deployee should not chair the meeting'. Reachable certainly made her presence felt. 'When the deployee realised that the voting numbers were tipped in favour of one presidential candidate [presumably Ramaphosa] she sabotaged the meeting and the vote counting process by starting several vote counting processes until members got so frustrated that they left the meeting.'[8]

The 'bare denials' proffered by the respondents did not convince the High Court that the irregularities did not occur. The court found that Magashule and his fellow respondents 'also failed to deal with the conduct of the respective PEC deployees'. The court case also highlighted the troubling phenomenon of prohibiting certain branch members from attending meetings. For example, branches in the eastern Free State's Thabo Mofutsanyana region were subjected to 'extreme gatekeeping'. At one branch, a private security firm 'controlled ... who entered the venue of the meeting'. The security guards allegedly allowed 'people who were not [branch] members, and whose names did not appear on the attendance register … to enter the venue', while 'members in good standing were denied access despite having had proof of their credentials and copies of their membership forms'. Things subsequently got out of hand. 'As a result of an altercation that ensued because of the refusal of [the security firm] to allow access to members in good standing, [the security guards] fired rubber bullets. A member in good standing … was pepper sprayed and his wife was shot in the back with a rubber bullet.'[9]

Sources told me that the security firm mentioned in the court filings was allegedly loyal to Vusi Tshabalala, the mayor of the problem-ridden Maluti-a-Phofung local municipality. Maluti-a-Phofung falls within the Thabo Mofutsanyana region. Branded as a 'gangster mayor' by opposition politicians, Tshabalala was one of Magashule's foremost political allies.[10] The same security firm was called into action at another BGM, this time in Ward 17 in Thabo Mofutsanyana. 'A councillor … accused one of the applicants … as being part of the "CR17" faction, which is a general reference to members who support Mr Cyril Ramaphosa … The … applicant was then intimidated by [the security firm] because of the association with Mr Ramaphosa. Any person belonging to the "CR17" faction or who raised a contentious issue relating to the procedural irregularities at the meeting was removed by [the security firm] and, at times, in a violent manner.'[11]

This tactic seemingly became the norm at branches all over this region. 'Similarly, in wards 6, 8, 13 and 22, if members were suspected of belonging to the "CR17" faction or indicated so during the meetings, they were excluded from partaking in the meeting or removed from the venue.'[12] Magashule and his fellow respondents tried to convince the court that the security firm had been appointed 'to secure all members of the ANC', but the High Court would have none of it. '[C]ontrary to the alleged reason why [the firm] was appointed, they were part of the cause of violence and became part and parcel of it, instead of preventing it,' the court found.[13]

The court case also exposed the pro-Magashule camp's other preferred methods of sidelining rivals. In this regard, 'inadequate notice and/ or a complete failure to notify members of an upcoming BGM' were the order of the day, as was 'the manipulation of membership numbers in certain wards'. The latter ploy allowed certain branches 'to reach the required quorum or appoint more delegates than [the] branch would legally be entitled to'. What transpired at a branch in the Mangaung region illustrates this tactic. According to the court papers, Ward 8 was scheduled to hold a BGM on 21 October 2017, but 'the venue was changed without proper notice', which resulted in many branch members not attending. And those members who did make it to the BGM were barred from entering. 'The meeting was scheduled to start at 9h00, but when members arrived, they were informed that the process had already begun at 6h00. [Other] people were allowed to enter and participate without proper credentials. The gate that allowed access to the venue was locked before all members could enter.' The unnamed PEC member who presided over the meeting was either up to some serious mischief or was in desperate need of an eye examination. 'Ward 8 has 426 audited members. The PEC deployee announced that there were 214 signatures on the register and that a quorum had therefore been reached. However, there were only approximately 80 people at the venue. Despite the fact that there was no quorum, a delegate from this ward was chosen.'[14]

Magashule and co.'s reply in this regard did not impress the High Court. 'The respondents attached the attendance register for Ward 8 in an attempt to refute the allegations pertaining to the lack of a quorum. However, in addition to the fact that the contents thereof were again not confirmed under oath, the attendance register in fact did not confirm that a quorum was reached,' the court found.[15] The applicants highlighted similar problems at a number of other branches in the Mangaung region, and each time the respondents failed to convince the court that such irregularities did not occur. In fact, the High Court had few kind words for the manner in which the respondents tried to defend themselves. They 'attempted to present countermanding evidence to rebut allegations made by the applicants, but dismally failed to do so,' the court found. Their 'bare denials' were 'vague, lacking in specificity and made in a generalised fashion'. Their answering affidavits therefore 'failed to raise genuine bona fide disputes of fact'. As a result, the court ruled that the applicants' rights to participate in the ANC's democratic processes were 'blatantly and grossly violated by the occurrence of the established irregularities'.[16]

The court further ruled that the provincial conference could not go ahead until the affected branches held new meetings that were in line with the ANC's rules and the country's Constitution. The decision had a bearing on twenty-nine branches in four regions.

This placed Magashule in a bind. The provincial conference was scheduled to take place over the first weekend of December, and Magashule and his supporters needed the gathering to proceed in order to formalise the province's support for the Dlamini-Zuma slate. They must have suspected that the court would rule against them, because they concocted another plan to ensure that their slate got some form of official backing from the province before Nasrec. Two days before the judgment, the party sent out a notice that there would be a Provincial General Council meeting in Parys the following day, Tuesday 28 November.[17] The PGC had the power to rubber-stamp the disputed branch decisions to support Dlamini-Zuma and Magashule. According to a former Magashule backer and erstwhile MEC in the province, this move was vintage Ace. 'Whenever he felt that his leadership or power was being threatened, he convened meetings or conferences in his hometown,' this person told me. 'He felt that he had more control over things in his own backyard.'

His detractors cried foul, saying that the announcement of the PGC had caught them off guard, and that it was a desperate attempt by Magashule to have the Free State back the Dlamini-Zuma slate amid the unresolved disputes. 'This is the chair's only path to a national career in the ANC,' a former provincial leader told News24.[18] Naturally, many of the party members who supported the Ramaphosa slate decided to boycott the PGC. Few observers were therefore surprised when the PGC delegates overwhelmingly voted in favour of the Dlamini-Zuma slate. Magashule received 216 votes against 36 cast in favour of former KwaZulu-Natal premier Senzo Mchunu, the Ramaphosa bloc's choice for secretary-general.[19]

Later developments suggest that Magashule did not view this questionable victory as enough of a guarantee to ensure his political future. In an apparent attempt to secure a fall-back position in case he got routed at Nasrec, Magashule and his PEC pressed ahead with plans to convene a provincial conference, despite the High Court's firm warning not to do so until all branches affected by the judgment had held lawful BGMs.

The latest provincial conference was held in Magashule's hometown on Monday 11 December, less than a week before the Nasrec conference was scheduled to start. Thabo Manyoni, the former mayor of Mangaung, was supposed to challenge Magashule for the position of provincial chairperson,[20] but he and his backers boycotted the conference, adamant that the problems at the disputed branches had not been resolved.[21] With his only challenger absent, Magashule secured a landslide victory.[22] But it would prove to be short-lived. On the Friday before the national conference was due to begin, the Bloemfontein High Court yet again ruled in favour of disgruntled party members who sought to have the Parys conference declared unlawful and its decisions void. The court found that fourteen of the twenty-nine disputed branches could not send delegates to Nasrec.[23] This translated into a loss of about eighty voting delegates for the province. Although the voting at Nasrec for some of the Top Six positions ended up being extremely close, the Free State's 'lost' votes alone would not have changed the outcome in any of those contests.[24]

Magashule's victory at Nasrec over his challenger Senzo Mchunu certainly deserves scrutiny. The result surprised not only onlookers and commentators, but conference delegates too. Mchunu had received more branch nominations than Magashule and was widely expected to win.[25] Many delegates therefore struggled to contain their shock when the outcome was announced.[26] The battle for secretary-general yielded the tightest result of all the major races. Exactly 4696 votes were tallied, and Magashule won by just twenty-four.[27] But the new secretary-general barely had time to soak up his success before trouble brewed once again. While the Nasrec delegates were still casting their ballots for the ANC's new NEC, there were strong indications that Magashule's victory may have been secured through the same political dark arts that had kept him in power in the Free State.

Some delegates noticed that the numbers released by the EleXions Agency, a private service provider that oversaw the voting, did not add up. Word quickly spread through the venue that there were sixty-eight votes that had not been factored into the result.[28] Most concerning, it appeared that the 'missing' ballots were those of delegates who represented pro-Mchunu branches in Limpopo and KwaZulu-Natal.[29] As it turned out, the missing votes had been placed in 'quarantine' amid uncertainty over the affected delegates' credentials. The sixty-eight conference-goers had accreditation tags, but their names were not on the voters' roll.[30] Mchunu was both furious and dejected. His chief campaigner, Jomo Sibiya, insisted that the affected delegates had been 'properly accredited'.[31]

The issue threatened to derail the entire conference. Some of the sixty-eight delegates indicated that they would take legal action.[32] Eventually, the conference steering committee decided that fifteen of the sixty-eight votes were legitimate and could be added to Mchunu's tally.[33] But he still came up short. Mchunu probably would have pursued the matter, but his support within the Ramaphosa camp began to dwindle. Some Ramaphosa backers were afraid that further pressure to probe the issue could spark calls for a recount of the votes for the entire Top Six, possibly jeopardising Ramaphosa's own narrow victory over Dlamini-Zuma.[34] In the end, Mchunu relented. He took up a job at Luthuli House in early 2018, after which the controversy over the uncounted votes died down.[35]

But mere days after news broke of Mchunu's move to the ANC's headquarters, a fresh scandal engulfed the party. The *Mail & Guardian* revealed that the Maluti-a-Phofung municipality, stronghold of Magashule ally Vusi Tshabalala, had suddenly appointed about 200 new 'assistant general workers' the previous December. Some of these new 'employees' were also Nasrec delegates from branches in the Maluti-a-Phofung region. Four of them told the newspaper that they scored the jobs in exchange for supporting Dlamini-Zuma, and that they received their first salaries a day before the conference kicked off. Others claimed their appointments were in no way related to Nasrec and strongly denied that it was a 'jobs for votes' scandal.[36]

A senior political figure provided me with a list of the Maluti-a-Phofung region's Nasrec delegates. There were about fifty of them representing thirty-six branches. I found the names of twelve on a list of municipal workers fired by the Maluti-a-Phofung municipality in May 2018, after an investigation by the provincial Department of Cooperative Governance and Traditional Affairs. Most of them said they could not talk to me without permission from their branches. One of them denied that any of the Maluti-a-Phofung workers who attended Nasrec voted for the Dlamini-Zuma slate in exchange for a job. He claimed that the allegation was 'political propaganda' from the province's anti-Magashule faction, and that their employment at the municipality had been 'unfairly terminated'. But a delegate from another branch who also scored a municipal job sang a different tune. This person claimed that he had been instructed to vote not only for Dlamini-Zuma, but also for 'the full slate', which of course included Magashule as secretary-general. He did not want to divulge who had issued the order.

The DA reported the alleged 'jobs for votes' scandal to the Hawks in January 2018, but it remains to be seen whether anyone will be brought to book. The Hawks told me they had completed an 'initial investigation' and submitted the docket to the NPA for possible prosecution. However, according to an update sent to me by the law-enforcement agency in January 2019, in July 2018 'the case was returned to the Hawks for further investigation, which is still underway'.

30

New dawn, old guard

After Cyril Ramaphosa's victory at Nasrec, his promised 'new dawn' broke unexpectedly early, or so it seemed.

The new ANC leader had not even formally taken over the country's reins from Jacob Zuma when, in late January 2018, the Hawks raided the Bloemfontein offices of outgoing premier Ace Magashule. They were searching for possible evidence related to the Gupta-linked dairy venture in Vrede. They also hit the offices of the Department of Agriculture and Rural Development that same morning. 'We are looking for documents and any electronic information pertaining to our investigation,' Hawks spokesperson Hangwani Mulaudzi told reporters. 'We are going to be here the whole day.'[1]

Many South Africans welcomed this dramatic turn of events. The Hawks, other law-enforcement bodies and the country's prosecutions authority were all widely criticised for their apparent lethargy and inaction during Zuma's time in power, especially regarding politically sensitive cases. The raid on the offices of the ANC's newly elected secretary-general suggested that the police and the National Prosecuting Authority were finally being released from the clutches of Zuma and his allies. The raids in Bloemfontein were followed by one at the powerful Gupta family's estate in Johannesburg, sparking further optimism about the new regime's willingness to pursue corrupt politicians and their state-capture partners.

But there is a disconcerting backstory to the Hawks' operations in early 2018.

About two weeks before the law-enforcement body rolled into the Free State, Kopung Ralikontsane, the director-general in Magashule's office, allegedly warned fellow provincial officials about the pending raids. 'We knew the Hawks were coming well in advance,' one current MEC told me. 'Ace's DG told us to be ready.' Someone within the law-enforcement environment must have tipped off Magashule or one of his colleagues.

The sources I spoke to were not surprised by allegations that Magashule's office knew about the raid beforehand. 'Ace was in total control of the Hawks and the police in the Free State,' Beatrice Marshoff, Magashule's predecessor as premier, said when I interviewed her about Noby Ngombane's murder. A former senior Hawks officer told me that this influence stretched beyond the Free State's borders. 'There were top-level people in the Hawks and the SAPS who were looking out for Ace all these years,' this person alleged. 'Whenever a member of the public or a government official laid a criminal complaint that involved Ace or one of his associates, that news would very quickly reach Ace's ears.'

Judging by an event that occurred shortly before the raid, it seems Magashule had indeed been tipped off. Allegedly, a small group of men removed heaps of documents, computers, printers and other items from the Office of the Premier a few days before the raid. Two sources familiar with the development claimed the men had been instructed to get rid of material that could have implicated Magashule and some of his colleagues in dodgy government deals. My sources gave me the name of a former staffer in Magashule's office who allegedly oversaw the operation. They also showed me photographs of the computers, documents and other items. It was enough material to fill a small room. A bar code on a computer captured in one of the photos showed that the item belonged to the 'Department of the Premier – Free State'. The small mountain of potential evidence was allegedly taken to a house located in one of the townships on the outskirts of Bloemfontein. I was given an address.

Tiisetso Makhele, the spokesperson at the Office of the Premier, said the Free State provincial government rejected the allegations 'with the contempt that they deserve'. He claimed the Hawks 'seized all the items they were searching for as part of their investigation'.

My contacts in the police and in the province's political set-up, however, said they were sure Magashule had been warned about the raid. They also feared that future police investigations would be similarly compromised. One of my sources, the former senior Hawks officer, said Magashule's influence over key personnel in the law-enforcement environment did not end when he vacated his Bloemfontein office for his new position at Luthuli House. 'As SG, Ace is still making himself heard within the SAPS and the Hawks,' alleged this source. 'He is close to some very senior people in the police's national structures.'

If these allegations are anything to go by, it is interesting that both the national police commissioner, Khehla Sithole, and the deputy commissioner for crime detection, Lebeoana Tsumane, are former Free State provincial commissioners. Sithole, who served as Free State commissioner between 2011 and 2013, became national commissioner in November 2017.[2] This was one of Zuma's final major appointments. Sithole subsequently appointed Tsumane as one of his deputy commissioners. Tsumane had led the SAPS in the Free State from late 2016 until his promotion to the national office in December 2017.[3]

Of particular concern is the fact that the two former Free State commissioners are implicated in an alleged plot to buy votes at the 2017 Nasrec conference using 'laundered' funds from a dubious Crime Intelligence (CI) operation. The Independent Police Investigative Directorate (IPID), which is investigating the matter, has alleged in court papers that Sithole, Tsumane and other SAPS and CI officers pushed for the procurement of surveillance equipment shortly before the ANC's elective conference. The equipment was reportedly valued at about R7 million, but the SAPS and CI head honchos were allegedly willing to pay R45 million for the device. The difference of about R38 million would then have been used to buy votes for an unnamed 'faction' at Nasrec, IPID has claimed.[4] The court filings do not specify which faction was to benefit from the alleged scheme, but they offer pretty strong hints. King Bhoyi Ngcobo, one of the CI officers implicated in the saga, is one of Jacob Zuma's former bodyguards.[5]

If Magashule does have a few top cops on his side, South Africa remains in peril, especially in light of his apparent contempt for the outcome of the Nasrec conference. At an ANC Youth League gathering in January 2018, Magashule urged party members to 'work hard' so that 'the ANC that we know returns'.[6] The alleged Durban plot of September 2018 by Zuma, Magashule and others to challenge Ramaphosa's leadership spells more trouble.[7] Any suggestion that Magashule's faction has allies within police or intelligence structures needs to be probed and dealt with immediately, lest these vital agencies get sucked into a dangerous political battle.

For Magashule, there is more at stake than political power. The ANC secretary-general is alleged to have presided over a decades-long state-capture scheme in his home province. This may yet land him in some serious trouble. This book and the myriad media reports over the years should contain enough material to at least prompt the authorities to begin looking in the right places. But that will only happen once the Hawks, the SAPS and the NPA are released from the clutches of their captors. In this regard, Ramaphosa's 'new dawn' has so far been just that – a faint glimmer of hope peeking over the horizon. What this country needs now is direct sunlight. The ANC's secretary-gangster and his cohort need to feel the heat of a truly independent and unfettered law-enforcement environment.

Acknowledgements

My first word of gratitude has to go to the Taco Kuiper Fund for Investigative Journalism, administered by Wits Journalism. A generous grant from the Taco Kuiper Fund allowed me to work on this book full time for almost a year. I hope *Gangster State* will encourage other journalists and authors to embark on a similar writing journey and broaden the body of literature that shines a light into this country's darkest corners.

Investigating and writing about politicians' secret lives can be a lonely, daunting and at times risky business. Fortunately, I am able to rely on a solid support base that consists of family, friends and colleagues in the media industry. I am thankful for each and every person who has in some way helped, supported or encouraged me.

Politicians, government officials, businesspeople and a myriad other sources collectively dedicated hours of their time to help me better understand my subject and to share vital information with me. Many of them have asked to remain anonymous due to the climate of fear that permeates politics in South Africa. But they know who they are, and I owe them much gratitude for their time and assistance.

Those who can be named and whom I would like to thank include the DA's Leona Kleynhans and Roy Jankielsohn, and COPE's Dennis Bloem and Papi Kganare. Former Bloemfontein mayor Thabo Manyoni deserves special acknowledgement for the courage he demonstrated by sharing with me his recollections of his trip with Ace Magashule to the Guptas' Saxonwold estate in Johannesburg. Mxolisi Dukwana was also willing to share some of his experiences in the Free State on the record. Beatrice Marshoff, Magashule's predecessor as premier, committed her name to the important information she shared with me. Nokwanda Ngombane spoke to me about an extremely painful and distressing period in her life – I am truly thankful for her time and courage. Basildon Peta's insights were also invaluable. If I have forgotten anyone, please forgive me!

Finally, I must thank the team at Penguin Random House, and attorney Willem de Klerk and his candidate attorney, Charl du Plessis. These are the smart and talented people who worked tirelessly in the background to help get this book on the shelves.

PIETER-LOUIS MYBURGH
FEBRUARY 2019

Notes

INTRODUCTION

1. Pieter-Louis Myburgh, 'Onmin broei oor sport se Oscars', *Rapport*, 9 June 2013.
2. Pieter-Louis Myburgh, 'Exclusive: Man killed in Sandton "hit" linked to R255m Free State contract', *News24*, 19 April 2018, available at https://www.news24.com/SouthAfrica/News/exclusive-man-killed-in-sandton-hit-linked-to-r255m-free-state-contract-20180419 (last accessed 12 February 2019).
3. Sapa, 'Criminals within ANC: Magashule', *IOL*, 31 July 2012, available at https://www.iol.co.za/news/politics/criminals-within-anc-magashule-1353140 (last accessed 12 February 2019).

CHAPTER 1: THE TUMAHOLE 'TREASONIST'

1. Interview with Elias Ace Magashule by Moses Mzwandile Hadebe, for the ANC Oral History Project, n.d.
2. If this is correct, Magashule would have turned seventeen in his Grade Eight year.
3. Fiona Forde, 'Magashule: premier in waiting', *Sunday Independent*, 12 October 2008, https://www.iol.co.za/news/politics/magashule-premier-in-waiting-419845 (last accessed 11 September 2018).
4. Tshepo Cyril Moloi, 'Black politics in Kroonstad: Political mobilisation, protests, local government, and generational struggles, 1976–1995', PhD thesis, University of the Witwatersrand, 2012.
5. Interview with Elias Ace Magashule by Moses Mzwandile Hadebe, for the ANC Oral History Project, n.d.
6. 'Who is Ace Magashule?', official website of Dr Ace Magashule, 1 October 2017, available at https://acemagashule.co.za/wp/2017/10/01/who-is-ace-magashule/ (last accessed 11 September 2018).
7. Diphoko Senokoane, 'Cosas is born, schools stand together', *Express*, 23 September 2015, available at https://www.news24.com/SouthAfrica/Local/Express-News/Cosas-is-born-schools-stand-together-20150922 (last accessed 11 September 2018).
8. 'Minutes of the UDF held on 10 and 11 September 1983 at Phoenix Settlement in Durban', Collection No. AK2117, Historical Papers, University of the Witwatersrand, 2012, available at http://www.historicalpapers.wits.ac.za/inventories/inv_pdfo/AK2117/AK2117-J2-4-D1-001-jpeg.pdf (last accessed 11 September 2018).
9. See http://www.anc.org.za/officials/elias-sekgobelo-magashule (last accessed 11 September 2018).
10. Judge A.J. Lamprecht, *S v Bhekibutho Vincent Nxumalo*, case no. CC 94/14 (High Court of South Africa, Gauteng Division, Eastern Circuit, Ermelo), 6 August 2015, available at www.saflii.org/za/cases/ZAGPPHC/2015/660.rtf (last accessed 11 September 2018).
11. Rico Devara Chapman, *Student Resistance to Apartheid at the University of Fort Hare: Freedom Now, a Degree Tomorrow* (Lanham: Lexington Books, 2016), p. 58.
12. 'Fort Hare students get final warning', *Daily Dispatch*, 5 May 1982.

13. '20 on violence charges', *Daily Dispatch*, 19 May 1982.
14. 'CCIS man tells of shots at Fort Hare', *Daily Dispatch*, 12 January 1983.
15. Bheki Mlangeni, South African History Online, available at http://www.sahistory.org .za/people/bheki-mlangeni (last accessed 11 September 2018).
16. Interview with Elias Ace Magashule by Moses Mzwandile Hadebe, for the ANC Oral History Project, n.d.
17. *S v Dingiswayo and Others* 1985 3 SA 175, Ciskei General Division.
18. 'CCIS man tells of shots at Fort Hare'.
19. 'Ciskei terror trial postponed', *Daily Dispatch*, 24 August 1982.
20. Interview with Elias Ace Magashule by Moses Mzwandile Hadebe, for the ANC Oral History Project, n.d.
21. Forde, 'Magashule: premier in waiting'.

CHAPTER 2: HILLBROW DAYS

1. Setjhaba Maphalla and Mondli Mvambi, 'A man of the people', *Public Sector Manager*, January 2014, pp. 56–61.
2. Ibid., pp. 56–57.
3. Fidelis Hove, 'Bias in MK analysis leaves much to be desired', *Mail & Guardian*, 2 March 2017, available at https://mg.co.za/article/2017-03-01-omissions-in-mk -analysis-leave-much-to-be-desired (last accessed 12 September 2018).
4. J. Brooks Spector, 'The UDF at 30: An organisation that shook apartheid's foundation', *Daily Maverick*, 22 August 2013, available at https://www.dailymaverick .co.za/article/2013-08-22-the-udf-at-30-an-organisation-that-shook-apartheids -foundation/ (last accessed 12 September 2018).
5. Interview with Elias Ace Magashule by Moses Mzwandile Hadebe, for the ANC Oral History Project, n.d.
6. 'Let us respect the legacy of Mama Winnie Madikizela-Mandela', media release by Dennis Bloem MP, 9 April 2018.

CHAPTER 3: EXILE

1. Interview with Elias Ace Magashule by Moses Mzwandile Hadebe, for the ANC Oral History Project, n.d.
2. Jeremy Seekings, *The UDF: A History of the United Democratic Front in South Africa, 1983–1991* (Cape Town: David Philip, 2000), p. 212.
3. Bloem statement.
4. 'Seipei's mother says she forgave Winnie long ago', *eNCA*, 8 April 2018, available at https://www.enca.com/south-africa/watch-stompie-seipeis-family-welcomes-anc -into-their-home (last accessed 13 September 2018).
5. Interview with Elias Ace Magashule by Moses Mzwandile Hadebe, for the ANC Oral History Project, n.d.
6. Nico Gous, 'Manuel rips into Magashule about restoration of Winnie's Brandfort home', *TimesLive*, 5 April 2018, available at https://www.timeslive.co.za/news/ south-africa/2018-04-05-manuel-rips-into-magashule-about-restoration-winnies -brandfort-home/ (last accessed 13 September 2018).
7. Mahlatse Mahlase, 'Magashule hits back at Trevor Manuel over Winnie's Brandfort home', *News24*, 10 April 2018, available at https://www.news24.com/SouthAfrica/ News/magashule-hits-back-at-trevor-manuel-over-winnies-brandfort-home -20180410 (last accessed 13 September 2018).
8. Ayanda Dlodlo, 'Magashule can never be erased from the history of the struggle', *Sunday Independent*, 22 April 2018.

9. 'Tumahole (Parys) 698-714', Document ID AK2117-K2117-L9-22, Historical Papers, University of the Witwatersrand, 2009, available at http://www.historicalpapers.wits .ac.za/inventories/inv_pdfo/AK2117/AK2117-L09-22-01-jpeg.pdf (last accessed 13 September 2018).
10. *S* v *Patrick Mabuya Baleka and 21 others*, case no. CC 482/85, Transvaal High Court, Pretoria, 15 February 1988, available at https://repository.up.ac.za/bitstream/handle/ 2263/63853/delmas_trial_vol347_1988.pdf?sequence=7 (last accessed 13 September 2018).
11. Dlodlo, 'Magashule can never be erased from the history of the struggle'.
12. Christa Kuljian, *Sanctuary: How an Inner-city Church Spilled onto a Sidewalk* (Johannesburg: Jacana, 2013), p. 78.
13. Sapa, 'Winnie started assault on abducted youths, TRC hears', 26 November 1997, available at http://www.justice.gov.za/trc/media%5C1997%5C9711/s971126b.htm (last accessed 14 September 2018).
14. Sapa, 'Stompie killed on Winnie's orders to cover up assaults, TRC told', 3 December 1997, available at http://www.justice.gov.za/trc/media%5C1997%5C9712/s971203f.htm. See http://www.justice.gov.za/trc/special%5Cmandela/mufc7b.htm for transcript (both last accessed 14 September 2018).
15. Sapa, 'MDM distanced itself from Winnie after she ignored Mandela', 27 November 1997, available at http://www.justice.gov.za/trc/media%5C1997%5C9711/s971127g.htm (last accessed 14 September 2018).
16. Birthdate appears on a UAE tourist visa for Thato Magashule, contained in the #GuptaLeaks emails.
17. Interview with Elias Ace Magashule by Moses Mzwandile Hadebe, for the ANC Oral History Project, n.d.
18. Ibid.
19. Ibid.

CHAPTER 4: AN EARLY SCANDAL

1. Chitja Twala, 'The demon of factionalism in an African National Congress (ANC)-led Free State Province (1994–2004): A reality?', *Journal for Contemporary History*, 30 (3), January 2005, pp. 109–131.
2. 'Resolutions by ANC, 20 December 2007, 52nd National Conference, Polokwane', South African History Online, available at https://www.sahistory.org.za/archive/ resolutions-anc-20-december-2007-52nd-national-conference-polokwane (last accessed 17 September 2018).
3. Rapule Tabane, 'Drive to finesse "Ace"', *Mail & Guardian*, 15 April 2005, available at https://mg.co.za/article/2005-04-15-drive-to-finesse-ace (last accessed 17 September 2018).
4. Tom Lodge, *South African Politics Since 1994* (Cape Town: David Philip, 1999), p. 19.
5. Ibid.
6. Twala, 'The demon of factionalism in an African National Congress (ANC)-led Free State Province (1994–2004)'.
7. Marianne Merten, 'Magashule aces entrenchment of power', *Sunday Independent*, 24 June 2012, available at https://www.iol.co.za/news/politics/magashule-aces -entrenchment-of-power-1326234 (last accessed 17 September 2018).
8. Qaanitah Hunter, 'NDZ bid to be No 1 hits bumps in NEC and Ace', *Sunday Times*, 24 September 2017.
9. Twala, 'The demon of factionalism in an African National Congress (ANC)-led Free State Province (1994–2004)'.
10. Ibid.

11. Mark Gevisser, 'Patrick "Terror" Lekota, Free State premier, in', *Mail & Guardian*, 8 August 1996, available at https://mg.co.za/article/1996-08-08-patrick-terror-lekota -free-state-premier-in (last accessed 17 September 2018).

12. Staff reporter, 'Lekota uncovers corruption in Free State', *Mail & Guardian*, 8 August 1996, available at https://mg.co.za/article/1996-08-08-lekota-uncovers-corruption-in -free-state (last accessed 17 September 2018).

13. Lodge, *South African Politics Since 1994*, p. 21.

14. Twala, 'The demon of factionalism in an African National Congress (ANC)-led Free State Province (1994–2004)'.

15. 'Commission finds R3-m irregularities', *The Star*, 13 December 1996.

16. National Party media statement, undated, sourced from the Archive for Contemporary Affairs (ARCA) at the University of the Free State.

17. Staff reporter, 'Lekota uncovers corruption in Free State'.

18. Staff reporter, 'Lekota row stews in Free State', *Mail & Guardian*, 24 January 1997, available at https://mg.co.za/article/1997-01-24-lekota-row-stews-in-free-state (last accessed 17 September 2018).

19. Staff reporter, 'Lekota's foe implicated in dubious deals', *Mail & Guardian*, 20 June 1997, available at https://mg.co.za/article/1997-06-20-lekotas-foe-implicated-in-dubious -deals (last accessed 17 September 2018).

20. Lodge, *South African Politics Since 1994*, p. 19.

21. Ibid.

22. Staff reporter, 'Confusion reigns over race for premier', *Mail & Guardian*, 22 November 1996, available at https://mg.co.za/article/1996-11-22-confusion-reigns -over-race-for-premier (last accessed 17 September 2018).

23. Personal profile of Mosiuoa Lekota, available at http://www.armsdeal-vpo.co.za/ special_items/profiles/profile_lekota.html (last accessed 17 September 2018).

24. Twala, 'The demon of factionalism in an African National Congress (ANC)-led Free State Province (1994–2004)'.

25. Lodge, *South African Politics Since 1994*, p. 22.

26. Twala, 'The demon of factionalism in an African National Congress (ANC)-led Free State Province (1994–2004)'.

27. Staff reporter, 'Lekota's nemesis goes to Parliament', *Mail & Guardian*, 24 June 1997, available at https://mg.co.za/article/1997-06-24-lekotas-nemesis-goes-to-parliament (last accessed 17 September 2018).

28. Twala, 'The demon of factionalism in an African National Congress (ANC)-led Free State Province (1994–2004)'.

29. Lodge, *South African Politics Since 1994*, p. 22.

30. Jonny Steinberg, 'Magashule and allies sweep the floor in Free State ANC election', *Business Day*, 24 August 1998, available at https://allafrica.com/stories/199808240103 .html (last accessed 17 September 2018).

31. Ibid.

32. Twala, 'The demon of factionalism in an African National Congress (ANC)-led Free State Province (1994–2004)'.

33. Ibid.

34. Sapa, 'ANC disbands split Free State executive', *IOL*, 3 June 2000, available at https://www.iol.co.za/news/politics/anc-disbands-split-free-state-executive-39408 (last accessed 17 September 2018).

35. Rapule Tabane, 'Free State snubs ANC, elects Magashule', *IOL*, 29 July 2002, available at https://www.iol.co.za/news/politics/free-state-snubs-anc-elects-magashule-90529 (last accessed 17 September 2018).

CHAPTER 5: FREE STATE CAPTURE AND THE 'CATTLE THIEF'

1. 'From premier to scrub nurse', *City Press*, 24 February 2013, available at https://www.news24.com/Archives/City-Press/From-premier-to-scrub-nurse-20150430 (last accessed 17 September 2018).
2. Sapa, 'Marshoff names new Free State council', *IOL*, 3 May 2004, available at https://www.iol.co.za/news/politics/marshoff-names-new-free-state-council-211941 (last accessed 18 September 2018).
3. Ainsley Moos, 'Staat gryp in vir swart boer', *Landbou Weekblad*, 4 March 2005, available at http://m24lbargo1.naspers.com/argief/berigte/landbouweekblad/2005/03/4/81/3.html (last accessed 18 September 2018).
4. Nico van Burick, 'DA waarsku oor bevriesde projekte', *Landbou Weekblad*, 25 June 2004, available at http://m24lbargo1.naspers.com/argief/berigte/landbouweekblad/2004/06/25/89/3.html (last accessed 18 September 2018).
5. Sapa, 'Parties question Free State reshuffle', *IOL*, 7 August 2007, available at https://www.iol.co.za/news/politics/parties-question-free-state-reshuffle-365355 (last accessed 18 September 2018).
6. 'Marshoff axe hits top ANC man', *News24*, 7 April 2005, available at https://www.news24.com/SouthAfrica/News/Marshoff-axe-hits-top-ANC-man-20050407 (last accessed 18 September 2018).
7. Tabane, 'Drive to finesse "Ace"'.
8. Adriaan Basson, 'Bloem land price blows up', *Mail & Guardian*, 1 June 2009, available at https://mg.co.za/article/2009-06-01-bloem-land-price-blows-up (last accessed 18 September 2018).
9. Sapa, 'Parties question Free State reshuffle'.
10. Loyiso Sidimba, 'R11m down the drain', *Sowetan*, 9 January 2015.

CHAPTER 6: CRUSHING THE SCORPIONS

1. Sibusiso Ngalwa, 'Line-up of ANC's would-be kingmakers', *IOL*, 28 October 2007, available at https://www.iol.co.za/news/politics/line-up-of-ancs-would-be-kingmakers-376681 (last accessed 19 September 2018).
2. Sapa, 'Court action against F State ANC "counter-revolutionary"', *Mail & Guardian*, 23 April 2007, available at https://mg.co.za/article/2007-04-23-court-action-against-f-state-anc-counterrevolutionary (last accessed 19 September 2018).
3. Sapa, 'F State ANC hits out at reports of split', *IOL*, 29 April 2007, available at https://www.iol.co.za/news/politics/f-state-anc-hits-out-at-reports-of-split-350676 (last accessed 19 September 2018).
4. *Mayekiso and Others v Magashule and Others* (2567/2008, 5614/2008) [2009] ZAFSHC 31 (19 March 2009), available at http://www.saflii.org/za/cases/ZAFSHC/2009/31.html (last accessed 19 September 2018).
5. Ibid.
6. 'Surprise support for Zuma', *News24*, 25 November 2007, available at https://www.news24.com/SouthAfrica/Politics/Surprise-support-for-Zuma-20071125 (last accessed 19 September 2018).
7. Charles Molele, 'ANC delegates forced to cough up for Zuma's defence', *Sunday Times*, 27 July 2008, available at https://www.pressreader.com/south-africa/sunday-times/20080727/281633891014018 (last accessed 19 September 2018).
8. Anna Majavu, '"Scorpions targeted Free State ANC leader"', *Sowetan*, 22 December 2008, available at https://www.sowetanlive.co.za/news/2008-12-22-scorpions-targeted-free-state-anc-leader/ (last accessed 19 September 2018).
9. Andre Grobler, 'Dissent and disgust at hearing on Scorpions' future', *Mail &*

Guardian, 14 August 2008, available at https://mg.co.za/article/2008-08-14-dissent-and-disgust-at-hearing-on-scorpions-future (last accessed 19 September 2018).

10. 'Scorpions officially disbanded', *News24*, 30 January 2009, available at https://www.news24.com/SouthAfrica/News/Scorpions-officially-disbanded-20090130 (last accessed 19 September 2018).

11. Mcebisi Ndletyana, 'Congress of the People: A promise betrayed', *Journal of African Elections* 9 (2): 32–55, available at https://eisa.org.za/pdf/JAE9.2Ndletyana2.pdf (last accessed 20 September 2018), p. 48.

12. Sapa, 'Free State "realigns" cabinet', *Mail & Guardian*, 22 October 2008, available at https://mg.co.za/article/2008-10-22-free-state-realigns-cabinet (last accessed 20 September 2018).

CHAPTER 7: THE ASSASSINATION OF NOBY NGOMBANE

1. Twala, 'The demon of factionalism in an African National Congress (ANC)-led Free State Province (1994–2004)'.

2. Rapule Tabane, 'Power behind Free State throne', *Mail & Guardian*, 30 July 2004, available at https://mg.co.za/article/2004-07-30-power-behind-free-state-throne (last accessed 22 October 2018).

3. Ibid.

4. Ibid.

5. Ibid.

6. T. Geldenhuys, 'Local business, government meet', *Netwerk24*, 26 May 2015, available at https://www.netwerk24.com/ZA/Kroonnuus/Nuus/Local-business-government-meet-20150525 (last accessed 22 October 2018).

7. Sapa, 'Top Free State official gunned down at home', *IOL*, 23 March 2005, available at https://www.iol.co.za/news/politics/top-free-state-official-gunned-down-at-home-237091 (last accessed 22 October 2018).

8. Ibid.

9. Ibid.

10. Rapule Tabane, 'ANC hit by post-poll turmoil', *Mail & Guardian*, 17 December 2004, available at https://mg.co.za/article/2004-12-17-anc-hit-by-postpoll-turmoil (last accessed 22 October 2018).

11. Sapa, 'Cool reception for claims of political killing', *Mail & Guardian*, 29 March 2005, available at https://mg.co.za/article/2005-03-29-cool-reception-for-claims-of-political-killing (last accessed 22 October 2018).

12. Ibid.

13. Matefu Mokoena, 'Twist in ANC man murder', *City Press*, 3 April 2005, available at https://www.news24.com/SouthAfrica/News/Twist-in-ANC-man-murder-20050403 (last accessed 22 October 2018).

14. Andre Grobler, 'More arrests expected in Ngombane murder case', *IOL*, 22 July 2005, available at https://www.iol.co.za/news/politics/more-arrests-expected-in-ngombane-murder-case-248849 (last accessed 22 October 2018).

15. Hopewell Radebe, '"No political motive" in ANC official's killing', *Business Day*, 22 July 2005.

16. Nomboniso Gasa, 'We're bound together by spilt blood', *City Press*, 20 May 2018, available at https://www.news24.com/Columnists/GuestColumn/were-bound-together-by-spilt-blood-20180520-3 (last accessed 22 October 2018).

17. Jimmy Seepe, 'Slain ANC man insured for R20m', *City Press*, 24 July 2005.

18. Ibid.

19. Sapa, 'State working "non-stop" on Ngombane murder', *Mail & Guardian*,

19 September 2005, available at https://mg.co.za/article/2005-09-19-state-working
-nonstop-on-ngombane-murder (last accessed 23 October 2018).

20. Julian Rademeyer, 'Family furious as coffin dug up in bizarre search for gun', *Sunday Times*, 16 October 2005.

21. Andre Grobler, 'Ngombane murder: New facts may lead to acquittal', *Mail & Guardian*, 13 March 2006, available at https://mg.co.za/article/2006-03-13-ngombane
-murder-new-facts-may-lead-to-acquittal (last accessed 23 October 2018).

22. Sapa, 'Prisoner claims to have been Ngombane hit man', *Mail & Guardian*, 18 July 2007, available at https://mg.co.za/article/2007-07-18-prisoner-claims-to-have-been
-ngombane-hit-man (last accessed 23 October 2018).

23. Julian Rademeyer, 'The man who rules from the grave', *Sunday Times*, 17 April 2005.

24. Baldwin Ndaba, '"Prisoner's claim won't be investigated"', *IOL*, 19 July 2007, available at https://www.iol.co.za/news/south-africa/prisoners-claim-wont-be-investigated
-362613 (last accessed 23 October 2018).

25. 'Ngombane: State drops charges', *News24*, 27 September 2009, available at https://www
.news24.com/SouthAfrica/News/Ngombane-State-drops-charges-20060927 (last accessed 23 October 2018).

26. Ibid.

27. Sapa, 'Inquiry postponed into Free State official's murder', *Mail & Guardian*, 9 May 2008, available at https://mg.co.za/article/2008-05-09-inquiry-postponed-into-free
-state-officials-murder (last accessed 23 October 2018).

28. Sapa, 'Ngombane "family unfairly treated"', *IOL*, 15 May 2008, available at https://
www.iol.co.za/news/south-africa/ngombane-family-unfairly-treated-400628 (last accessed 23 October 2018).

29. Rademeyer, 'Family furious as coffin dug up in bizarre search for gun'.

30. 'Noby-killing evidence in camera', *News24*, 14 May 2008, available at https://www
.news24.com/SouthAfrica/News/Noby-killing-evidence-in-camera-20080513 (last accessed 23 October 2018).

31. Ibid.

CHAPTER 8: 'BRING YOUR PEOPLE'

1. The department was formerly known as the Department of Local Government and Housing, but was reconfigured after the 2009 general election to constitute the Department of Cooperative Governance, Traditional Affairs and Human Settlements. The portfolio is generally split into the Department of Cooperative Governance and Traditional Affairs and the Department of Human Settlements.

2. Auditor-general of South Africa. Go to https://www.agsa.co.za/Reporting.aspx to view the general PFMA reports on the provincial audit outcomes of the Free State, 2011/12 to 2016/17, and the annual reports for the Free State Department of Human Settlements.

3. Gauteng Department of Human Settlements annual report 2013/14, available at http://www.gauteng.gov.za/government/departments/human-settlements/
Annual%20Reports/GDHS%20ANNUAL%20REPORT%202013-2014.pdf (last accessed 9 October 2018).

4. Free State Department of Human Settlements annual report 2013/14, available at https://provincialgovernment.co.za/department_annual/149/2014-free-state-human
-settlements-annual-report.pdf (last accessed 9 October 2018).

5. Free State Department of Human Settlements annual reports for 2015/16 and 2011/12, available at http://www.humansettlements.fs.gov.za/?page_id=1720 (last accessed 9 October 2018).

6. *The MEC of the Department of Co-operative Governance, Human Settlements and Traditional Affairs (Free State Province)* vs *Scenic Route Trading 802 CC and others*, case 241/2016, Bloemfontein High Court.

7. Staff reporter, 'Free State provincial ministers announced', *Mail & Guardian*, 11 May 2009, available at https://mg.co.za/article/2009-05-11-free-state-provincial-ministers -announced (last accessed 9 October 2018).

8. *The MEC of the Department of Co-operative Governance, Human Settlements and Traditional Affairs (Free State Province)* vs *Scenic Route Trading 802 CC and others*, case 241/2016, Bloemfontein High Court.

9. Ibid.

10. Ibid.

11. Ibid.

12. Mandy de Waal, 'Ace Magashule's Potemkin villages of the Free State', *Daily Maverick*, 6 March 2013, available at https://www.dailymaverick.co.za/article/ 2013-03-06-ace-magashules-potemkin-villages-of-the-free-state/ (last accessed 19 October 2018).

13. 'State and party colours', Public Protector Report No. 1 of 2016/17, available at http://www.pprotect.org/sites/default/files/legislation_report/SKMBT_C55416050601 050.pdf (last accessed 19 October 2018).

14. Free State Department of Human Settlements annual report 2016/17, available at http://www.humansettlements.fs.gov.za/wp-content/uploads/2018/04/Annual%20 Report%202016-2017.pdf (last accessed 19 October 2018).

15. *The MEC of the Department of Co-operative Governance, Human Settlements and Traditional Affairs (Free State Province)* vs *Scenic Route Trading 802 CC and others*, case 241/2016, Bloemfontein High Court.

16. Ibid.

17. Sue Cullinan and Sello Mabotja, 'South Africa: Sexwale, the apprentice', *Africa Report*, 22 March 2010, available at http://www.theafricareport.com/News-Analysis/ south-africa-sexwale-the-apprentice.html (last accessed 10 October 2018).

18. *The MEC of the Department of Co-operative Governance, Human Settlements and Traditional Affairs (Free State Province)* vs *Scenic Route Trading 802 CC and others*, case 241/2016, Bloemfontein High Court.

19. Ibid.

20. Ibid.

21. Ibid.

22. Progress report on FSHS 2010/11 projects.

23. *The MEC of the Department of Co-operative Governance, Human Settlements and Traditional Affairs (Free State Province)* vs *Scenic Route Trading 802 CC and others*, case 241/2016, Bloemfontein High Court.

24. Qaanitah Hunter, 'Hlaudi sued in R1bn housing "fraud" spree', *Sunday Times*, 15 January 2017.

25. 'Magashule shuffles MEC's', *News24*, 4 February 2011, available at https://www .news24.com/southafrica/politics/magashule-shuffles-mecs-20110204 (last accessed 10 October 2018).

26. Angelique Serrao, 'State capture arrests: Who are the accused and what are the charges?', *News24*, 15 February 2018, available at https://www.news24.com/SouthAfrica/News/ state-capture-arrests-who-are-the-accused-and-what-are-the-charges-20180215 (last accessed 10 October 2018).

27. Parliamentary Monitoring Group, 'Fetsa Tlala Food Production initiative & conditional grants: Provincial departments reporting day 1', Agriculture, Forestry and Fisheries,

21 September 2016, available at https://pmg.org.za/committee-meeting/23331/ (last accessed 10 October 2018).

28. Beauregard Tromp, 'Thousands mourn Tatane', *Sunday Independent*, 24 April 2011, available at https://www.iol.co.za/news/south-africa/free-state/thousands-mourn -tatane-1060727 (last accessed 10 October 2018).

29. Sipho Masondo, Khutso Tsikane and Amukelani Chauke, 'Police use rubber bullets to disperse protesters', *TimesLive*, 12 July 2011, available at https://www.timeslive.co.za/ news/south-africa/2011-07-11-police-use-rubber-bullets-to-disperse-protesters/ (last accessed 10 October 2018).

30. Ntwaagae Seleka, 'Unfinished RDP houses leave residents fuming', *Sowetan*, 20 June 2012, available at https://www.sowetanlive.co.za/news/2012-06-20-unfinished-rdp -houses-leave-residents-fuming/ (last accessed 10 October 2018).

31. 'Power struggle in anti-Magashule group', *The Weekly*, 9 March 2012, available at http://theweekly.co.za/?p=3797 (last accessed 10 October 2018).

32. Greg Nicolson, 'The cast of the holy EFF', *Daily Maverick*, 12 July 2013, available at https://www.dailymaverick.co.za/article/2013-07-12-the-cast-of-the-holy-eff/ (last accessed 16 October 2018).

33. Sapa, 'Free State premier fires MEC', *IOL*, 22 February 2012, available at https://www .iol.co.za/news/politics/free-state-premier-fires-mec-1240513 (last accessed 10 October 2018).

34. Baldwin Ndaba, 'No sleepless nights over victory', *IOL*, 7 August 2016, available at https://www.iol.co.za/news/politics/no-sleepless-nights-over-victory-2054391 (last accessed 10 October 2018).

35. Maluti-a-Phofung Water (Pty) Ltd annual report 2011/12.

36. 'Housing scam exposed', *The Weekly*, 6 July 2012, available at http://theweekly. co.za/?p=8132 (last accessed 10 October 2018).

37. Free State Department of Human Settlements annual report 2012/13, available at http://www.humansettlements.fs.gov.za/wp-content/uploads/2012/07/2012-2013 -Annual-Report.pdf (last accessed 9 October 2018).

38. 'SIU approached to look into Free State housing', *South African Government News Agency*, 23 August 2012, available at https://www.sanews.gov.za/south-africa/ siu-approached-look-free-state-housing (last accessed 10 October 2018).

39. 'Housing scam exposed'.

40. *The MEC of the Department of Co-operative Governance, Human Settlements and Traditional Affairs (Free State Province)* vs *Scenic Route Trading 802 CC and others*, case 241/2016, Bloemfontein High Court.

41. 'Sexwale briefs portfolio committee on housing challenges in the Free State', SA government media statement, 22 August 2012, available at https://www.gov.za/ sexwale-briefs-portfolio-committee-housing-challenges-free-state (last accessed 10 October 2018).

42. SIU annual report 2015/16, available at https://www.siu.org.za/wp-content/uploads/ 2017/11/SIU-Annual-Report-2015-2016.pdf (last accessed 10 October 2018).

43. 'Sexwale briefs portfolio committee on housing challenges in the Free State'.

44. *The MEC of the Department of Co-operative Governance, Human Settlements and Traditional Affairs (Free State Province)* vs *Scenic Route Trading 802 CC and others*, case 241/2016, Bloemfontein High Court.

45. 'Sexwale briefs portfolio committee on housing challenges in the Free State'.

46. 'Sexwale not leaving ANC – report', *News24*, 24 December 2012, available at https:// www.news24.com/SouthAfrica/Politics/Sexwale-not-leaving-ANC-report-20121224 (last accessed 10 October 2018).

47. Sapa, 'Pule, Sexwale axed in cabinet reshuffle', *IOL*, 9 July 2013, available at https://www.iol.co.za/news/politics/pule-sexwale-axed-in-cabinet-reshuffle-1544397 (last accessed 10 October 2018).

CHAPTER 9: FALL GUYS AND FAT CATS

1. *The MEC of the Department of Co-operative Governance, Human Settlements and Traditional Affairs (Free State Province)* vs *Scenic Route Trading 802 CC and others*, case 241/2016, Bloemfontein High Court.
2. Ibid.
3. Ibid.
4. 'Five top officials dismissed', *New Age*, 5 June 2015.
5. *The MEC of the Department of Co-operative Governance, Human Settlements and Traditional Affairs (Free State Province)* vs *Scenic Route Trading 802 CC and others*, case 241/2016, Bloemfontein High Court.
6. Ibid.
7. 'State land release gains momentum', Housing Development Agency, 10 May 2013, available at http://thehda.co.za/index.php/news/single-article/state-land-release-gains-momentum (last accessed 15 October 2018).
8. Free State Department of Social Development annual report 2015/16, available at https://provincialgovernment.co.za/department_annual/402/2016-free-state-social-development-annual-report.pdf (last accessed 15 October 2018).
9. Staff reporter, 'PAC's De Lille names "spies"', *Mail & Guardian*, 23 October 1997, available at https://mg.co.za/article/1997-10-23-pacs-de-lille-names-spies (last accessed 15 October 2018).
10. Sam Sole and Stefaans Brümmer, 'Ngcuka vs Zuma: Inside the spy wars', *Mail & Guardian*, 28 November 2003, available at https://mg.co.za/article/2003-11-28-ngcuka-vs-zuma-inside-the-spy-wars (last accessed 15 October 2018).
11. *The MEC of the Department of Co-operative Governance, Human Settlements and Traditional Affairs (Free State Province)* vs *Scenic Route Trading 802 CC and others*, case 241/2016, Bloemfontein High Court.
12. Steve Motale, 'Company denies any wrongdoing in SAA multimillion-rand tender', *Sunday Independent*, 9 July 2017, available at https://www.iol.co.za/news/politics/company-denies-any-wrongdoing-in-saa-multimillion-rand-tender-10203856 (last accessed 15 October 2018).
13. amaBhungane, 'CSIR's supercomputer tender and the theatre of the absurd that followed it', *Daily Maverick*, 1 July 2016, available at https://www.dailymaverick.co.za/article/2016-07-01-amabhungane-csirs-supercomputer-tender-and-the-theatre-of-the-absurd-that-followed-it/ (last accessed 6 November 2018).
14. Ibid.
15. Vicki Robinson, '"Heavy hand" behind hotel deal', *Mail & Guardian*, 15 September 2005, available at https://mg.co.za/article/2005-09-15-heavy-hand-behind-hotel-deal (last accessed 6 November 2018).
16. Vicki Robinson, 'E Cape ruling exposes political ploy', *Mail & Guardian*, 23 September 2005, available at https://mg.co.za/article/2005-09-23-e-cape-ruling-exposes-political-ploy (last accessed 6 November 2018).
17. amaBhungane, 'CSIR's supercomputer tender and the theatre of the absurd that followed it'.
18. Arbitration matter GPBCI 1385/2015, Bloemfontein.
19. *The MEC of the Department of Co-operative Governance, Human Settlements and*

Traditional Affairs (Free State Province) vs *Scenic Route Trading 802 CC and others*, case 241/2016, Bloemfontein High Court.

20. Qaanitah Hunter, 'Hlaudi, Mrs M off house-fraud hook', *Sunday Times*, 29 January 2017.
21. Progress report on FSHS 2010/11 projects.
22. Pieter-Louis Myburgh, 'Magashule and daughter in money-for-jam property scandal', *News24*, 31 January 2018, available at https://www.news24.com/SouthAfrica/News/magashule-and-daughter-in-money-for-jam-property-scandal-20180131 (last accessed 16 October 2018).
23. Adriaan Basson and Mandy Rossouw, 'Premier's R3-million casino "bribe"', *Mail & Guardian*, 26 June 2009, available at https://mg.co.za/article/2009-06-26-premiers-r3million-casino-bribe (last accessed 16 October 2018).
24. Centlec annual report 2013/14.
25. Centlec annual report 2015/16, available at http://cms.centlec.co.za/documents/ANNUAL%20REPORT%202015-16.pdf (last accessed 16 October 2018).
26. Progress report on FSHS 2010/11 projects.

CHAPTER 10: REWARDING FRIENDS AND PUNISHING FOES

1. Qaanitah Hunter, 'Hlaudi sued in R1bn housing "fraud" spree', *Sunday Times*, 15 January 2017.
2. Luyolo Mnkemtane, 'Mbalula's wife denies R1bn tender fraud,' *Daily News*, 22 January 2017.
3. Charles Molele, 'Ace Magashule accused of taking revenge', *Mail & Guardian*, 24 August 2012, available at https://mg.co.za/article/2012-08-23-ace-magashule-accused-of-taking-revenge (last accessed 16 October 2018).
4. Niren Tolsi, 'Concourt declares ANC Free State's PEC unlawful', *Mail & Guardian*, 14 December 2012, available at https://mg.co.za/article/2012-12-14-concourt-declares-anc-free-states-pec-unlawful (last accessed 16 October 2018).
5. 'Free State ANC to rerun PEC election', *News24*, 8 May 2013, available at https://www.news24.com/southafrica/politics/free-state-anc-to-rerun-pec-election-20130508 (last accessed 16 October 2018).
6. 'Premier on course to reclaim party reins', *Free State Times*, May 2013.
7. 'Free State ANC to rerun PEC election'.
8. 'Ramakatsa faces ANC expulsion', *Free State Times*, May 2013.
9. Twala, 'The demon of factionalism in an African National Congress (ANC)-led Free State Province (1994–2004)'.
10. 'Daggers out in leadership battle', *The Weekly*, 20 April 2012, available at http://theweekly.co.za/?p=5342 (last accessed 17 October 2018).
11. Jane Steinacker, 'Free State tenderpreneur scores big', *Sunday Times*, 4 April 2010.
12. Ibid.
13. 'ANC whip sentenced for homicide', *News24*, 17 September 2008, available at https://www.news24.com/SouthAfrica/News/ANC-Whip-sentenced-for-homicide-20080917, and Sapa, 'ANC mayors, officials get the boot', *IOL*, 4 November 2008, available at https://www.iol.co.za/news/politics/anc-mayors-officials-get-the-boot-423017 (both last accessed 17 October 2018).
14. Sarah Sarabjiet, 'Pietermaritzburg Business Support Centre visits India', *Maritzburg Sun*, 9 December 2013, available at https://maritzburgsun.co.za/7836/pietermaritzburg-business-support-centre-visits-india/ (last accessed 17 October 2018).
15. Carol Paton, 'Only Damascene conversion will save Eskom', *Daily Dispatch*, 25 January 2018, available at https://www.pressreader.com/south-africa/daily-dispatch/20180125/281706910107282 (last accessed 30 October 2018).

16. Progress report on FSHS 2010/11 projects.
17. Mr Seiso Mohai (ANC), People's Assembly profile, available at https://www.pa.org.za/blog/mr-seiso-mohai-anc (last accessed 17 October 2018).
18. Progress report on FSHS 2010/11 projects.
19. Sapa, 'MEC's husband guilty of fraud', *IOL*, 29 January 2007, available at https://www.iol.co.za/news/south-africa/mecs-husband-guilty-of-fraud-312921 (last accessed 17 October 2018).
20. Selloane Khalane, 'Tsopo ook betrek by VS-huisskandaal', *Volksblad*, 25 January 2017.
21. Progress report on FSHS 2010/11 projects.
22. Ibid.
23. Progress report on FSHS 2010/11 projects.
24. 'Fouriesburg female contractor scoops award', *The Weekly*, 18 May 2012, available at http://theweekly.co.za/?p=6382 (last accessed 17 October 2018).
25. Sapa, 'FState Tourism Authority "a disaster"', *IOL*, 5 February 2013, available at https://www.iol.co.za/news/politics/fstate-tourism-authority-a-disaster-1464735 (last accessed 17 October 2018).
26. Progress report on FSHS 2010/11 contracts.
27. *Group Ywo Trading Enterprise CC* v *Construction Industry Development Board* (44681/08) [2009] ZAGPPHC 124 (5 August 2009), available at http://www.saflii.org/za/cases/ZAGPPHC/2009/124.html (last accessed 17 October 2018).
28. Pieter-Louis Myburgh, 'Exposed: ANC secretary general Magashule and daughter involved in dodgy R150 million RDP housing scam', *News24*, 28 March 2018, available at https://www.news24.com/SouthAfrica/News/exposed-magashule-and-daughter-in-r150m-rdp-housing-scandal-20180328 (last accessed 17 October 2018).
29. N. Mokhesi (HOD FSHS) submission to Free State Provincial Legislature, 4 August 2015.
30. N. Mokhesi (HOD FSHS) submission to Free State Provincial Legislature, 31 July 2018.

CHAPTER 11: REGIME UNCHANGED
1. 'Exclusive: Report condemns Free State government tenders', *eNCA*, 12 February 2014, available at https://www.enca.com/south-africa/damning-report-business-usual-letlaka (last accessed 11 December 2018).
2. Free State Department of Public Works and Rural Development, 2010/11 budget vote tabled by MEC Fezi Ngubentombi, available at https://www.gov.za/free-state-department-public-works-and-rural-development-201011-budget-vote-tabled-mec-fezi (last accessed 11 December 2018).
3. Free State Department of Police, Roads and Transport annual report 2014/15, available at https://provincialgovernment.co.za/department_annual/275/2015-free-state-police-roads-and-transport-annual-report.pdf (last accessed 11 December 2018).
4. Charles Molele, 'The Free State's teflon premier', *Mail & Guardian*, 17 May 2013, available at https://mg.co.za/article/2013-05-17-00-the-free-ace-magashule-nimbly-dodges-political-and-financial-controversy-to-hold-on-to-his-positionstates-teflon-premier (last accessed 11 December 2018).
5. Ntwaagae Seleka, 'Magashule confident of re-election as Free State ANC chair', *Sowetan*, 21 May 2012, available at https://www.sowetanlive.co.za/news/2012-05-21-magashule-confident-of-re-election-as-free-state-anc-chair/ (last accessed 11 December 2018).
6. Ibid.
7. Sibusiso Ngalwa, 'Line-up of ANC's would-be kingmakers', *IOL*, 28 October 2007, available at https://www.iol.co.za/news/politics/line-up-of-ancs-would-be-kingmakers-376681 (last accessed 11 December 2018).

8. Kingdom Mabuza, 'ANC power struggle threatens premier', *Sowetan*, 22 September 2011, available at https://www.sowetanlive.co.za/news/2011-09-22-anc-power-struggle-threatens-premier/ (last accessed 11 December 2018).

9. *Mpho Ramakatsa and Others v Elias [Ace] Magashule and Others*, Constitutional Court of South Africa, case CCT 109/12, judgment delivered on 14 December 2012, reasons on 18 December 2012.

10. Ibid.

11. Bloemfontein High Court, case number 5942/2017, *Tumelo John Mokoena and Others v Elias Magashule and Others*.

12. Kingdom Mabuza, 'Premier assaulted us', *Sowetan*, 24 March 2011, available at https://www.sowetanlive.co.za/news/2011-03-24-premier-assaulted-us-/ (last accessed 11 December 2018).

13. 'Ace plot revealed', *The Weekly*, 11 May 2012, available at http://theweekly.co.za/?p=6121 (last accessed 11 December 2018).

14. Mabuza, 'Premier assaulted us'.

15. 'Ace plot revealed'.

16. 'ANC leadership battle looms', *The Weekly*, 25 November 2011, available at http://theweekly.co.za/?p=924 (last accessed 11 December 2018).

17. Charles Molele, 'Faction aims to unseat Magashule', *Mail & Guardian*, 26 April 2012, available at https://mg.co.za/article/2012-04-26-faction-aims-to-unseat-magashule (last accessed 11 December 2018).

18. George Matlala, 'ANC's Besani says he was undermined', *Sunday Independent*, 5 March 2012, available at https://www.iol.co.za/sundayindependent/ancs-besani-says-he-was-undermined-1248851 (last accessed 11 December 2018).

19. Molele, 'Faction aims to unseat Magashule'.

20. *Mpho Ramakatsa and Others v Elias [Ace] Magashule and Others*, Constitutional Court of South Africa, case CCT 109/12, judgment delivered on 14 December 2012, reasons on 18 December 2012.

21. Ibid.

22. Matuma Letsoalo, 'Magashule defies ANC resolution and endorses Zuma', *Mail & Guardian*, 23 June 2012, available at https://mg.co.za/article/2012-06-23-defies-anc-resolution-and-openly-endorses-zuma (last accessed 11 December 2018).

23. SABC Digital News, 'Free State re-elects Magashule as ANC chair', 22 June 2012, available at https://www.youtube.com/watch?v=dYtX5pYO4og (last accessed 11 December 2018).

24. Charles Molele, 'Ace Magashule accused of taking revenge', *Mail & Guardian*, 24 August 2012.

25. 'Terror campaign unmasked', *The Weekly*, 4 May 2012, available at http://theweekly.co.za/?p=5871 (last accessed 11 December 2018).

26. *Ramakatsa and Others v Magashule and Others*, Free State High Court, case no. 3453/2012, judgment delivered on 26 October 2012, available at http://www.saflii.org/za/cases/ZAFSHC/2012/207.html (last accessed 11 December 2018).

27. *Mpho Ramakatsa and Others v Elias [Ace] Magashule and Others*, Constitutional Court of South Africa, case CCT 109/12, judgment delivered on 14 December 2012, reasons on 18 December 2012.

28. Ibid.

29. Ibid.

30. Ibid.

31. Ibid.

32. Ibid.

33. Niren Tolsi, 'Free State ANC PEC barred from voting at Mangaung', *Mail & Guardian*, 15 December 2012, available at https://mg.co.za/article/2012-12-15-free-state-anc-prohibited-from-voting-at-mangaung-conference (last accessed 11 December 2018).

34. *Mpho Ramakatsa and Others* v *Elias [Ace] Magashule and Others*, Constitutional Court of South Africa, case CCT 109/12, judgment delivered on 14 December 2012, reasons on 18 December 2012.

35. Tolsi, 'Free State ANC PEC barred from voting at Mangaung'.

36. Matuma Letsoalo and Niren Tolsi, 'Rigged: Fake members boost Jacob Zuma', *Mail & Guardian*, 12 October 2012, available at https://mg.co.za/article/2012-10-12-00-fake-members-boost-jacob-zuma (last accessed 11 December 2018).

37. Niren Tolsi, 'Audits reveal ANC membership numbers soar', *Mail & Guardian*, 17 December 2012, available at https://mg.co.za/article/2012-12-17-anc-membership-numbers-soar (last accessed 11 December 2018).

38. *Mpho Ramakatsa and Others* v *Elias [Ace] Magashule and Others*, Constitutional Court of South Africa, case CCT 109/12, judgment delivered on 14 December 2012, reasons on 18 December 2012.

39. Sapa, 'ANC announces Free State task team members', *Mail & Guardian*, 16 December 2012, available at https://mg.co.za/article/2012-12-16-anc-free-state-task-team-members-named (last accessed 11 December 2018).

40. Selloane Khalane, 'ANC gaan teen afvalliges optree', *Volksblad*, 13 May 2013.

41. 'Ramakatsa faces ANC expulsion', *Free State Times*, May 2013.

42. 'Free State ANC elects top 5 unopposed', *News24*, 11 May 2013, available at https://www.news24.com/southafrica/news/free-state-anc-elects-top-5-unopposed-20130511 (last accessed 11 December 2018).

43. SABC Digital News, 'Ace Magashule has been elected ANC chairperson of the Free State', 11 May 2013, available at https://www.youtube.com/watch?v=r6eqIKkxGZU (last accessed 11 December 2018).

44. *Mpho Ramakatsa and Others* v *Elias [Ace] Magashule and Others*, Constitutional Court of South Africa, case CCT 109/12, judgment delivered on 14 December 2012, reasons on 18 December 2012.

45. 'Ramakatsa faces ANC expulsion'.

46. Khalane, 'ANC gaan teen afvalliges optree'.

47. Ntokozo Sindane, 'Malema announces interim leadership of EFF', *Public News Hub*, 12 July 2013, available at http://www.publicnewshub.com/malema-announces-interim-leadership-of-eff/ (last accessed 11 December 2018).

CHAPTER 12: FOURTH ESTATE CAPTURE

1. National Treasury report, 'Investigation into the appointment of Letlaka Media Services by the department of the Free State Premier', 2013.

2. Ibid.

3. Ibid.

4. Ibid.

5. 'Exclusive: Report condemns Free State government tenders', *eNCA*, 12 February 2014, available at https://www.enca.com/south-africa/damning-report-business-usual-letlaka (last accessed 14 January 2019).

6. National Treasury report, 'Investigation into the appointment of Letlaka Media Services by the department of the Free State Premier', 2013.

7. Ibid.

8. Ibid.

9. Selloane Khalane, 'LUR beweer eienaar van koerante wou hom omkoop', *Volksblad*, 28 October 2013.
10. 'Exclusive: Report condemns Free State government tenders'.
11. 'EL Magashule Draft Response [to] Questions for Written Reply', Free State Provincial Legislature, 30 September 2015.
12. 'Letlaka Media and Communications vs. Volksblad', ruling by the Press Ombud, 13 December 2017, available at https://presscouncil.org.za/Ruling/View/letlaka-media -and-communications-vs-volksblad-4215 (last accessed 14 January 2019).
13. Media statement, 'Free State provincial government integrated website project', 5 March 2013, available at https://www.gov.za/free-state-provincial-government -integrated-website-project (last accessed 14 January 2019).
14. Marietjie Gericke, 'Ace gee R95 miljoen aan "vrugtelose projek"', *Volksblad*, 8 November 2017.
15. Faranaaz Parker and Nickolaus Bauer, 'Tender process trashed by R48m Free State website bid', *Mail & Guardian*, 7 March 2013, available at https://mg.co.za/ article/2013-03-07-tender-process-trashed-by-r48m-free-state-website-bid (last accessed 14 January 2019).
16. 'Exclusive: Report condemns Free State government tenders'.
17. Mabuza, 'Premier assaulted us', *Sowetan*, 24 March 2011.
18. 'Ace plot revealed', *The Weekly*, 11 May 2012.
19. Ibid.
20. Ibid.
21. Ibid.
22. 'Attack on *The Weekly* shows *Free State Times* is becoming more desperate daily', *The Weekly*, 25 November 2011, available at http://theweekly.co.za/?p=1038 (last accessed 14 January 2019).
23. Wendy Jasson da Costa, '"Zuma assassination plot is serious"', *IOL*, 16 May 2007, available at https://www.iol.co.za/news/politics/zuma-assassination-plot-is-serious -353164 (last accessed 14 January 2019).
24. 'Inside regime change war room', *The Weekly*, 30 March 2012, available at http:// theweekly.co.za/?p=4618 (last accessed 14 January 2019).
25. Ibid.
26. Ibid.
27. 'Terror campaign unmasked', *The Weekly*, 4 May 2012, available at http://theweekly .co.za/?p=5871 (last accessed 14 January 2019).
28. Steve Nale, '*Free State Times* perpetuates a sinister agenda that projects Magashule as corrupt', Letters to the Editor, *The Weekly*, 18 November 2011, available at http:// theweekly.co.za/?p=787 (last accessed 14 January 2019).
29. Tiisetso Makhele, 'Open letter to Ace Magashule', *The Weekly*, 6 March 2015, available at http://theweekly.co.za/?p=12539 (last accessed 14 January 2019).
30. Sidwell Guduka, 'Premier gets new spokesperson', *Express*, 2 December 2015, available at https://www.news24.com/SouthAfrica/Local/Express-News/premier-gets-new -spokesperson-20151201 (last accessed 14 January 2019).
31. Gericke, 'Ace gee R95 miljoen aan "vrugtelose projek"'.
32. 'Volksblad vs. The Weekly', ruling by the Press Ombud, 13 December 2017, available at https://presscouncil.org.za/Ruling/View/volksblad-vs-the-weekly-4214 (last accessed 14 January 2019).
33. Ibid.
34. Ibid.
35. Nale, '*Free State Times* perpetuates a sinister agenda that projects Magashule as corrupt'.

36. Thabo Rapoho, 'We must reject yellow journalism', Letter to the Editor, *The Weekly*, 4 May 2012, available at http://theweekly.co.za/?p=6084 (last accessed 14 January 2019).

37. 'ANCYL blasts Free State Times', *The Weekly*, 16 March 2012, available at http://theweekly.co.za/?p=4059 (last accessed 14 January 2019).

38. Sally Evans and Thabang Matjama, 'Press buyout a victory for Magashule', *Mail & Guardian*, 23 March 2013, available at https://mg.co.za/article/2013-03-22-00-press-buyout-a-victory-for-magashule (last accessed 14 January 2019).

39. As seen on the *Free State Times*'s Facebook page.

40. 'Court orders *The New Age* to pay', *Business Day*, 18 March 2011.

CHAPTER 13: TEA WITH ATUL

1. Mondli Makhanya, 'Sunset for the ANC Premier League', *News24*, 11 March 2018, available at https://www.news24.com/Columnists/Mondli-Makhanya/sunset-for-the-premier-league-20180309 (last accessed 6 February 2019).

2. Sam Mkokeli, 'Zuma increasingly relying on backing of rural "premier league"', *Mail & Guardian*, 9 December 2016, available at https://mg.co.za/article/2016-12-09-zuma-increasingly-relying-on-backing-of-rural-premier-league (last accessed 6 February 2019).

3. See https://wazimap.co.za/profiles/province-FS-free-state/ (last accessed 23 October 2018).

4. Owen Kock, 'New town to rise next to airport', *Bloemfontein Courant*, 24 April 2013, availble at https://www.bloemfonteincourant.co.za/new-town-to-rise-next-to-airport/ (last accessed 24 October 2018).

5. '#GuptaLeaks: How Multichoice paid the Guptas millions', *News24*, 24 November 2017, available at https://www.news24.com/SouthAfrica/News/guptaleaks-how-multichoice-paid-the-guptas-millions-20171124 (last accessed 24 October 2018).

6. 'ANC announces its mayoral candidates for 2016 local elections', *Mail & Guardian*, 19 June 2016, available at https://mg.co.za/article/2016-06-19-anc-announces-its-mayoral-candidates-for-2016-local-elections (last accessed 24 October 2018).

7. Mr Thabo Moses Manyoni, People's Assembly profile, available at https://www.pa.org.za/person/thabo-manyoni/ (last accessed 24 October 2018).

8. Setume Stone, 'Guptas offered me R2m a month for 10 years', *City Press*, 21 October 2018.

9. Ibid.

10. Ibid.

11. SAARF AMPS July 2011–June 2012, Average issue readership of newspapers and magazines, available at http://saarf.co.za/amps-readership/2012/AMPS%20JUNE%2012-%20SUMMARY.pdf (last accessed 25 October 2018).

12. Sarah Evans and Lionel Faull, 'New Age: Dawn of advertising riches with no circulation figures', *Mail & Guardian*, 25 January 2013, available at https://mg.co.za/article/2013-01-25-00-new-age-dawn-of-advertising-riches-with-no-circulation-figures/ (last accessed 25 October 2018).

13. Sapa, 'New Age garners government ads', *Mail & Guardian*, 23 September 2010, available at https://www.mg.co.za/article/2010-09-23-new-age-garners-government-ads (last accessed 25 October 2018).

14. Glenda Daniels, 'Fancy digs, but is New Age moving enough copies?', *Mail & Guardian*, 18 March 2011, available at https://mg.co.za/article/2011-03-18-fancy-digs-but-is-new-age-moving-enough-copies (last accessed 25 October 2018).

15. amaBhungane, 'Gupta-owned newspaper in line of fire of new Nielsen report', *Daily*

Maverick, 15 February 2017, available at https://www.dailymaverick.co.za/article/2017
-02-15-amabhungane-gupta-owned-newspaper-in-line-of-fire-of-new-nielsen
-report/#.WzNAQ6czZPY (last accessed 25 October 2018).

16. Jeanette Chabalala, '#StateCaptureInquiry: Gupta-owned media houses bagged
R260m from govt, with Free State dishing out the most', *News24*, 10 September 2018,
available at https://www.news24.com/SouthAfrica/News/statecaptureinquiry-gupta
-owned-media-houses-bagged-r260m-from-govt-with-free-state-dishing-out-the
-most-20180910 (last accessed 25 October 2018).

17. Poloko Tau, 'Motsoaledi: Mediosa served as an ATM card for the Guptas', *City Press*,
2 March 2018, available at https://city-press.news24.com/News/motsoaledi-mediosa
-served-as-an-atm-card-for-the-guptas-20180302 (last accessed 25 October 2018).

18. Gosebo Mathope, 'Free State health department pays Gupta-linked Mediosa R25m',
Citizen, 5 March 2018, available at https://citizen.co.za/news/1845045/free-state-
health-department-paid-gupta-linked-mediosa-r25m/ (last accessed 25 October 2018).

CHAPTER 14: A FAMILY OF FIXERS

1. Budget vote speech for Free State Department of Agriculture and Rural Development,
tabled by MEC M.J. Zwane, 22 March 2012.

2. Ibid.

3. Ibid.

4. Ibid.

5. 'Allegations of maladministration against the Free State Department of Agriculture
– Vrede Integrated Dairy Project', Public Protector Report No. 31 of 2017/18, available
at http://www.pprotect.org/sites/default/files/legislation_report/Vrede%20Report.pdf
(last accessed 18 February 2019).

6. Vicus Burger, 'Guptas se VS-bande ontbloot', *Netwerk24*, 22 May 2013, https://www
.netwerk24.com/Nuus/Guptas-se-VS-bande-ontbloot-20130522 (last accessed
18 February 2019).

7. 'Intended beneficiaries of Gupta-linked farm speak out', *eNCA*, 22 January 2018,
available at https://www.enca.com/south-africa/gupta-linked-farm-saga-beneficiaries
-speak-out (last accessed 18 February 2019).

8. Lindi van Rooyen, 'MPO appalled by failed Vrede dairy project', *Farmer's Weekly*, 20
February 2014, available at https://www.farmersweekly.co.za/agri-news/south-africa/
mpo-appalled-by-failed-vrede-dairy-project/ (last accessed 18 February 2019).

9. amaBhungane and *Daily Maverick*'s Scorpio, '#GuptaLeaks: The Dubai laundromat
– how millions milked from the Free State government paid for Sun City wedding',
News24, 30 June 2017, available at https://www.news24.com/SouthAfrica/News/
guptaleaks-the-dubai-laundromat-how-millions-milked-from-free-state
-government-paid-for-sun-city-wedding-20170629 (last accessed 29 January 2019).

10. Charles Smith, 'Onthul: Omvang van Guptas se plundering by Vrede', *Volksblad*,
13 February 2019.

11. Karyn Maughan, 'NPA provisionally withdraws Estina case', *Business Day*,
4 December 2018, available at https://www.businesslive.co.za/bd/national/2018-12-04
-breaking-news-npa-provisionally-withdraws-estina-case/ (last accessed 18 February
2019).

12. Pieter-Louis Myburgh, 'Exclusive: Gupta associate "advised" Magashule on Vrede dairy
project – court papers', *News24*, 12 July 2018, available at https://www.news24.com/
SouthAfrica/News/exclusive-gupta-associate-advised-magashule-on-vrede-dairy
-project-court-papers-20180712 (last accessed 18 February 2019).

13. Siwe Feketha, 'Magashule: My son is not involved in Vrede dairy farm project', *IOL*,

22 January 2018, available at https://www.iol.co.za/news/politics/magashule-my-son-is-not-involved-in-vrede-dairy-farm-project-12857580 (last accessed 18 February 2019); 'Magashule: No secret my son works for Guptas', *News24*, 22 January 2018, https://www.news24.com/Video/SouthAfrica/News/magashule-no-secret-my-son-works-for-guptas-20180122 (last accessed 18 February 2019).

14. Jan Gerber, '#GuptaEmails: Guptas asked to buy airtime for ANC election agents', *News24*, 2 June 2017, available at https://www.news24.com/SouthAfrica/News/guptaemails-guptas-asked-to-buy-airtime-for-anc-election-agents-20170602 (last accessed 25 October 2018).

15. Marietjie Gericke, 'Vrae oor Ace se huis in Woodlands', *Volksblad*, 5 June 2015.

16. Ibid.

17. Thanduxolo Jika, 'Exposed: Explosive Gupta e-mails at the heart of state capture', *Sunday Times*, 28 May 2017, available at https://www.timeslive.co.za/sunday-times/news/2017-05-28-exposed-explosive-gupta-e-mails-at-the-heart-of-state-capture/ (last accessed 25 October 2018).

18. See letter from James Lorimer MP to S. Luzipo, 4 November 2016, available at http://pmg-assets.s3-website-eu-west-1.amazonaws.com/161109daletter.pdf (last accessed 25 October 2018).

19. Allan Seccombe and Genevieve Quintal, 'Dismay at new head of mining department', *Business Day*, 3 March 2017, available at https://www.businesslive.co.za/bd/national/2017-03-03-dismay-at-new-head-of-mining-department/ (last accessed 25 October 2018).

20. Allan Seccombe, 'Regional manager "fired at behest of Guptas"', *Business Day*, 16 February 2018, available at https://www.businesslive.co.za/bd/national/2018-02-16-union-furious-as-zwane-fires-regional-manager-for-trying-to-close-gupta-linked-mine/ (last accessed 25 October 2018).

21. 'Sweeping changes to the boards of key state companies', *ujuh*, 11 December 2014, available at https://www.ujuh.co.za/sweeping-changes-to-the-boards-of-key-state-companies/ (last accessed 25 October 2018).

22. Kyle Cowan, Sikonathi Mantshantsha and Genevieve Quintal, 'Is the senior bureaucrat at public enterprises a Gupta spy?', *Sunday Times*, 4 June 2017, available at https://www.timeslive.co.za/sunday-times/news/2017-06-04-is-the-senior-bureaucrat-at-public-enterprises-a-gupta-spy/ (last accessed 25 October 2018).

23. Ibid.

24. Poloko Tau, 'Gupta-linked public enterprises DG Richard Seleke quits', *Sowetan*, 4 October 2018, available at https://www.sowetanlive.co.za/news/south-africa/2018-10-04-gupta-linked-public-enterprises-dg-richard-seleke-quits/ (last accessed 25 October 2018).

25. 'Inside the rise of Hlaudi Motsoeneng at the SABC', *Sunday Times*, 3 July 2016, available at https://www.businesslive.co.za/rdm/politics/2016-07-05-inside-the-rise-of-hlaudi-motsoeneng-at-the-sabc/ (last accessed 30 October 2018).

26. Angelique Serrao and Jeanette Chabalala, 'Investigation: King Hlaudi's rise to power', *News24*, 23 September 2016, available at https://www.news24.com/SouthAfrica/News/investigation-king-hlaudis-rise-to-power-20160923 (last accessed 30 October 2018).

27. Stephan Hofstatter, Mzilikazi wa Afrika and Rob Rose, 'Massive looting at SABC exposed', *Sunday Times*, 7 October 2012, available at https://www.timeslive.co.za/news/south-africa/2012-10-07-massive-looting-at-sabc-exposed/ (last accessed 30 October 2018).

28. Ibid.

29. See one such TNA Business Briefing at https://www.youtube.com/watch?v=bRM5aq

OuW6g, 'Unpacking the SOPA and education – Free State', SABC Digital News, published 16 February 2016 (last accessed 30 October 2018).

30. amaBhungane and Scorpio, '#GuptaLeaks: A tale of two captures: Alexkor, Gupta Inc and "WMC"', *Fin24*, 13 December 2017, available at https://www.fin24.com/Companies/Industrial/a-tale-of-two-captures-alexkor-gupta-inc-and-wmc-20171213 (last accessed 30 October 2018).

31. 'Who the Guptas wanted', *Sunday Times*, 18 June 2017.

32. Carol Paton, 'Only Damascene conversion will save Eskom', *Daily Dispatch*, 25 January 2018.

33. Pieter-Louis Myburgh, 'Exclusive: Gupta associate "advised" Magashule on Vrede dairy project - court papers', *News24*, 12 July 2018.

CHAPTER 15: REDDY TO RUMBLE

1. Abram Mashego, 'Reddy's City Power deal "irregular"', *City Press*, 16 July 2017.

2. Wendy Jasson da Costa, 'I lent Zuma money for Nkandla – Reddy', *Mercury*, 19 November 2012, available at https://www.iol.co.za/news/politics/i-lent-zuma-money-for-nkandla-reddy-1425914 (last accessed 6 February 2019).

3. Adriaan Basson and Mandy Rossouw, 'Premier's R3-million casino "bribe"', *Mail & Guardian*, 26 June 2009.

4. Amanda Khoza, 'Reddy's R10m birthday bash', *Sunday Tribune*, 24 February 2013, available at https://www.iol.co.za/news/south-africa/kwazulu-natal/reddys-r10m-birthday-bash-1475895 (last accessed 6 February 2019).

5. Free State Provincial Treasury 2015/16 annual report, available at http://www.agsa.co.za/Portals/0/Reports/PFMA/201516/GR/FS/FSTreasuryAnnualReport2015-16.pdf (last accessed 6 February 2019).

6. Jessica Bezuidenhout, 'Zuma pals clinch first nuclear deal', *Mail & Guardian*, 16 September 2016, available at https://mg.co.za/article/2016-09-16-00-zuma-pals-clinch-first-nuclear-deal (last accessed 6 February 2019).

7. Ibid.

8. Jessica Bezuidenhout, 'Energy exec on ice over nukes', *Mail & Guardian*, 9 June 2017, available at https://mg.co.za/article/2017-06-09-00-energy-exec-on-ice-over-nukes (last accessed 6 February 2019).

9. National Treasury letter to Department of Energy Director-General Thabane Zulu, 8 December 2016.

10. Linda Ensor, 'Key nuclear contracts are "irregular", documents reveal', *Business Day*, 23 August 2017.

11. Bezuidenhout, 'Energy exec on ice over nukes'.

12. Ibid.

13. Press Council of South Africa, 'Appeal hearing decision: Mail & Guardian vs Vivian Reddy', 5 April 2017, available at https://presscouncil.org.za/Ruling/View/appeal-hearing-decision-mail--guardian-vs-vivian-reddy-4075 (last accessed 6 February 2019).

14. List available at http://www.ameu.co.za/Portals/16/Conventions/Convention%202015/Delegate%20List%20-%20Final.pdf (last accessed 6 February 2019).

15. Qaanitah Hunter and Jeff Wicks, 'Exposed: Zuma plot to oust Cyril', *Sunday Times*, 9 September 2018, available at https://www.pressreader.com/south-africa/sunday-times/20180909/281530816912060 (last accessed 6 February 2019).

CHAPTER 16: ZUMA'S VREDE 'THANK-YOU FEE'

1. 'Developing a better future', *Tame Times*, 15 September 2017.

2. Khaya Readykit website, https://www.readykit.co.za/.

3. 'Developing a better future', *Tame Times*, 15 September 2017.
4. VNA website, http://www.vnac.co.za/
5. *Progressive Leader*, Issue 7, 2012.
6. *The State* v *Jacob Gedleyihlekisa Zuma and 2 Others*, High Court of South Africa (Natal Provincial Division), List of State Witnesses in Terms of Section 144(3)(a) of Act 51 of 1977, available at http://www.armsdeal-vpo.co.za/special_items/jacob_zuma _trial02/zuma_List%20of%20state%20witnesses%20Zuma%20Thint%20-%20 MASTER%20FINAL%20FOR%20SUMMONS.pdf (last accessed 29 January 2019).
7. amaBhungane, 'Nkandla: Reddy an unapologetic benefactor', *Mail & Guardian*, 23 November 2012, available at https://mg.co.za/article/2012-11-23-00-nkandla-reddy -an-unapologetic-benefactor (last accessed 29 January 2019).
8. 'Khaya Readykit – Innovative building solution', *SA Affordable Housing*, Issue 39, July 2013.
9. 'Developing a better future'.
10. 'President Jacob Zuma hands over houses built by Sizakele MaKhumalo Zuma Foundation', uploaded by GovernmentZA, 13 August 2013, available at https://www .youtube.com/watch?v=7jl77WCcNXI (last accessed 29 January 2019).
11. Phethogo Consulting report – Proposed establishment of a new extension in Thembalihle, Vrede, 10 June 2014.
12. amaBhungane, 'Gupta-linked farm milks Free State coffers', *Mail & Guardian*, 7 June 2013, available at https://mg.co.za/article/2013-06-07-00-gupta-dairy-project-milks -free-state-coffers (last accessed 29 January 2019).
13. 'Developing a better future'.
14. Free State Department of Human Settlements annual report 2013/14, available at https://provincialgovernment.co.za/department_annual/149/2014-free-state-human -settlements-annual-report.pdf (last accessed 9 October 2018).
15. Ibid.
16. Ibid.
17. Marcus Low and Anso Thom, 'Spotlight: Free State doctors battle with sub-standard theatre equipment', *Daily Maverick*, 16 May 2018, available at https://www .dailymaverick.co.za/article/2018-05-16-84321/ (last accessed 29 January 2019).
18. Free State Development Corporation annual report 2012/13, available at http://www .fdc.co.za/images/2018/downloads/annual_reports/fdc_annual_report_2012_2013_1st _proof.pdf (last accessed 29 January 2019).
19. Lodge, *South African Politics Since 1994*, p. 21.
20. Free State Province Provincial Gazette No. 93, 7 March 2014.
21. Free State Department of Human Settlements annual report 2013/14.
22. Free State Department of Human Settlements annual report 2014/15, available at https://provincialgovernment.co.za/department_annual/274/2015-free-state-human -settlements-annual-report.pdf (last accessed 29 January 2019).
23. Free State Department of Human Settlements annual report 2013/14.
24. Phethogo Consulting report – Proposed establishment of a new extension in Thembalihle, Vrede, 10 June 2014.
25. Free State Department of Human Settlements annual report 2013/14.
26. Thembalihle Ext 4 housing project progress report, June 2015.
27. Themablihle Ext 4 housing project progress report, February 2015.
28. Vrede 1 000 housing project progress report, June 2015.
29. Ibid.
30. Vrede 1 000 housing project progress report, October 2015.
31. 'Developing a better future'.

32. Vrede 1 000 housing project progress report, October 2015.
33. Vrede EPHP progress report, VNA Consulting, February 2015.
34. Metric Group, 'Project management fees', available at https://www.metricgroup.co.za/our-services/project-management/project-management-fees/ (last accessed 29 January 2019).
35. Pieter-Louis Myburgh, 'R51bn train tender has interesting beneficiaries', *City Press*, 15 May 2015, available at https://city-press.news24.com/Business/R51bn-train-tender-has-interesting-beneficiaries-20150516 (last accessed 29 January 2019).
36. Amanda Khoza, 'Zuma defends Myeni, quashing rumours of a romantic relationship', *News24*, 12 December 2015, available at https://www.news24.com/SouthAfrica/News/zuma-defends-myeni-quashing-rumours-of-a-romantic-relationship-20151212
37. Qaanitah Hunter and Jeff Wicks, 'Exposed: Zuma plot to oust Cyril', *Sunday Times*, 9 September 2018.
38. FSHS Budget Vote Speech 2017/18, presented by MEC Sisi Ntombela, 23 March 2017, available at https://www.gov.za/sites/default/files/speech_docs/FS-Human-Settlements_0.pdf (last accessed 29 January 2019).
39. Free State Provincial Gazette No. 114, 9 February 2018.
40. Karabo Ngoepe, 'ANC will rule until Jesus comes, Zuma says again', *News24*, 5 July 2016, available at https://www.news24.com/elections/news/anc-will-rule-until-jesus-comes-zuma-says-again-20160705 (last accessed 29 January 2019).

CHAPTER 17: THE R9-MILLION FREEBIE

1. Pieter-Louis Myburgh, 'Magashule and daughter in money-for-jam property scandal', *News24*, 31 January 2018; Pulane Choane, '"Ace's daughter got tenders on merit"', *Bloemfontein Courant*, 22 February 2018, available at https://www.bloemfonteincourant.co.za/aces-daughter-got-tenders-on-merit/ (last accessed 17 January 2019).
2. Pulane Choane, '"I sleep well," says Ace', *Bloemfontein Courant*, 1 March 2018, available at https://www.bloemfonteincourant.co.za/i-sleep-well-says-ace/ (last accessed 17 January 2019).
3. Ngwathe Local Municipality draft annual report 2013/14, available at http://mfma.treasury.gov.za/Documents/06.%20Annual%20Reports/2013-14/02.%20Local%20municipalities/FS203%20Ngwathe/FS203%20Ngwathe%20Annual%20Report%202013-14.pdf (last accessed 17 January 2019).

CHAPTER 18: VOGELFONTEIN

1. Pieter-Louis Myburgh, 'Exposed: ANC secretary general Magashule and daughter involved in dodgy R150 million RDP housing scam', *News24*, 28 March 2018.
2. Tladi Moloi, 'Ace: No to "kasi"', *Eastern Free State Express*, 20 November 2013.
3. Tladi Moloi, 'Residents will have to wait longer for houses', *Eastern Free State Express*, 15 October 2014.
4. Report on Vogelfontein by Dihlabeng Democratic Alliance Task Team, compiled between July and September 2017, released in 2018.
5. Auditor-general of South Africa, 'Auditor-general consolidated general report on the audit outcomes of local government', MFMA 2014–15, available at http://www.agsa.co.za/Portals/0/MFMA%202014-15/Section%201-9%20MFMA%202014-2015/fullReport MFMA2014-15.pdf (last accessed 21 January 2019).
6. Dihlabeng council document, item R4/2015, special meeting of the mayoral committee held on 25 November 2016.
7. Ibid.

8. Pieter-Louis Myburgh, 'Exclusive: Court battle implicates ANC secretary general Magashule in daughter's R150m RDP contracts', *News24*, 28 March 2018, available at https://www.news24.com/SouthAfrica/News/exclusive-court-battle-implicates-anc -secretary-general-magashule-in-daughters-r150-million-rdp-contracts-20180328 (last accessed 21 January 2019).

9. Housing Development Agency Catalytic Projects Summary Fact Sheet for Baken Park Ext 5, 6 and 7 (Vogelfontein), available at http://thehda.co.za/pdf/uploads/ multimedia/fs_baken_park_rev_1_gov.pdf (last accessed 21 January 2019).

CHAPTER 19: PAVED WITH GOLD

1. Free State MEC for Police, Roads and Transport Thabo Manyoni, Budget Vote Speech, 25 March 2011, available at https://www.gov.za/free-state-mec-police-roads -and-transport-mr-thabo-manyoni-presents-budget-vote-speech (last accessed 23 January 2019).

2. National Treasury, Presentation to the Portfolio Committee on Public Service and Administration: Financial status of provincial departments under administration, 6 June 2012, available at http://pmg-assets.s3-website-eu-west-1.amazonaws.com/ docs/120606treasury.pdf (last accessed 23 January 2019).

3. Ibid.

4. Free State Department of Police, Roads and Transport, annual report 2017/18.

5. Sidwell Guduka, 'Premier gets new spokesperson', *Express*, 2 December 2015, available at https://www.news24.com/SouthAfrica/Local/Express-News/premier-gets-new -spokesperson-20151201 (last accessed 23 January 2019).

6. Olebogeng Motse, 'FS Road and Transport HOD dies', *OFM*, 28 December 2017, available at https://ofm.co.za/article/local-news/254632/fs-road-and-transport-hod -dies (last accessed 23 January 2019).

7. Hlengiwe Nhlabathi, 'Ace's bizarre poison claims', *City Press*, 7 January 2018, available at https://www.news24.com/SouthAfrica/News/aces-bizarre-poison-claims-20180106 (last accessed 23 January 2019).

8. Tabelo Timse, 'Ace Magashule ally's property bonanza', *City Press*, 11 March 2018, available at https://www.news24.com/SouthAfrica/News/ace-magashules-allys -property-bonanza-20180311-2 (last accessed 23 January 2019).

9. Ibid.

10. Free State Department of Police, Roads and Transport presentation on Contractor Development Programme, April 2017, available at www.cpsi.co.za/wp-content/uploads/ 2017/04/CPSI-Awards-Launch-FS-CDP-2017.pdf (last accessed 23 January 2019).

11. Ibid.

12. Free State Department of Police, Roads and Transport, annual report 2013/14, available at https://provincialgovernment.co.za/department_annual/150/2014-free -state-police-roads-and-transport-annual-report.pdf (last accessed 23 January 2019).

13. Free State Department of Police, Roads and Transport presentation on Contractor Development Programme, April 2017.

14. Pieter-Louis Myburgh, 'Ace Magashule and new Free State premier's families score cars, contracts in R300m government programme', *Daily Maverick*, 10 July 2018, available at https://www.dailymaverick.co.za/article/2018-07-10-ace-magashule-and -new-free-state-premiers-families-score-cars-contracts-in-r300m-government -programme/ (last accessed 23 January 2019).

15. Free State Province Tender Bulletin No. 61, 11 November 2016, available at https:// www.greengazette.co.za/documents/tender-bulletin-for-free-state-61-of-11 -november-2016_20161111-TFS-00061.pdf (last accessed 23 January 2019).

16. Myburgh, 'Ace Magashule and new Free State premier's families score cars, contracts in R300m government programme'.
17. Marietjie Gericke, 'Ace, Sisi se familie kry kontrakte', *Volksblad*, 12 July 2018.

CHAPTER 20: ENTER IGO

1. Ignatius Mpambani's online LinkedIn profile.
2. Catherine Bond, 'S. Africa's mining towns fight for survival', *CNN World News*, 17 March 1998, available at http://edition.cnn.com/WORLD/9803/17/s.africa.gold/ (last accessed 27 November 2018).
3. Ignatius Mpambani's online LinkedIn profile.
4. Ibid.
5. Patience Bambalele, 'Fun for the stay-at-homes', *Sowetan*, 15 December 2010, available at https://www.sowetanlive.co.za/entertainment/2010-12-15-fun-for-the-stay-at-homes/ (last accessed 27 November 2018).
6. Edna, 'Beach on the Track: What a way to start a new year', *SA Vibe*, 1 January 2013, available at http://savibeza.co.za/2013/01/beach-on-the-track-what-a-way-to-start-a -new-year/ (last accessed 27 November 2018).
7. 'Scandal case of R20m postponed until May 2016', *Vista*, 19 November 2015.
8. 'Free State Premier's statement on withdrawal of criminal charges against MEC Mathabo Leeto', issued by Tiisetso Makhele, Free State premier's spokesperson, 7 November 2016, available at http://www.politicsweb.co.za/news-and-analysis/ mathabo-leeto-cleared-of-corruption-charges--ace-m (last accessed 27 November 2018).
9. Jeanette Chabalala and Iavan Pijoos, 'Free State MEC and Bloem Water CEO arrested for fraud, corruption', *News24*, 16 February 2018, available at https://www.news24 .com/SouthAfrica/News/free-state-mec-and-bloem-water-ceo-arrested-for-fraud -corruption-20180216 (last accessed 27 November 2018).
10. Canny Maphanga, 'Free State MECs off the hook after NPA withdraws corruption charges over a technicality', *News24*, 31 October 2018, available at https://www.news24 .com/SouthAfrica/News/free-state-mecs-off-the-hook-after-npa-withdraws -corruption-charges-over-a-technicality-20180731 (last accessed 27 November 2018).
11. *Mpambani* v *Sekununu Construction and Trading CC and Others* (3959/2008) [2008] ZAFSHC 81 (14 August 2008), available at http://www.saflii.org/cgi-bin/disp .pl?file=za/cases/ZAFSHC/2008/81.html&query=%20sechaba%20solutions (last accessed 27 November 2018).
12. Free State Department of Human Settlements expenditure records.
13. Ibid.
14. Ibid.
15. Free State Tourism Authority 2011/12 and 2012/13 annual reports.
16. Mohokare Local Municipality 2010/11 annual report.

CHAPTER 21: PLUNDER PLOT

1. Free State provincial government briefing document for Cuba visit, January 2015.
2. 'DA asks Labour Minister to investigate "slave labour" of Ace's Cuban engineers', statement issued by Roy Jankielsohn, leader of the Democratic Alliance in the Free State Provincial Legislature, 7 January 2016, available at https://www.dampl.co.za/2016/ 01/da-asks-labour-minister-to-investigate-slave-labour-of-aces-cuban-engineers/ (last accessed 27 November 2018).
3. Marietjie Gericke, 'Kubane kos SA baie geld', *Netwerk24*, 1 April 2015, available at https://www.netwerk24.com/Nuus/Kubane-kos-SA-baie-geld-20150401 (last accessed 27 November 2018).

4. Free State provincial government briefing document for Cuba visit, January 2015.
5. Government Tender Bulletin No. 2796, 18 October 2013, Vol. 580, p. 60, available at https://www.greengazette.co.za/pages/tender-bulletin-2796-of-18-october-2013-vol-580_20131018-TBN-02796-00060 (last accessed 27 November 2018).
6. Court filings, Bloemfontein High Court, case 3101/2015, *The Democratic Alliance* v *the Head of Department of Human Settlements, Free State Province and Others.*
7. 'Energy department appoints controversial director general', *Fin24*, 8 October 2015, available at https://www.fin24.com/Economy/Energy-department-appoints-controversial-director-general-20151008 (last accessed 27 November 2018).
8. Gcwalisile Khanyile and Piet Rampedi, 'DG's R1.4m "bribe"', *Sunday Independent*, 2 April 2012, available at https://www.iol.co.za/sundayindependent/dgs-r14m-bribe-1268185 (last accessed 27 November 2018).
9. 'Businessman loves the high life', *Sunday World*, 6 September 2015, available at https://www.pressreader.com/south-africa/sunday-world/20150906/281556584596736 (last accessed 28 November 2018).
10. Sipho Masondo, '"Watergate": Noose tightens around Nomvula Mokonyane', *City Press*, 3 August 2016, available at https://city-press.news24.com/News/noose-tightens-around-nomvula-20160730 (last accessed 28 November 2018).
11. Auditor-general of South Africa, PFMA report 2016/17, 'Pushbacks by the Department of Water and Sanitation', Water and Sanitation portfolio committee briefing, 2 November 2017, available at http://pmg-assets.s3-website-eu-west-1.amazonaws.com/180327AGSA-Pushbacks.pdf (last accessed 28 November 2018).
12. Court filings, North Gauteng High Court, case 68385/17, *Blackhead Consulting* v *Diamond Hill Trading 71 and Others.*
13. 'Deviations in terms of Regulation 16A6 of Treasury Regulations to the PFMA', *Boqwana Burns*, 25 July 2016, available at http://www.boqwanaburns.com/deviations-in-terms-of-regulation-16a6-of-treasury-regulations-to-the-pfma/ (last accessed 28 November 2018).
14. Court filings, Bloemfontein High Court, case 3101/2015, *The Democratic Alliance* v *The Head of Department of Human Settlements, Free State Province and Others.*
15. 'Exodus in Gauteng premier's office blamed on predecessor', *Cape Times*, 10 November 2014.
16. Court filings, Bloemfontein High Court, case 3101/2015, *The Democratic Alliance* v *The Head of Department of Human Settlements, Free State Province and Others.*
17. Letter from Thabane Zulu to Tim Mokhesi, 13 August 2014.
18. Court filings, North Gauteng High Court, case 68385/17, *Blackhead Consulting* v *Diamond Hill Trading 71 and Others.*
19. Matthew le Cordeur, '#StateCapture: I was used for something very perverse – whistleblower', *Fin24*, 31 October 2017, available at https://www.fin24.com/Economy/Eskom/live-statecapture-trillian-contracts-with-eskom-under-microscope-20171031 (last accessed 28 November 2018).
20. Court filings, Bloemfontein High Court, case 3101/2015, *The Democratic Alliance* v *The Head of Department of Human Settlements, Free State Province and Others.*
21. 'State of Capture', Public Protector Report No. 6 of 2016/17, available at https://www.politicsweb.co.za/documents/state-of-capture-full-text-of-thuli-madonselas-rep (last accessed 4 December 2018).
22. Amil Umraw, 'Treasury wants the Hawks to investigate Koko and Singh', *TimesLive*, 16 November 2018, available at https://www.timeslive.co.za/news/2018-11-16-treasury-wants-the-hawks-to-investigate-koko-and-singh/ (last accessed 4 December 2018).

23. Court filings, North Gauteng High Court, case 68385/17, *Blackhead Consulting* v *Diamond Hill Trading 71 and Others.*

CHAPTER 22: A BLUEPRINT FOR BRIBES

1. 'Malema exposé: #NomvulaLikesEmYoung, Mabala Noise', *IOL*, 5 August 2016, available at https://www.iol.co.za/entertainment/music/malema-expose-nomvulalike semyoung-mabala-noise-2054008 (last accessed 28 November 2018).

CHAPTER 23: HAVANA NIGHTS

1. Tax Justice Network, Financial Secrecy Index 2018, 'Narrative report on Cayman Islands', available at http://www.financialsecrecyindex.com/PDF/CaymanIslands.pdf (last accessed 29 November 2018).
2. Pieter-Louis Myburgh, 'The great art heist: ANC secretary-general Ace Magashule in "stolen" Pierneef painting debacle', *Daily Maverick*, 22 October 2018, available at https://www.dailymaverick.co.za/article/2018-10-22-the-great-art-heist-anc-secretary -general-ace-magashule-in-stolen-pierneef-painting-debacle/ (last accessed 30 November 2018).

CHAPTER 24: ACE SHOWS HIS HAND

1. Marietjie Gericke, 'Ace se tentakels "ook om Macufe geslaan"', *Netwerk24*, 18 October 2018, available at https://www.netwerk24.com/Nuus/Politiek/ace-se-tentakels-ook -om-macufe-geslaan-20181018 (last accessed 3 December 2018).
2. 'Free State premier takes Operation Hlasela to Kroonstad', *FS News Online*, 4 August 2017, available at http://fsnewsonline.co.za/free-state-premier-takes-operation-hlasela -to-kroonstad/ (last accessed 3 December 2018).
3. Refiloe Mokoena SARS profile, available at http://www.sars.gov.za/About/PeopleSARS/ Exco/Pages/Refiloe-Mokoena.aspx (last accessed 3 December 2018).
4. Pauli van Wyk, 'Scorpio: The Moyane Dossier, Part 1 – How SARS boss disregarded the law to pay Guptas' VAT refund', *Daily Maverick*, 16 March 2018, available at https://www .dailymaverick.co.za/article/2018-03-16-scorpio-the-moyane-dossier-part-1-how-sars- boss-disregarded-the-law-to-pay-guptas-vat-refund/ (last accessed 3 December 2018).

CHAPTER 25: THE ANC'S ASBESTOS BENEFITS

1. Tiisetso Makhele, 'Lessons from Cuba', *The Weekly*, 3 June 2016, available at http:// theweekly.co.za/?p=19660 (last accessed 3 December 2018).
2. SABC Digital News, 'Mantashe calls on municipalities to do an audit of redistributed land', 6 February 2016, available at https://www.youtube.com/ watch?v=VSwzyyWX8zE (last accessed 3 December 2018).
3. Inge Strydom, 'Zuma won't run for third term, says ANC', *News24*, 10 February 2016, available at https://www.news24.com/SouthAfrica/Local/Express-News/zuma-wont -run-for-third-term-says-anc-20160209 (last accessed 3 December 2018).
4. Kherbert, '"All must share in wealth"', *Express*, 10 February 2016, available at https:// www.news24.com/SouthAfrica/Local/Express-News/all-must-share-in-wealth -20160209 (last accessed 3 December 2018).

CHAPTER 26: ZIZI

1. Sibongakonke Shoba, 'Premier's man says it's time to spin good news', *Sunday Times*, 29 September 2013.
2. Kyle Cowan, 'Bosasa ran "the country like an underworld, like a mafia" state – ANC's Kodwa', *News24*, 25 January 2019, available at https://www.news24.com/SouthAfrica/

News/bosasa-ran-the-country-like-an-underworld-like-a-mafia-state-ancs-kodwa
-20190125 (last accessed 3 February 2019).

3. Ibid.

CHAPTER 27: THE LAST CASH RUN

1. Free State Government Tender Bulletin No. 24, 24 June 2016, p. 3, available at https://
www.greengazette.co.za/documents/tender-bulletin-for-free-state-24-of-24-june
-2016_20160624-TFS-00024.pdf (last accessed 4 December 2018).
2. Presentation by 605 Consulting Solutions to FSHS, 'Implementation of Water and
Sewer Networks in the Free State Province', 29 August 2016.
3. Mahlatse Gallens, 'Mbalula tweets slam Magashule', *News24*, 15 June 2017, available at
https://www.news24.com/SouthAfrica/News/mbalula-tweets-slam-magashule-20170615
(last accessed 4 December 2018).
4. Afro World View TV, 'Magashule responds to Mbalula', 17 June 2017, available at
https://www.youtube.com/watch?v=KdzpUkIzb_g (last accessed 4 December 2018).

CHAPTER 29: NAS(W)REC(K)

1. Mahlatse Gallens, 'Mbalula tweets slam Magashule', *News24*, 15 June 2017.
2. Matuma Letsoalo and Govan Whittles, 'Cyril to Supra: Step down or be fired', *Mail &
Guardian*, 4 May 2018, available at https://mg.co.za/article/2018-05-04-00-cyril-to
-supra-step-down-or-be-fired (last accessed 18 December 2018); Aphiwe Deklerk,
'North West Premier Supra Mahumapelo to take "early retirement"', *TimesLive*,
23 May 2018, available at https://www.timeslive.co.za/politics/2018-05-23-supra
-mahumapelo-on-early-retirement/ (last accessed 18 December 2018).
3. Gallens, 'Mbalula tweets slam Magashule'.
4. Afro World View TV, 'Magashule responds to Mbalula', 17 June 2017.
5. Bloemfontein High Court, case number 5942/2017, *Tumelo John Mokoena and Others
v Elias Magashule and Others*.
6. 'Mbalo eyes top ANC post', *The Weekly*, 13 April 2012, available at http://theweekly
.co.za/?p=5112 (last accessed 4 December 2018).
7. Bloemfontein High Court, case number 5942/2017, *Tumelo John Mokoena and Others
v Elias Magashule and Others*.
8. Ibid.
9. Ibid.
10. 'Zuma-supporting Free State "gangster" mayor due to make a comeback – DA', *The
Citizen*, 3 August 2018, available at https://citizen.co.za/news/south-africa/1990903/
zuma-supporting-free-state-gangster-mayor-due-to-make-a-comeback-da/ (last
accessed 18 December 2018); Juniour Khumalo, 'Ace Magashule still a divisive figure
in the Free State', *City Press*, 12 November 2018, available at https://city-press.news24
.com/News/ace-magashule-still-a-divisive-figure-in-the-free-state-20181112 (last
accessed 18 December 2018).
11. Bloemfontein High Court, case number 5942/2017, *Tumelo John Mokoena and Others* v
Elias Magashule and Others.
12. Ibid.
13. Ibid.
14. Ibid.
15. Ibid.
16. Ibid.
17. Tshidi Madia, 'ANC Free State holds "surprise" provincial general council', *News24*,
28 November 2017, available at https://www.news24.com/SouthAfrica/News/

anc-free-state-holds-surprise-provincial-general-council-20171128 (last accessed 4 December 2018).

18. Ibid.

19. Tshidi Madia, 'Free State endorses team Nkosazana Dlamini-Zuma', *News24*, 28 November 2017, available at https://www.news24.com/SouthAfrica/News/ free-state-endorses-team-nkosazana-dlamini-zuma-20171128 20171128 (last accessed 4 December 2018).

20. Tshidi Madia, 'Ace Magashule stays on as ANC chairperson in the Free State', *News24*, 11 December 2017, available at https://www.news24.com/SouthAfrica/News/just-in -ace-magashule-stays-on-as-anc-chairperson-in-free-state-20171211 (last accessed 18 December 2018).

21. Dineo Bendile, 'Still no start in sight for ANC Free State conference', *Mail & Guardian*, 10 December 2017, available at https://mg.co.za/article/2017-12-10-still-no -start-in-sight-for-anc-free-state-conference (last accessed 18 December 2018).

22. Madia, 'Ace Magashule stays on as ANC chairperson in the Free State'.

23. Lizeka Tandwa, 'ANC Free State PEC, several branches barred from attending elective conference', *News24*, 15 December 2017, available at https://www.news24.com/ SouthAfrica/News/just-in-anc-free-state-pec-several-branches-barred-from -attending-elective-conference-20171215 (last accessed 18 December 2018).

24. The only unsuccessful Top Six contender who could have surpassed his opponent with the help of eighty additional votes was Magashule's challenger, former KwaZulu -Natal premier Senzo Mchunu. However, the Free State branch members who were barred from attending Nasrec most likely would have been Magashule supporters.

25. Paddy Harper, 'Senzo yields but the fight goes on', *Mail & Guardian*, 21 December 2017, available at https://mg.co.za/article/2017-12-21-00-senzo-yields-but-the-fight -goes-on (last accessed 18 December 2018).

26. Ra'eesa Pather, 'Supra Mahumapelo: If they recount SG votes, they must recount entire top six', *Mail & Guardian*, 19 December 2017, available at https://mg.co.za/ article/2017-12-19-supra-mahumapelo-if-they-recount-sg-votes-they-must-recount -the-entire-top-six (last accessed 18 December 2018).

27. 'Here is the ANC's new top 6', *News24*, 18 December 2017, available at https://www .news24.com/SouthAfrica/News/meet-the-ancs-new-top-6-20171218 (last accessed 18 December 2018).

28. Tshidi Madia and Mahlatse Mahlase, 'Mchunu supporters question his defeat as ANC SG', *News24*, 19 December 2017, available at https://www.news24.com/SouthAfrica/ News/mchunu-supporters-question-his-defeat-as-anc-sg-20171219 (last accessed 18 December 2018).

29. Genevieve Quintal and Claudi Mailovich, 'Ace Magashule claws onto ANC secretary -general role after another recount', *Business Day*, 20 December 2017, available at https://www.businesslive.co.za/bd/politics/2017-12-20-ace-magashule-claws-onto-anc -secretary-general-role-after-another-recount/ (last accessed 18 December 2018).

30. Lizeka Tandwa and Mahlatse Mahlase, 'Ramaphosa camp admits defeat over SG votes, but Mchunu expected to go to court', *News24*, 20 December 2017, available at https:// www.news24.com/SouthAfrica/News/ramaphosa-camp-admits-defeat-over-sg-votes -but-mchunu-expected-to-go-to-court-20171220 (last accessed 18 December 2018).

31. Bheki Mbanjwa, Khaya Koko and Lebogang Seale, 'Bid to save ANC conference', *The Star*, 20 December 2017.

32. Naledi Shange, 'ANC to meet lawyers of 68 "missing voters"', *Business Day*, 22 December 2017, available at https://www.businesslive.co.za/bd/politics/2017-12-22 -anc-to-meet-lawyers-of-68-missing-votes/ (last accessed 18 December 2018).

33. Ziyanda Ngcobo, Barry Bateman and Rahima Essop, 'Magashule to remain ANC secretary-general as vote discrepancy clarified', *EWN*, 20 December 2017, available at https://ewn.co.za/2017/12/20/magashule-to-remain-anc-secretary-general-as-vote -discrepancy-clarified (last accessed 18 December 2018).

34. Tandwa and Mahlase, 'Ramaphosa camp admits defeat over SG votes, but Mchunu expected to go to court'.

35. Tshidi Madia and Lizeka Tandwa, 'Mchunu to work full time at Luthuli House – Magashule', *News24*, 25 February 2018, available at https://www.news24.com/ SouthAfrica/News/mchunu-to-work-full-time-at-luthuli-house-magashule-20180225 (last accessed 18 December 2018).

36. Athandiwe Saba, '"Jobs for votes" scandal rocks ANC', *Mail & Guardian*, 9 March 2018, available at https://mg.co.za/article/2018-03-09-00-jobs-for-votes-scandal-rocks-anc (last accessed 18 December 2018).

CHAPTER 30: NEW DAWN, OLD GUARD

1. Ernest Mabuza, 'Magashule's office cooperating with Hawks', *TimesLive*, 26 January 2018, available at https://www.timeslive.co.za/politics/2018-01-26-magashules-office -cooperating-with-the-hawks/ (last accessed 6 February 2019).

2. Bernadette Wolhuter and Thami Magubane, 'Mixed reaction to new top cop General Khehla John Sithole', *IOL*, 23 November 2017, available at https://www.iol.co.za/news/ mixed-reaction-to-new-top-cop-general-khehla-john-sithole-12124242 (last accessed 6 February 2019).

3. 'National commissioner appoints two deputy national commissioners', media statement from National Media Centre, Corporate Communication, South African Police Service, 1 December 2017, available at https://www.saps.gov.za/newsroom/ selnewsdetails.php?nid=13624 (last accessed 6 February 2019).

4. Juniour Khumalo, 'Mbalula: I had nothing to do with plan to syphon millions from SAPS', *City Press*, 22 January 2019, available at https://city-press.news24.com/News/ mbalula-i-had-nothing-to-do-with-plan-to-syphon-millions-from-saps-20190122 (last accessed 6 February 2019).

5. Marianne Thamm, 'Nasrec plot: IPID targets senior SAPS members and former ministerial adviser in ANC vote-buying scandal', *Daily Maverick*, 7 January 2019, available at https://www.dailymaverick.co.za/article/2019-01-07-nasrec-plot-ipid -targets-senior-saps-members-and-former-ministerial-adviser-in-anc-vote-buying -scandal/ (last accessed 6 February 2019).

6. Eric Naki, 'Ace is sweet-talking Cyril "because he knows he's being watched"', *Citizen*, 2 October 2018, available at https://citizen.co.za/news/south-africa/2016610/ace-is-sweet -talking-cyril-because-he-knows-hes-being-watched/ (last accessed 6 February 2019).

7. Qaanitah Hunter and Jeff Wicks, 'Exposed: Zuma plot to oust Cyril', *Sunday Times*, 9 September 2018.

Abbreviations

ABT: alternative building technologies
AG: auditor-general
ANC: African National Congress
AZASO: Azanian Students Organisation
BGM: branch general meeting
CDP: Contractor Development Programme
CEO: chief executive officer
CFO: chief financial officer
CIDB: Construction Industry Development Board
CIPC: Companies and Intellectual Property Commission
COO: chief operating officer
COPE: Congress of the People
COSAS: Congress of South African Students
DA: Democratic Alliance
DG: director general
DPRT: Department of Police, Roads and Transport
EFF: Economic Freedom Fighters
EPHP: Enhanced People's Housing Process
ERP: expenditure recovery plan
FDC: Free State Development Corporation
FSHS: Free State Department of Human Settlements
HOD: head of department
HSS: housing subsidy system
ILC: Interim Leadership Committee
IPW: instruction to perform work
JV: joint venture
KZN: KwaZulu-Natal
MEC: member of the executive council
MK: Umkhonto we Sizwe
MP: member of Parliament

MPL: member of the provincial legislature
NCOP: National Council of Provinces
NEC: National Executive Committee
NIA: National Intelligence Agency
NPA: National Prosecuting Authority
NURCHA: National Urban Reconstruction and Housing Agency
NWC: National Working Committee
PEC: Provincial Executive Committee
PFMA: Public Finance Management Act
PGC: Provincial General Council
PHP: people's housing process
PRASA: Passenger Rail Agency of South Africa
PRTs: professional resource teams
RDP: Reconstruction and Development Programme
SABC: South African Broadcasting Corporation
SABS: South African Bureau of Standards
SACC: South African Council of Churches
SACP: South African Communist Party
SALGA: South African Local Government Association
SAMAs: South African Music Awards
SAPS: South African Police Service
SG: secretary-general
SIU: Special Investigating Unit
SOE: state-owned entity
SRC: student representative council
TTC: Tshwara Thebe Construction
UAE: United Arab Emirates
UDF: United Democratic Front

Index